RESEARCH IN SOCIAL MOVEMENTS, CONFLICTS AND CHANGE

Volume 6 • 1984

RESEARCH IN SOCIAL MOVEMENTS, CONFLICTS AND CHANGE

A Research Annual

Guest Editor: **RICHARD E. RATCLIFF**
Department of Sociology
Syracuse University

Series Editor: **LOUIS KRIESBERG**
Department of Sociology
Syracuse University

VOLUME 6 • 1984

104819

 JAI PRESS INC.

Greenwich, Connecticut   *London, England*

CONTENTS

LIST OF CONTRIBUTORS

Richard G. Braungart

Department of Sociology
Syracuse University

Gerard J. Grzyb

Department of Sociology
University of Alabama

Alexander Hicks

Department of Sociology
Northwestern University

James H. Johnson, Jr.

Department of Geography
University of California at
Los Angeles

Clarence Y. H. Lo

Department of Sociology
University of California at
Los Angeles

Theodore J. Majka

Department of Sociology and
Anthropology
University of Dayton

Linda C. Majka

Department of Sociology and
Anthropology
University of Dayton

Melvin L. Oliver

Department of Sociology
University of California at
Los Angeles

Dietrich C. Reitzes

Department of Sociology
Roosevelt University

Donald C. Reitzes

Department of Sociology
Georgia State University

Joyce Rothschild-Whitt

Department of Sociology
University of Louisville

Duane H. Swank

Department of Sociology
Marquette University

Herman Turk

Department of Sociology
University of Southern California

Bert Useem

Department of Sociology
University of Illinois at
Chicago

John F. Zipp

Department of Sociology
Washington University at
St. Louis

Lynne G. Zucker

Department of Sociology
University of California at
Los Angeles

INTRODUCTION

As is to be expected in an annual review in a series aimed to cover a broad field, this volume offers a diverse set of articles concerned with "social movements, conflict and change." Certainly, no argument can be made that the scholarship presented here emphasizes any one theoretical or methodological approach or attempts to solve any single set of interrelated substantive problems. Instead, the articles range widely. Nevertheless, there are three topics that do receive considerable attention here. The first of these topics concerns local political conflicts and community organizing; the second involves issues of the American labor movement in the context of modern economic and political changes; and the third deals with the social bases and the impact of recent right-wing political mobilization. For each of these topics the articles in this volume reflect an important, though often overlooked, dialectical tension between the impacts of conscious action and of more impersonal historical forces in shaping social movements. Thus, the analyses look at some consciously organized attempts to establish and strengthen social movements, and alternatively at other attempts to weaken and destroy movements, and also examine how broader social and economic transformations "determine" social movements and their outcomes.

In important ways, all of these articles deal with the issues of social movements and the conflicts such movements reflect and stimulate. However, for some readers, much of the work might seem to reach beyond the normal boundaries of "social movements" research. As with many other topics in the social sciences, the area of social movements has come to be a recognized subfield with a defined literature, extensively debated theoretical and definitional issues and a network of recognized specialists. Unfortunately, as the field of social movements evolved, it has also suffered from an increasing narrowness in its substantive concerns and theoretical approaches. Current work in this field often seems far removed from the classic questions of class conflict and of the social turbulence that arises from political and economic transformations which stimulated earlier interest in the area.

The field of social movements is currently in some disarray, as indicated by active debates between adherents of more established collective behavior approaches and the recently emergent advocates of the "resource mobilization" perspective. Work in the collective behavior tradition has typically emphasized social psychological research concerned with the determinants of social movement participation. From this viewpoint, the critical factors are often seen as the patterns of individual distress, grievances and beliefs that then merge into organized collective behavior. While these issues are of obvious importance, the recent critiques have identified a number of limitations in such studies. The focus on the aggrieved or disturbed individual as the basic unit of social movement activity tends to ignore organizational factors that are often more important in determining which social movements will grow and become important social forces and which will fail, or perhaps never even appear. The critiques make the valid point that there always exists a diversity of distresses and grievances felt by individuals and groups in the society and that the depth and fervor of such sentiments are poor predictors of which will grow into social movements. Rather, it is claimed that it is more critical to understand which organizational resources are available to be "mobilized" in order to develop and promote particular sets of grievances. Moreover, it has been pointed out that the social psychological approaches often imply an aura of pathology and aberrant behavior for participation in social movements. The suggestion is that "normal" people do not get involved in social movements. According to the resource mobilization perspective, social movement participation is better viewed as a normal extension of established political activity.

The resource mobilization perspective has decided strengths as an analytical approach. Since research on social movements has shown a great diversity in the individual characteristics and dispositions of participants (Zurcher and Snow, 1981), this perspective correctly, it seems, shifts the focus to those organizational factors that both shape the emergence of social movements and are critical determinants of their outcomes (cf. McCarthy and Zald, 1977). This model also distinguishes social movement organizations from the more diffuse notion of a "social movement" and helps focus analyses on those features of organizations associated with the success or failure of efforts to promote particular causes. Similarly, work pursuing this model has looked more carefully at the important roles played by external resources in social movement activities.

Still, the resource mobilization perspective has its own important limitations. In the effort to make the valid point that the marshalling of resources is usually more important, and more problematic, than the existence of serious grievances, the resource mobilization advocates have understated the importance of such grievances. Just as the historical landscape is well littered with instances of deeply felt grievances that have not produced social movements, there also have been innumerable seriously organized attempts to build social movements which have failed because their agendas, or ideologies, have not proven attractive to their intended social bases. And there are valid questions regarding whether such vastly successful social movements as those that put communists in power in Russia and China or fascists in power in Germany were more a result of the competent use of organizational resources or rather were largely the beneficiaries of historically specific strains and transformations in the social structure. Thorough analyses would suggest that these movements were jointly shaped by the convergence of organizational resources and underlying social forces.

The resource mobilization perspective has also been limited by its rather narrow, and unrealistically formalized, notions of how social movement participants are motivated (Ferree and Miller, forthcoming). Especially in the formulation offered by McCarthy and Zald, the idea of rational calculation and economic self-interest seems out of touch with the diversity of forces that propel social movement participation.

Given the stated emphases of the resource mobilization perspective, and even given the title of this approach, it is peculiar that in this area so little attention has been paid to actual mobilization processes involving social movements. In fact, even the notion of "resources" has been left so broadly defined as to have little clear meaning. It is here that much important, and potentially fascinating, work needs to be done. For example, there is the question of just what organizational factors are critical in causing particular grievances of individuals to be crystallized into some sort of group consciousness and social movement ideology, and in facilitating the formation of organized social movement activities. In a more classic Marxist context, this issue has been posed as the question of how a class "in itself" makes the transformation into a class "for itself."

While such questions have been little handled in the collective behavior tradition, the general notion that "external" and "internal" resources are vital that is offered in resource mobilization formulations is not by itself very helpful. What is needed are more concrete models and propositions of how social movement activities occur that can be examined in regard to specific historical situations. In order to provide some contrast with the rather vacuous generalities that have pervaded the field, it is useful to examine in some detail an example of such a concrete model.

One idea that merits far more attention than it has had in this field is that in a broad range of insurgent situations the critical factor has been the existence of a cadre of commited grass-roots level "militants" who carry a particular movement's worldviews, ideological messages and programs for action to potentially organizable social groups. These militants are not the top leadership group, but rather local level activists who provide an organizational infrastructure for the movement. They certainly can be seen as a "resource" that is available to be mobilized. An argument can be made that the existence and active mobilization of such militants is a necessary condition for the emergence of powerful social movements. According to this viewpoint, political ideas that stimulate "radical" political views and behaviors are most effectively communicated in face-to-face interactions in which the message is carried by a militant, a particularly appropriate term for such an intermediary in a social movement context, who is both committed and socially on a similar level to the people being mobilized.

This model of how movements are mobilized is supported by empirical research both on how radical socialist and communist ideas have been transmitted among the poor (Petras and Zeitlin, 1967) and on how the fascist movement arose in Germany (Hamilton and Wright, 1975). Work on the importance of social networks in recruiting social movement participants also is consistent with this model (Snow, et al., 1980). It is even related to seemingly distant studies on the "two-step flow" of influence from media messages and to research on the ways in which innovations are spread by an infrastructure of local leaders. In a more politically relevant context, the notion of the critical role of militants in social movements is linked to longstanding debates among both Marxist theoreticians and others regarding the roles played by "vanguard" groups in political transformations. But, surprisingly, the idea has never really caught on in modern social movement research.

The reasons for this lack of attention probably come from a number of sources. One practical problem has been the difficulties in doing empirical research on grass-roots processes in revolutionary settings. Moreover, the level of generality sought in many treatments of social movements, even by those promoting the resource mobilization approach, has precluded attention to such specific phenomena. Also, due to more practical concerns, the notion of militants has been avoided by liberal social scientists wishing to dispel conservative claims that all social turbulence and insurgency is the result of "outside agitators"; and has also been avoided by some left intellectuals who want to promote the notion that the exploited masses are quite capable of arising on their own. Still, it is notable that the idea of the importance of the conscious intervention by activists was not avoided by Trotsky who made the notable observation, generally consistent with the premise of the resource mobilization model, that if poverty and exploitation by themselves were enough to stimulate revolution then "the masses would be always in revolt" (1959: 249).

One of the benefits of pursuing focused models of how change occurs is that one is forced by empirical realities to consider complexities in a more specific context. Here the idea of the role of grievances, that has been actively debated but with little specificity in regard to the resource mobilization perspective, naturally arises. The issue that is posed is whether militants, if they are vital, can carry "any" message into "any" context and produce a social movement. The answer is undoubtably negative in general but it is arguable that in almost any context they can produce some converts to the cause. Still, the general thesis would be that militants are necessary but not sufficient for social movements to emerge. In order to be successful, the message and political program must be compatible with the situations of those they seek to organize and to be truly effective they must run parallel with strongly felt grievances or frustrations that have been produced in the setting by social and economic transformations.

Were organizing by militants sufficient by itself to produce strong social movements, there would be far more Jehovah's Witnesses and Mormons among us than there are, to mention two religious groups that have engaged in extensive door-to-door organizing. Similar observations could be made for the many political and other organizations that have devoted themselves to face-to-face organizing from time to time. Similarly, it is notable that in Third World contexts in the 1960s the CIA was quite unsuccessful when, inspired by the successes of left insurgency and oriented to more subtle interventions than its typical covert programs, it tried to introduce community organizers as a means to better communicate defenses of the status quo and to shore up the positions of generally unrepresentative governments. Nevertheless, while in general effective organizing by militants does seem to depend on some reasonable degree of correspondence between the messages carried by the militants and the personal situations of those to be organized, there is quite probably a broad range of possible directions in which a given set of popular views can be mobilized. Such flexibility is suggested in the analyses in this volume concerning anti-tax and anti-busing organizing and concerning struggles going on in industrial work settings.

Stepping back from the specific notion of militants, it is possible to offer a few observations on the factors crucial to social movement mobilization. Drawing on the views considered here, the emergence of social movements certainly seems to depend on a context in which structural dislocations have occurred in social and economic relations so as to produce groups of people with strong grievances or frustrations regarding the existing relations in society. Given such potential social bases, which as the resource mobilization advocates point out are quite prevalent, the actual formation of social movements then depends on a range of organizational factors. The one such factor that has been discussed here is the existence of an organization that can field and support an infrastructure of mobilized militants, who have both an ideology or worldview and a program of political action that "makes sense" to the affected groups. Among issues not discussed here, a range of material and nonmaterial resources, both internal and external to engaged social movement organizations, could be vital. Furthermore, some weaknesses and divisions in the dominant groups in the relevant areas of the society might also be necessary if the movement is to have more than the most transitory of successes.

The variety of ways in which such factors can interact to affect the evolution of specific social movements provides the substance for many concrete analyses of social change. The studies contained in this volume reflect a diversity of findings in this area. Perhaps the clearest unifying themes presented here concern how planned and conscious human political activity and broader historical forces interrelate in shaping movements pushing for social change. A number of these studies deal directly with focused efforts to "organize" in ways that promote social change. The analysis by Donald Reitzes and Dietrich Reitzes treats most extensively the notion that planned programs to organize can be used to build social movements in working class communities. It is notable that the area of "community organizing," discussed here by Reitzes and Reitzes, has been so little examined by social scientists. This topic should be of particular relevance to those exploring the resource mobilization perspective. The disdain that Saul Alinsky had for academic social science has been amply reciprocated by the indifference that researchers have shown not only to the many efforts he and his direct followers have initiated but also to the rich diversity of similar community organizing programs pursued by groups such as ACORN and Massachusetts Fair Share (Boyte, 1980). With few exceptions (cf. Bailey, 1972), this area of social movement activity has simply been ignored.

The article by Theo Majka and Linda Majka also deals with issues of the impact of working class organizing but here the emphasis is more on the ways in which such efforts are shaped by external factors. A related theme is pursued in the analysis of Joyce Rothschild-Whitt who reveals the seemingly contradictory constellation of forces that has promoted and organized for the "progressive" idea of worker ownership. Gerard Grzyb and John Zipp also consider planned attempts to bring social change but here, however, the "organizers" are the agents of capital who have worked to take advantage of changing economic conditions to gain greater control over labor. Bert Useem and Clarence Lo also examine the context and impact of organizing but in their studies the "militants" have a generally reactionary or right-wing character. Nevertheless, both analyses make clear that the promoters of such efforts are not an upper class elite. Rather, they emerge from more marginal economic interests and ethnic groups adversely affected by economic and social changes. The analysis of Herman Turk and Lynne Zurker shows that organized political efforts can prove effective in shaping outcomes even for groups appearing to be in vulnerable minority positions. While not dealing with the organizing process as such, Swank and Hicks do provide evidence that insurgent political action does shape the flow of economic resources in the society.

All of the articles deal with the impact of larger historical forces on the emergence and outcomes of social movements. The analysis by Richard Braungart represents an ambitious theoretical treatment of how the political character of generational groups is shaped by the historical context within which they emerge. This model is also related to the issue of political organizing as Braungart argued that the ways in which generations of youth incorporate the political "messages" of their historical situations are shaped by the conscious efforts at political mobilization they experience. Grzyb, Zipp and Majka and Majka all consider how economic and technological changes affect the nature of the conflict between labor and capital. However, in each analysis it is also shown, in contrast to often-accepted rigid notions of technological determinism, that the resulting relations between labor and capital reflect the conscious and planned efforts by contending parties to gain greater control over each other. The study by Melvin Oliver and James Johnson examines how underlying economic forces shape the urban ethnic conflicts that are too often portrayed as mainly resulting from social and cultural factors. Similarly, Useem and Lo show how historically shifting economic strains provide the context within which broader political struggles emerge.

The scholarly efforts presented here provide both a large and valuable base of case materials on different movements and social conflicts and important explorations of how planned and unplanned forces interact to shape social movements. The questions they raise identify and help illuminate the key processes at work. The pursuit of a better understanding of these processes must, of course, continue.

Richard E. Ratcliff
Guest Editor

REFERENCES

Bailey, Robert J.
  1972 Radicals in Urban Politics: The Alinsky Approach. Chicago: The University of Chicago Press
Boyte, Harry C.
  1980 The Backyard Revolution: Understanding the New Citizen Movement. Philadelphia: Temple University Press
Ferree, Myra Marx and Frederick D. Miller
  Forth- "Mobilization and meaning: toward an integration of social psychological and resource coming perspectives on social movements." Sociological Quarterly

Hamilton, Richard F. and James Wright
  1975   New Directions in Political Sociology. Indianapolis: Bobbs-Merrill
McCarthy, John D. and Mayer N. Zald
  1977   "Resource mobilization and social movements: a partial theory." American Journal of Sociology 82:1212–1241.
Petras, James and Maurice Zeitlin
  1967   "Miners and agrarian radicalism." American Sociological Review 32:578–586.
Snow, David A., Louis A. Zurcher, Jr. and Sheldon Ekland-Olson
  1980   "Social networks and social movements: a microstructural approach to differential recruitment." American Sociological Review 45:787–801.
Zurcher, Louis A. and David A. Snow
  1980   "Collective behavior: social movements." Pp. 447–482 in Morris Rosenberg and Ralph H. Turner, (eds.) Social Psychology: Sociological Perspectives. New York: Basic Books

MILITANCY, NEED AND RELIEF:

THE PIVEN AND CLOWARD AFDC CASELOAD THESIS REVISITED

Duane H. Swank and Alexander Hicks

I. INTRODUCTION

In recent decades social scientists have shown increasing concern with the disadvantages experienced by lower class groups in the institutionalized political competitions of capitalist democracies (e.g., Schattschneider, 1960; Bachrach and Baratz, 1970; Lindblom, 1977). This awareness has led to considerable interest in whether these disadvantages can be overcome. One resulting focus has been upon the effectiveness of direct action as a political strategy for lower class groups. Systematic inquiry into this question has accelerated since the late 1960s (e.g., Lipsky, 1968; Gamson, 1975; Gurr, 1980). Much of this work has concerned how political turbulence affects social welfare policies (e.g., Jackman, 1975; Button, 1978; Swank, 1983), and more specifically, the relationship between direct action by black Americans and periods of growth in U.S. social welfare programs in the decades following World War II (e.g., Feagin and Hahn,

Research in Social Movements, Conflict and Change, Vol. 6, pages 1–29.
Copyright © 1984 by JAI Press Inc.
All rights of reproduction in any form reserved.
ISBN: 0-89232-311-6

1973; Welch, 1975; Button, 1978). A large share of the controversy in this literature has been shaped around the arguments made in Frances Fox Piven and Richard A. Cloward's widely-read *Regulating the Poor* (1971) and *Poor People's Movements* (1977) concerning governmental responsiveness to "poor peoples'" political activities. Indeed, Jennings (1980; 1981), Albritton (1979a), and Isaac and Kelly (1981) all attempt to test Piven and Cloward's thesis that increases in caseloads for the Aid to Families with Dependent Children (hereafter AFDC) program have been a result of direct political action.

Piven and Cloward's arguments concerning the linkage between direct action and government welfare policies is of considerable importance because it challenges a number of widely accepted notions concerning why welfare programs expand and contract. Unfortunately, extant attempts to explicitly test Piven and Cloward's explanation of increases in AFDC rolls are all marked by one or both of the following shortcomings: (1) oversimplifications of Piven and Cloward's propositions about the causes of AFDC caseload growth; and (2) methodological inadequacies in the testing of propositions, particularly in the use of subnational units of analysis, cross-sectional modes of analysis, and misspecified models of changes in AFDC rolls.

In these pages, we will present a more comprehensive evaluation of the Piven and Cloward thesis. First we provide a summary of Piven and Cloward's theory of "poor people's movements" and what might be termed the disruptions/mobilization thesis of AFDC caseload increases. We also elaborate the above criticisms of the principal prior attempts to test the Piven and Cloward argument. We then present our own test of their thesis. In concluding, we will discuss the implications of our findings for the study of welfare policy determination, social movements, and outcomes of political protest by lower class groups.

II.   PIVEN AND CLOWARD ON RELIEF AND AFDC ROLLS

A.   On Poor People's Movements and the State

Piven and Cloward (1977: Ch. 1) argue that the institutionalized political routines of capitalist societies are so biased that only disruptive forms of political action provide the poor with any reasonable hope of obtaining ameliorative policy concessions. Piven and Cloward's argument can briefly be summarized as follows. Socioeconomic crises such as depressions, rapid changes in labor force composition, migration of large populations, and so on, may lead to severe socioeconomic dislocations among specific lower class groups, to increasing experiences of relative deprivation and consequently to the disorganization of the regulating, "comforting" banalities and routines of everyday life (Piven and Cloward, 1977:9–14). The extent of this disorganization may be increased if certain elite groups, which sense their own position undermined by ongoing changes, attempt to seek support from the dislocated by proclaiming the dislocation affecting the poor to be an injustice and by proposing or enacting policies for the redress of the dislocated's grievances. Such responses from among the elite may help the dislocated articulate normative justifications for their protests, and thus, broaden and intensify mass political demands.

The discontentments of the dislocated are typically expressed either through the vote or through institutional disruption. While expressions of unrest by the poor through electoral means may trigger elite concessions (Piven and Cloward, 1971:38–40), Piven and Cloward (1971: Chapters 2, 4, and 8; 1977: Chapter 1) place the greatest emphasis upon expressions of discontent in the form of civil disruptions. While these disruptions might provoke repressive responses, they are also likely to yield new relief measures and other policy concessions directed at the dislocated groups. Piven and Cloward do not claim that these concessions are particularly substantial, let alone permanent. In fact they stress that many are withdrawn when elites see the threat of disruption diminish. Moveover, they note that new concessions often promote the cooptation of protest leadership and energies, channeling these into routine and ineffective modes of political activity (Piven and Cloward, 1977:29–34). Nevertheless, however limited elite concessions to the poor's institutional and electoral disruptions may be, Piven and Cloward argue that they entail the greatest state responsiveness that those in subordinate class positions may realistically expect (Piven and Cloward, 1977:34–36, 341–348).

Piven and Cloward assert in general that the poor will not benefit from ameliorative policies unless they engage in protest. In particular, they deny that mere need for welfare will foster ameliorative policies except when the need gives rise to civil disorders (Piven and Cloward, 1971:183–250; 1977:9–26, 181–286). With these claims, Piven and Cloward distinguish their thesis from previous theories of welfare state expansion that emphasize a nearly automatic state responsiveness to emergent public needs.

B.   On Poor People's Movements and AFDC Relief Rolls

1.   Hypothesized Determinants

Piven and Cloward make specific claims regarding the relationship between black protest activity, relief mobilization, and the expansion of welfare, especially AFDC caseloads, in the post-World War II United States. In their view, this crisis had its origins in the crisis of Southern agricultural reorganization and massive black ejection from the South which led to the relocation and concentration of blacks in the urban North and West. This transition from rural to urban settings for blacks, and the resulting dislocations, coincided with and contributed to the emerging civil rights movement. This movement raised black consciousness of discriminatory injustice (Piven and Cloward, 1977: Ch. 4). The movement also stimulated forms of support from Democratic elites, which in effect, helped legitimate black grievances, helped justify black demands, and helped create for blacks opportunities for governmentally assisted redress. During the Kennedy and Johnson administrations, liberal intellectuals and politicians helped articulate the political and economic plight of blacks with War-on-Poverty rhetoric, promises, and programs. According to Piven and Cloward, much of this support reflected an attempt to secure the electoral support of the great majority of black voters with a minimal focus on black socio-political emancipation and thus a minimal alienation of Southern whites (Piven and Cloward, 1971: 250–252; 1977:225–228).

All of these factors contributed to blacks' sense of remediable injustice and to their disposition to engage in direct political action. According to Piven and Cloward, blacks responded to their sense of injustice in those sites in which they had most ready political leverage—in the streets, stores, and welfare offices. They did so with the disruptiveness of peaceful protest (Piven and Cloward, 1971:269–270), riots (Piven and Cloward, 1971:226–239; 1977:274–275), and more frequent and aggressive welfare application (1971:220–284).[1] Federal, state, and local officials responded to pressures from direct political action and mass welfare applications, from political superordinates and their own liberal consciences and from their fears and uncertainties regarding further upheavals with new programs and increased utilization of old ones (Piven and Cloward, 1979:1013). The most important elements of elite response, according to Piven and Cloward (1979:1013), consisted of the initiation and expansion of "community action" services and the acceptance of the expansion of AFDC rolls. These responses often had additional effects. For example, "community action" workers mobilized potential welfare recipients and legal resources for their assistance, generating yet further responses in the form of expanding welfare rolls (Piven and Cloward, 1971:250, 285–330; 1979:1013). "Community action" workers carried out these mobilizations *via* counseling, organizing, legal activism and related "community action" activities (1977:272–273). A notable feature of Piven and Cloward's thesis, however, is that it does not project increasing levels of militancy and of government response. According to Piven and Cloward, by the early 1970s, political repression of black political activists, increased lobbying and electoral political orientations of blacks and cooptation had dampened the politics of disruption (Piven and Cloward, 1977:316–333).

2. Hypothesized Non-Determinants

Piven and Cloward (1971:189–196) argue that the increased need for relief manifested by expanding pools of persons eligible for it does not generate increased relief rolls. They so argue on the basis of a perusal of some data on need and welfare rolls and of the argument that relief policy is constrained by a general policy orientation toward maintaining supplies of cheap labor which overly generous relief policies would reduce (Piven and Cloward, 1977: Ch. 1). The authors' conclusion that need does not directly augment welfare roll levels is contradicted by arguments in a considerable volume of literature linking the sizes of needy populations to the scale of welfare services directed toward such populations. The purported link between need and welfare is argued to consist of various mechanisms including the legitimation requirements of governments in industrial and post-industrial societies (or "political systems"), the existence of opportunities for the effective articulation and realization of citizen demands in such societies and, perhaps most forcefully, the legal right to welfare provided for certain sub-populations by welfare legislation. Such general aspects of needs as unemployment, and pools of program-eligible persons as program-specific aspects of need, are principal explanatory factors in this literature (e.g., Fry and Winters, 1970; Wilensky, 1975).

Piven and Cloward's writing on AFDC caseload increases has recently been expanded to include an explicit denial of Robert Albritton's challenge to their thesis (Piven and Cloward, 1979). This alternative explanation emphasizes a set of 1965 amendments to the Social Security Act. Albritton argues that these amendments, enacted before the Watts riot led to a "rapid expansion of the scope of welfare assistance in the form of AFDC rolls" (1979a:1010). According to Albritton, the 1965 amendments, which "extended coverage and incentives to add eligibles to welfare rolls" (1970b:1022), were the cause of the increase in welfare rolls in the subsequent decade. Albritton offered a statistical analysis in support of his thesis (1975:61–65). Piven and Cloward's (1979) denial of 1965 Social Security Act amendment effects, like their denials of commonly hypothesized need effects, merits consideration in any test of Piven and Cloward's caseloads thesis.

III. TESTS OF PIVEN AND CLOWARD'S AFDC CASELOAD EXPLANATION

A. Review

Several recent studies have systematically examined the Piven and Cloward thesis. In a study of variations in AFDC growth across 108 urban counties, Albritton (1979a) finds no support for riot, robbery and burglary effects on AFDC roll increases. In a study of both state and national level changes in AFDC rolls, Jennings (1980) reports modest cross-state and national time-series effects of major riots on AFDC rolls. Jennings' (1981) pooled data and time-series data analysis of AFDC rolls in the American states provides additional evidence of fairly consistent and often strong impacts of major state *and* national riots upon state roll expansions. Isaac and Kelly (1981) report national time-series evidence for riot effects upon AFDC caseload expansion although complementary cross-city analyses do not uncover significant riot impacts upon AFDC growth. Finally, while three of these four studies lend support to the Piven and Cloward thesis, some alternative explanations of AFDC caseload expansion also receive notable support. Effects of measures of need for relief—a *direct* cause of disruptions rather than of rolls in Piven and Cloward—are prominent in Jennings (1980; 1981). "Incrementalism" rather than disruption effects dominate Isaac and Kelly's findings. In short, these four studies yield conflicting findings with mixed implications for the Piven and Cloward thesis.

B. Critique

One problem with these attempts to evaluate Piven and Cloward's argument has been their narrowness of focus. Albritton (1979a), Jennings (1980; 1981), and Isaac and Kelly (1981) all confine their tests to empirical relationships that include only subsets of the factors highlighted in Piven and Cloward's suggested civil disruptions/mobilization thesis. Albritton (1979a) tests only for riot effects and crime effects on AFDC caseload growth. (The latter is only barely hinted at by Piven and Cloward, as noted in Note 1.) However, Jennings (1980; 1981) tests only for "overall" and "major" riot effects and for community action expenditure effects. Moreover, he tests for the latter only in his cross-state analysis, which we criticize below. Isaac and Kelly (1981) confine their attention exclusively to the impact of riots, examining the effect of riot frequency and riot severity on AFDC caseload expansion. Furthermore, Jennings (1980; 1981) and Isaac and Kelly (1981) largely ignore Piven and Cloward's conclusion that need for welfare relief is not directly related to welfare policy outputs. Albritton (1979a) completely ignores any consideration of need. Both Piven and Cloward's claims concerning non-violent protest effects and their denial of 1965 Social Security Act amendment effects on AFDC rolls, as suggested by Albritton (1979a), remain untested, with the exception of an interrupted time-series analysis of potential amendment effects performed without statistical control by Albritton (1975). In short, no author has systematically investigated more than a fraction of the relevant factors involved in Piven and Cloward's disruptions/mobilization thesis of AFDC roll expansion.

A second problem in these empirical tests involves the governmental levels for which effects are examined. Piven and Cloward's discussion of the causes of the dramatic expansion of AFDC rolls entails discussion of governmental perceptions and responses at local, state, *and federal* levels of analysis and interrelations of these, as does any discussion of formal authority over AFDC benefits (e.g., Piven and Cloward, 1971:245, 261). A key factor in the protests of the 1960s is that they had a fundamentally national character that makes it very questionable whether localities can be studied independently and as if events within them were of local origins. Furthermore, as Isaac and Kelly (1981) point out:

We think it quite reasonable to hypothesize that local political officials were as concerned with averting the onset of rioting in cities where it had not yet occurred, as officials were with quelling any further outbreaks in cities where substantial rioting has already taken place.

The multi-level character of processes determining AFDC rolls implies that any subnational analysis of AFDC-roll determinants may be distorted—at least in the absence of complex specifications of contextual effects. The national character that riots and protests appear to have acquired due to the dissemination of news on them *via* the national media suggests that a severe case of Galtung's problem may render any subnational analysis of disturbance impacts on AFDC rolls problematic (see Naroll, 1970:974–989 on Galtung's problem).

All of Albritton's (1979a) analyses and roughly half of Jennings' (1980) analyses are done cross-sectionally with counties and states, respectively. Consequently, conclusions of these authors about disorder-caseload linkages are open to doubt if we assume that they were all subject simultaneously to influences of "national" as well as of "local" events. A national, time-series analysis of annual variations in AFDC rolls provides a simple, potent solution to these problems by controlling for spatial variations and diffusion effects, aggregating information from all relevant levels, and focusing attention at the national level on which Piven and Cloward themselves place greatest stress (see Piven and Cloward, 1979:1012).

IV. CONCEPTUAL AND OPERATIONAL MODELS

A. Piven, Cloward and Their Opponents

In review, Piven and Cloward (1971; 1977) argue that a sequential process involving economic development and crisis, black out-migration from the rural South, black social and economic dislocation, and new stresses and needs gave rise to conditions which produced mass mobilization, protest and, ultimately, violent rioting (e.g., 1971:337–338). Mass black civil disturbances, in combination with the impact of "community action" programs officially legislated to contain them, in turn, culminated in elite policy concessions in the form of AFDC caseload increases. In addition, Piven and Cloward argue that "community action" programs also contributed to the expansion of AFDC caseloads (1971:285–339; 1970:1013).

Crises and migrations are interpreted by us to be *indirect* causes of roll increases. Effects of these factors upon rolls are conceptualized to be channeled by two major types of conduits. One, drawn from Piven and Cloward (1971: esp. 189–191, 335–339), consists of civil disturbances and state responses to them. The second, drawn from sources noted in the following paragraph, consists of needs for relief and state reactions to these. In line with our reading of relevant literature, such crises and migrations are assumed to be potentially indirect

sources of roll expansions without direct effects upon caseloads once the disturbance and need factors explicitly considered in this paper's analyses are taken
into account.[2] In addition, the governmental linkages—attitudes, decision making and so on—connecting disturbances and other explanatory factors considered
here to caseloads are regarded as micro-mechanisms or intervening variables for
the transmission of such factors' effects. In econometric terms, they are regarded
as components of our equations' implicit reduced forms. In summary, a number
of need and demand factors still to be introduced, plus the following core factors
from Piven and Cloward, constitute the heart of our initial model: riots, protests,
and "community action" activities. Each of the three preceding factors is hypothesized to positively affect increases in AFDC caseloads.

Like the crises of Southern agriculture and black migrations out of the South,
"needs" for relief are viewed by Piven and Cloward as indirect causes of AFDC
caseload expansion (1971:335–339). Here, however, Piven and Cloward are
denying more direct effects in the face of contrary claims and evidence in a large
number of works which emphasize the policy-generating role of welfare-needs in
industrial and post-industrial political systems (e.g., Rakoff and Schaeffer, 1970;
Wilensky, 1975; Jennings, 1980). Hence, alternative hypotheses representing
competing theoretical claims are in order. We specify these for those aspects of
need that have been related to welfare outputs in the "industrial systems"
literature and have been identified as relevant to the Piven and Cloward thesis.
These are poverty, unemployment and program-specific pools of those eligible
for AFDC benefits. In line with Piven and Cloward, poverty, unemployment,
and AFDC-eligibility (as operationalized below) are hypothesized to have no
direct effect upon AFDC rolls, net of other factors. If one adopted the "industrial
systems" literature's perspective, each of these factors would be hypothesized to
positively affect increases in AFDC caseloads.

Rival hypotheses are also appropriate for Piven and Cloward and Albritton's
conflicting evaluations of the impact of the 1965 Social Security Act amendments on AFDC roll increases. In line with Piven and Cloward's expectations,
the 1965 Amendments (as operationalized below) are predicted to have no effect
on AFDC caseload expansion, net of other factors. From Albritton's perspective,
the hypothesis is altered: the 1965 amendments are hypothesized to positively
affect AFDC roll expansion.

B.   Change and Incrementalism

Consistent with Piven and Cloward's emphasis on "welfare explosions,"
Jennings (1980; 1981), Albritton (1979a) and other previous tests of Piven and
Cloward's thesis have focused on increases in AFDC rolls.[3] The study of increases or, more generally, changes in a variable requires consideration of previous levels of the variable.

Changes in a variable are quite likely to be related to previous levels in the variable, particularly because of regression-toward-the-mean effects (e.g., Markus, 1979). In general, a correlation between a change and its base is likely enough that neglecting to control for its base year may introduce specification bias of an "omitted variable" sort into statistical analysis. Changes in a variable are commonly studied by means of regression equations of the following form:

$$Y_t = a + b_0 Y_{t-1} + b_1 X_1 + b_2 X_2 + \ldots + b_j X_j + e. \tag{1}$$

As demonstrated by Marcus (1979:45–48) and others, slope coefficients (b's) for regressors other than Y_{t-1} in such models express *changes in changes* in Y, or changes in $Y_t - Y_{t-1}$, for each unit change in the regressor. To clarify:

$$Y_t - Y_{t-1} = a + (b_0 - 1)Y_{t-1} + b_1 X_1 + \ldots + b_j X_j + e, \text{ or}$$
$$\Delta Y = Y_t - Y_{t-1} = a + b_0^* Y_{t-1} + b_1 X_1 + \ldots + b_j k X_j + e, \tag{2}$$

where $b_0^* = b_0 - 1$. Across equations (1) and (2), unstandardized coefficients for the same variables are identical. Coefficients b_1 through b_j can be interpreted as predicting changes in $Y_t - Y_{t-1}$ in equation (1) as well as in equation (2). Significance tests for these coefficients are also identical in equations (1) and (2). b_0 and b_0^* will differ, but systematically according to the formula $b_0^* = b_0 - 1$. Standardized coefficients for X_1 through X_j will differ because a standardized coefficient B_{yx} equals its unstandardized analogue b_{yx} times the ratio of the standard deviation of X to the standard deviation of Y, and because the standard deviations of the dependent variable $Y_t - Y_{t-1}$ and Y are distinct. For most purposes, then, equations (1) and (2) are identical. To sustain clear links between Piven and Cloward's focus upon welfare "explosions," or changes, and our empirical analyses we shall emphasize equations of type (2), which focus more clearly on year-to-year *changes* in AFDC caseloads.

Coefficients for lagged values of a dependent variable, such as the coefficient b_0 are commonly used to index and to test for so-called incrementalism effects. These are typically defined to involve small shifts in budgeting outputs—most commonly, expenditure outputs—from one budgetary measurement period to the next. The marginal shifts may be in increments and/or decrements depending upon the specific formulation. Incremental shifts are interpreted as indicators of bureaucratic and legislative processes that constrain the magnitude of period-to-period changes in outputs. These constraints primarily involve various costs of abrupt change such as costs of information processing and costs of readjusting expectations among politicians, bureaucrats and influential clients and constituents. (See, e.g., Wildavsky, 1975; Padgett, 1980.) These processes all involve inertia in policy-making and delivery.

Such inertia may be studied in terms of b_0. (The closer b_0 is to 1.00, the greater the inertia in shifts in AFDC rolls.) However, because $b_0^* = b_0 - 1$, such inertia may also be studied in terms of b_0^*. (The closer b_0^* is to .00, the greater the inertia in caseload change.) We expect to find marginal shifts in rolls, or a small b_0^*, because of constraints upon abrupt changes in caseloads. With respect to the supply of AFDC beneficiary statuses by government, we expect that politicians and bureaucrats attempt to constrain caseload changes in an effort to keep changes in AFDC program delivery levels, workloads, administrative costs, and payment costs within technically and politically manageable bounds. We also expect that the relative stability of eligibility criteria for benefits will have an inertial effect. On the demand side, we expect that the tendency for AFDC beneficiaries to remain beneficiaries from year to year will have an inertial effect. (On these points, see Goodwin and Moen (1980).)

Our exact hypothesis is that b_0^* will be greater than -0.25 and less than 0.25. This hypothesis involves a "modified" form of incrementalism because it does not directly pertain to budgetary outputs and because it is based upon and interpreted in terms of assumptions about AFDC clients, political and bureaucratic decision-making, and because it is operationalized in terms of b_0^* and Δy (or ΔAFDC) instead of b_0 and y. (Recall that $b_0^* = b_0 - 1$.)

C. Operational Models

1. Measures

The central dependent variable and the three key explanatory factors in Piven and Cloward's disruptions/mobilization thesis of AFDC roll expansion were operationalized as follows. Annual data for each of these variables and all variables discussed below were collected for the period 1947 to 1977. Aid to Families with Dependent Children caseloads (Re: AFDC) were measured in terms of thousands of families receiving AFDC benefits.[4] (ΔAFDC, equal to $AFDC_t -$ $AFDC_{t-1}$, is our principal regressand.) Community Action Program activities (COMACT) were measured indirectly by collecting information on Community Action Program expenditures in millions of dollars. Black riots (RIOTS) were measured in terms of riot frequency.[5] This method of measuring riots is the most commonly used in previous studies of the policy impacts of black riots. Nonviolent protest (PROT) was measured in terms of the frequency of black civil rights-related protest demonstrations.[6]

Variables included in supplementary and alternative hypotheses were operationalized through the following procedures. Following Atkinson's (1975) suggestion, poverty (POV) was measured as the percentage of persons below one-half of the median income. Unemployment (UNEMP) was measured as the proportion of the economically active population unemployed. Eligibility pools for the AFDC program were operationalied using female-headed households below the poverty line (FHHP). Direct data on FHHP was unavailable prior to 1959. Consequently, we relied on estimates or proxies for the period 1948 to 1958.[7]

With respect to the impact of the 1965 Social Security Act amendments, Albritton (1970a:1010) states "abrupt changes in AFDC spending coincide with the implementation of the 1965 legislation.'' Given that our regressand is a change measure, such an abrupt change can be captured by means of dummy variables coded one for *circa* 1965 and zero for other years. Regression slopes for such dummy variables will capture the extent to which, adjusting for control variables, mean caseload changes circa 1965 exceed mean caseload changes for other years. Our principal dummy variable (SSA65) for capturing the abrupt changes hypothesized to follow the 1965 amendments is coded 1 for 1966, zero for other years. However, in order not to overlook possible increases in changes in rolls during the year of the amendments, a variable (SSA6566) coded 1 for 1965 and 1966 will also be employed. Furthermore, rather than neglect possible *sustained* post-amendment increases in changes in rolls, two more dummies will be used, one (SSA66PLUS) coded 1 for 1966 and after, another (SSA65PLUS) coded 1 for 1965 and after.[8]

2. Design and Techniques

Parameters for hypothesized determinants of AFDC caseload increases are estimated, and corresponding hypotheses tested, within a multiple regression framework using annual time-series data. Lagging explanatory variables one or more periods in a model including a lagged dependent variable safeguards slope estimates for the explanatory variables against simultaneity bias and against some other forms of specification bias. Since our model for AFDC is algebraically equivalent to a model with a lagged dependent variable (see equations 1 and 2), lagging regressors provides the same safeguard. Accordingly, we lag our explanatory variables one or more time periods, except in cases of compelling reasons for specifying a contemporaneous rather than a lagged effect. UNEMP, POV, and FHHP were not lagged for just such reasons. Each of these variables is judged to affect AFDC caseloads contemporaneously (i.e., with a lag period of less than one year) by increasing or decreasing the pool of persons who may either directly or indirectly make claims or exert pressures upon AFDC delivery personnel for AFDC benefits. For example, increased unemployment is likely to decrease job prospects for female-household heads, increase their adult dependents, and pressure them to pressure delivery personnel for AFDC enrollment. Poverty is expected to exert similar indirect pressures. Both poverty and unemployment rates are also expected to tap some of the secular variance in female-headed households below the poverty line that FHHP may miss because of measurement error. FHHP should capture most secular variations in the pool of persons eligible for AFDC benefits, and, along with COMACT, index most direct pressure on the part of applicants for increased enrollment.[9]

Specification of delays, or lags, in the operation of possible effects of 1965 Social Security Act amendments was intrinsic to the above specification of SSA6566, SSA66 and other variables used to test the 1965 Social Security amendment hypothesis. However, specification of lags for possible RIOTS,

PROT and COMACT effects on caseload increases has yet to be addressed. One and/or two year lags seem appropriate for capturing the lengths of time necessary for variations in black rioting, black protest and Community Action Agency funding to modify the attitudes and application behaviors of potential AFDC beneficiaries; to alter the goals, strategies and policy choices of AFDC policy-making and delivery personnel; and to register black rioters', black protesters' and "community action" personnel's main impacts upon changes in AFDC caseloads. To assist in the choice of one, the other or both of the lag options for each disruption/mobilization variable, the zero-order correlations between AFDC and each of these variables, lagged one and lagged two periods, were examined. On the bases of these correlations and some ancilliary statistical information, $RIOTS_{t-2}$, $PROT_{t-2}$ and $COMACT_{t-1}$ were chosen as our disturbance/mobilization regressors for the analyses to follow.[10]

Regressions were estimated using a backward stepwise regression procedure. The backward stepwise procedure was designed to exclude regressor variables with F-statistics for slope coefficients of less than 1.00. Backward stepwise regression routinizes the practice of reestimating equations after the exclusion of variables that fail to meet some statistical significance criterion for inclusion in a final equation. Indeed, it improves upon this convention by removing variables sequentially in order of their significance (see Efroymson, 1960). In addition, the exclusion criteria employed—an F-statistic less than one—is a very conservative one in terms of the risk of omitting variables which, despite insignificant effect-parameter estimates, may have non-zero "true" effects. Despite its conservativeness, it guards against the retention of regressors with such insignificant effects that their inclusion would reduce a regression's goodness-of-fit (Haitovsky, 1969).

In our principal regression analysis, we estimate the following regression equation:

$$\triangle AFDC = a + b_0 AFDC_{t-1} + b_1 RIOTS_{t-2} + b_2 PROT_{t-2}$$
$$+ b_3 COMACT_{t-1} + b_4 SSA66_t + b_5 UNEMP_t + b_6 POV_t +$$
$$b_7 FHHP_t + e. \tag{3}$$

The 0.05 level of significance will be considered sufficient to provide some support for a hypothesis, despite scant degrees of freedom. Results that fail to attain 0.05 level significance but that do attain F-values of at least 1.00 and that are retained in equations are judged indeterminate. Our decision to use tests of statistical significance for data on an apparent population is based upon arguments and assumptions presented by Camilleri (1970), Hogood (1970) and Kruskal (1974).

The presence of a lagged dependent variable makes the Durbin h-statistic (rather than the Durbin-Watson d-statistic) appropriate for tests for serially correlated errors. Our equations—of type (2) and (3) above—do not contain explicit lagged dependent variables. However, these equations are simple algebraic transformations of equations of type (1), above. These equations are usefully regarded as "disguised" versions of type (1) equations. Our equations' coefficients and coefficient estimates are either identical to, or errorless functions of, coefficients and coefficient estimates for equations of type (1). Consequently, Durbin's h is the appropriate test-statistic for our tests for serially correlated error (see Johnston, 1972).[11]

V. ANALYSIS AND FINDINGS

A. Principal Analyses

Results from the regression analysis described above are displayed in Table 1. The statistics reported in the table are taken from the final equations that emerged from the backward stepwise regression procedure. This procedure deleted variables whose F-statistics were less than 1.00.[12] The equation for $\triangle$AFDC fits the data well. Its coefficient of determination corrected for degrees of freedom ($\bar{R}^2$) is .754. Its Durbin's h equals .189, indicating a probability of first-order serial error correlation of less than .15 (See P_h in Table 1).[13]

Overall, Piven and Cloward's disruption/mobilization thesis receives only mixed support from our initial analysis. Evidence for the hypothesized positive black rioting and "community action" effects emerges, although evidence for the hypothesized positive non-violent protest effect does not. The estimate of the standardized slope ($\hat{B}$) for RIOTS$_{t-2}$ equals .984 and has a probability value (p)

Table 1.   Results of Regressions of $\triangle$AFDC on Hypothesized
Determinants*

Independent Variables	$\hat{B}$	$\hat{b}$	F	P
AFDC$_{t-1}$	−.892		17.5	.000
RIOT$_{t-2}$	.984		11.8	.001
PROT$_{t-2}$	−.341		4.8	.032
COMACT$_{t-1}$	.577		3.5	.037
UNEMP$_t$	.517		15.6	.000

N = 30 $\bar{R}^2$ = .754   a = −147.12   Durbin's h .189 P_h = .144

Notes:
$\hat{B}$ = estimated standardized regression slope coefficient.
$\hat{b}$ = estimated unstandardized regression slope coefficient.
F   = F-statistic.
p   = probability value of $\hat{b}$ for null hypothesis that b = 0.
$\hat{a}$ = intercept estimate.
$\bar{R}^2$ = coefficient of determination corrected for degrees of freedom.
P_h = probability that first-order error serial correlation is not equal to zero.
*   = Only those hypothesized determinants which were not deleted by backward stepwise procedure because of F-statistic values of less than 1.00 are included in Table 1.

of .001. The standardized parameter estimate and significance for "community action" activity are weaker ($\hat{B}$ = .577; p = .037). Contrary to expectations, civil rights-related black protests appear to have negatively affected AFDC expansion ($\hat{B}$ = −.341; p = .032).[14]

While this negative non-violent protest finding is inconsistent with our overall reading of Piven and Cloward, it is not entirely inconsistent with their writing, nor entirely implausible as a reflection of the linkages between non-violent protests and AFDC caseload changes. First, portions of Piven and Cloward's (1977:267–270) discussion of peaceful black protests suggest that the impact of protests upon AFDC roll expansion may have been confined to a brief (1962–1963) period during the Kennedy Administration.[15] Secondly, the preponderantly civil rights emphasis of the protests may have directed the political attention of black Americans and U.S. governmental leadership and personnel away from the immediate amelioration of poverty by means of welfare policy. Thirdly, protests may have primarily affected roll expansion *indirectly* by contributing to the rise of black rioting and "community action" programs and activities. Consistent with this view, one and two year lagged values of the frequency of non-violent protests are substantially correlated with riot frequency and "community action" expenditures (zero-order correlations vary from .58 to .82). Moreover, a highly significant positive protest effect ($\hat{B}$ = .395; p = .017) emerges if the equation of Table 1 is reestimated after substitution of $PROT_{t-3}$ for $PROT_{t-2}$ and deletion of the "intervening" variables, $RIOTS_{t-2}$ and $COMACT_{t-1}$. In sum, Table 1's non-violent protest results are substantively plausible and not entirely inconsistent with Piven and Cloward (1971; 1977). However, final conclusions about the implications of this negative protest effect should be deferred until after an examination of further empirical analyses presented below. Moreover, our evidence for *indirect,* positive protest effects should be viewed as no more than suggestive *in lieu* of thoroughly specified models of riot frequency and "community action," the variables suggested as channeling possible *indirect* protest effects. (Filling these lacunae is beyond the scope of this paper.)

Two variables not included in Piven and Cloward's set of explanatory factors have substantial effects on changes in AFDC caseloads. The first is unemployment ($UNEMP_t$), which has a statistically significant effect on AFDC roll changes ($\hat{B}$ = .517). This result lends support to those who have viewed "need" as a determinant of welfare outputs. The result entails a rejection of the hypothesis drawn from Piven and Cloward that need does not affect relief, net of mass collection action by the needy. However, results for the other two need variables, poverty and female-headed households below the poverty line, have opposite implications. Effects of POV_t or $FHHP_t$ are not significant enought to yield F-statistics of one or greater. The Piven and Cloward position in the debate over need effects receives some support from our findings for these two variables. However, even this support is substantially undercut by the possibility that POV_t

and FHHP$_t$ effects—primarily a POV$_t$ effect—might have been suppressed by multicollinearity.[16]

The second variable ignored by Piven and Cloward for which we find substantial evidence of an effect is AFDC$_{t-1}$, the "incrementalism" regressor. The parameter estimate for this variable is most cogently described in terms of AFDC$_{t-1}$'s unstandardized slope estimate ($\hat{b} = -.130$). This indicates that the typical year-to-year change in AFDC caseloads, net of all explanatory factors except the prior year's caseload level, is a 13 percent decrease in caseloads from the prior year's level. In other, more speculative words, inertial tendencies in the behaviors of politicians, bureacrats and clients relative to AFDC caseloads tend, net of other forces, to hold year-to-year changes in AFDC caseloads to marginal shifts. More specifically they tend to hold these changes to 13 percent *decreases*. This shift is within the $\pm.25$ range predicted: it is significantly greater than a $-.25$ shift at the .05 level. The very considerable consequentiality of variations in AFDC$_{t-1}$ for variations in $\triangle$AFDC is suggested by the high absolute magnitude of the standardized slope estimate ($\hat{B}$) for AFDC$_{t-1}$. This estimate equals $-.891$. (See footnote 13 for analogous information on b$_0$.)

Finally, the hypothesized effect of the 1965 Social Security Act amendments, or the "Albritton" proposition, receives no support. Similar to the "industrial systems" need variables POV$_t$ and FHHP$_t$, the Albritton variable SSA65, has consistently positive signs in the early stages of the stepwise estimation, but its F-values are always trivial. The three additional operationalizations—SSA6566, SSA65PLUS and SSA66PLUS—all yield similarly trivial results in parallel analyses.

Before proceeding to a final summary and an extended discussion of the above findings, we shall turn to a topic deferred until now. This is the specification of alternative hypotheses. Factors emphasized in "industrial systems" literature referred to above are emphasized. Such factors involve the "capacities" to provide welfare services and benefits and the "demands" for welfare. In addition to "capacity" and "demand" alternatives, we examine the impact of several other hypothesized sources of AFDC increases that have received notable attention in the literature on post-World War Two welfare determination.

B.   Capacities and Demands

At this point, it is useful to return to the "industrial systems" literature, which in contrast to Piven and Cloward's explicit denial of "need" effects, served as a source of the "need" hypotheses above. This literature argues that demands for welfare and the capacity for its provision complement needs for welfare as sources of welfare policy outputs (e.g., Schaeffer and Rakoff, 1970; Jackman, 1975). Our test of Piven and Cloward's explanation of changes in AFDC caseloads has already investigated possible "need" effects explicitly denied by Piven and Cloward (1971:183–196). A look at "capacity" hypotheses conspicuously lacking in Piven and Cloward's discussion of welfare increases, as well as at "demand" hypotheses closely linked to arguments stressing "need" and "capacity" determinants of welfare policy, will round out our consideration of the "industrial systems" explanations of welfare.

Economic Capacity. Piven and Cloward (1971:183–250; 1977:8–29) discuss indirect effects of economic development upon welfare that are channeled *via* civil disruptions. However, they conspicuously neglect reference to more direct development effects, although such direct effects are commonly considered in the "industrial systems" and development/modernization literatures (e.g., Cutright, 1965; Fry and Winters, 1970; Jackman, 1975). Most commonly, relatively high or rapidly increasing levels of economic affluence are argued to entail relatively high or increasing citizen willingness to finance increased welfare outputs (see Cameron, 1978:1245). That is, economic affluence and growth increase state capacities to finance welfare. We tested a number of "capacity" propositions which we adapted to our study of AFDC caseload increases. We hypothesized that levels of and annual percentage changes in per capita real GNP, both lagged and unlagged, positively affect changes in AFDC caseloads.[17] The capacity variables were entered into the equation of Table 1 separately and in all possible sequences. Two capacity measures enter the equation. One is the percentage change in GNP from "t − 1" to "t" ($\%\triangle GNP_t$); the second is the percentage change in GNP from "t − 2" to "t − 1" ($\%\triangle GNP_{t-1}$). Contrary to expectations, each of these has a significant *negative* effect upon AFDC caseload increases (see Table 2, especially column I). These estimates involve no substantial multicollinearity and have a simple interpretation. The measures of percentage changes in GNP are operating as additional (albeit inverse) indicators of need: higher rates of year-to-year economic growth yield decreases in caseloads because such growth connotes declining need. The addition of the two GNP measures improves the fit of our evolving model. The $\bar{R}^2$ increases from .754 to .834. This addition also greatly attenuates the size and significance of UN-EMP$_t$'s effect estimates (F = 1.01 in Table 2, column I).[18] The new economic growth regressors actually cause COMACT$_{t-1}$ to be deleted from our equation.[19] Ironically, the addition of two need effects is accompanied by an augmentation of the black rioting effects (see Table 2).

Electorally Mediated Demands. Demands are not entirely omitted from the hypothesized determinants and the statistical analyses presented above, given that Piven and Cloward's concern with black collective behavior is, in political systems parlance, a concern with the transmission of demands. Nevertheless, our consideration of demands, until now, has emphasized the transmission of demands *via* direct action. It has ignored the transmission of demands by means of electoral processes and organizations such as voting and parties. These are the primary channels for popular influence on U.S. public policy identified by most of the policy determination literature (see, e.g., Rakoff and Schaeffer, 1970; Frey and Schneider, 1978).

Although direct time-series data on demands and their electoral transmission is virtually non-existent, means for capturing the influence of mass demands on public policy are not lacking (see Isaac and Kelly, 1981; Frey and Schneider, 1978; Golden and Poterba, 1980). We tested several propositions which we adapted to our model of AFDC caseload increases from works with a broader and somewhat distinct focus upon income transfer payments. We hypothesized that Democratic presidential administrations (operationally, DEM) positively affect AFDC caseload increases (e.g., Isaac and Kelly, 1981). Popularity levels of presidential incumbents of both major parties (operationally, POP), Democratic incumbents (DEMPOP) and Republican incumbents (REPPOP) are hypothesized to negatively affect AFDC roll increases (e.g., Golden and Poterba, 1980). Popularity deficits (POPDF) and Democratic popularity surpluses (DROPSR) should positively affect AFDC caseloads, while Republican popularity surpluses (RPOPSR) should negatively affect AFDC rolls (Frey and Schneider, 1978).

These hypotheses were tested by including the demand variables in a regression equation containing regressors from the first equation in Table 2.[20] Demand variables were *included in the following four sets:* DEM; POP; DEMPOP, REPPOP; POPDF, DPOPSR, RPOPSR. This was done to preserve degrees of freedom, limit potential multicollinearity, and avoid simultaneous tests for inconsistent hypotheses (e.g., for POP and POPDF). Only one of the demand variables— DEMPOP—achieves an F-value of greater than 1.00, as indicated by the second equation in Table 2. As hypothesized, the impact of DEMPOP is negative, although DEMPOP is barely retained in the equation because of its F-value of only 1.02 ($p = .162$). (See Table 2, column II.) Nevertheless, a negative impact of Democratic popularity is not only consistent with the literature that stresses the importance of demands as determinants of transfer payments. It is consistent with the theorizing of Piven and Cloward as well. As noted above, Piven and Cloward (1971:253–256; 1979:1012–1015) suggest that elite electoral vulnerability, or declining electoral support for Democratic Party candidates during the 1950s, provided the context and initial impetus for concessionary responses to black disruptions and relief mobilizations. While DEMPOP by no means captures the complex interplay of electoral forces, blacks' insurgency, and policy responses suggested by Piven and Cloward (1971, 1979), the weak negative impact of DEMPOP upon AFDC roll changes is consistent with their observations concerning policy consequences of Democratic elite vulnerability.[21] The inclusion of DEMPOP in the "capacities" equation has three consequences. Specifically, the presence of DEMPOP moderately decreases the effects of the GNP regressors, enhances the effect of the unemployment variable, and, most notably, renders the coefficient for non-violent black protests insignificant. ($PROT_{t-2}$ still retains its negative sign and is arguably of marginal significance ($p = .059$).)

Table 2. Results of Regressions of ΔAFDC on Hypothesized Determinants of Table 1 Plus Additional Controls*

Type of Variable Considered for First Time

Independent Variable	Capacities (I)	Demands (II)	Miscellany (III)
$AFDC_{t-1}$	-.363 (-.05) 6.12 (.010)	-.44 (-.06) 7.08 (.007)	-.42 (-.06) 7.01 (.008)
$RIOTS_{t-2}$	1.15 (113.5) 54.43 (.000)	1.17 (114.9) 55.40 (.000)	1.22 (120.00) 63.27 (.000)
$PROT_{t-1}$	-.29 (-24.81) 5.7 (.025)	-.254 (-21.59) 3.9 (.059)	-.18 (-15.40) 1.96 (.176)
$COMACT_{t-1}$	* *	* *	* *
$UNEMP_t$	.152 (16.79) 1.00 (.163)	.255 (24.85) 1.80 (.097)	.193 (21.31) 1.4 (.123)
$\%\Delta GNP_t$	-.364 (-18.15) 17.14 (.000)	-.321 (16.03) 10.87 (.002)	-.348 (-17.39) 13.55 (.000)
$\%\Delta GNP_{t-1}$	-.236 (-11.68) 5.30 (.015)	-.191 (-9.47) 2.94 (.051)	-.196 (-9.69) 3.35 (.04)
$DEMPOP_t$	—	-.11 (-.580) 1.02 (1.62)	-.147 (-.782) 1.9 (.089)
$MILTEXP_t$	—	—	-.75 (-1.81) 2.96 (.050)
â**	55.61	23.88	119.56
$\bar{R}^2$	.834	.834	.848
Durbin's h**	.246	.103	.070
P_h**	.344	.078	.056

Notes:
*Only those hypothesized determinants which were not deleted beause of F-statistics less than 1.00 are included in columns. These report standardized slope estimates followed by their F-statistic values, with unstandardized estimates in parentheses under standardized ones and with p-values of slope estimates under F-statistics.

**For definitions of these symbols see Table 1.

C. Alternative Explanations of AFDC Caseload Expansion

A number of additional explanations of welfare expenditure growth have received support in recent empirical analyses of welfare expansion in the post-World War Two United States. In addition to the hypothesized sources of AFDC expansion treated above, Isaac and Kelly (1981) found evidence to suggest that differences over time in levels of average-monthly payments and military expenditures have important impacts upon welfare expenditure and caseload increases. Various studies have suggested that the poor in the urban North and North Central portions of the United States are disproportionately likely to enter welfare rolls (Long, 1974:46–56, esp. 46). As suggested by several scholars (e.g., Winegarden, 1973), increased benefit levels may supply increased incentives to non-enrolled, potential welfare beneficiaries to more actively seek admission to the rolls. As suggested in Long (1974) and elsewhere, a more positive orientation toward welfare utilization on the part of the "Northern" poor, together with a more liberal orientation toward admissions to welfare rolls (and toward benefit levels) on the part of welfare decision makers in the North may have led to a greater responsiveness of Northern (and North Central) rolls to poverty.[22] Another possibility is that increased military spending may have squeezed out spending for welfare expansion (e.g., Russett, 1970).[23]

In order to test for the hypothesized effects of the above factors upon increases in AFDC rolls, both lagged and unlagged levels of the preceding variables were entered into the "demand" equation of Table 2, column II. No variable but unlagged military spending levels ($MILTEXP_t$) is retained. Not even "average monthly AFDC payments" is retained, although this variable had a sizeable estimated effect upon rolls in Isaac and Kelly (1981).[24] The $MILTEXP_t$ effect estimate just attains the .05 significance level and is negative as anticipated ($B = -.75$).

With the inclusion of $MILTEXP_t$ a number of parameter estimates are modified. $RIOT_{t-2}$'s slope attains a strong standardized value of 1.22, a strong unstandardized one of 63.3 (and an $F=120$). The former effect estimate, though very strong, contains an element of arbitrariness. If we substitute $AFDC_t$ for the explicit measure of change AFDC, the standardized slope estimates for $RIOTS_{t-2}$ (like those for other X variables) decline because of the greater standard deviation of $AFDC_t$. The standardized slope estimate for $RIOTS_{t-2}$ for the final (Table 2, column III) specification of explanatory variables become .167.[25] However, the unstandarized riot slope, which is invariant with respect to changes between the regressands $AFDC_t$ and $\triangle AFDC$, is clearly and strikingly strong. Given our natural logarithmic transformation of riot frequency it has the following interpretation: a one percent increase in riot frequency from its mean generates 63,300 more AFDC caseloads. The effect of economic growth—or, more tellingly, recession—is slightly increased, as is the effect of Democratic popularity, which attains the marginal .10 level of significance ($p = .029$). The initially significant but always somewhat questionable effect estimate for non-violent black protest diminishes, falling below all conventional standards for statistical significance. Interestingly, evidence for an *indirect* $PROT_{t-3}$ effect is strengthened with the addition of $MILTEXP_t$. If $PROT_{t-3}$ is substituted for $RIOTS_{t-2}$ (in the equation of Table 2, column III), $PROT_{t-3}$ achieves a B of .597, and a p-value of .003. (There is still no indication of any effect with a protest variable in the presence of a control for $RIOTS_{t-2}$, and the equations with $PROT_{t-2}$ simply substituted for $RIOTS_{t-2}$ "explain" roughly *30 percent less* variance than those with $RIOTS_{t-2}$.) The final equation of our analyses explains 84.7 percent of the variance in $\triangle AFDC$ after adjustment for degrees of freedom, and it has a very small probability of error autocorrelations. If we substitute $AFDC_t$ for $\triangle AFDC$, R^2 rises to .997.

VI. SUMMARY AND DISCUSSION

Our findings have mixed implications for Piven and Cloward's explanations of post-war AFDC caseload growth. Several of our findings are inconsistent with assertions made by Piven and Cloward, and others suggest inadequacies and incompleteness in Piven and Cloward's treatment of the sources of AFDC caseload variations. Contrary to explicit assertions by Piven and Cloward that need does not directly impact on welfare provision, changing levels of need for relief benefits appear to have generated variations in caseload changes net of any impacts that need might have had upon civil disruptions. This point is underscored by our findings involving strong impacts of economic growth (or declining need) and the marginal effects of unemployment upon welfare caseloads. Furthermore, Piven and Cloward's suggestion that increasing levels of "community action" activity generated substantial increases in AFDC rolls receives little support from our analysis. As demonstrated above, effects of "community action" funding become trivial, net of our full array of controls for disruptions, "incrementalism" and need (see Table 2).[26] Past levels of AFDC caseloads and relatively high military spending also appear to have been consequential for changes in AFDC caseloads, although Piven and Cloward have been silent regarding "incrementalism" and "guns-versus-butter" constraints on welfare caseload variation. Our findings imply not only weaknesses in Piven and Cloward's explanation of AFDC caseload growth but inaccuracies in their broader treatments of welfare provision in advanced capitalist societies. For example, Piven and Cloward's counterfactual claim that AFDC rolls decreased following the early 1970s cessation of black riots follows logically from their view that AFDC roll increases were generated by disruptions alone.

Several of our findings do lend noticeable support to Piven and Cloward's claims concerning the determinants of post-World War Two United States welfare expansions. First, Robert Albritton's explanation of caseload increases in terms of 1965 amendments to the Social Security Act receives no support, consistent with Piven and Cloward's (1979) comments on the Albritton thesis. Secondly, Piven and Cloward's suggestion that black non-violent protests may have *indirectly* affected increases in AFDC caseloads receives at least marginal support. This stems from our finding that non-violent protests may have indirectly contributed to increases in AFDC caseloads *via* effects channeled through violent disruptions. Most important, Piven and Cloward's thesis that *black riots functioned to expand AFDC rolls* receives strong support. Finally, Democratic administrations appear—consistent with Piven and Cloward—to have responded to declines in mass public support by accelerating the provision of AFDC beneficiary statuses.

The most striking of the diverse findings to emerge from our analysis is the one linking riots to AFDC rolls. At the core of Piven and Cloward's theorizing is the argument that relief concessions such as increases in AFDC rolls were responses to riots as cues to possible black electoral defections during Kennedy and Johnson administrations, as indicators of the distresses and tensions targeted for amelioration by anti-poverty programs, as signs and sources of relief demands upon street-level bureaucrats, and as threats of general governmental delegitimation. Our estimates of riot effects are at least consistent with such responses and suggest that these effects were quite strong, stronger than previous quantitative studies of AFDC caseloads have suggested.

Systematic empirical evidence of black riot effects upon increases in AFDC caseloads in the post-World War Two United States has now been found in several studies (see Jennings, 1980; 1981; Isaac and Kelly, 1981). This evidence supports the contention of Piven and Cloward (1977:5) and Goldstone (1980) that substantial formal organization of social movements is not a necessary precondition for obtaining policy objectives or concessionary policy responses from the state. (See Gusfield, 1970:453, for a contrary view.) This evidence also adds to a rapidly strengthening empirical case for the occurrence of policy-effective "direct action" by materially disadvantaged groups, particularly in post-1945 advanced capitalist polyarchies (see, also, Gamson, 1975; Button, 1978; Swank, 1983). New theorizing and research concerning conflictual as well as organizational political activities is suggested by our findings and by their theoretical implications.

It should be emphasized that the results of our analyses do not solely support Piven and Cloward's riot thesis. They also support propositions neglected or challenged by Piven and Cloward. First, as has been the case in many previous studies of policy determination, inertial, marginally shifting, policy trajectories emerge as important aspects of the policy process. We find that AFDC caseloads exhibit great uniformity across typical year-to-year periods, despite some successive, relatively big changes during the 1964–1971 period. We also find that decreases in the growth rate of real GNP, as an indicator of "need" for relief, positively affected AFDC caseload increases. Thus, the relative empirical novelty and theoretical unorthodoxy of policy effects of disruptive collective action by the poor should not be read to indicate irrelevance for hypothesized causal factors from the "budgetary" and "industrial society and welfare state" literatures on policy determination.

Neither should the relevance of such relatively unconventional public-policy determinants be read to imply the desirability of unbridled eclecticism in the study of policy determination. Even though non-institutionalized political conflict has not been central to conventional political science treatments of public policy determination, it is hardly inconsistent with pluralistic, industrial society frameworks (e.g., Dahrendorf, 1958:231–240). Similarly, although incrementalism and need effects on policy fit neatly into a developmental, industrial society orientation, they are also interpretable in less orthodox terms. For example, bureaucratic inertia is not inconsistent with the emergent neo-Marxist emphasis on state structures, and unemployment effects upon policy are interpretable in terms of politicians' efforts to buoy state legitimacy (see O'Connor, 1973). A principal challenge confronting social scientists is to assimilate the diverse compelling insights about the sources of state policies into coherent theoretical frameworks. This must be done without inhibiting the intellectual dynamism and safeguards against error that diversity promotes. It is becoming increasingly evident that political conflict and direct action are among those factors that theorists of policy determination can ignore only at risk of considerable distortion (Swank, 1983; Griffin et al., forthcoming).

ACKNOWLEDGMENT

The authors share equally in the paper's authorship. Special thanks are offered to Robert Lineberry, Larry Isaac, Robert Albritton and Ted R. Gurr, and also to Sheldon Danziger, Neil Fligstein, Herbert Jacob, and Christopher Winship for comments and criticism of earlier writing on the topic of this paper. Thanks are also expressed to the National Institute of Mental Health, and the National Opinion Research Center for support for portions of this project.

NOTES

1. For research on Piven and Cloward's (1971:226–31) vague suggestion that crime may have affected welfare policy, see Swank (1981).

2. Regional specification of poverty to the North and North Central regions of the United States are employed in tests in the section on "Alternative Explanations . . ." (also see note 22). Such "Northern" poverty is likely to have been partially determined by South-to-North migration (Long, 1974). Its use in analyses provides a particularly sensitive test of poverty as a potential conduit for indirect migration effects upon AFDC expansion.

3. Isaac and Kelly (1981) control for lagged AFDC caseloads in their analysis of caseloads, converting it into an analysis of change. (See "Change and Incrementalism" section.)

4. AFDC caseload data were collected from U.S. Bureau of the Census (1972: esp. Series H,

346–347; 1949–1979a). A measure of caseloads as a proportion of the population of potential AFDC beneficiaries that standardizes on, and controls for, demographic variations in the population of eligibles, might be preferred. One direct measure of beneficiary households as proportions of households eligible for AFDC benefits is available for 1967 and 1969–1977 (see Michael, 1980). This measure correlates .98 with our caseload measure (for 1967–1977 after inclusion of a 1968 value estimated *via* simple linear interpolation). Thus, our measure of AFDC caseloads may be interpreted as a proxy for the *mobilization of eligible beneficiaries*.

5. Community action expenditure data were collected from selected annual volumes of the Office of Management and Budget (1966–1978). All expenditure data were adjusted for inflation (see Bureau of the Census 1949–1979a, esp. 1979). 1960–1970 riot frequency data are from the raw data files of Ted Robert Gurr. (See also ICPSR data set 7531.) Pre-1960 and post-1970 data are from the *New York Times Index*. Our black riot data exludes what Janowitz (1979) terms communal riots and concentrates on what he terms commodity or anti-establishment riots. These are riots initiated by blacks against property or perceived symbols of ''the white Establishment.'' Our riot frequency variable was sufficiently skewed to merit use of its *natural logarithm*.

6. Data on protest frequency are from the *New York Times Index* and logged (like riots) to offset skewness.

7. Poverty was measured using interpolative estimates of percentages computed with data from U.S. Bureau of the Census (1949–1979b). Unemployment data are from U.S. Bureau of the Census (1976; 1949–1979a, especially 1978). The measurement of FHHP for the years 1948–1958 was done as follows. Female-headed households below the poverty line were regressed upon a number of 1959–1977 measures not used in our principal analysis. It was found to be well predicted by three measures not used in our analysis: military expenditures, black unemployment rates and a counter for years (R= .98). The resulting equation in combination with 1948–1958 values on these three variables was used to generate predicted values of female-headed households for 1948–1958. These values were used to complete the 1948–1958 portion of the poor female-headed households time-series. 1959–1977 data on female-headed households below the poverty line are from Table 18 of Bureau of Census (1979). Data on black unemployment and military spending are from U.S. Bureau of Census (1949–1979a).

8. Let us emphasize that SSA66PLUS and SSA65PLUS test for year-to-year *changes* for *every* year following 1965 and 1964, respctively. With these two dummies, we test *extensions* of Albritton's formulation below.

9. Analyses with lagged measures of need were also performed. One-year-lagged measures of each need variable were entered both one-at-a-time and together into equations containing (1) the variables entered into the analyses reported in Table 1, and (2) the variables in columns 3a and 3b of Table 2. In every case, effects of the lagged need terms were insignificant or weaker than those for the need terms for which they were substituting.

10. Correlations with $AFDC_t$ were .626 for $RIOTS_{t-1}$ and .751 for $RIOTS_{t-2}$; .309 for $PROT_{t-1}$ and .325 for $PROT_{t-2}$; .664 for $COMACT_{t-1}$ and .661 for $COMACT_{t-2}$. We chose $PROT_{t-2}$ over $PROT_{t-1}$ and $COMACT_{t-1}$ over $COMACT_{t-2}$ only after exploratory analyses consistently revealed somewhat larger and more significant effects for the eventual choices. These explorations included estimations with each option included alone and with one- and two-period lags included simultaneously.

11. As for all models with autoregressive lagged endogenous variables, estimates for our model will be inconsistent if equation *errors* are autocorrelated. As for all models of our type that are estimated with small samples (i.e., with less than roughly 30 degrees of freedom), our estimates will suffer from some small-sample bias even if error autocorrelation is not present. However, for the sample size (i.e., 30) and the numbers of degrees of freedom (i.e., 21 to 24) present in our analyses, the amounts of such small-sample bias that will arise *in lieu* of error autocorrelation will be demonstrably small (see Johnston, 1972, Chapter 10, especially equation 10-3). If our Durbin's h's reveal low (and, better yet, consistently low) probabilities that first-order autocorrelation is equal to zero,

we may be fairly confident that the properties of our estimates are not distorted as a result of error autocorrelation and lagged endogenous variables.

12.   The difference between our backward stepwise regression procedure and forward stepwise regression must be emphasized. *Forward* stepwise regression starts off by considering variables for inclusion in a regression on the basis of the significance levels of lower-order coefficients. (For example, it begins with zero-order coefficients for a, so far, regressorless equation, first-order coefficients for a so-far bivariate or one-regressor equation, and so on.) The coefficients considered to determine inclusion with the *forward* procedure are thus particularly likely to suffer from specification bias due to the omitted-relevant-variable problem (see Rao and Miller, 1971).

13.   A couple of technical notes are appropriate here. First, readers may be interested to know that variables in the equation of Table 1 are identical to those with slope estimates with F-values greater than one in the initial round of stepwise estimations in which all of the variables of equation (3) are included. Second, tests for heteroscedasticity, including one suggested by Jackman (1980), were performed. They revealed no heteroscedasticity. Third, the fit of the algebraically identical model with $AFDC_t$ rather than $\triangle AFDC$ as a regressand is predictably very strong ($R^2 = .995$), while, standardized slopes in this alternative model (except that for $AFDC_{t-1}$ which equals .831) are smaller in absolute values than are their Table 1 analogues. They are .137 as large as the standardized slopes of Table 1 because of the much greater variance in $AFDC_t$ (than in $\triangle AFDC$). (See the discussion following equations 1 and 2.)

14.   It should be noted that two of the variables in our analyses, $RIOTS_{t-2}$ and $COMACT_{t-1}$, are highly collinear. Each shares *circa* 90 percent of its variance with the other regressors of equation (3) and of Table 1. (Much of this multicollinearity is a result of these two variables' zero-order correlation of .81.) Although no given level of multicollinearity *per se* signals severe estimation problems, these levels of multicollinearity are sufficient to raise the possibility of seriously inflated standard errors of estimates, the principal multicollinearity problem (see, Klein, 1962:50; Theil, 1971: 162–168; Johnston, 1972:163–164). Inflated standard errors may rob parameter estimates of desired levels of precision, attenuating the power of these statistics and denying the analyst the ability to detect theoretically designated differences between parameter *estimate* values and parameter values set in null hypotheses (e.g., zero). Fortunately, multicollinearity in Table 1 is not sufficient to hinder rejection of the null hypotheses that slopes for $RIOTS_{t-2}$ and $COMACT_{t-1}$ equal zero. However, in an analysis to follow, $COMACT_{t-1}$ will fall well below statistical significance and be deleted from our equations (see Table 2, especially column I). We shall return to this instance of multicollinearity in our discussion of Table 2. To conclude the present discussion of potentially multicollinearity-induced problems, let us note that $AFDC_{t-1}$ and POV_t also are quite multicollinear, respectively sharing 90 and 85 percent of the variances with the other regressors of equation (3). Since standard errors for $AFDC_{t-1}$ slopes are in all instances less than a quarter (the absolute value of) the sizes of $AFDC_{t-1}$ slopes, and, thus, more than precise enough for any uses we have for them, we do not regard $AFDC_{t-1}$'s multicollinearity as problematic. Possible problems due to POV_t's multicollinearity are dealt with in note 16.

15.   We tested for interaction between protests and dummy variables for the Kennedy administration and Kennedy-Johnson administration. While these tests yielded positive coefficients for the protest-administration interactions, F-values were consistently of a trivial magnitude (i.e., $F < 1.00$).

16.   Readers might suspect considerable multicollinearity among and involving the "need" variables. Indeed, as stated in footnote 14, POV_t is quite multicollinear with the regressors from the Table 1-related analyses. (It also correlates .72 with $UNEMP_t$.) As it turns out, multicollinearity for $UNEMP_t$ and $FHHP_t$ is not severe and collinearity between $FHHP_t$ and two other need variables is low. Nevertheless the equation of Table 1 was reestimated with each combination of need variables taken two-at-a-time in order to uncover possible multicollinearity-induced supression of need effects. The two reestimations including $UNEMP_t$ yield the same results presented in Table 1. Reestimation with POV_t and $FHHP_t$ yields an equation with a significant POV_t effect estimate ($\hat{B} = .383$; p $= .034$), a very marginal $FHHP_t$ effect estimate ($\hat{B} = .176$; p $= .159$; F $= 1.04$), and $AFDC_{t-1}$, riot

and "community action" effects nearly identical to those reported in Table 1. However, the fit of the equation with POV_t and $FHHP_t$ ($\bar{R}^2 = .652$) is markedly inferior to that with only $UNEMP_t$ ($\bar{R}^2 = .753$). This information, in combination with the extremely low F-statistics of *circa* .34 for POV_t and FHHP when these variables are added to the Table 2 equation, suggests that $UNEMP_t$ is far and away the most consequential of the three need variables for AFDC expansion. Moreover, it suggests that there is little indication of a POV_t or an $FHHP_t$ effect or of a multicollinearity-induced suppression of such effects, and that potential POV_t and $FHHP_t$ effects are more plausibly viewed as controlled away by $UNEMP_T$ than as suppressed by their multicollinearity with $UNEMP_t$.

17. Data on per capita real GNP for 1947–1977 are from U.S. Bureau of Census (1949–1979a).

18. Attenuation of the $UNEMP_t$ effect by the addition of two GNP-change variables (with negative effects on rolls) into our regressions suggests that changes in GNP may longitudinally tap variations in need better than unemployment rates. Certainly, the latter's omission of "discouraged" former job-seekers, and underemployment and its neglect of changing labor force composition have cast doubts upon unemployment statistics. (The GNP-change measures are *not* multicollinear and they do *not* notably augment the extent of multicollinearity for $UNEMP_t$.) In addition, investigations into possible effects of change measures of unemployment and lagged measures of unemployment rates and their changes reveal *no* new evidence for unemployment-related effects. Let us note that the negative economic growth effects need not solely be interpreted as need effects. For example, Wilensky (1975:55) suggests that economic growth augments individualistic, laissez-faire (as opposed to statist and welfare) citizen approaches to economic problems.

19. As suggested above, this diminution of any sign of a statistically significant $COMACT_{t-1}$ effect might be due to $COMACT_{t-1}$'s high multicollinearity, in particular, with $RIOTS_{t-2}$ (see footnote 14). To check on this possibility, various relevant regressions were estimated, yielding the following results. First, $COMACT_{t-1}$ is always significant (F *circa* 17.0, p *circa* 0.00) *when* the equations of Table 2 are reestimated with $COMACT_{t-1}$ substituted for $RIOTS_{t-2}$. However, "RIOTS equations" consistently explain about 15 percent more variance in $\triangle AFDC$ than do "COMACT equations" (e.g., *circa* 83 percent as opposed to *circa* 68 percent). Secondly, if $COMACT_{t-1}$ and $RIOTS_{t-2}$ are orthoganilized by residualizing $COMACT_{t-1}$ on $RIOTS_{t-2}$ (allocating all of the two variables' common variance to $RIOTS_{t-2}$) and the residualized $COMACT_{t-1}$ is added to Table 2's regression, this orthogonalized $COMACT_{t-1}$ has no remotely significant effects. Yet, if $RIOTS_{t-2}$ is residualized on $COMACT_{t-1}$ and included in analogous regressions with $COMACT_{t-1}$, effects of the residualized variant of $RIOTS_{t-2}$ persist. These are about as significant as effects of $COMACT_{t-1}$ (F's *circa* 26.0), despite allocation of *all* shared variance to $COMACT_{t-1}$. From the results we conclude: (1) riot effects are stronger and more robust than any reasonably construed "community action" effects; and (2) the possibility of some "community action" effects cannot be unequivocally rejected, even though evidence *for* "community action" effects can only be "identified" by biasing analyses toward such effects.

20. Democratic administrations (DEM) were coded one, Republican administrations (REP), zero. Popularity (POP) was measured as the average proportion of respondents answering "yes" to the famed Gallup Poll Presidential approval question. Democratic popularity (DEMPOP) equals POP for Democratic administrations, zero for Republican administrations. Republican popularity (REPPOP) equals POP for Republican administrations, otherwise zero. Following Frey and Schneider (1978) popularity deficits (POPDEF) equal $(POP - POP^*)^2$ for POP less than or equal to POP^*, otherwise zero. Democratic popularity surpluses (DEMPOPSURP) equal $(POP - POP^*)^2$ for POP greater than POP^* and DEM equal to one; otherwise they equal zero. Republican popularity surpluses equal $(POP - POP^*)^2$ for POP greater than POP^* and DEM equal to zero; otherwise they equal zero. Because DEM is expected to tap roughly contemporaneous effects of administrations and because popularity-related variables have typically been lagged one *quarter* year, no lags were deemed appropriate for operationalizing "demand" with our annual data. (Lags were examined and have no effect on demand results.)

21. An effective operationalization of Piven and Cloward's claims concerning and consequences

of Democratic elite electoral vulnerability for AFDC caseload expansions was, in principal, desirable. However, Piven and Cloward's claims involve strategic early-1960s Democratic policy responses to both black and Southern-white electoral defections throughout the 1950s, at the very least, *plus* possible interactions between responses to defections and disruption. No adequate operationalization of Piven and Cloward's vulnerability formulation was devised nor seemed devisable within an aggregate longitudinal analytic framework.

22. It should be noted that Piven and Cloward (1971:191–192) briefly dismiss any effect of average monthly payments or of "Northern" poverty and benefit liberalism upon AFDC rolls. However, payment effects are suggested in several studies (e.g., Isaac and Kelly, 1981), and "Northern" poverty-benefit effects on rolls are at least consistent with the findings of several studies (e.g., Feagin, 1972). It should also be noted that the Northern poverty-benefits argument is viewed both by its advocates and critics (sic. Piven and Cloward) as a crucial component of cases for the existence of migration effects upon AFDC rolls. Northern and North Central poverty are measured in terms of families with less than one-half of the U.S. median income as proportions of families. Data limitations required that denominators as well as numerators of regional poverty measures be confined to numbers of regional families and that Northern and North Central poverty be measured separately. (See note 23.)

23. Data on average monthly payments to AFDC families are from U.S. Bureau of the Census (1972, 1949–1979b, Series H). Data on proportions of Northern and North Central families below one-half the U.S. median income are from U.S. Bureau of the Census (1947–1979b). Those data are only available for our 1953–1977 time series and were run on separate 1954–1977 equations with and without the significant lagged military spending variable.

24. It might be argued that SSA66 and related Social Security Amendments measures, CO-MACT$_{t-1}$, and average monthly AFDC payments all tap the increasing social legislation, social spending and social welfare liberalism of the 1964–1971 period of greatest AFDC expansion. If that is true, our tests for these variables have been conservative, biased toward the rejection of null hypotheses.

25. See "Change and Incrementalism" section and note 13.

26. As noted in notes 14 and 19, the triviality of "community action" effects in part may be due to COMACT$_{t-1}$'s collinearity with other regressors (esp. RIOTS$_{t-2}$). This collinearity militates against any unequivocal conclusion that "community action" was inconsequential for AFDC roll expansion.

REFERENCES

Albritton, Robert B.
1975 "Simulation of welfare spending: some approaches to public policy analysis." Pp. 52–72 in Dorothy B. James (ed.), Analyzing Poverty Policy. Lexington, MA.: D. C. Heath.
1979a "Social amelioration through mass insurgency: a reexamination of the Piven and Cloward thesis." American Political Science Review. 73:1003–1011.
1979b "A reply to Piven and Cloward." American Political Science Review. 73:1020–1923.
Atkinson, Anthony Barnes
1975 The Economics of Inequality. Oxford: Clarendon Press.
Bachrach, Peter and Morton Baratz
1970 Power and Poverty: Theory and Practice. New York: Oxford University Press.
Button, James W.
1978 Black Violence: Political Impact of the 1960's Riots. Princeton, NJ: Princeton University Press.
Cameron, David R.
1978 "The expansion of the public economy: a comparative analysis." American Political Science Review 72:1243–1261.

Camilleri, Santo F.
  1970   "Theory, probability and induction in social research." Ch. 16 in Denton E. Morrison and Ramon E. Henkel (eds.), The Significance Test Controversy. Chicago: Aldine.
Cutright, Phillips
  1965   "Political structure, economic development and social security programs." American Journal of Sociology 70:537–550.
Dahrendorf, Ralph
  1959   Class and Class Conflict in Industrial Society. Stanford: Stanford University Press.
Efroymson, M. A.
  1960   "Multiple regression analysis." Pp. 191–203 in R. Ralston and H. Will (eds.), Mathematical Models in Digital Computers. New York: Wiley.
Feagin, J. R.
  1972   "Poverty: we still believe that God helps those who help themselves." Psychology Today 6:101–111.
Feagin, J. R. and H. Hahn
  1973   Ghetto Revolts: The Politics of Violence in American Cities. New York: MacMillan.
Frey, Bruno S. and Friedrich Schneider
  1978   "An empirical study of politico-economic interaction in the United States." Review of Economics and Statistics 60:174–183.
Fry, Brian R. and Richard F. Winters
  1970   "The politics of redistribution." American Political Science Review 49:508–522.
Gamson, William A.
  1975   The Strategy of Social Protest. Homewood, ILL.: Dorsey Press.
Golden, David and James Poterba
  1980   "The price of popularity: the political business cycle reexamined." American Journal of Political Science. 24:696–714.
Goldstone, Jack
  1980   "A new look at Gamson's strategy of social protest." American Journal of Sociology. 85:1428–1432.
Goodwin, Leonard and Phyllis Moen
  1980   "The evaluation and implementation of family welfare policy." Policy Studies Journal 8:633–651.
Griffin, Larry J., Joel Devine and Michael Wallace
  1983   "On the politics and economics of welfare expansion in the post World War II United States." Politics and Society, forthcoming.
Gurr, Ted Robert
  1980   "On the outcomes of violent conflict." Pp. 238–294 in T. R. Gurr (ed.), Handbook of Political Conflict: Theory and Research. New York: Free Press.
  1983   Special issue on conflict outcomes.: American Behavioral Scientist. 26:283–416.
Gusfield, Joseph R., (ed.).
  1970   Protest, Reform and Revolt: A Reader in Social Movements. New York: John Wiley and Sons.
Hagood, Margaret Jorman
  1970   "The notion of a hypothetical universe." Ch. 4 in Denton E. Morrison and Ramon E. Henkely (eds.), The Significance Test Controversy. Chicago: Aldine.
Haitovsky, Y.
  1969   "A note on the maximization of R-square." American Statistician 23:20–21.
Isaac, Larry and William R. Kelly
  1981   "Racial insurgency, the state and welfare expansion: local and national level evidence from the post-war United States." American Journal of Sociology 86:1348–1386.
Jackman, Robert
  1975   Politics and Social Equality. New York: Wiley.

1980   "Note on the measurement of growth rates in cross-national research." American Journal
        of Sociology 86:604–617.
Janowitz, Morris
1979   "Collective racial violence: a contemporary history." Pp. 261–285 in T. R. Gurr and H.
        Graham (eds.), Violence in America. Beverly Hills, CA.: Sage.
Jennings, Edward T.
1980   "Urban riots and welfare policy change." Pp. 111–144 in Helen Ingram and Dean Mann
        (eds.), Why Policies Succeed or Fail. Beverly Hills, CA.: Sage Publications.
1981   "Social amelioration through mass insurgency revisited: another look at the welfare conse-
        quences of urban riots." Paper presented at the annual meeting of the Midwest Political
        Science Association, April 16–18, Cincinnati, Ohio.
Johnston, John
1972   Econometric Methods, 2nd ed. New York: McGraw Hill.
Klein, Lawrence Robert
1962   An Introduction to Econometrics. Englewood Cliffs, NJ: Prentice Hall.
Kruskal, William
1974   "The ubiquity of statistics." American Statistician 28:3–6.
Lindblom, Charles E.
1977   Politics and Markets: The World's Political-Economic Systems. New York: Basic Books.
Lipsky, Michael
1968   "Protest as a political resource." American Political Science Review 62:114–158.
Long, Larry H.
1974   "Poverty status and receipt of welfare among migrants and nonmigrants in large cities."
        American Sociological Review 39:46–56.
Markus, Gregory B.
1979   Analyzing Panel Data. Beverly Hills, CA.: Sage Publications.
Michael, R.
1980   "Participation in the aid to families with dependent children program, part I: national
        trends from 1967 to 1977." Washington, D.C.: The Urban Institute, working paper 1387–
        1402.
Naroll, Raoul
1970   "Galton's problem." Pp. 974–978 in Raoul Naroll and Ronald Cohen (eds.), Handbook of
        Methods in Cultural Anthropology. Garden City, NJ: Natural History Press.
New York Times Index.
1948–   New York: The New York Times Company.
1977
O'Connor, James
1973   The Fiscal Crisis of the State. Boston: St. Martin's Press.
Office of Management and Budget
1966–   Special Analyses: Budget of the United States Government. Washington, D.C.: U.S.
1978   Government Printing Office.
Padgett, John F.
1980   "Bounded rationality in budgetary research." American Political Science Review
        74:354–372.
Piven, Frances Fox and Richard A. Cloward
1971   Regulating the Poor: The Functions of Social Welfare. New York: Vintage, Random
        House.
1977   Poor People's Movements: Why They Succeed, How They Fail. New York: Pantheon
        Books.
1979   "Electoral instability, civil disorder and relief rises: a reply to Albritton." American
        Political Science Review 73:1012–1019.

Rakoff, Stuart H. and Schaeffer, Guenther F.
  1970   "Politics, policy and political science: theoretical alternatives." Politics and Society 2:51.
Rao, Potluri and R. L. Miller
  1971   Applied Econometrics. Belmont, CA: Wadsworth.
Russett, Bruce M.
  1970   What Price Vigilance? New Haven, Conn. Yale University Press.
Schattschneider, Elmer Eric
  1960   Two Semi-Soverign People, A Realistic View of Democracy in America. New York: Holt.
Swank, Duane H.
  1981   "Does crime really pay? The state, social instability and the growth of social welfare in the
         post-World War II United States." Presented at the annual meeting of the American
         Political Science Association, New York.
  1983   "Between incrementalism and revolution: protest groups and the growth of the welfare
         state in advanced industrial democracies." American Behavioral Scientist 26:291–310.
Theil, Henri
  1971   Principles in Econometrics. New York: Wiley.
U.S. Bureau of the Census
  1972   Historical Statistics of the United States, Colonial times to 1970. Washington, D.C.:
         Government Printing Office.
  1949– Statistical abstract of the United States. Washington, D.C.: Government Printing Office.
  1979a
  1949– Current population reports: consumer income, Series P-60. Washington, D.C.: Govern-
  1979b. ment Printing Office.

Welch, Susan
  1975   "The impact of urban riots on urban expenditures." American Journal of Political Science
         19:741–760.
Wildavsky, Aaron
  1975   Budgeting: A Comparative Theory of Budgeting Processes. Boston: Little Brown.
Wilensky, Harold L.
  1975   The Welfare State and Equality. Berkeley: University of California Press.
Winegarden, C. R.
  1973   "The welfare explosion: Determinants of the size and recent growth of the AFDC Popula-
         tion." American Journal of Economy and Society. 32:245–256.

ALINSKY'S LEGACY:
CURRENT APPLICATIONS AND EXTENSIONS
OF HIS PRINCIPLES AND STRATEGIES

Donald C. Reitzes and Dietrich C. Reitzes

I.   INTRODUCTION

The death of Saul D. Alinsky in 1972 is one of a series of possible benchmarks for locating the conclusion of an era of vibrant community organization and experimentation in grass roots citizen participation. A period of social and political upheaval was ending. It signalled the decline of vocal protest, radicialism, and massive federal aid to urban areas, including support of city and community job, education, and housing programs. Alinsky was remarkably successful in generating broad public interest and enthusiasm for community organization through a combination of well publicized community organization ventures, popular books, and a flamboyant personal style. He emerged as a national figure advocating and defending community organization as a mix of protest and conflict ideologies with involvement in social programs and a goal of local citizen participation.

Research in Social Movements, Conflict and Change, Vol. 6, pages 31–55.
Copyright © 1984 by JAI Press Inc.
All rights of reproduction in any form reserved.
ISBN: 0-89232-311-6

Ten years later the social and political climate appears very different and the lasting significance of Alinsky's work has been questioned. His orientation and programs may seem distant, inappropriate, and unworkable under the current conditions of a sluggish to stagnant economy, the growth and aggressiveness of conservative organizations and conservative politicians, and the massive cuts in federal spending on social and urban programs. This perspective suggests that Saul Alinsky has become an historical figure, whose approaches and organizations are of limited utility. An alternative interpretation, however, suggests that the Alinsky style of community organization did not die with him but is still being applied, modified, and extended. There has not emerged a successor of national stature capable of arousing wide public interest in community organizing or in maintaining an orthodox and unified Alinsky approach. However, the basic concepts Alinsky developed are being used and their implementation suggests that Alinsky's principles and strategies are as relevant today as they were in the 1960s.

This analysis explores Alinsky's legacy by reviewing and assessing the underlying principles and current applications of his work. The investigation covers three related topics. We begin by developing Alinsky's major orientations and tenets in order to better understand his strategies and to establish the criteria for reviewing current community organization ventures. Alinsky, despite his publications and public presentations, failed to clearly articulate the goals and purposes of his activities. His alienation from the academic social sciences prevented his use of current concepts and formulations necessary to clarify his intuitive grasp of community, organization, and power. The second step in the analysis is to investigate some contemporary community organizations and to see how they have applied, modified, and extended his principles and strategies. Examples are limited to Chicago-based organizations or organizations formerly located in Chicago. We will investigate national organizations which were either established by Alinsky or which base their strategies on Alinsky principles. Finally, the review of Alinsky's orientation and current community organization activities provides the foundation for assessing both Alinsky's relevance and the direction of contemporary community organizations.

II.   THEORETICAL BACKGROUND: AN OVERVIEW OF ALINSKY'S ORIENTATION

Alinsky was clearly impatient with theoretical discussions and chided academics to apply their attention to the task of community building. Thus, he wrote that "Asking a sociologist to solve a problem is like prescribing an enema for diarrhea" (Alinsky, 1972:64). Yet, today his importance lies in his vision of the promise and potential of community organization and his weaving together of a penetrating analysis of urban social conditions with a masterful sense of the strategies necessary to accomplish change. According to one current observer of community politics, "Alinsky is to community organizing as Freud is to psycho-analysis" (Boyte, 1980:39). The themes of urban social structure, organization, and community power provide the basis for unraveling Alinsky's orientation and establish the framework for the investigation of current applications of his work.

A. Community

Alinsky's understanding of urban social structure and community is probably the least well articulated theme in his writings but is, nevertheless, absolutely central both to an appreciation of his strategies and to any analysis of the success of his organizational ventures. Embedded in his rhetoric, observations, and rules for organizers is the recognition of: (1) the complex and multifaceted character of urban social structure; (2) the need to purposively generate and continuously support community-wide ties and attachments; and (3) the use of conflict to heighten cohesiveness within the community and to create a working instrumental organization.

Alinsky's understanding of the complex character of community is apparent in his awareness of the interdependence of units of social structure and the fragmentary and often competitive character of local attachments. Alinsky (1941, 1946, 1971) consistently argued that communities are not autonomous and self-sufficient entities but reflect the consequences of urban and national processes and policies. Alinsky pointed out with pride, as early as 1941, that his Back Of the Yards Neighborhood Council made residents aware that many of their problems stemmed from external sources and that the organization members became involved in city-wide and national issues. Alinsky is completely in line with the current understanding that community is a "uniquely linked unit of social/spatial organization between the forces and institutions of the larger society and the localized routines of individuals in their everyday lives" (Hunter, 1979:269).

He was keenly aware that abstract references to "community" often belie the heterogeneous and fragmented character of localities. Alinsky notes (1969:64-75) that relationships among local groups and leaders may often be hostile with competition among groups for the economic resources and social commitments of the same set of residents. Hostilities may also arise between heterogeneous groups over the political control and dominance of the community. Similarly, local groups with external affiliations such as unions and churches may also vie for influence among overlapping or competing memberships. The result is a community pattern which ranges from minimal participation in the locality to intense rivalry and competition among groups which prevent unified action or community organization. Alinsky (1971) used the term "organized apathy" to refer to this pattern of multiple and fragmented ties which encouraged intra-community conflict and discouraged participation in cooperative community. His success as an organizer stems, in part, from his recognition of the complexity of urban social structure and therefore the difficulty of community organization. Alinsky realized that common interests, and not territory, is the key to unifying residents and creating a vital community (Alinsky, 1972: 115-116, 120).

The complexity of urban social structure highlights the dilemma of community-wide attachment and organization. On one hand, the local community is typically linked in a dependent fashion to the economic and political institutions of the larger society. Residents of the locality are confronted with the employment, housing, and educational problems and policies of the city and nation but have little or no influence on the institutions that powerfully affect community life. Equally important, on the other hand, is the problem that the smaller, more intimate networks and groups in the locality often have greater salience and influence with residents than do community-wide groups. Nevertheless, community-wide attachments are extremely important as the local units most capable of representing and defending community needs and interests. The emphasis Alinsky placed on the role of the community-wide organization as spokesman for local interests complements emerging sociological perspectives of urban social structure (Bates and Bacon, 1972; Hunter and Suttles, 1972) and parallels Jacobs' (1961) insight that the role of the district (community) is to mediate between the inherently powerless street neighborhoods and the inherently powerful city as a whole.

Alinsky not only held a realistic understanding of the complex character of urban social structure, but extended current perspectives by emphasizing that the creation and maintenance of community-wide attachments and organization requires purposive and continuous action. Unlike models (see Hunter and Suttles, 1972) that assume that community attachments and identification are products of crescive or "natural" processes, Alinsky sees the organizer as an active agent for the conscious and intentional creation of community. In his view, the planned intervention of the organizer is of vital importance. He argues that combating organized apathy requires "community disorganization," and that "present arrangements must be disorganized if they are to be displaced by new patterns that provide the opportunities and means for citizen participation" (Alinsky, 1971:116). Part of Alinsky's strategy of community organization was the realignment of community interests toward interests and problems which were shared concerns of local residents. The maintenance of community-wide ties requires continuous action. Alinsky noted that it is the organizer's job to create issues and the community organization requires a constant stream of issues which appeal to the different and divergent segments of the community. "Organizations are built on issues that are specific, immediate, and realizable. . . . Organizations must be based on many issues" (Alinsky, 1971:120). Alinsky's emphasis on the purposive social construction of community is one of his unrecognized contributions to the understanding of urban social structure.

The third significant feature of Alinsky's understanding of urban social struc-

ture was his brillant use of non-violent conflict to heighten community cohesiveness. Hunter and Suttles (1972) argue that the intentional and unintentional
actions of outside advocates and antagonists aid in boundary maintenance and
community identity formation. Alinsky grasped the potential use of outsiders as a
common enemy to intensify local attachment and provide an issue for unified
community action. For example, upon arrival in Rochester, New York, where he
had been invited by white church leaders to organize the black community,
Alinsky publicly attacked a major company, the largest local newspaper, and the
local university. He maintained that his purpose was to provoke a negative
response from city leaders which would aid in winning local black acceptance of
him as an organizer and gain support for a locally based community organization. Alinsky argued (1969) that the task of the organizer was to use conflict with
external antagonists to demonstrate to local residents that their private discontents were shared social problems requiring a cooperative and organized community response. Thus, conflict was initially used to create a situation more conducive to positive community development.

B.   Organization

Alinsky's emphasis on organization as the catalyst for community development is the second theme which is vital to an understanding of his orientation.
The creation and maintenance of a community-wide and community-controlled
organization is the most salient feature of Alinsky's approach. Alinsky shares
with a resource mobilization approach (McCarthy and Zald, 1977; Zald and
McCarthy, 1979) an interest in the organization character and properties of a
social or community movement and an interest in the complex interplay of
external and internal factors on the development of instrumental action.
Alinsky's scheme may be divided into three parts: (1) the emergence of the community organization; (2) the mobilization of community resoures; and (3) the
application of community resources.

Alinsky's goal of community development shares with a resource mobilization
approach the emphasis on community (social movement) organization. It is the
organization which provides the structure, leadership, and policy direction which
both coordinates the action of members and influences the relationship between
the community and outside institutions. The first task of the organizer is to
develop the organization. This requires generating: (1) an awareness among local
residents that many of their private troubles are shared social problems, originat-
ing from structural conditions and best attacked through cooperative social and
political action; (2) acceptance of the organizer as an advisor to the emerging
organization; and (3) the funds necessary to establish a secure financial base for
the organization. An Alinsky trademark was a formal invitation extended by
local leaders to the organizer to highlight the community-controlled character of
the organization and to gain local acceptance for the organizer.

The next phase of the organizing venture is to broaden local acceptance and generate further interest in community-participation by provoking a hostile public reaction to the organizer by some external city-wide leader or spokesman. The strategy, as noted earlier, parallels Hunter and Suttles (1972) argument that community-wide boundaries and attachments are mobilized in response to the policies and organizational units of external adversaries. The negative reception by external adversaries not only aids in establishing the legitimacy and credibility of the organizer within the local community, but also heightens a community-wide identification. In Rochester, external advocates were also identified and organized through the establishment of "friends of FIGHT," an associated group of 400 white liberals, which provided funds, moral support, legal advice, and instructors for our community training projects (Alinsky, 1972:176). Alinsky typically tried to establish in advance the necessary funding for the organization. Often he sought and received support from local and national religious organizations or from private foundations. However, financial support from within the community to be organized was also actively solicited to generate commitment and a sense of investment in the organization, as well as to establish the organization's responsibility to local residents. Initial fund drives were often an early community-wide activity which encouraged cooperative action and generated common ties.

Alinsky was a master in the mobilization and control of local resources. After the organizer succeeded in gaining local acceptance, Alinsky (1946, 1969:77-83) suggested a period of quiet observation similiar to a sociological study. This time was to be used to identify local leaders, patterns of formal and informal interaction, local customs and traditions, and issues of particular importance to residents. Alinsky's strategies exemplify Fireman and Gamson' (1979) recognition of the importance of existing community groups for the establishment of solidarity and the need for an organization to obtain support from local leaders. Alinsky used three types of activities to maintain residents' interest and participation in the organization. First, in the Chicago community of Austin, the Alinsky organizer spent his first year establishing a network of block clubs (Bailey, 1972:66). In addition to continuing the process of introducing local residents to community action and a shared approach to individual troubles, the network of block clubs provided a foundation for organization on the community-wide level. Whenever possible, Alinsky used existing groups, particularly church groups and unions to demonstrate that community organization is compatible with local interests. Second, was a call for a community congress or convention. Its main purpose was to transform the coalition of groups into a broad-based, multiple issues and permanent community organization. The first convention ratified the constitution, approved the budget, and selected representatives and executive officers. Succeeding annual conventions were to keep the community up-to-date on the activities of the organization. An important aspect of the structure was the multiple standing committees dealing with salient local issues. This permitted the organization to pursue multiple issues simultaneously and to mobilize the interests of the many residents.

Third, Alinsky used small scale conflicts with internal antagonists, such as local merchants and realtors, to further demonstrate to local residents the effectiveness of joint action and base appeals for local participation on self-interest. He urged that initial issues should be highly visible and concrete, salient to local residents but not divisive or antagonistic to other local groups, and easy to win (Alinsky, 1971:114-159). He consistently argued that the first set of issues is particularly important when the organizations and leaders are inexperienced, when members are tentative in their commitment, and when acceptance of the organization and of the organizer are still in question. A series of successful specific and localized confrontations built confidence among leaders and members and demonstrated the organization's ability to improve the quality of neighborhood life. The target of confrontations was typically outside agencies, which defined their service and market areas within the local community. Thus, outside merchants, realtors, landlords, hospitals, social service agencies, and municipal services with local branches were frequent targets, in part, because they were dependent on the local community for clients, customers, employees and constituents.

The application of mobilized resources highlights Alinsky's goal of investing the community organization with the means to enter interest group politics as a spokesman and bargaining agent for the local community. Alinsky's use of nonviolent conflict directly reflects Oberschall's (1979:46) point that nonconventional conflict, harassment, and coercion may be the only means of influence available to relatively powerless groups facing powerful and legitimate opponents. Alinsky was also a master at using population size and the availability of people as a main resource to pressure and harass antagonists. He used the tactic of picketing in situations where public relations were a valued commodity for his opponent and the tactic of boycotts on educational systems whose financial support was based on attendance. The use of coercive tactics reflects an attempt to create a situation where antagonists perceive that it is in their best interests to negotiate with the community organization, while the community organization is in the position to offer the cessation of conflict in exchange for concessions and a settlement.

C. Power

Power and a commitment to democratic pluralism combine to form the third underlying theme vital to an understanding of Alinsky's orientation. Alinsky's use of confrontation tactics and his self-proclaimed radicalism are by far the most widely known but also the most misunderstood and misinterpreted facets of his work. Power and instrumental community action linked Alinsky's analysis of urban social structure with his emphasis on organization and the mobilization of community resources. The importance Alinsky placed on community power and the ability of the instrumental community organization to mobilize local resources is a direct outcome of his pluralist view of urban power. Alinsky saw urban politics and power as a continuous, changing, and dynamic interaction among economic, political, religious, and social or ethnic groups. Groups sought to maintain or expand control over their constituency and resources, while defeating antagonists and achieving instrumental goals. As issues arise, groups with parallel sets of interests create alliances and confront opponents in the appropriate political, economic, legal, and social areas. New issues generate new alliances, city-wide decisions and patterns of influence emerge as a product of power and not as a matter of rational planning. The problem for Alinsky was not the "system," but rather that major segments of the population were being excluded or not fully represented in the process.

Alinsky (1941, 1946, 1971) consistently maintained that one of the major structural weaknesses of most communities, and especially minority and poor communities, was the absence of instrumental community-wide organizations capable of exerting pressure on external institutions and resolving community problems. Unlike middle class residents, whose political and economic interests may be served by a host of voluntary or professional associations, poor people are more dependent on their residental areas as a basis of political and interest-group representation. The absence of strong local instrumental organizations in lower class neighborhoods may lead to an increased sense of alientation and powerlessness, or in some cases, such as in Boston's West-End (Gans, 1962) or Chicago's Addams' Area (Suttles, 1968), to the physical destruction of parts of the community. Alinsky felt that one of his major accomplishments in Chicago's Woodlawn area was to provide the community with an organization capable of mobilizing community resources into an effective interest or power group and using its influence to bargain with representatives of city government, social service agencies, and private business and industry:

> perhaps our most important accomplishment in Woodlawn was intangible; by building a mass power organization, we gave the people a sense of identity and pride. After living in squalor and despair for generations, they suddenly discovered the unity and resolve to score victories over their enemies, and to take their lives back into their own hands and control their own destinies (Alinsky, 1972:169-1970).

In addition to solving specific community problems, one of the central goals of community organization was to use conflict and confrontation strategies to gain recognition from outside organizations and institutions that the organization was the legitimate spokesman and bargaining agent for the community. The long term goal was to enable the community, through the organization, to broaden its voice and participation in city-wide decision making and to establish direct lines of influence with external organizations whose programs and policies directly influence the local community. Alinsky (1971) stated that he was ready to leave a community, and consider his mission a success, when its place in the city power structure was secure enough that it could lose a few issues and still retain credibility with local residents and viability with city-wide institutions.

Alinsky, beyond any other label, was a democrat and advocate of grass roots pluralism. His ideology and political program were closer to De Tocqueville than to Marx. Despite his proclaimed "radicalism", his political goal was not to overthrow existing institutions but rather to make them more democratic and responsive to a broader set of interests. Alinsky was distrustful of central authority, whether corporate or government, and feared that it limited the scope of participation and range of citizen involvement:

> I do no believe that democracy can survive except as a formality if the ordinary citizen's role is limited to voting, and if he is incapable of initiative or all possibility of influencing the political, social, and economic structures that surround him (Alinsky, 1969:217-218).

Similarly, on the city level, Alinsky believed that local interests would be best maintained and preserved by active, local voluntary associations. In Alinsky's view, "The democratic process cannot function lacking the essential prime mix of legitimate, bona fide representatives to meet accredited representatives of other sectors of society in the pushing, hauling, dealing, and temporary compromises before the process begins to repeat in the perpetual process of pressure of the democratic way" (Alinsky 1968:293). Finally, Alinsky was proud that his organizations were democratically structured and able to endure as active voluntary associations. He proposed that to be legitimate, a community organization must have a political structure based on indigenous leadership and citizen participation; an economic structure which ensures financial independence; and a social commitment to rigorously defend local interests.

III. CONTEMPORARY APPLICATIONS: REGIONAL AND NATIONAL TRAINING ORGANIZATIONS

The previous section presented a brief theoretical background which organized Alinsky's underlying assumptions and principles. Its purpose is to provide a better understanding of the goals and rationale of Alinsky's actions. The next step is to return to our central issue concerning the current applications and significance of Alinsky and his work. The question, again, is how appropriate is Alinsky's orientation today and what are some of the directions of Alinsky's legacy? This section presents three national organizations, located in Chicago or formerly located in Chicago, which train local leaders or establish community organizations. The task is to review their activities, discuss their applications, modifications, and extensions of Alinsky principles and strategies, and to assess Alinsky's relevance to their activities.

A.   The Industrial Areas Foundation (IAF)

The Industrial Areas Foundation (IAF) was started by Alinsky early in the 1940s. Marshall Field III became interested in Alinsky's Back of the Yards activities and provided the initial financial support to enable Alinsky to continue as a full-time, professional community organizer. The IAF was the organization which accepted contracts for Alinsky's services and which in turn paid him as its Executive Director. By 1969 Alinsky had decided to transform the IAF into a central training institute to which groups sent local leaders and staff to be trained as community organizers. When Alinsky died in 1972, Edward Chambers, an Alinsky-trained organizer and long-time staff member, became the Executive Director. Chambers moved the IAF to Huntington, New York in 1979 and returned the emphasis of the organization to on-site community organization. The IAF today is involved in community organization activities in 19 cities (Chambers, 1982).

Chambers' approach to community organization is clearly based on Alinsky's basic concepts, extended and further developed to deal with current conditions and problems. He is critical of social movements in the 1960s and 1970s, describing them as ineffective and unstable. Each tended to be built on a single issue, led by a charismatic leader with a very loose organizational structure and often a precarious financial foundation. If the leader died, or the issue was settled, or the public lost interest, then the movement died (Chambers, 1978). In contrast, he notes with pride the durability and organizational integrity of IAF organizations. Chambers (1978) identifies eight important features of community organization:

1.   a secure financial base, initially created by a two to three year contract with the IAF;
2.   knowledgeable and experienced guidance provided by a full-time, profes- sional organizer;
3.   well-trained local leaders and staff;
4.   skillfully managed campaigns representing the interests of residents;
5.   a community-controlled and community-led instrumental organization;
6.   engagement in multiple issues or projects reflecting the diverse concerns and interests of residents;
7.   a capability for quick and continuous actions to maintain interest in the organization and community; and
8.   enough flexibility to change leaders and tactics to meet organizational and community goals.

Chambers focuses on the crafting of a community organization and the technical expertise of the IAF.

Recently the IAF has been successful in organizing Mexican-American communities. Ernie Cortes was sent by the IAF to San Antonio early in the 1970s with funds provided by the Catholic Church. An organization was begun by tapping existing leadership in local churches, PTAs, and women's clubs. He extensively trained local leaders in the tasks of breaking down problems into manageable parts including researching issues, planning strategies, initiating action and evaluating strategies (Boyte, 1980:64). Over 2,000 people were then interviewed, as an organizing aid, to identify local opinions, issues, informal groups, and networks. The interviews also served as a means for the organizer to initiate contact with local residents and to begin the process of generating interest and enthusiasm for the organization. Communities Organized for Public Service (COPS) was founded in 1974 and by 1976 was one of the largest community organizations in the country with over 6,000 delegates attending the annual convention.

An emerging issue concerned the city's use of community development and revenue-sharing funds. COPS proposed an alternative city budget, interviewed candidates for mayor and city council, and began an extensive voter registration drive which netted more than 18,000 new voters. All of the COPS-backed candidates won, and the 1977 election was hailed as a major victory for the organization. COPS has since announced that it will no longer endorse candidates but has monitored issues and called community meetings to present community concerns to city officials (Boyte, 1980:165). The organization also takes credit for having lobbied for over $200 million worth of capital improvement for central city neighborhoods and for leading a successful campaign to block a Chamber of Commerce drive to attract new businesses that specialize in low skill, low wage labor (Crowder, 1981c).

COPS has spawned two additional IAF organized ventures in Mexican-American communities. The El Paso Interdenominational Sponsoring Organization was created by forty Catholic and Protestant churches and spent most of 1979 and 1980 raising $100,000 for an IAF organizer. Since December, 1980, over twenty churches have pledged to support the community organization with yearly dues ranging from $750-$6,000 (Crowder, 1981b). The organization has begun to mobilize Mexican-American residents by calling a community meeting where 200 people requested two local aldermen to propose a ban on drinking in a local park. Actions are underway to improve social services for public housing residents, upgrading city maintenance of local streets, and to prevent the closing of a neighborhood hospital (Crowder, 1981a).

Ernie Cortes moved to East Los Angeles and has been organizing Mexican-American residents into the United Neighborhood Organization (UNO). He began with the moral and financial support of the local bishop and used area Catholic churches as organizing centers for extensive training of local leaders and residential interviewers (Boyte, 1980:65). Early UNO activities have focused on extending the scope and quality of police and social services in the area (Leff, 1981:1). Two special campaigns have mobilized local support for the

organization. Three thousand residents met with state insurance officials to protest redlining by auto insurance companies and won a promise for immediate
action (Boyte, 1980:66-67), and three hundred UNO members descended on the
Merrill Lynch offices in Los Angeles to pressure the Safeway supermarket chain
to expand service and upgrade its commitment to the area (Leff, 1981). Since
then UNO has met with more than seventy top executives of Los Angeles
companies to request financial support for their community (Leff, 1981).

Returning to Alinsky's legacy, Chambers and the IAF staff extend and elaborate Alinsky's principles and strategies in each of the three areas of community,
organization, and power. Alinsky understood well both the fragmentary and
competitive character of local attachments, as well as the interdependence and
multifaceted nature of the linkage between local community and larger units of
social structure. While Alinsky often relied on national church organizations for
financial support and on local churches for leaders or aid in generating community support, Chambers (1978) has formalized the connection and requires parish
support as one of the conditions for IAF acceptance of an organizing contract.
Local parishes provide a fledgling organization with:

1. an experienced set of leaders, who are accustomed to responsibility and
    hold the trust and confidence of residents;
2. local loyalty to the church, which aids in winning acceptance for the
    organizer in a new community and legitimacy for the organization;
3. entry to church affiliated groups and contact with local community social
    networks which are necessary for identifying salient issues and possible
    foundations for community-wide participation;
4. an institutional home and community base for the organization.

IAF success in Mexican-American and other predominantly Catholic communities may be due, in part, to church support. Gans (1962) and Suttles (1968)
note that churches are among the few external institutions serving a locality with
extensive vertical or extra-community ties and resources which may become
locally controlled or influenced. Indeed, they found that church leaders in working class Italian neighborhoods served as both community spokesman in dealing
with external adversaries and as mediators of local disputes. Chambers' reifica-
tion of the linkage between local churches and community may aid the organizing process but it also limits the range and scope of community organization.
Further, it fails to identify or sensitize organizers to situations where other
institutions, such as unions, political parties, or existing instrumental organizations, may provide comparable resources and support.

Chambers extends and elaborates Alinsky's community organization procedures in at least two ways. First, he is actively creating and spreading a legend
to cultivate the connection between the IAF and Alinsky. He is using Alinsky's
reputation to generate publicity about the IAF and its community ventures by
telling stories about Alinsky's outrageous remarks and famous antics. News-

paper accounts, particularly early in the development of an organization, may introduce people to the organization and aid in generating interest and enthusiasms in community-wide participation. Ties to Alinsky may aid in legitimatizing the organization by highlighting the accomplished history, proud tradition, and long experience of the IAF in developing community organizations. Chambers wants to convince people that since Alinsky was successful, so can the new IAF ventures succeed (Crowder, 1981a). Secondly, Chambers (1982) points out that the IAF no longer follows Alinsky's practice of totally severing ties and withdrawing from an organization after the expiration of a contract. The IAF now maintains a role in the selection of local leaders and insists that leadership be changed every two years. Chambers (1982) argues that leaders in the community organization may become entrenched and more involved in protecting their role or prestige than in further developing the organization. The prolonged IAF-community contract permits cancellation by either party and Chambers has used the threat of cancellation to influence local leaders.

Turning to the area of power, Chambers (1978) modifies and extends Alinsky's approach by eliminating references to "radicalism," which often peppered Alinsky's rhetoric. Indeed, Chambers pragmatically appeals to church or family values and to the need of citizens to actively defend their beliefs through participation in locally controlled community organizations. The appeal to traditional values is an attempt to broaden the base of community organization and to reduce any alienation or hesitancy on the part of middle class or conservative residents which could prevent participation in the organization. Similarly, conflict as a strategy has been de-emphasized. Even confrontation tactics now do not go beyond meeting with local officials in order to express grievances and to request action. Finally, Lancourt (1979:172-173) argues that for organizations to achieve lasting structural changes and influence they must get actively involved in local politics. It is fascinating that COPS ended its direct involvement in politics after successfully backing candidates and establishing a close working relationship with the newly elected city officials. The maintenance of community-wide ties and the role of the organization as a defender of local interests may require its direct involvement in local elections and politics. Chambers and the IAF may have to substantially extend their conception of the role of community organization in a participatory democracy and enter pluralist politics.

B. National People's Action (NPA) and National Training and Information Center (NTIC)

While Chambers is a direct descendent, Alinsky's lessons have also been disseminated by a number of other Alinsky-trained organizers. One of the most influential is Thomas Gaudette, who, through his Mid-America Institute, has actively been training organizers since the 1960s. Today he runs training sessions from his headquarters in Chicago and from centers in Pasadena, Philadelphia, and New Orleans (Gaudette, 1982). Gaudette (1981) was personally recruited and trained by Alinsky. He was assigned to organize the northwest side of Chicago (Northwest Community Organization) and later was responsible for the development of Organization for a Better Austin (OBA). OBA, although no longer in existence, is important, in part for several reasons. One reason is that OBA had a book written about it. Gaudette allowed the organization to be observed and the resulting investigation is one of the most comprehensive accounts of Alinsky tactics and strategies (Bailey, 1972). Also, OBA is significant because it became one of the leading organizations to publicize and attack banking and insurance redlining. OBA also, has a continuing legacy in the activities of two of its leaders. Gale Cincotta and Sheldon Trapp, went on to establish a new organization, National People's Action (NPA) which represents a major extension and development of Alinsky techniques and principles.

Gale Cincotta was an Austin housewife who became involved in neighborhood affairs through her concern with the education of her children. She became the first president of OBA and actively led the organization in a series of confrontations aginst slum landlords and real estate speculators who were block-busting and frightening white homeowners as the area was beginning to undergo racial transition. The organization was not able to maintain an integrated neighborhood but did claim responsibility for the absence of violence or a major racial disturbance. The fight against redlining led Cincotta to form a city-wide coalition and in 1972 Cincotta and Trapp called together a national conference on the problems of central city housing. The conference was attended by more than 2,000 people representing neighborhoods in 37 states. An outgrowth of the conference was the formation of National People's Action (NPA) which was envisioned as a national coalition of neighbors which could collectively represent the common issues that concerned neighborhood groups. In addition, the National Training and Information Center (NTIC) was formed to provide a structure for the training of local leaders. Cincotta was elected the first president of NPA and Trapp the national coordinator of NTIC (Cincotta, 1982; Swanson, 1982).

NPA is today a coalition of 200 neighborhood organizations engaged in a variety of lobbying and confrontation activities. NPA's first activities were centered on redlining, and the organization extensively lobbied for the passage of three pieces of legislation between 1972 and 1975: (1) the Illinois anti-redlining law, which was the first in the nation; (2) the National Mortgage Disclosure Act, which requires lending institutions to reveal where they make loans; and (3) a national moratorium on mortgage foreclosures on Federal Housing Authority Loans (Trapp, 1982a). In 1976 NPA pressured the Law Enforcement Assistance Administration (LEAA) for a fund to support local community efforts in anti-crime programs and LEAA allocated $32 million for community anti-crime programs. Since then NPA has used sit-ins and mass visitations to directly confront officials in HUD, the Department of Justice, the Department of Energy, and the Federal Reserve Board (Trapp, 1982b).

Recently, NPA has directed its attention to the private sector and to large corporations and other private business organizations. School buses filled with supporters have "visited" meetings of the Business Roundtable, National Association of Manufacturers, American Council for Life Insurance, and the American Petroleum Institute. In the fall of 1981, the American Petroleum Institute held its annual meetings in Chicago and NPA led a counter-meeting where over 5,000 people participated in the two days of activities. Workshops, strategy sessions, and meetings of a Congressional delegation, including the chairman of the House energy committee, focused national attention on the negative consequences of deregulation of natural gas prices for senior citizens and others living on fixed or low incomes (DeZutter, 1981, Cincotta, 1982). NPA planned a series of rallies for the Fall of 1982 in Chicago, Cleveland, Washington, and Philadelphia, culminating in New York City. The purpose of these demonstrations was to demand greater citizen participation in and local opposition to governmental and corporate economic policy decisions.

The leaders of NPA and NTIC demonstrate a fascinating mixture not only of applying and extending, but also of neglecting, Alinsky principles and strategies. Unlike Chambers and the IAF, Cincotta and Trapp are not intentionally using Alinsky's legacy as a vehicle for legitimatizing their activities nor are they actively using Alinsky as a role model for a professional organizer. Therefore, Alinsky's themes of community, organization, and power are interesting benchmarks to assess the strength and weakness of Cincotta's and Trapp's ventures and to identify the ways in which they have modified and extended Alinsky's principles and strategies. Their example also further highlights the vicissitudes of current community organization practices.

Beginning with the theme of community, none of the current practioners incorporate the depth and sophistication of Alinsky's understanding of urban social structure. Chambers reduces Alinsky's awareness of the complex and fragmented internal character of local communities and its social structure to a practical recognition of the need for the support of local churches. Cincotta and Trapp highlight the other fact of Alinsky's understanding: namely that community is not a self-contained, isolated, or complete social system, but linked to and interdependent on larger units of social structures. Trapp (1982a) notes that the lesson of NPA is that concerns of localities are often not unique or idiosyncratic. They are common problems which are shared with other areas, in part, because their origin rests with city-wide or national processes and policies. Further, while Alinsky argued that common interests and not common territory create the bonds of community, the experience of NPA highlights the possibility and promise of coordinated action and participation of multiple communities in issues of common concern and salience. The development of a network of communities is an important extension of Alinsky community organization.

The most significant organizational feature of NPA has been its ability to endure for over ten years as a national coalition of neighborhoods. Alinsky (1946, 1972) repeatedly paid lip service to the utility of a coalition of community organizations which could pursue shared interests on a national level. However, there is no evidence that he ever seriously attempted to create such a coalition. Indeed, Lancourt (1977) argued that Alinsky's emphasis on local, independent organizations made it unlikely that his organizations would be willing to sacrifice their local autonomy for participation in either a central national movement or even a more federated coalition. In fact, Lancourt (1977) points out that Alinsky community organizations did not act jointly even when several existed in the same city.

NPA's success in developing its coalition appears to rest on three well established strategies which are very much in the Alinsky tradition. First, the issues that NPA tackles are common concerns and in the self-interests of community residents. Further, the national focus on issues such as redlining, inflationary economic policies, or the exploitative practices of national corporations are meant to complement but not be competitive with the programs or initiatives of local organizations. Second, a strong bond uniting NPA is the dynamic, aggressive, and charismatic leadership of Gale Cincotta. She definitely has a flair for coining a phrase and presenting herself for NPA in a manner which can captivate an audience, as well as generate broad media coverage. Cincotta, more than most other community organization leaders, uses her presence and appeal as a tactic to generate and maintain organizational cohesiveness. Finally, NPA has persisted as a coalition, in part, because it has used a series of external antagonists as common enemies to create loose ties across a heterogeneous set of community organizations. Periodic protests and confrontation activities require less continuous and extensive coordination than commonly administered service programs or community development activities. Further, limiting common action to protest enables NPA to avoid facing the realization that the self-interest of some member organizations may directly conflict with the interest of other member organizations.

It is in the area of power and the exerting of influence that NPA appears weakest and has not really extended Alinsky principles or strategies. The major success of the organization has been its lobbying, especially the early campaign against redlining. Since then the activities of the organization have moved through a series of large confrontations which appear to capture media attention and may aid in citizen awareness but do not seem to exert much pressure on antagonists. Indeed, the confrontations typically have occurred during the annual convention and NPA has not been able to encourage antagonists to negotiate or enter a stage of serious bargaining with the organization. NPA has been ineffective as a power broker. The confrontation has been more successful as a means of generating internal cohesion than as an instrumental activity geared toward institutional change. Similarly, the NTIC staff, as reflected by its published materials (Trapp, 1976), seems to grasp only the most general and elementary features of Alinsky's principles and strategies for the development of issues and leaders capable of effectively exercising community power. NTIC appears considerably less sophisticated than the IAF staff in understanding and teaching the skills necessary for developing an organization's ability to participate in city-wide decision making and for representing the interests of community residents.

C. Citizens Action Program (CAP), Midwest Academy, Illinois Public Action Council (IPAC)

The Citizens Action Program (CAP) was the last community organization project initiated by Alinsky before his death. Although no longer in existence, it is important for two reasons. First, CAP was one of the most unusual and innovative of the Alinsky organizations and suggested some of Alinsky's new directions and experimentations. Second, key people in CAP went on to form new organizations and became involved in activities which have contributed interesting modifications and extensions of basic Alinsky strategies and principles.

Pollution was becoming a major issue in the late 1960s. A severe temperature inversion for more than a week in November, 1969 trapped polluted air over Chicago. The local news media and several citizens groups used the situation to focus public attention on pollution and the need for improved air quality controls. Mike Royko, a nationally-known popular columnist, wrote a stinging column on air pollution and turned over to Alinsky the 300 letters of support he received from angry citizens (Shearer, 1973). Alinsky gave the letters to trainees studying community organization with the IAF. Thirty of the letter writers, together with representatives of concerned civic associations, local churches, and area university personnel created Campaign Against Pollution which later was renamed Citizens Action Program. The structure of the organization entailed local, neighborhood chapters which sent representatives to a steering committee empowered to make decisions and initiate direct action. The IAF provided the staff. Paul Booth, a former SDS organizer, and Leonard Dubi, a Catholic priest, served as co-chairpersons from 1970 to 1973.

CAP began a three-pronged campaign focusing on Commonwealth Edison, the local utility company; the Illinois Commerce Commission, which establishes utility rates; and the Chicago City Council, which has the authority to regulate air quality standards. A variety of confrontation tactics were employed. Fifty housewives entered the bank which housed the utility company's main offices and distributed pennies taped to a news release entitled, "Commonwealth Edison Pinches Pennies on Pollution." At another point, 1,000 CAP members went to City Hall to request Mayor Daley's support for an anti-pollution ordinance. Similarly, 800 CAP members entered the Edison annual meeting with 1,000 stock proxies to demand company action on pollution reduction measures. The three major CAP demands were all met by the end of the summer of 1971: (1) the City Council passed a new and strong anti-pollution ordinance; (2) the ICC cut Commonwealth Edison's rate increase and made future rate increases contingent on reduced pollution; and (3) the utility company started using coal with a lower sulfur content (Boyte, 1980). CAP next took on U.S. Steel, a major source of air and water pollution, and released research findings showing that the company was being underassesed in its taxes by $16.5 million. Eventually, the President of U.S. Steel met with CAP leaders to assure them that the Company would speed up the installation of pollution controls. Other CAP activities included a senior citizens visitation and sit-in at the Abbott Laboratories to pressure the company to market low-cost generic drugs, a meat boycott to protest increases in food prices and excess profits by supermarket chains, and an education drive to inform voters of the positions of gubernatorial candidates on the construction of an expressway project which was strongly opposed by CAP (Shearer, 1973).

Heather Booth participated in the anti-war and student movements and was active in CAP. She left CAP in 1972, in part, because she felt that the IAF staff was insensitive to women's needs and the women's movement. The Midwest academy was founded by Booth in 1973. It represents a continuation of Alinsky's goal of developing a central facility for the initial training of local leaders and the advanced training of professional staff members. Chambers abandoned the central training function of the IAF but under Booth's leadership the Academy provides both leadership training services and a resource center for coordinating citizen participation and community organization activities. Training courses include a basic two week session covering the history of grass roots organizing ventures, techniques for efficiently running meetings, press relations, leaflet writing, and methods for holding demonstrations. Sessions also highlight the overall political and economic context of citizen participation and some of the principles of social democracy. Boyte (1980:110) notes that the three elements stressed in the Academy's approach is that the organization must: (1) win real victories that improve people's lives; (2) develop a community power base and an enduring source of influence; and (3) practice democracy and contribute to the broadening of democratic practices.

The Midwest Academy, in addition to training sessions, also offers on-site workshops and consulting services which were used by 47 organizations in 1981 and sponsors an annual meeting which in 1982 attracted 650 organizers to share experiences and discuss new issues and approaches (Thomas, 1981). One of the emerging activities of the Academy is to coordinate the programs and activities of a network of community associations, senior citizens' organizations, women's groups, and some labor unions. Women Employed (WE) begun in 1973, represents one of the new groups which have developed with the aid and support of the Midwest Academy. WE is an organization dedicated to fighting discrimination against women office workers. It uses basic community organization principles and practices to encourage women to identify shared problems and probe collective solutions. The group initiated, in 1976, a national campaign to prevent the Ford administration from dismantling affirmative action procedures. WE advises groups of women and aids them in the establishment of grievance procedures, lobbying for fair pay schedules, and publicizing promotion opportunities for women (Boyte, 1980:114). WE's activities highlight some of the innovative directions and new opportunities to apply Alinsky's organizing strategies and techniques.

Dissatisfaction with CAP also spawned another organization. Some of the local leaders of CAP, in 1975, felt that the IAF had become heavy-handed in the manipulation of the CAP board and were operating from a "hidden agenda" in dealing with local personnel (Schakowsky, 1982). Robert Creamer launched the Illinois Public Action Council (IPAC) in 1976, as a coalition of community organizations, senior citizens groups, labor, and conservation associations (Creamer, 1982). Heather Booth became a member of the organization's Board and the Midwest Academy became its official training center. IPAC is state-wide in its scope and includes 115 affiliated member organizations.

There are five components in the organizational structure of IPAC which reflect a masterful blend of innovative approaches and established Alinsky principles. First, IPAC is structured to be a state-wide organization of organizations sharing resources and initiating common actions, just as Alinsky community organizations were structured to be umbrella community-wide organizations. However, IPAC is a federated coalition. Affiliated organizations may select the programs and issues in which they care to participate and to which they may financially contribute. The intention is to support local autonomy and to enable affiliates to meet the particular needs of their constituents while IPAC provides the institutional framework for coordinated action. Second, IPAC is committed to pursuing multiple issues and many simultaneous campaigns. Alinsky advised that multiple issues enabled an organization to satisfy diverse and divergent interests and IPAC contains a very heterogeneous set of member organizations. Initially, IPAC identified state-wide programs for monitoring energy and utility rates and tax reforms as cross-cutting common issues and a pooling of resources and skills to aid individual members in their particular programs for neighborhood preservation. Recently, IPAC has also moved to coordinate action in the areas of health care, consumer rights and protection, as well as unemployment and manpower development (Creamer, 1978; Schakowsky, 1982). Third, IPAC has actively been engaged in trying to broaden its membership. The organization has created a department to aid local groups in developing their organizations and in initiating local actions. Further, regional councils have been established on the energy and tax issues to pursue the special interests and problems of four areas in the state.

IPAC has also experimented with two new sources of funding. The organization has pioneered in the use of direct canvassing and solicitation to supplement yearly membership fees for affiliated organizations. Teams of canvassers go door to door, explaining the activities of the organization and requesting a contribution. The approach has the benefits of increasing the organization's independence from either large private donors or government grants; it encourages public

awareness and enhances the organization's name recognition, as well as educat-
ing the public (Boyte, 1980:102). In addition, IPAC began a consumer service
program which offers two hours of legal services at lower than average rates.
Both plans are revenue generating services (Creamer, 1978).

Fifth and finally, IPAC has branched out into two new directions. Since 1979,
IPAC has been a member of Citizen Action, a federation of state citizen action
organizations which work together in projects such as plant relocations, taxes,
and energy, as well as serving as a forum for sharing experiences and new
approaches to problem solving. Today, Citizen Action includes state-wide organizations in nine states with organizing projects underway in nine additional
states (Midwest Academy Annual Report, 1981). Further, IPAC organized in
1981 the Citizen Action Non-Partisan Political Action Committee (CANPAC)
which has begun to recruit and support candidates for public office. In the Illinois
primary election held in the spring of 1982, the major CANPAC-backed candidate narrowly lost but CANPAC went on to actively support many candidates in
the general election.

The experiences of CAP, the Midwest Academy, and IPAC represent some of
the most interesting modifications and extensions of Alinsky's strategies and
principles. The themes of community, organization, and power provide the
framework for tracing their innovations and assessing their accomplishments.
Beginning with the theme of community and urban social structure, the three
organizations represent a systematic move away from territorially based community as the foundation for the organization. Alinsky (1971:120) noted that, "to
organize a community you must understand that in a highly mobile, urbanized
society the word 'community' means community of interests, *not* physical community." CAP was Alinsky's own experimentation in organizing a city-wide,
non-territorial community based on a common concern for a clean environment.
IPAC is even further removed from a locality-based organization by coordinating
groups which share common interests throughout the state of Illinois.

Alinsky began as a labor organizer and the Midwest Academy breaks new
ground, or rather completes the circle, by returning Alinsky organizing practices
to the work site. Indeed, organizations such as WE, which focus on the concerns
of office workers and women, highlight an entirely new direction for the application of Alinsky strategies and for the development of non-territorial communities
of interest. Further, while Chambers and the IAF have stressed the importance of
the local church as a community resource, the Midwest Academy and IPAC have
stressed the importance of unions in developing communities of interest. Unions
offer financial backing, material and institutional resources, and experienced
leadership to fledgling organizations and young coalitions.

Alinsky's organizational practices are taught at the Midwest Academy and are
central to the organizational development ventures of IPAC. Organizational
strategies have expanded in two directions. First, the Midwest Academy and
IPAC are firmly committed to creating cross-cutting and horizontal ties with

other organizations. IPAC is an organization of organizations and is affiliated with other state-wide organizations through Citizen Action. Networks and coalitions enable organizations to create specialized facilities, such as the training services or the Midwest Academy, which would be beyond the means of any single organization; to share resource and experiences so as to avoid duplicating mistakes; and cooperative action which may improve the efficiency and strengthen the power of the organizations. The second new direction deals with the use of new funding sources. IPAC has pioneered in the use of canvassing and revenue generating consumer services. The Woodlawn Organization (TWO), an Alinsky created organization and IPAC member, runs a community newspaper, automotive service center, movie theater, shopping center, supermarket, and two housing complexes (Fish, 1973; Finnerty, 1982).

Some organizational problems have occurred. CAP folded in 1976 in large part because of the difficulties between the local leaders and the IAF staff (Schakowsky, 1982). Alinsky was always troubled by the difficulties that a professional organization encounters in gaining local acceptance. It appears that later in the development of the organization the issue of control and jurisdiction boundaries may also create organizational difficulties. The training of community leaders in centers such as the Midwest Academy may be one way of reducing the strains between staff and local leaders. Greater sensitivity on the part of the professional staff is probably also needed. A second organizational problem deals with the maintenance of local interests, attention, and participation as the scale of issues and action increases. Galluzzo (1982) feels that IPAC, in its emphasis on broad issues, sometimes neglects the concerns of members of local constituent organizations. Organization members often do not get a sense of increased power from coalitions such as IPAC. The partial and temporary interest in large scale projects is a constraint on community programs and must be faced realistically if the organization tactics is to retain local loyalty. Confrontation tactics are not a major part of IPAC but may provide an important source of internal cohesion.

Finally, it is in the area of power that current organizations have had their most significant development. The leaders of the Midwest Academy have dropped Alinsky's radical rhetoric and are now directly advocating grass roots pluralism and expanded democratic practices. It has been in the pursuit of expanded citizen participation that the organizations have moved in two new directions. First, the Midwest Academy and IPAC are committed to entering electoral politics. The Midwest Academy has launched a drive to train individuals and organizations in the techniques and skills of political organizing. More than one third of the 650 participants at the 1982 annual meeting of the Academy are actively engaged in political campaigns. Similarly, one of IPAC's goals is to create cross-community and cross-consistency alliances to support shared issues and candidates. IPAC has been active in trying to create a "majoritarian" organization which can appeal to a broad cross-section of the electorate. Second, the organizations which have grown out of CAP are appealing increasingly to issues which highlight the rights of consumers and the social and ecological responsibilities of private corporations and industry. Alinsky began his community organization activity by using the large meat-packing companies as a common enemy to unite a fragmented community. Today, consumer and energy issues provide common concerns which IPAC is using to mobilize ties and maintain a durable coalition.

IV. SUMMARY AND CONCLUSION

This analysis has addressed itself to the appropriateness of Alinsky's community organization orientation under present conditions and to current applications, modifications, and extensions of his principles and strategies. The review of the principles controlling the activities of IAF, NPA, NTIC, Midwest Academy, and IPAC strongly suggests the persistent and lasting impact that Alinsky has on the practice and theory of community organization. Chambers and the IAF use Alinsky's name as well as his concepts to educate a public about the opportunities of collective action, to inspire confidence in the expertise of the IAF, and to stimulate interest in community participation. The training programs of the Midwest Academy and NTIC use Alinsky principles and refer to him as the prime example of a professional organizer and to his community organization activities as classic cases to be studied and emulated. Alinsky is still recognized as a role model or founding father of current community organization. His training programs contributed to the vitality of his legacy in that all leaders of the organization studied were either trained by Alinsky or by Alinsky-trained organizers.

Alinsky's themes of community, organization, and power provide the framework for presenting and assessing the community organization practices and the training of local leaders of each of the national groups studied. Alinsky's sophisticated understanding of the fragmentary character of local attachments and the interdependence of the community with larger units of urban social structure remains the least developed or appreciated facet of his orientation. Chambers retains Alinsky's awareness of the difficulty entailed in creating a community-wide organization by insisting on the financial backing and participation of local church leaders. Cincotta and the other leaders of NPA have learned well the lesson that many individual troubles may best be attacked as shared social problems and that a federation or coalition of communities may be an efficient means of solving local concerns: Similarly, Heather Booth and the leaders of IPAC have recognized the importance of cooperative action and have expanded the domain of community organization to include non-territorial communities of interest.

Leaders of all of the groups studied praise Alinsky's organizational expertise and incorporate structural and strategic elements of his model to strengthen and extend their own organizations. Chambers and the IAF retain the basic Alinsky organizational model but have extended the duration of their commitment to local communities to aid organizations in adjusting to leadership changes and problems of succession. Cincotta and Booth have used basic Alinsky strategies to develop the commitment of members to the organization and have extended Alinsky by creating enduring coalitions or neighborhood and other organizations. NPA and IPAC have forged their coalitions by lobbying for state and federal housing and anti-pollution legislation, and by pressuring city, state, and federal government agencies for more local funds and control over programs. These organizations also have confronted national corporations and industries to acknowledge their responsibility for the preservation and improvement of local communities and their quality of life.

Finally, all organizations studied have declared their commitment to grass roots participation and social democracy. Alinsky's radical rhetoric has been dropped but his ideology is clearly in line with the direction and goals of these current organizations. Alinsky and the organizations share an interest in making city, state, and federal governments more responsive to citizens and to make commerce and industry more responsible to consumers and employees. IPAC has extended Alinsky's orientation by moving into electoral politics. Grass roots participation in the political and electoral processes may become the most significant activity of the 1980's. The application of Alinsky's principles and strategies is an impressive and clear demonstration of his current significance. It is ironic that for all of Alinsky's impatience with academics and "theory", his lasting contribution may very well be his understanding and sociological analysis of the structures and processes of community, organization, and power.

REFERENCES

Alinsky, Saul D.
    1941   "Community analysis and organizations." American Journal of Sociology 46:797-808.
    1946   Reveille for Radicals. Chicago: University of Chicago Press.
    1968   "What is the role of community organization in bargaining with the establishment for health care services?" Pp. 291-299 in J.C. Norman (ed.), Medicine in the Ghetto. New York: Appleton-Century-Croft.
    1969   Reveille for Radicals (2nd edition). New York: Vintage Books.
    1971   Rules for Radicals. New York: Random House.
    1972   "Playboy interview: Saul Alinsky." Playboy Magazine (March):59-178.
Bailey, Robert J.
    1972   Radicals in Urban Politics: The Alinsky Approach. Chicago: The University of Chicago Press.
Bates, Frederick L. and Lloyd Bacon
    1972   "The community as a social system." Social Forces 50:371-379.
Boyte, Harry C.
    1980   The Backyard Revolution: Understanding the New Citizen Movement. Philadelphia: Temple University Press.

Chambers, Edward
    1978   Organizing for Family and Congregation. Huntington, New York: Industrial Areas
            Foundation.
    1982   Interview. Huntington, New York: February 5.
Cincotta, Gale
    1982   Interview. Chicago, Illinois: May 6.
Creamer, Robert
    1978   "The public action difference: a new model." Just Economics 6(7):1–3.
    1982   Interview. Chicago, Illinois: May 7.
Crowder, David
    1981a   "Religious leaders quietly hire troublemakers to better city." The El Paso Times. July 5:
            1A, 16A.
    1981b   "Citizens band together for quick results." The El Paso Times. July 7: 1A, 8A.
    1981c   "San Antonio citizens break power hold." The El Paso Times. July 7,: 1A, 2A.
DeZutter, Hank
    1981   "Community organizing for the 80's: taking it to boardrooms." Chicago Reader. Septem-
            ber 25.
Finnerty, Thomas
    1982   Interview. Chicago, Illinois: August 17.
Fireman, Bruce and William A. Gamson
    1979   "Utilitarian logic in the resource mobilization perspective." Pp. 8-44 in M.N. Zald and
            J.D. McCarthy (eds.), The Dynamics of Social Movements. Cambridge, Massachusetts:
            Winthrop Publishers.
Fish, John Hall
    1973   Black Power/White Control. Princeton, New Jersey: Princeton University Press.
Galluzzo, Gregg
    1982   Interview. Chicago, Illinois: August 5.
Gans, Herbert J.
    1962   The Urban Villagers. New York: The Free Press.
Gaudette, Thomas
    1981   Interview. Chicago, Illinois: November 3.
    1982   Interview. Chicago, Illinois: August 16.
Hunter, Albert and Gerald Suttles
    1972   "The expanding community of limited liability." In Gerald Suttles (ed.), The Social
            Construction of Communities. Chicago: The University of Chicago Press.
Jacobs, Jane
    1961   The Death and Life of Great American Cities. New York: Random House.
Lancourt, Joan E.
    1977   Evaluation and Analysis of Goals, Tactics and Results of Citizen Action Organizations:
            The Alinsky Model. Unpublished Ph.D. dissertation. Waltham, Massachusetts: Brandeis
            University.
    1979   Confront and Concede: The Alinsky Citizen-Action Organizations. Lexington, Mas-
            sachusetts: Lexington Books.
Leff, Laurel
    1981   "Community spirit: local groups that aid poor flourishing by using confrontation tactics."
            The Wall Street Journal. May 13: 1, 25.
McCarthy, John D. and Mayer N. Zald.
    1977   "Resource mobilization and social movements: a partial theory." American Journal of
            Sociology 82:1212-1241.
Midwest Academy
    1981   Midwest Academy Annual Report. Chicago: Midwest Academy.

Oberschall, Anthony
   1979 "Protracted conflict." Pp. 45-70 in M.N. Zald and J.D. McCarthy (eds.), The Dynamics
         of Social Movements. Cambridge, Massachusetts: Winthrop Publishers.
Schakowsky, Jan
   1982 Interview. Chicago, Illinois: August 3.
Shearer, Derek
   1973 "CAP: new breeze in the windy city." Ramparts. (Oct.):12-16.
Suttles, Gerald D.
   1968 Social Order of the Slum: Ethnicity and Territory in the Inner City. Chicago: University of
         Chicago Press.
Swanson, Stevenson O.
   1982 "She arose from grass roots to shake the tallest oaks." Chicago Tribune. March 18.
Thomas, Karen
   1981 Interview. Chicago, Illinois: November 27.
Trapp, Sheldon
   1976 Dynamics of Organizing. Chicago: A NTIC Publication.
   1982a "Dynamics of organizing in the 1980's." Disclosure. (Mar.): 1.
   1982b Interview. Chicago, Illinois: August 18.
Zald, Mayer N. and John D. McCarthy
   1979 The Dynamics of Social Movements. Cambridge, Massachusetts: Winthrop Publishers.

INTER-ETHNIC CONFLICT IN AN URBAN GHETTO:

THE CASE OF BLACKS AND LATINOS IN LOS ANGELES

Melvin L. Oliver and James H. Johnson, Jr.

I. INTRODUCTION

Over the past two decades considerable research attention has been devoted to racial conflicts between blacks and whites. Spurred by the rising tide of black aspirations for equality during the 1960s, sociologists and other social scientists have explored these inter-racial conflicts via a myriad of theoretical and conceptual approaches (Blauner, 1969; Geschwender, 1964; Himes, 1966; Marx, 1969). While the research efforts have increased and subsided in direct proportion to the ebb and flow of overt black-white confrontations, social scientists have largely ignored conflicts among non-white ethnic minorities. Such confrontations have achieved greater urgency in recent years as a result of the substantial influx of disadvantaged immigrants to the U.S. from Mexico, other parts of Latin America, and Southeast Asia (Blackwell, 1982; Guptan, 1983; Portes, 1979, 1977; Rose and Christian, 1982). In particular, the potential conflict between

Research in Social Movements, Conflict and Change, Vol. 6, pages 57–94.
Copyright © 1984 by JAI Press Inc.
All rights of reproduction in any form reserved.
ISBN: 0-89232-311-6

blacks and Latinos, two ethnically distinct but racially identified minorities, remains relatively unnoticed by the social scientific community (Jackson, 1979; Fairchild and Tucker, 1982).[1]

This lack of notice is all the more surprising given the events that occurred in Miami, Florida. In May, 1980 fourteen persons were killed and over a hundred million dollars of property destroyed in racial violence that mirrored the turbulent race rebellions of the 1960s. There were striking similarities in these events to those of earlier violent outbreaks in black America: high rates of black unemployment, wretched living conditions, and the precipitating event of police brutality or injustice. However, in addition to these more conventional factors, a new issue appeared, one which threatens to be a factor of urban inner city life for the next decade or more: the presence of a competing and visible ethnic group in the community. The Miami violence is unique in the way in which the impact of recently arrived Cubans affected the black community. Competing for similar jobs in the unskilled and service sectors of the city's economy, blacks found themselves losing to Cubans at an alarming rate. Cuban faces soon replaced blacks in such competitive sectors of the economy as hotels, hospitals and restaurants. Employers claimed to find the Cubans more willing to take menial jobs for minimum and below minimum wages. Blacks felt an extreme sense of injustice in the way in which they were being passed, economically and socially, by the more recent Cuban arrivals. The ire that blacks felt was expressed by one youthful participant in the violence:

> We can't get a job because they give them to Cubans who keep coming over here, so the only thing we can do is steal and sell dope (Sheppard, 1980: 4).

While whites were certainly the primary target of the violence in Miami, the Cuban factor was also present and an important source of the conflict.

While inter-ethnic urban conflict has not been expressed at that level in other American cities, the potential that it will is ever increasing. In many cities like New York, Detroit, Chicago, Houston, Dallas, and Los Angeles where considerable migration from Latin America and Asia has been occurring, low income black communities have increasingly felt the deleterious impact of this movement. In Los Angeles, for example, Latino movement into the traditionally black south central area of the city has set the stage for inter-ethnic conflict in innumerable ways. Cultural barriers lead each to blame the other for the problems they share like poverty, unemployment, inadequate housing and crime. Documenting these trends was a series of articles published in the *Los Angeles Times* entitled "Watts 1980: 15 Years After the Riots." In this series, they reported on the "new strain" emerging in this area between blacks and Latinos. The intensity of the situation was observed by one black leader who asks "How long can it last before the whole thing spills over into what caused the Watts situation 15 years ago'' (Hernandez and Scott, 1980: 22).

This grave concern is mirrored in a number of other ways. Competition for housing has turned intense. Public services that blacks feel they fought hard to earn are being utilized in large numbers by Latino newcomers. For example, nearly three out of every four children born at Martin Luther King Jr. County Hospital are Latino. Heavy Latino use of these facilities is frowned on by some blacks: "I don't think its proper. When we built some of these facilities in Watts, we didn't find anyone to help us . . . if they want their share of services they should get active in the community" (Hernandez and Scott, 1980: 22). Latinos on the other hand, do not feel welcome in these communities. Fear of violence and crime is an important factor. One Latino victim of an assault by a group of blacks expressed "fear and anger" about blacks after the assault. No more evidence of fear is more clear than to drive through Watts as school is ending for the day. The complexion of the community is transformed as the terrain is dominated by Latino mothers escorting their children home, fearful that black youths will assault them. While overt social conflict has not exploded, in the words of a close observer, "It's a potential powder keg . . . it's just a matter of time" (Hernandez and Scott, 1980: 22).

In this paper we shall explore the initial theoretical and empirical parameters of what has become popularly known as the "black-brown" conflict (Hernandez and Scott, 1980). To achieve some specificity we focus on the emerging "ethnic frontier" developing in formerly all black communities of south central Los Angeles (See Figure 1). From a theoretical perspective we attempt to understand the Los Angeles situation through a spatial orientation, emphasizing the role of residential invasion, concentration, and succession as preconditions for developing social conflicts. In this way, the analysis fits squarely within the tradition of early urban theorists who viewed racial conflict as symptomatic of the pains associated with predetermined stages of urban growth and development (Burgess, 1967; McKenzie, 1967; Park, 1975). We depart from this tradition, however, by emphasizing the specificity of black-Latino interaction, especially the significant constraints imposed by racial and economic factors which were not characteristic of the early American industrial city. In moving away from the deterministic emphasis which was the hallmark of early urban theorists, we attempt to specify the theoretical and empirical differences between the developing newer ethnic ghettos and earlier accounts of European ethnic communities (National Advisory Commission on Civil Rights, 1973; Blauner, 1969; Green et al., 1979; Willhelm, 1970; Lieberson, 1980). Toward this end, we draw on census data, public opinion surveys, and historical and impressionistic works to unravel the social and political implications of black-Latino antagonisms in Los Angeles. What we imply is that the urban context in which blacks and Latinos find themselves is one which is ripe for the development of mutual distrust and

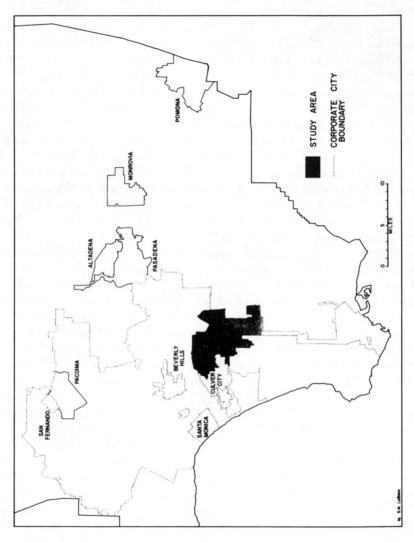

Figure 1. Los Angeles and the south central Los Angeles area

60

hostility. By focusing on the effects of a whole structural complex known as the "urban crisis," we show that inter-ethnic conflict between blacks and Latinos has a strong economic motor which is fueled by competition over scarce jobs, adequate housing, and government services.

II. SOME THEORETICAL CONSIDERATIONS

Our initial premise is that the experience of blacks and Latinos in U.S. cities is theoretically distinct from that of the European immigrants who arrived around the turn of this century. In this section, we try to specify those differences, insofar as they are basic to an understanding of the conflict reportedly emerging between blacks and Latinos in Los Angeles.

Newly arriving ethnic groups to American cities traditionally have settled in older transitional communities on the fringes of the central business district. For the European immigrant groups, residence in these "port of entry" communities usually was only temporary, followed by gradual, and in some instances, rapid social and economic integration and residential dispersion into mainstream American society. This dispersion was especially common when community ties in the initial core areas were weak. In instances where community linkages were fairly strong, as in the case of Italians (Gans, 1962), the groups tended to remain clustered but nevertheless were socially and economically integrated into society (Gans, 1962). In either case, assimilation was fairly extensive for European groups. The ability of European groups to integrate so thoroughly in American society was made possible by such factors as (1) their close resemblance to British Americans (the dominant group) in appearance and other visible symbols, (2) their arrival in either relatively small numbers or over a long period of time, and (3) their exposure to minimal discriminatory barriers.

For blacks and Latinos, however, assimilation has been much more difficult. Neither group resembles British Americans in physical appearance or other visible cultural symbols, and both arrived in urban America in large numbers and over a relatively short period of time. Partly for these reasons, both have been victims of significantly more overt discrimination and exploitation than their European counterparts. Here we focus on three aspects of the black-brown experience which appear to be responsible for the conflict reportedly emerging between these two groups in Los Angeles and other U.S. cities. They are: (1) structural changes in the U.S. economy, (2) discrimination in the metropolitan housing market, and (3) the two groups' images and attitudes towards one another.

A. Changing Structure of the American Economy

Distinguishing the black and Latino experiences in urban America from that of their European counterparts are issues which fall under the rubric of "political economy.'' Blacks and Latinos, unlike ethnic groups arriving earlier, appeared on the urban scene at precisely the time when the social structure of opportunities for low and semi-skilled labor had declined drastically (National Advisory Commission on Civil Rights, 1973; Blauner, 1969; Green et al., 1979; Willhelm, 1970; Lieberson, 1980), As the National Advisory Commission on Civil Rights (1973:99) pointed out:

> When the European immigrants were arriving in large numbers, America was becoming an urban-industrial society. To build its major cities and industries, America needed great pools of unskilled labor. The immigrants provided the labor, gained an economic foothold, and thereby enabled their children and grandchildren to move up to skilled, white collar and professional employment. . . . The Negro migrant, unlike the immigrant migrant, found little opportunity in the city; he had arrived too late, and the unskilled labor he had to offer was no longer needed.

By the time blacks and Latinos arrived in large numbers in urban areas, the transition from labor intensive to capital intensive production processes in industries was well advanced. Capitalists, attempting to increase both profit and their control of the labor process had made investments that mechanized large segments of the industrial economy, and in turn eliminated many of the labor intensive production processes traditionally performed by the unskilled (Braverman, 1974; Castells, 1977; Gordon, 1978). Even though at the same time white collar jobs that required high levels of education and specific skills were being created at unprecedented rates, blacks and Latinos who had little education and training were not eligible for jobs of this type (Bell, 1973).

One enduring feature of the labor force experience of minorities in the U.S. is that employment opportunities improve significantly, even while discrimination in wages and promotion persist, when the overall demand for labor is high. The importance of the economy's labor demands for blacks and Mexican Americans is easily documented by examining the timing of their migration from the south and Mexico respectively. For blacks, migration from the south was greatest during and just after the World Wars when, due to the curtailment of European immigration, the demand for labor in wartime industries was high (Johnson and Brunn, 1980; Farrell and Johnson, 1978; Farley, 1970). Similarly Mexican Americans were encouraged to cross the border during the 1920s under the auspicies of mining, railroad, and agricultural interests in the American southwest to serve as ''. . . an abundant source of cheap and exploitable labor'' (Estrada et al., 1981: 114). Likewise, the ''Bracero'' program, re-established in 1942, also brought in Mexican American workers to fill labor shortages generated first by World War II and, later by the Korean War. Whatever the gains of minorities during times of high labor demand, the losses can be even sharper when labor demands decline. During such times blacks and Latinos are among the first to suffer rates of high unemployment. For Latinos, the costs can be even more drastic than just the loss of jobs. For example, during periods of low demand official action has been taken to "repatriate" surplus labor. In such times, Latinos, including U.S. citizens and others legally in this country have been forced to leave the U.S. Pointing to the powerlessness of Mexican and Mexican Americans, Estrada et al. (1981: 116) note:

> It is estimated that in the early years of the Depression (1929–34) more than 400,000 Mexicans were forced to leave the country under "voluntary repatriation." Those who applied for relief were referred to "Mexican Bureaus," whose sole purpose was to reduce the welfare rolls by deporting applicants. Indigence, not citizenship, was the criterion used in identifying Mexicans for repatriation.

Other structural changes in the economy also distinguish the black-Mexican American experience from that of their European counterparts. In addition to the absolute decline of manufacturing jobs due to automation, many of the remaining unkilled and semi-skilled jobs originally concentrated in central cities decentralized by the time blacks and Latinos arrived in cities (Kain, 1968; Sternlieb and Hughes, 1975; DeVise, 1976; Scott, 1982; Castells, 1977). Freed of the need to be centrally located in central cities, manufacturers have chosen to decentralize and take advantage of existing technologies that allow horizontal assembly line modes of production, truck transport, fast and efficient transportation arteries, and governments that provide greater incentives in terms of lower taxes, new infrastructure, and new housing developments for its employees in suburban, exurban, and, more recently, non-metropolitan areas (Scott, 1982; Phillips and Brunn, 1978). These developments have adversely affected the structure of employment opportunities in the inner city where blacks and Latinos are concentrated (DeVise, 1976; Green et al., 1979; Davies and Huff, 1972). Whereas the growth industries (aircraft, aerospace and electronics) have, for the most part, located in metropolitan ring communities, manufacturing jobs in the inner city have not kept pace with the population needs (Wilson, 1978:93).

Potentially more damaging to the economic opportunities of minorities than job shifts within the U.S. is the move toward a "new international division of labor" (Bonacich, 1976; Castells, 1977; Cohen, 1981; Bluestone and Harrison, 1982). In recent decades, the economic organization of business has shifted away from small, privately owned local enterprises, which dominated the early industrial period, to large corporations whose production capabilities are not limited by national boundaries. These multinational corporations operate on the basis of a world market, relying on a complex infrastructure of corporate related services (including multinational banks and law, accounting, advertising and contracting firms), and thus are able to establish various components of their production system wherever cheap labor may exist (Cohen, 1981:288–90). For instance, automobiles are no longer manufactured in a single country; instead auto makers take advantage of cheap labor in underdeveloped countries to manufacture parts, and assembly takes place in advanced industrialized nations where the cars will be marketed. This strategy of relocating parts of the production process has led to what Bluestone and Harrison (1982) call the "deindustrialization of America." Large corporations have tended to flee advanced industrial nations like the U.S. and establish production facilities in underdeveloped countries where a cheap and controllable labor force exists. Meanwhile, corporate activities related to servicing these multinationals becomes increasingly concentrated in the large urban centers like New York, Los Angeles, and Tokyo (Cohen, 1981:305). While these developments create employment opportunities for the highly skilled and educated, they do little to provide jobs for the unskilled and poorly educated blacks and Latinos in the urban ghettos.

Those jobs that are left behind which match the education and skill requirements of lower and working class blacks and Mexican Americans are concentrated in the "secondary" or "competitive" sectors of the economy (Baron and Hymer, 1968; Bluestone, 1970; Gordon, 1972; O'Conner, 1973). Firms in these sectors exist only to the extent that their prices stay competitive vis à vis national and inter-national firms. One result of the efforts of these firms to stay competitive is that they usually offer low wages and have unattractive working conditions. Moreover, employers in the competitive sector often structure their work force in illegal ways. For example, a recent inspection showed that 83 percent of the garment manufacturers in California had systematically evaded state wage and hour laws (Moore, 1981:284). Because their "illegal" status makes them less likely to complain of unfair treatment and more likely to accept economic exploitation and "dirty work," undocumented (particularly those of Latino origin) workers have become a favored employee of the nation's most competitive sectors of industry (i.e. garment manufacturers, sub-contractors and fast food restaurants) (Jackson, 1979). It has been claimed that the availability of undocumented workers further depresses wages in the secondary sectors. However, the effects can be felt unevenly. Given the comparatively "high" cost of black labor vis à vis much Latino labor (Bonacich, 1972,1976), it has been suggested that the job competition that emanates from the concentration of these two groups in the competitive sector has had a deleterious effect on access of blacks to employment, contributing in part to the high rates of unemployment among blacks, particularly young blacks (Jackson, 1979). In the past one could actually see the progressive movement of ethnic groups into the inner city as a "queuing" process in which the arrival of a new group upgraded the occupational status of ethnic groups higher on the queue (Lieberson, 1980:376–84); but, today, blacks who were on the bottom of the queue are not experiencing an upgrade because of continued discrimination, the contracting employment opportunities in the economy, and the undercutting of black labor by recent immigrants to the city (Jackson, 1979). Blacks are not alone in finding the ethnic assimilation process thwarted. Instead of an orderly process of adaptation and residential dispersion as described by Park and his colleagues (Park and Burgess,

1967), it appears that a permanent "underclass" composed largely of blacks, Latinos, and other recent immigrants to U.S. cities is emerging (Moore, 1981; Wilson, 1978).

B. Housing Discrimination

Once the European immigrants obtained sufficient capital they were able to move freely within the residential sector, if they chose to do so (Brown, 1981). However, for blacks and Latinos, regardless of socioeconomic status, only selected parts of the metropolitan housing market have been accessible (Morrill, 1965; Rose, 1971). While whites often move from an area when minorities move in (Clark, 1980), there have also been a series of techniques and procedures that whites have employed to maintain the homogeneity of Anglo neighborhoods by excluding blacks, Latinos, and other non-white minorities. These include race-restrictive covenants (Long and Johnson, 1947), block busting and panic peddling tactics (i.e. racial steering) on the part of real estate agents (Osofsky, 1963; Pearce, 1979), government public housing and highway projects (Ford and Griffin, 1979), and discriminatory lending practices on the part of banks, savings and loan, and insurance companies (Darden, 1980; Squires and DeWolfe, 1981). While most of these techniques and procedures, termed "ghettomakers" by Ford and Griffin (1979), have been outlawed, blacks and Latinos nevertheless remain highly segregated in American cities. They are often forced to compete for housing in the same areas, in part due to less overt forms of discrimination in the metropolitan housing market, such as exclusionary zoning practices in suburban communities (Johnston, 1981), and in part due to these groups' common low economic status.

C. Black-Latino Political and Cultural Conflicts

In addition to the structural and institutional forces which have constrained black-Mexican American access to jobs and housing in U.S. cities, there are also political and cultural differences between the two groups which also must be considered as a source of potential conflict. These issues have come to the fore recently, in the spate of literature which examines the possibilities of a black-brown political coalition (Henry, 1980; Dreyfuss, 1979; Calhoun, 1980; Arias, 1980). What all of these analyses conclude is that a better understanding of the different cultural and political perspectives of the two groups is necessary before a successful coalition can be forged.

While on the face of it blacks and Latinos occupy basically the same social and economic position in U.S. society, their political attitudes and behavior differ markedly. Blacks are decidedly "democratic" and "liberal" in their party affiliation and outlook. Latinos, on the other hand, tend to be much more heterogeneous in their political affiliation and political ideology. Thus, blacks through "bloc" voting and higher voter turnout, have translated their numbers into significantly more political power than Mexican Americans. As Henry (1980:225) notes:

> Blacks have advanced further politically. California, a state in which Chicanos outnumber Blacks 2 (16 percent) to 1 (8 percent), is a prime example. Blacks hold eight seats in the state legislature and three in Congress. This compares favorably to the six Chicanos in the state legislature and one in Congress. In Los Angeles, the mayor and three members of the city council are Black, while there are no Chicano members.

This greater success in elections has led to suspicion on the part of Latinos that blacks have "too much" political power. Latinos are also hesitant to forge a coalition with blacks for fear that their interests will be overlooked by the more politically astute and experienced black leadership.

More important than political differences are the perceived social differences between the two groups. Henry (1980:224) notes, for example, that "Mexican-Americans have historically viewed Blacks as 'black Anglo-Saxons' in the negative sense of their being an inferior imitation [of] and having an affinity for Anglo culture." Further, Spanish culture traditionally denigrated "dark skin" and "inferiorized" its possessors. The legacy of that culture persists and translates into a desire on the part of some Mexican Americans to be considered as being "white" and for others into negative attitudes toward contact with blacks. Studies by Grebler et al. (1970) and Williams et al. (1964) reveal, for example, that on practically all indicators of social distance (e.g. whether you would find it distasteful to eat with, to socialize with, to marry a member of the respective ethnic group) Mexican Americans were from two to three times more likely to express xenophobic attitudes towards the respective groups than vice versa. And for Mexican-Americans, controlling for sex, region, ethnicity and class does not appreciably change these relationships. As Grebler et al. (1970:394) note "There is really no reason . . . to expect Mexican Americans to be particularly tolerant toward Negroes. The Mexican tradition is not one of tolerance."

Blacks, on the other hand, tend to discount Mexican Americans as a fellow minority, citing as the reason for this stance the ease with which some Mexican Americans are apt to blend into mainstream American society. Bereft of physical characteristics that distinguish them as a member of a minority group, some Mexican Americans indeed can "Anglicize" themselves and thoroughly assimilate. As one black activist interested in forming a coalition between black and Latino police officers noted:

> Given the similar circumstances that Blacks and Hispanics find themselves in it would be advantageous to both groups to work together on some issues. It has been our experience, over the years that all too often, Hispanic police officers lean toward trying to be white (Calhoun, 1980:14).

In sum, the potential for conflict between blacks and Latinos is not only intensified by their common dearth of economic opportunities but also their different perceptions and attitudes toward each other which are grounded in different historical and cultural legacies.

On the theoretical level we have argued that real and important distinctions exist between the European immigrant experience in urban America and the more recent experience of blacks and Latinos. Both groups have been the object of intense personal and institutional forms of racism with attendant consequences being the residential segregation and ghettoization of these two groups. More insidious, however, have been changes in the political economy of urban America that have lessened opportunities for social and economic mobility. Trapped in inner city communities with less than adequate housing, poor employment opportunities, meager public services, and a fear of violence, these problems become touchstones of conflict. As Latinos move into formerly all black enclaves competition for housing, jobs, public and government services like assistance, education and health intensify. Negative experiences with blacks, derived from competition over scarce resources, can initiate, or reinforce Latino racial antipathy. Black residents trapped in wretched conditions and forced to compete for a limited supply of needed goods and services, assuage their powerlessness by scapegoating their problems upon an identifiable but relatively helpless object. The key point here is that environmental conditions determined by structural forces are the major cause of this conflict.

In order to provide additional insights into this phenomenon we conducted an empirical examination of the experience of blacks and Mexican Americans in Los Angeles. In the section which follows, we will examine the concrete factors which led to the formation of the nearly all-black south central Los Angeles ghetto, emphasizing the importance of personal and institutional discrimination in its evolution and maturation. We then examine the recent movement of Latinos (particularly Mexican Americans) into the area, which has established the population prerequisites for conflict; and finally, we scrutinize survey data on the perceptions of black and Latinos toward each other in the south central Los Angeles ghetto. The objective is to assess the nature and magnitude of hostility as well as the issues upon which conflict may arise between the two groups. In the final section, we discuss the implications of our findings within the broader context of inter-ethnic conflict in urban America.

III.   THE LOS ANGELES CASE STUDY

A.   Ghettoization of Blacks in Los Angeles

Blacks began migrating into southern California after the Santa Fe railroad was built and the land boom of 1887 (de Graaf, 1962: 32–33). The factors luring blacks to the region up to 1940 were not unlike those attracting whites to the state. For example, advertisements by realtors and other businessmen described the moderate climate and the overall prosperity of the city (indeed the entire state), especially the prospects of obtaining employment. Blacks were barred from jobs in the rapidly growing motion picture and oil industries, but housing construction, transportation, and domestic services were major areas of employment. More important than the jobs themselves, however, were the wages offered in the city. A black artisan could earn up to $14 per day and a semi-skilled worker up to $5 per day. Between 1910 and 1930, wage rates in California were the highest in the nation. And during the 1930s, when the nation was in the throes of the Great Depression, wages remained relatively high, and blacks stood a better chance of obtaining work relief in California than in any other state. In short these "pull" factors, together with the decline of the cotton economy, the shift to livestock farming, and heightened racial oppression (i.e. lynching and mob violence) in the south, were largely responsible for the growth of Los Angeles' black population to 75,000 in 1940 (Collins, 1980).

Early black migrants were widely dispersed throughout the city. As one early migrant intimated in an interview with Bond (1936): "When I came to Los Angeles, Negroes lived anywhere they could afford to live. Homes were rented to anyone who had money." In a similar vein, J. B. Loving, editor of the *Liberator,* a local black newspaper, stated in 1904 that:

> The Negroes of the city have prudently refused to segregate themselves into any locality, but have scattered and produced homes in sections occupied by wealthy, cultured White people, thus not only securing the best fire, water, and police protection but also the more important benefits that accrue from refined and cultured surroundings (Bass, 1961).

Developments occurring between 1910 and 1930 had significant impact on black settlement patterns and employment opportunities in Los Angeles, however (Tolbert, 1980). During this period Los Angeles became a "diversified metropolis" as a result of a major influx of foreign immigrants (Mexican, Oriental, and Philippino) and native (primarily southern born) whites (McWilliams, 1946). Foreign born immigrants competed with blacks for skilled and semi-skilled jobs, and the in-migration of southern born whites coincided with the onset of racial discrimination in housing and other social and economic activities in Los Angeles (de Graaf, 1962). Because the southern born whites vehemently opposed "mixing" of the races, race restrictive covenants were established to stem the tide of black settlement in all white areas. Thus, after 1920 blacks were no longer able to settle wherever they so desired, even if they had the economic means to do so.

As a result of the establishment of race restrictive covenants and widespread discrimination in other social and economic activities, by 1940 in Los Angeles three well defined black communities were evolving in the Central-Avalon, Santa Barbara, and Watts districts of the city (Figure 2a). While most of Los

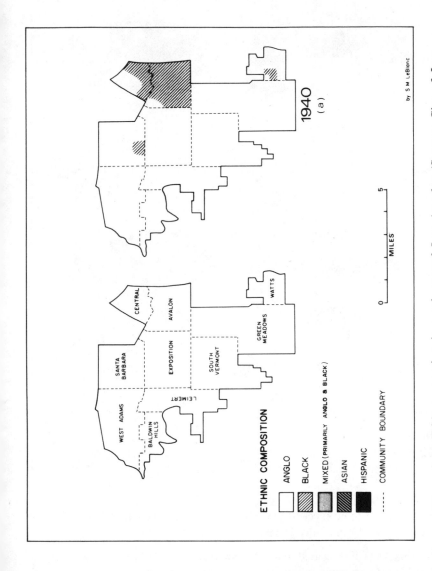

Figure 2a. Ethic succession in south central Los Angeles (Source: City of Los Angeles Community Development Department (1977, 1982)

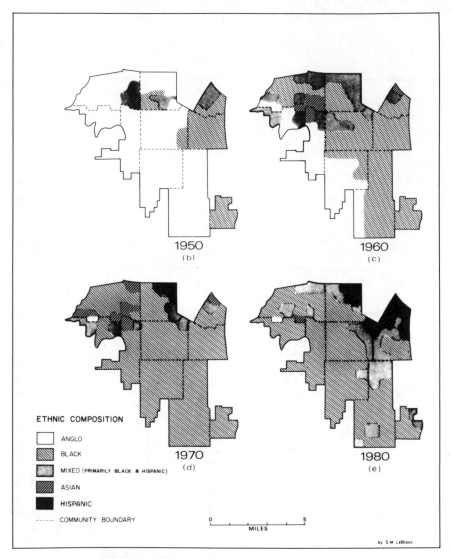

Figure 2b–2e.   Ethnic succession in south central Los Angeles (Source: City of
   Los Angeles Community Development Department (1977–1982)

Angeles' blacks (70%) resided in the Avalon district (called the Furlong Tract in
the 1920s), the Central community was the center of economic and socio-cultural
life. Likened to New York's black Harlem, over 86 black businesses, ranging
from advertising to wholesale watch manufacturing, were located along Central
avenue (the main street transecting the area) as early as the 1920s' (Tolbert,
1980).

Attracted by the prospects of obtaining jobs in the wartime shipbuilding and aircraft construction industries, approximately 289,000 blacks migrated to California during the 1940s, and the majority settled in Los Angeles (Collins, 1980; Bullock, 1972). Because of the rigid real estate and property owner's segregation policies (approximately 95 percent of the housing stock was covered by race restrictive covenants), living conditions for blacks became increasingly more congested during the 1940s (Spaulding, 1946). As Figure 2b shows, housing availability was limited to units vacated by Anglos in the Central, Avalon, Santa Barbara, and West Adams Districts and in Watts where three public housing projects were built between 1942 and 1944, largely to accommodate the massive influx of black migrants. Although these housing projects—Hacienda Village (1942), Imperial Courts (1944), and Jordan Downs (1944)—provided much needed additional housing, by locating them in Watts the city actually contributed to further isolation and ghettoization of blacks (Collins, 1980; Bullock, 1972). Moreover, the number of units built fell far short of the estimated 11,000 to 12,000 needed to ease the tension mounting among blacks and between them and other ethnic groups (particularly in Watts) as a result of congested and deplorable living conditions (Spaulding, 1946; Fisher, 1947).

In 1947 the City Planning Commission of Los Angeles described Watts as:

> an obsolescent area in which all the social and physical weakness of urban living are to be found. Some streets are unpaved, others have fine concrete roadways and ornaments; some structures seem about to fall apart, while next to them exist new standard buildings. In some areas, a great number of 25 foot lots stood vacant, while in others six or more dwellings are crowded into a similar parcel. Recreational facilities in certain sections are few in number and limited in area. Schools are located in places where the maximum walking distance, rather than the minimum, is required of a great number of children. The shopping district on 103rd Street has little provision for off-street parking, and during business hours the street is cluttered with double parked vehicles and is almost closed to traffic movement. . . . The low rental pattern, the high disease and delinquency rates, all reflect the blighted character of this district (Cited in Bullock, 1972: 285).

Two years later in 1949, Robinson described Watts in the following manner:

> This area is surrounded by strong Anglo-American Communities which in the past have manifested discriminatory practices-even physical aggression. The Latin American residents are disturbed by the rapidly growing Negro majority. The native Negroes are disturbed by the incoming "southern" Negroes . . . (Cited in Bullock, 1972:284–285).

The only housing open to the large number of new arrivals during the 1940s outside of the existing black enclave was in Little Tokyo (not shown on the map), the Japanese community, which became available when the Japanese were relocated to internment camps during World War II. As a result of the massive influx of blacks into Little Tokyo, the name was changed to "Bronzeville" and the area became the worst example of congestion and slums in the city (Collins, 1980).

Living conditions in the area were described in the following manner by the Los Angeles Housing Authority:

> Records of our applications show families piling up to a congestion of four, five and six persons per bedroom. In one case a family of 5 was living in a dirt-floored garage with no sanitary facilities whatsoever. In an abandoned storefront and two nearly windowless storage rooms in Little Tokyo 21 people were found to be living—and paying approximately $50 a month for these quarters (Holtzendof, 1943:1764).

In the aftermath of World War II, the Japanese-Americans returned to reclaim their community, forcing those blacks to search elsewhere for housing.

While the city was fully aware of the poor living conditions existing in Watts and other black residential areas during the 1940s, little was done to ameliorate the situation (Collins, 1980). Race restrictive covenants were relaxed in 1945 in the "Sugar Hill Decision" and were ruled unenforceable by the U.S. Supreme court in 1948, but little additional housing became available to blacks. Thus by the end of the decade a majority of the city's black population, totaling 175,000, resided in three identifiable "mini-ghettos" (See Figure 2b).

Although race restrictive covenants were ruled unenforceable in the late 1940s, discriminatory practices of realtors and community resistance in large parts of the metropolitan area restricted blacks to areas where whites were either leaving or avoiding during the 1950s. Largely as a result of extensive "White flight" and "White avoidance," by 1960 the central city mini-ghettos had coalesced, to form one major "ghetto," encompassing all, or a substantial portion of housing in the Central, West Adams, Santa Barbara, Exposition, Avalon, Green Meadows and Watts Districts (Figure 2c).

During the early 1960s, attempts were made to enact open housing legislation in California (Becker, 1964). For example, William Rumford, a black Assemblyman from Oakland, proposed legislation which would outlaw racial and religious discrimination in the sale or rental of housing in the state; any property owner found guilty of such acts would be subject to a $500 fine. Passed in 1963, the Rumford Act was opposed by the State Real Estate Association and the Apartment Owner's Association of California. They argued that property owners should have the right to sell or rent "to whomever they choose," and gathered over 1 million signatures on a petition to force a referendum on the issue. In November, 1964, the Rumford Act was repelled by the California electorate by a margin of 2 to 1. The repeal essentially prohibited all legal restrictions on the "absolute discretion" of owners to choose to whom they would sell or rent (*New York Times*, 1964). The repeal of the Rumford Act essentially authorized housing discrimination against minorities, especially blacks (*New York Times*, 1964:38).

Meanwhile, living conditions in Los Angeles' black ghetto, especially in Watts, grew progressively worse during the early-to-mid-1960s. Overcrowded and deteriorated housing, animosities between blacks and the police, poor public transit service, inadequate health care and shopping facilities, high unemployment, and a general lack of concern about these problems by city officials sparked the Watts rebellions of 1965: 11 days of violence, looting and burning which left 34 dead, 1032 injured, and property damage and loss totaling $40 million (McCone Commission, 1965; Fogelson, 1969). Many Anglos responded to the Watts disturbances by leaving the city and some of the housing vacated by them, particularly on the fringes of the ghetto, filtered down to blacks, continuing the contagious pattern of ghetto expansion north and westward within the city (Figure 2d).

B.   Ethnic Succession in the Black Ghetto

One of the major and largely unnoticed developments of the 1960s' undoubtedly overshadowed by the Watts rebellions, was the significant influx of Spanish speaking households into the central city black ghetto. Los Angeles' Hispanic population increased sharply during the decade, largely due to increased migration into the city. As a consequence of this population increase, new arrivals were forced to seek housing outside of the established Latino communities of east Los Angeles. By 1970, approximately 50,000 Hispanics had settled in south central Los Angeles, accounting for nearly 10 percent of the ghetto's total population. As Table 1 shows, in 1970 approximately 40 percent of the Hispanics were concentrated in three formerly all black communities—Central, Santa Barbara, and Exposition—and the rest were fairly well dispersed in other ghetto communities (Figure 2d). In 1970, 10 percent of the central city's Spanish speaking population resided in south central Los Angeles.

During the 1970s the number of Hispanics settling in south central Los Angeles continued to increase, totaling over 100,000 in 1980, or nearly 21 percent of the area's population by the decade's end. It is important to note that these figures, based on the census, substantially understates the total number of Spanish speaking households in this area. Given that an unestimated number are undocumented workers, it follows that they are not represented in the census figures in Table 1. Of the total number of Hispanics in south central Los Angeles which were counted in the U.S. census, approximately two thirds (67%) were clustered in 1980 in four formerly all black communities (Figure 2e): Santa Barbara (26%), Exposition Park (14.5%), Avalon (13.8%), and Central (12.7%). While the Hispanic population in the black ghetto was increasing, the black population actually declined by 8 percent, with those communities experiencing the largest Hispanic increase also registering the most significant black losses. This pattern of ethnic succession is often cited by blacks as evidence that Latinos are displacing them from their traditionally all black communities. The 1980 census data do show that part of the black loss in the central city ghetto has been offset by a significant increase in the number of blacks in other parts of the

Table 1. Distribution of Black and Hispanic Population in Los Angeles' Black Ghetto: 1970 and 1980

Statistical Area	Total Population			Black Population			Hispanic Population		
	1970	1980	Percent Change	1970	1980	Percent Change	1970	1980	Percent Change
Avalon	45,328	48,510	+7.0	41,883	33,005	−22.2	2,357	15,194	+544.6
Baldwin Hills	24,665	23,215	−5.9	15,885	20,386	+27.0	1,381	657	−52.4
Central	16,296	20,568	+26.2	9,892	5,766	−42.7	4,742	13,962	+194.4
Exposition Park	70,705	71,715	+1.4	58,544	53,251	−10.6	5,798	15,802	172.5
Green Meadows	98,704	88,696	−9.9	87,056	74,331	−15.6	6,317	13,207	+109.1
Leimert	48,883	46,263	−5.4	33,240	39,587	+17.8	3,422	2,411	−29.5
Santa Barbara	61,741	67,766	+9.8	34,205	29,564	−15.6	13,707	28,201	+105.7
South Vermont	73,105	67,082	−8.2	60,092	57,030	−3.0	5,775	6,383	+105.7
Watts	29,661	27,500	−7.3	26,517	23,354	−12.0	2,581	4,032	+56.2
West Adams	70,710	67,387	−4.7	49,709	48,565	−2.3	4,547	10,029	+120.6
Ghetto	539,798	528,975	−2.0	417,001	382,486	−8.3	50,627	109,878	+117.0
Los Angeles City	2,811,801	2,966,850	5.5	503,606	495,723	−1.6	518,791	816,076	+57.3

Notes:
*1970 Definition.
**Percent of Total Ghetto Population.
***Percent of Total Central City Population.
Source: City of Los Angeles Community Development Department (1977, 1982).

metropolitan area which traditionally were inaccessible to minorities. During the 1970s, for example, the number of blacks living in the San Fernando Valley increased by 79 percent and in the suburbs by 66 percent, although much of the latter growth occurred in spillover communities adjacent to the central city ghetto. But the extent to which the growth of the black population in these areas is a function of coerced movement from south central Los Angeles communities experiencing black to brown succession is unclear and remains to be determined. What is very clear, however, is that the influx of Spanish speaking households into south central Los Angeles has created the conditions ripe for considerable conflict between blacks and browns.

In summary, historically a number of techniques and procedures, including race restrictive covenants and the location of public housing projects, were employed to restrict black access to housing primarily in south central Los Angeles. More recently, since 1950, the growth and spread of the central city black community has reflected a contagious-diffusion process in which upwardly mobile blacks have moved into housing vacated by whites fleeing the city in response to the Watts riots, neighborhood racial transition, mandatory school busing, and a general perception of a declining quality of life in the central city. For those blacks left behind in older parts of the central city ghetto, the newly arriving Spanish speaking population has been a source of competition for affordable housing as well as other social and economic resources. In the section that follows, we explore the perceptions of ethnic antagonism emerging between these two groups in south central Los Angeles.

IV. PERCEPTIONS OF ETHNIC ANTAGONISM

In discussing racial and ethnic conflict, sociologists usually begin with a conceptual apparatus that assumes that the two groups involved are distinguishable in terms of the resources they possess, particularly power resources, with the dominant group being able to exclude the minority group from full participation in the culture and economy of the society (Barth and Noel, 1972; Berreman, 1969; Blalock, 1967; Lieberson, 1961; Merton, 1949; Myrdal, 1944; Noel, 1968). In the case of blacks and Latinos however, the differences are not necessarily as important as the similarities; both suffer from discrimination, are consigned to the lower rungs of the social order, and are subject to the ravages of the urban crisis (i.e. substandard city services, poor schools and unsafe environments). Therefore, any conflict that exists between these two groups is distinct from traditional black-white conflicts, particularly those associated with the ghetto rebellions of the 1960s. Moreover, these similarities logically should lead to cooperative rather than contentious relations. But in the context of urban America where opportunities for economic subsistence are declining and inner-city neighborhood life is deteriorating they can become the basis for inter-group conflict (Willhelm, 1970; Wilson, 1978).

In this section we will explore, through an analysis of survey data collected by the *Los Angeles Times,* the nature and extent of ethnic antagonism that these two groups have toward one another.[2] We are concerned primarily with the following questions: What are the critical expressions of ethnic antagonism between blacks and browns in Los Angeles? Is antagonism toward blacks and Latinos expressed more strongly by these two groups toward each other or by whites? In what ways are these expressions related to the personal characteristics of the two groups and to their perceptions and experiences of everyday urban life?

We have already identified a number of sources of potential conflict between blacks and Latinos. Two sources stand out. First, there are those which derive from the economic and political situation in which these two groups find themselves. Most prominent are perceptions of job competition between the two groups, and perceptions of unequal and unfair advantage in terms of political and economic resources between them. Second, there are those which derive from cultural differences, such as language and racial and ethnic antipathy resulting from sterotyped belief systems. We label such perceptions "ethnic antagonism," following Bonacich (1972:548) who notes that " 'antagonism' is intended to encompass all levels of intergroup conflict, including ideologies and beliefs . . . behaviors . . . and institutions." We stress in this exposition individual beliefs.

In Table 2 we see the survey responses of blacks, Latinos, and whites to what we term perceptions of ethnic antagonism. We present our findings below.

A.   Political and Economic Power

In the *Los Angeles Times* survey each respondent was asked to think about the "economic power" and "political power" that some groups "have or don't have." They were then given the name of two groups, blacks and Mexican Americans, and asked whether that "particular group has too much, just enough, or too little" political or economic power. Given the well documented fact that both blacks and Latinos have little or no economic and political power compared to the majority group in U.S. society, we took an individual response of "too much" as an indicator of ethnic antagonism toward the other group by the respondent. Blacks were the least likely group to express the view that Mexican Americans had "too much" political or economic power" (4%). This contrasted significantly with Latino perceptions of blacks in terms of political power (Chi Square=14.06, sig<.001); 12 percent of the Latinos surveyed expressed the belief that blacks had "too much political power." Whites concurred with Latinos in their perception of the political power of blacks. However the differences between black and Latino perceptions of each other's economic power showed little differences. Thus it appears that Latinos and whites are more concerned about the political power of blacks than blacks and whites are of the political power of Mexican Americans.

Table 2. Expressions of Ethnic Antagonism by Race

Perceptions of:	Political and Economic Power		Stereotypes			Interaction	Black-Brown Relations	Job Competition
	Percent "Too Much Political Power"	Percent "Too Much Economic Power"	Percent Agreeing "More Violent Than Other Groups"	Percent Agreeing "Blacks Not As Intelligent As Other Groups"	Percent Agreeing "Mexican Americans Don't Try To Speak English"	Percent Who "Prefer Not to Have Blacks/Mexican Americans As Neighbors"	Percent Who Agree "Black/Mexican American Relations are Getting Worse"[1]	Percent Who Agree that "Undocumented Mexicans Take Away Jobs From U.S. Citizens"
1. Black Perceptions of Mexican Americans	4 (582)	4 (583)	20 (586)	NA[2]	35 (587)	16 (589)	19 (589)	66 (587)
2. Latino Perceptions of Blacks	12 (161)	9 (162)	39 (161)	21 (162)	NA	22 (162)	13 (162)	34 (162)
3. White Perceptions of Blacks	9 (474)	7 (440)	14 (468)	15 (478)	NA	14 (474)	28 (471)	79 (478)
4. White Perceptions of Mexican Americans	13 (471)	9 (476)	35 (476)	NA	59 (473)	21 (471)		
Chi-Square between:								
Groups 1 and 2:	14.06***	1.43	24.32***	—	—	2.02	2.15	52.84***
Groups 1 and 4:	11.15***	3.88	24.20***	—	61.36***	.79	10.93***	5.95*
Groups 2 and 3:	.01	.00	28.36***	2.23	—	4.32*	12.45***	—

*p < .05
**p < .01
***p < .001

Notes:
[1]Responses to these questions do not indicate a perception of a particular group, per se, but rather just a response to the particular question posed.
[2]Question not posed to the indicated group.

B.   Stereotypes and Interaction

Next we examine expressions of ethnic antagonism which refer to each group's agreement with common stereotypes about the other group and with each group's willingness to interact with each other. Once again a similar pattern persists; Latinos are generally more antagonistic toward blacks than blacks are to Latinos.

Each respondent was asked whether they agreed or disagreed with certain "statements that have been made by different kinds of people from time to time." They were further instructed that while "some statements are positive and some . . . negative . . . you can be sure that there are other people who feel the same as you do" in order to facilitate the securing of the respondent's true feelings, even though they might be socially disapproved views. There were seven items: four related to blacks and three related to Mexican Americans. We chose to analyze two stereotypes from each group (others elicited similar patterns, but did not have as strong face validity as those chosen). One stereotype was similar for each group: the notion that blacks and Mexican Americans "are more violent than other people." This is the only stereotype item for which direct comparisons can be made. In this case Latinos are almost twice as likely (39%) as blacks (20%) to agree that the other group is more violent than the average group. Once again these differences are statistically significant (Chi Square = 24.32, sig<.001). Moreover, blacks express this form of antagonism toward Mexican Americans much less often than whites (20% to 35%). Clearly Latinos' antagonism towards blacks and white antagonism towards Mexican American stand out when this item is examined.

Latino antagonism is further noted when we examine the responses to the item which ask respondents whether or not they believe "blacks aren't as intelligent as other people." This item taps what is usually thought of as the ideological bedrock of racism: the belief in the inherent inferiority of people (Gould, 1981). We find that about one fifth (21%) of the Latinos surveyed agreed that blacks were not as intelligent as other people. The origin of this belief is not apparent. We do not know whether this is a belief rooted in the everyday experiences of Latinos or part of a "Spanish" cultural heritage that has been transmitted through socialization. Indeed it could very well represent the degree of cultural similarity of the Spanish cultural heritage with the norms of American society, as white and Latino responses to this item show no statistical difference (although Latinos are slightly more likely to agree than whites).

The second stereotype which measures blacks prejudgements about Mexican Americans concerns their feelings about Mexican Americans' desire to learn and speak English. Communication in Watts between blacks and Latinos is a major problem. As two journalists note:

Language poses an insurmountable barrier between the Latino newcomers and their black neighbors. Though they live side by side, they remain strangers to one another . . . Spanish is the second language of Watts. Spanish language masses are celebrated in most Catholic churches. Spanish is the language of children at play in the streets and the shadows of decaying tenements where Latinos have gained a stronghold (Hernandez and Scott, 1980:22).

About one third of the blacks surveyed (35%) thought that "Mexican Americans don't try hard to speak English." Lack of communication, or a perception that communication is not possible, only leads to isolation and suspiciousness between groups. However, whites are significantly more likely (59%) than blacks to think that "Mexican Americans don't try hard to speak English." This softens considerably the perception that blacks are highly antagonistic toward Mexican-Americans. For these two stereotype items, at least, blacks were less likely than whites to express feelings of antagonism toward Latinos.

As an indicator of the extent to which social interaction between each group is tolerated, we chose a question which asked each respondent "How would you feel about having" Blacks and Mexican Americans "in your neighborhood." A response indicating that they would prefer not to have blacks or Mexican Americans as neighbors was taken as a central expression of ethnic antagonism. Once again Latinos were more antagonistic toward blacks (22%) than vice versa (16%). However the difference is not statistically significant and is among the smallest set of differences in the table between these two groups. To put this in perspective, we note that 21 percent of the whites indicated that they would "prefer not" to have Mexican Americans as neighbors. This is contrasted to their more lenient attitude toward blacks; only 14 percent of the whites expressed a preference to not have blacks as neighbors.

C. Job Competition

The most significant expression of ethnic antagonism, from our perspective, revolves around economic issues, particularly job competition. Most commentators who have recognized ethnic hostility between blacks and Latinos have usually emphasized the role of economic competition. Most pointedly, the issue has been treated as one in which Latinos, usually undocumented aliens, are seen as *taking* away low status, menial jobs from blacks who had previously been employed in similar positions. Some commentators even go so far as to claim that the impact of undocumented workers, particularly Spanish-speaking ones, upon blacks "is a major reason for the employment crisis among . . . young black men" (Jackson, 1979: 34). While we view this as a hyperbolic generalization, it is, nevertheless, a highly representative viewpoint in many urban black communities across the country. The survey taken by the *Los Angeles Times* confirms this view. Two thirds (66%) of the black respondents agreed that "undocumented Mexicans living in the U.S. take jobs away from American citizens.'' It is worth noting that almost four out of ten of the Latinos (39%) responded similarly. This is indicative of the non-ethnic character of this dimension; the threat of a low priced, powerless labor pool threatens Latinos also, who must compete for vanishing unskilled jobs that barely pay a decent standard of living. Moreover, the impact of black antagonism is somewhat blunted by the overwhelming percentage of whites (79%) who also indicate a concern with ''undocumented workers'' taking jobs away from American citizens. However, it is clear that black antagonism towards Latinos centers almost exclusively on economic grounds.

D.   Black-Mexican American Relations

The final expression of ethnic antagonism that was tapped is a general summary measure. Respondents were asked the following: ''During the past fifteen years, do you think the relationship between Black people and Mexican Americans has gotten better—worse—or don't you think there has been any change in the relationship between Blacks and Mexican Americans.'' In contrast to all the recent concern about potential black-brown conflict the percentage of respondents who indicated things were getting worse between blacks and Mexican Americans was relatively small. Blacks were somewhat more likely (19%) than Latinos (13%) to express pessimism over the developing black-Mexican American relationship during the last fifteen years. However, this was once again overshadowed by the responses of whites to the item. Whites were significantly more likely to express pessimism over black-Mexican American relationships than either blacks or Latinos. Indeed, it is clear from this whole review that whites are more antagonistic toward Latinos than blacks. Moreover, Latinos appear slightly more antagonistic toward blacks than vice versa. The predicted antagonism of blacks towards Latinos has not materialized, at least in these data.

The fact that inter-ethnic antagonism between blacks and Latinos was found to be quite modest in these data does not invalidate our concern with urban inter-ethnic conflict. However, these findings do put in perspective any notion that inter-ethnic antagonism has surpassed traditional racial antagonism in urban America. White antipathy toward minorities, both black and brown, is still quite strong and capable of producing heightened racial conflict. However, it is also clear that conditions in our nation's urban centers can ignite existing inter-ethnic antagonism into inter-ethnic conflict. Therefore, it is important to try and understand the basis of the inter-ethnic antagonism that has been uncovered.

E.   The Role of Social Background and Community Perceptions
on Ethnic Antagonism

The initial argument in this paper is that inter-ethnic conflict in the urban ghettos of Los Angeles is rooted primarily in forces associated with the political economy of the city. This political economy has functioned in such a way as to force various ethnic groups to compete for affordable housing, unskilled jobs, and public services. Our analysis of the residential changes that have taken place in black communities in Los Angeles during the last decade has empirically documented the movement of Mexican Americans into these communities in search of affordable housing and proximity to sources of low wage, unskilled employment. The resulting mixture of lower and working class blacks and Latinos living together in communities where public services have always been less than adequate, can lead to a socially undesirable atmosphere. Plagued by social problems of all sorts, these communities have the potential to drift into anomic wastelands (Bullough, 1967; Wilson, 1972). The fear of crime and personal safety can become rampant. Language differences can separate people so that inter-ethnic communication is hampered. The lack of confidence in others is reinforced by one's lack of faith in the efficacy of the public institutions that are there to serve you. Schools do little to educate one's children, public assistance is one large degradation ceremony, and health facilities are overcrowded and their services demeaning. It is this social context that sets in motion inter-ethnic conflict.

We want to explore whether our hypothesis concerning the relationship of the urban political economy to ethnic antagonism has any merit. We can conduct an indirect analysis of this proposition through further examination of the *Los Angeles Times* survey data. We have constructed an index from the two stereotype items and the one interaction item. These items are closest in content and form to traditional measures of prejudice and intergroup hostility. Each respondent was given 1 point for each response that indicated antagonism toward the other group. Therefore scores could range from 0 if no antagonistic responses were given to a high of 3 if all answers were negative toward the other group. In Table 3 we see the index for blacks and Latinos. Not surprising, nearly half of the respondents from both groups (45%) scored in the lowest category, having given

Table 3. Black and Latino Scores on
Index of Ethnic Antagonism

Index Score	Blacks	Latinos
Low 0	45	45
1	41	30
High 2 or more	14	25
	100%	100%
	(588)	(162)
	$x^2 = 12.45$, sig $< .01$	

Note:
The cases with information on at least two of the items in the index were dropped, thus leading to a reduced N for both indexes.

no antagonistic responses. However there were significant differences between the two groups in the extent to which they scored high on the indexes (answered 2 or more of the questions in an antagonistic manner). Latinos were significantly more likely to score high than blacks (Chi Square=12.45, p<.01). While one in four (25%) of the Latinos scored high, only about one in seven (14%) of the blacks were similarly classified. While these are still quite small percentages of the groups, we want to better understand who these antagonistic blacks and browns are, as well as attempt to see how their antagonisms are related to their perceptions of the community. It is our argument that these perceptions of the community can go a long way in explaining their perceptions of each other.

From the survey we have developed some measures of the respondent's perceptions of their community. These measures give us some indication of how the respondent experiences everyday life. We assume that daily life for many of our survey respondents is very much affected by the deleterious impact of the urban political economy. We have identified six measures related to the quality of urban life. They are: (1) Whether or not the respondent "feels trapped" in their community; (2) whether the respondent perceives the most important problems facing their community as one of either employment, housing or schools (three problems most often associated with the urban crisis); (3) whether the respondent or anyone else in the household was unemployed at the time of the survey; (4) whether the respondent "feels safe" in their community and home; (5) whether the respondent has confidence in a number of city services (city bureaus, public schools and the police); and (6) whether the respondent can trust neighbors and people around them. We would expect our index of ethnic antagonism to correlate strongly with feelings of being trapped in one's community, perceiving the urban crisis, experiencing the urban crisis through a loss of one's own job or someone close to them, feeling unsafe in one's community, having no confidence in public services, and having little confidence in one's neighbors. Likewise we would expect that background demographic variables of age, education, and income would also be related to ethnic antagonism in such a way that the younger respondents who compete against each other for jobs, the poorly educated who are consigned to the competitive labor market, and the low wage earners to express greater antagonism than older, more highly educated and high income respondents. In addition, we will determine how our index of ethnic antagonism relates to other types of ethnic antagonism, such as perceptions of too much political and economic power, job competition, and black-Mexican American relations.

In Table 4 we are able to examine these relationships. While the correlations are generally quite low, we will emphasize the pattern of significant relationships in this discussion. Examining the relationship of background variables first, we note that age (-.09) is significantly related to the black index of ethnic antagonism, while for Latinos, education (-.29) and income (-.15) are related to black antipathy. Younger blacks are more inclined to be antagonistic toward Latinos,

Table 4. Correlations Between Index of Ethnic Antagonism and Background and Community Perception Variables

	Blacks	Latinos
Background:		
Age	−.09**	.07
Education	.05	−.29***
Income	−.04	−.15*
Community Perceptions:		
Feel Trapped	−.03	−.30***
Perceive Urban Crisis	.04	−.07
Feel Urban Crisis	.01	.13*
Feel Unsafe	.02	.08
No Confidence in Public Services	.10**	.11
No Confidence in Neighborhood	.04	.09
Job Competition	−.22***	.09
Black-Brown Relations Getting Worse	.15***	.13*
Feel Blacks-Brown Have Too Much Economic Power or Political Power	.16***	.31***

*p < .05
**p < .01
***p < .001

Note:
The N for each correlation varies depending on whether or not full information was available.

while low education and low income Latinos are more likely to express antagonism towards blacks. This is somewhat consistent with our "urban crisis" thesis as we would expect younger blacks and Latinos competing in the job market currently alongside each other to be most affected by this sort of job competition.

Examining the relationship between community perceptions and ethnic antagonism reveals fewer differences in the patterns of relationships between blacks and Latinos, with those differences being only minor. Black antagonism toward Mexican Americans is more likely among those who express little confidence in public services like police, education and city services (.10), who feel that undocumented Mexican Americans take away jobs from American citizens (-.22), that black-Latino relations have worsened (.15), and that Mexican Americans have either too much political or economic power (.16). Not surprisingly the job competition variable is the strongest predictor. While for the Latinos, those who feel trapped in their communities (-.30), have felt the ravages of the urban crisis through unemployment in their households (.13), who see black-

Latino relations deteriorating (.13), and who view blacks as having too much economic or political power (.31) are those most inclined to have high scores on the Latino index of ethnic antagonism. Those perceptions of the community which are economically related seem to be the most consistently related to ethnic antagonism, although in different guises for each group. Blacks seem to be concerned with the direct threat of job competition from undocumented workers, while Latinos who feel powerless and economically vulnerable seem to have displaced some of their animosity upon blacks.

V.   SUMMARY, CONCLUSION, AND IMPLICATIONS

This analysis has explored the theoretical and empirical parameters of emerging "black-brown" conflict in the south central black ghetto of Los Angeles. We began by discussing the unique constellation of forces that distinguish the spatial and social patterns of black and Latino movement in urban America from that of earlier European immigrants. We stressed three important differences. First, we noted the changing structure of the economy and its effect on black and Latino job opportunities. Shrinking opportunities for entry level, un-skilled labor due to the growth of large multinationals, the movement of industry to the suburbs and, more recently, outside of the country, and the automation of assembly line work has led to a situation where inner city blacks and Latinos compete for a limited supply of available jobs. Second, we noted a legacy of discrimination in the metropolitan housing market which constrained black-Latino residential mobility, thus trapping them within areas deemed socially undesirable. More recently, institutionally based decisions by the mortgage, insurance, and the real estate industry have continued to adversely impact the opportunities of these groups to move, and thus inhibits their ability to recreate the residential movement of earlier immigrant groups. And third, we showed that there exists a strand of ethnic antipathy between blacks and Latinos that, when fueled by other factors, could also lead to conflict between these groups. With these differences in mind, we explored the social-historical and spatial development of the south central ghetto in Los Angeles.

Our discussion of the development of the black community in south central Los Angeles emphasized a whole array of "ghettomakers" that have been implicated in the genesis of these areas, among them race restrictive covenants, governmental policies, and real estate practices. Characterized by poor living conditions, the black community exploded in the Watts rebellion of 1965. At the same time, the black communities of south central Los Angeles began to feel the impact of a considerable influx of Latinos (primarily Mexican Americans) into the area. By 1980 Latinos constituted about one fifth of the area's population. It is this movement which set the stage for inter-ethnic conflict.

Our examination of survey data revealed that black and Latino expressions of antagonism toward each other are not that great, especially when compared to whites. Whites still express considerable antagonism and hostility toward both blacks and Latinos. Traditional racial and ethnic hostility is still important in urban America, and should not be overlooked or sidetracked by our concern with inter-ethnic conflict. Indeed, this is one of the major findings of our examination of the survey data.

However, the survey data also revealed that when we examine only blacks and Latinos some interesting information does emerge. For example, Latinos appear to be more antagonistic toward blacks than vice versa on almost every indicator. Black antagonism seems concentrated in one area. Blacks feel fairly strong that "undocumented Mexicans take jobs away from American citizens." The strong feelings on this issue provide a fairly clear indicator of the primacy of economic factors emanating from the structural changes that have taken place in the economy and which have contributed to what we now call the "urban crisis."

As initially hypothesized, we expected that those respondents who were most affected by the urban crisis would be those most likely to express ethnic antagonisms. To indirectly test this notion we built an "index of ethnic antagonism" for each group and attempted to relate it to the respondents' personal background and perceptions of urban life, including perceptions about each others' group. While not definitive, the analysis did show that younger, less educated respondents, those most likely to be in the secondary labor market, were more likely than older and more educated respondents to express ethnic antagonisms. Blacks who were not satisfied with city services were also more likely to score high on the index. In a most revealing manner, the strongest correlate of black antagonism toward Latinos was the job competition item. Among Latinos in this survey, those who felt trapped in their neighborhoods and who had experienced the most negative effect of the urban crisis in their household, unemployment, were most likely to express antagonism toward blacks.

This analysis points to the centrality of the economic context in percipitating and shaping ethnic antagonism between blacks and Latinos in the central city ghetto of Los Angeles. While the analysis also indicated the importance of social and political differences in shaping antagonistic perceptions, closer inspection of the data suggests that these differences may ultimately reflect economic causes. For example, it is clear that Latinos in the analysis perceive blacks to have too much political power. This is contrasted sharply with black views of Latinos on this issue. However, these discrepancies may reflect a realistic perception of the nature of political power in the local context of Los Angeles. While blacks do not have political representation in national and state politics proportional to their population, at least they have high visibility in electoral politics in Los Angeles: a black mayor, membership on city council, and administrative positions in the city bureaucracy. On the other hand, Latinos in Los Angeles county represent one of the least represented ethnic groups in the history of urban politics. In a city which has the largest Latino population in the Northern hemisphere, outside of

Mexico City and Guadalajara, there are no elected Latino officials in the City or County government (Moore et al., 1978:13–4). While the reasons for this pattern are complex, it is clear that Latino ethnic antagonism on the political dimension has some basis in reality, and more importantly, it is not at all separated from the economic dimension.

The potential for social conflict arising from these different perceptions is economically related. Historically, city politics has been a stepping stone for ethnic group mobility, particularly for European ethnic groups in the the east and midwest (Handlin, 1951; Cornwall, 1969). It is not at all clear that they serve this same purpose now; it has been argued that bureaucratic politics has replaced patronage politics to the extent that going through bureaucratic procedures (i.e. eligibility criteria such as schooling and exam scores) has replaced party loyalty as the basis for city employment (Erie, 1980). Latinos face the bureaucracy in Los Angeles as a sea of predominately white and black faces whose hands control employment and promotion criteria. Furthermore, just as economically blacks and Mexican Americans are squared off against each other for a limited set of spoils, politically, "quotas" for a specified percentage or presence of minorities in everything from government institutions to education, both elementary and higher, are potential battlegrounds between ethnic groups over how the percentage is to be divided among ethnic and racial groups. When Latinos view blacks as having more say in these decisions due to their superior political or economic status, the probability of ethnic conflict increases.

The foregoing analysis has implications beyond the particulars of the black-brown conflict in Los Angeles. Increasingly, urban conflict is based on issues of how scarce resources are to be allocated. Corporate decisions, made by distant executives, are becoming the shapers and major architects of the infrastructure of urban economic opportunities. Mechanisms for popular control and review of these decisions are non-existent. Effected in important ways by these decisions, the inhabitants of the ghettos of the nation's major cities deal with their frustration through displaced conflict. This conflict gets expressed as violence against one another, or potentially more damaging, as violence and conflict between disadvantaged groups who perceive each other as "causing" the problem.

While white racial and ethnic antagonisms are still strong, as our analysis shows, researchers should be sensitive and concerned with the potential for social conflict that exists between the have-nots who are increasingly forced to live together in our nation's ghettos (i.e. blacks, browns and Asians as well as other black immigrants e.g. Haitians) The impact of the "new immigration" is that the new groups, for the most part, are ethnically and culturally different from the traditional inhabitants of these areas and therefore, each are perfect targets for the others displaced hostility.

It is also clear that the potential for conflict between these groups is directly related to political decisions which effect not only local areas but also the national economy. The case of "undocumented workers" for example show the futility of purely political decisions. This issue will not lose its force in the black community until enough jobs are created by the economy to create opportunities for employment for all. The simple amnesty of undocumented workers now residing in the U.S., combined with penalities for employers who hire them in the future, will only lead to more competition for scarce jobs unless the structure of job opportunities is drastically altered. On the local level, it is important that inner city communities with the potential for inter-ethnic conflict receive more than adequate city and welfare services. Otherwise, local conditions could pre- cipitate and aggravate social conflict. As our data show, ethnic antagonism is related to perceptions of the adequacy of city services. And it is on local issues where back-brown coalitions can serve their most valuable role. Bringing to- gether these groups to work toward immediate, visible improvements in the community can help ameliorate, though not completely, the effects of economic forces. The survey results are encouraging as they relate to cooperative efforts between the two groups in Los Angeles. Almost half of both groups appear friendly and non-antagonistic toward each other. Thus the basis of a movement for cooperation appears more likely than conflict.

This study has brought forth a number of unresolved questions. Its exploratory nature suggests a number of directions for future research. First, the question of population succession in south central Los Angeles raises questions about the social dynamics involved. While the spatial movement patterns appear similar to classic descriptions, it is not at all clear that the social processes are the same (Rosenberg and Lake, 1976; Massey, 1983). Is the movement of blacks out of this area a consequence of voluntary or coerced movement? While no research explores this question, a probable hypothesis is that black movement is coerced by real estate agents and institutions who evict or raise rents precipitously to force blacks out and to rent to Latinos, who because of multiple wage earners or undocumented status are able to afford, but not able to challenge, the exorbitant rents. Examining the pattern of movement of a recent group of blacks from this area, Meyer (1983) noted that instead of moving to the outer edges of the ghetto as whites vacate, this recent cohort of movers showed no such pattern, but rather moved in a spraylike fashion all over the Los Angeles metropolitan area. This suggests a different pattern, as well as process, than described by Rose (1970) in examining ghetto growth and expansion. Future research should examine whether black movement is coerced or a result of the traditional forces which generated ghetto expansion.

The whole area of the impact of new immigrants to our nation's urban centers and their interaction with the resident population is in need of attention. While we have approached this topic through an analysis of conflict, studies which highlight the ways in which cooperative relations are established as well are also needed. Particularly absent are studies which could provide an in-depth under- standing of the social fabric and life in these communities. Survey methodologies are not adequate to tap these dimensions and need to be supplemented by participant and naturalistic observation research. These types of research would describe the subtle ways in which conflict and cooperation occur between blacks and browns within our inner cities, an issue which, as we have shown, is of considerable sociological and political significance.

ACKNOWLEDGMENTS

We would like to note the research support the authors received through grants from the UCLA Academic Senate and the Ford Foundation. Helpful research assistance was provided by Althea Silvera and Anita Garcia. Also, we would like to acknowledge the critical readings given to earlier versions of this paper by a group of conscientious colleagues: Melvin Seeman, Rodolfo Alvarez, Ivan Light, Susan Smith and Joan Moore. Of course, we are completely responsible for the interpretations and analyses presented. Send all communication to Oliver, Department of Sociology, University of California, Los Angeles, Los Angeles, CA 90024.

NOTES

1. Throughout the paper we use the term "Latino" to refer to Americans from Latin America, Central America and the Caribbean. While in the Los Angeles case, most of the Latinos we refer to are from Mexico, a significant proportion, probably 10 percent, are from such Central American, South American and Caribbean countries as El Salvador, Panama, Nicaragua, Columbia, Guatamala, Honduras, and Cuba. However, when reference is made to Mexican Americans or Hispanics specifically, we use those terms as well.

2. The *Los Angeles Times* survey was a telephone study of 1295 Los Angelenos conducted from July 27 through July 31, 1980. Done in conjunction with their series on Watts (*Los Angeles Times*, 1980), the survey was particularly concerned with the black communities of south central Los Angeles, which are the focus of this paper. Therefore, this area was purposefully over-sampled. Thus a random cross-section of 610 interviews were completed from the south central area, as well as a similar cross-section of 685 people from other parts of the city. Trained interviewers, as well as Spanish speaking interviewers, conducted the survey. The margin of error is computed at about four percent in either direction.

REFERENCES

Ambrecht, Biliana C. S. and Harry P. Panchon
    1974   "Ethnic mobilization in a Mexican American community: an exploratory study of East Los
            Angeles 1965" The Western Political Science Quarterly September:500–19.
Arias, Ron
    1980   "The coming Black/Hispanic coalition: a Hispanic view." Perspectives 12(1):12–18.
Baron, Harold and Bennet Hymer
    1968   "The Negro worker in the Chicago labor market." Pp. 232–285 in Julius Jacobson (ed.)
            The Negro in the American Labor Movement. New York: Harper and Row.
Barth, Ernest A. T. and Donald L. Noel
    1972   "Conceptual frameworks for the analysis of race relations: an evaluation." Social Forces
            50 (March):333–346.

Bass, Charlotta
  1961 Forty Years: Memoirs from the Pages of a Newspaper. Los Angeles: Charlotta Bass.
Becker, Bill
  1964 "Fair housing fought on coast." New York Times June 19:76.
Bell, Daniel
  1973 The Coming of Post-Industrial Society. New York: Basic Books.
Berreman, Gerald D.
  1969 "Caste in India and the United States." American Journal of Sociology 66:120–129.
Berry, Brian J. L.
  1980 "Inner city futures: an American dilemma revisited." Institute of British Geographers,
         Transactions 5:1–28.
Blackwell, James
  1982 "Persistence and change in intergroup relations: the crisis upon us." Social Problems
         29:325–346.
Blalock, Hubert M.
  1967 Toward a Theory of Minority Group Relations. New York: John Wiley and Sons.
Blauner, Robert
  1969 "Internal colonislism and ghetto revolt." Social Problems 16:393–408.
Bluestone, Barry
  1970 "The Tripartide Economy: Labor, Market, and the Working Poor." Poverty and Human
         Resources 5 (July–August):15–36.
Bluestone, Barry and Bennett Harrison
  1982 The Deindustrialization of America. New York: Basic Books.
Bonacich, Edna
  1972 "A theory of ethnic antagonism: the split labor market." American Sociological Review
         37:34–51.
  1976 "Advanced capitalism and Black-White relations in the United States: a split labor market
         interpretation." American Sociological Review 41:34–51.
Bond, J. Max
  1936 Negroes in Los Angeles. Unpublished doctoral dissertation, University of Southern
         California.
Braverman, Harry
  1974 Labor and Monopoly Capital: The Degradation of Work in the Twentieth Century. New
         York: Monthly Review Press.
Brown, Kevin
  1981 "Race, class and culture: towards a theorization of the 'choice-constraint' concept." Pp.
         185–203 in Peter Jackson and Susan J. Smith (eds.) Social Interaction and Ethnic Segrega-
         tion. London: Academic Press.
Bullock, Paul
  1972 "Watts: before the riots." Pp. 281–288 in Roger Daniels and Spencer E. Olin, Jr. (eds.)
         Racism in California: A Reader in the History of Oppression. New York: The Macmillan
         Co.
Bullough, Bonnie
  1967 "Alienation in the ghetto." American Journal of Sociology 72:469–478.
Burgess, Ernest W.
  1967 "The growth of the city: an introduction to a research project". Pp. 47–62 in R. E. Park
         [1925] and E. W. Burgess (eds.) The City. Chicago: University of Chicago Press.
Calhoun, Lillian
  1980 "The coming Black/Hispanic coalition: a black view." Perspectives 12(1):12/15.
Castells, Manuel
  1977 The Urban Question. Cambridge: MIT Press.

Clark, William A. V.
  1980   "Residential mobility and neighborhood change: some implications for racial residential
          segregation." Urban Geography 1:95–117.
Collins, Keith E.
  1980   Black Los Angeles: The Making of the Ghetto, 1940–1950. Saratoga, CA: Century Twen-
          ty One Publishing.
Cohen, R. B.
  1981   "The new international division of labor, multinational corporations and urban hierarchy."
          Pp. 287–315 in Michael Dear and Allen J. Scott (eds.) Urbanization & Urban Planning in
          Capitalist Society. London: Methuen.
Cornwall, Elmer
  1969   "Bosses, machines, and ethnic politics." Pp. 190–206 in Harry Bailey and Ellis Katz
          (eds.) Ethnic Group Politics. Columbus, Ohio: Charles Merrill Publishing Co.
Darden, Joe T.
  1980   "Lending practices and policies affecting the American Metropolitan System." Pp. 91–
          110 in Stanley D. Brunn and James O. Wheeler (eds.) The American Metropolitan System:
          Present and Future. New York: John Wiley and Sons.
Davies, Shane and David L. Huff
  1972   "Impact of ghettoization on black employment." Economic Geography 48:421–28.
de Graaf, Lawrence B.
  1962   Negro Migration to Los Angeles, 1930 to 1950. Unpublished doctoral dissertation, Univer-
          sity of California, Los Angeles.
De Vise, Pierre
  1976   "The suburbanization of jobs and minority employment." Economic Geography 52:348–
          362.
Dreyfuss, Joel
  1979   "Blacks and Hispanics: coalition or confrontation." Black Enterprise July:21–3.
Erie, Stephen P.
  1980   "Two faces of ethnic power: comparing the Irish and the Black experiences." Polity 13
          (2):261–84.
Estrada, Leobardo, F., F. C. Garcia, R. F. Macias, and L. M. Maldonado
  1981   "Chicanos in the United States: a history of exploitation and resistance." Daedalus
          110(2):103–132.
Fairchild, Halford and M. B. Tucker
  1982   "Black residential mobility: trends and characteristics." Journal of Social Issues 38:51–
          74.
Farley, Reynolds
  1970   Growth of the Black Population: A Study of Demographic Trends. Chicago: Markham
          Publishing Co.
Farrell, Walter C., Jr. and J. H. Johnson, Jr.
  1978   "Black migration as a response to social-psychological stress: a note on migrant letters;
          1916–1918." Geographical Survey 7:22–27.
Fisher, Lloyd H.
  1947   The Problems of Violence: Observations on Race Conflict in Los Angeles. Chicago:
          American Council on Race Relations.
Fogelson, Robert M.
  1969   Mass Violence in America: The Los Angeles Riots. New York: Arno Press.
Ford, Larry and Ernest Griffin
  1979   "The ghettoization of paradise." The Geographical Review 69:140–158.
Gans, Herbert
  1962   The Urban Villagers. New York: Free Press.

Geschwender, James A.
    1964   "Social structure and the Negro revolt: an examination of some hypotheses." Social
            Forces 43,2:248–256.
Gordon, David M.
    1972   Theories of Poverty and Underemployment. Lexington, MA: D. C. Heath.
    1978   "Capitalist development and American history." Pp. 25–63 in William K. Tabb and Larry
            Sawyers (eds.) Marxism and the Metropolis. New York: Oxford University Press.
Gould, Stephen Jay
    1981   The mismeasure of man. New York: Norton
Grebler, Leo and Joan W. Moore, Ralph Guzman
    1970   The Mexican-American People: The Nation's Second Largest Minority. New York: The
            Free Pres
Green, Robert L., Joe T. Darden, Jill Hurt, Cassandra Simmons, Thomas Ten brunsel, Francis S.
        Thomas, June M. Thomas, and Richard M. Thomas
    1979   "Discrimination and the welfare of urban minorities." Background paper prepared for the
            Urban Policy Task Force of the Department of Housing and Urban Development. Lansing,
            MI: Michigan State University.
Guptan, Udayan
    1983   "From other shores." Black Enterprise 13:51–54.
Handlin, Oscar
    1951   The Uprooted. Boston: Little, Brown and Company.
Henry, Charles P.
    1980   "Black-Chicano coalitions: possibilities and problems." Western Journal of Black Studies
            4:222–232.
Hernandez, Marita and Austin Scott
    1980   "Latino influx: new strains emerge as Watts evolves." Los Angeles Times, August, 24.
Himes, Joseph S.
    1966   "The functions of racial conflict." Social Forces 41(1):1–10.
Holtzendof, Howard L.
    1943   "Statement before the Izak subcommittee of the House Naval Affairs Committee investi-
            gating war housing conditions in Los Angeles, Nov. 10, 1943." Washington, D.C.: U.S.
            Government Printing Office.
Jackson, Jacquelyn Johnson
    1979   "Illegal aliens: big threat to Black workers. Ebony 34:33–36.
Johnson, James H. Jr. and Stanley D. Brunn
    1980   "Spatial and behavioral aspects of the counterstream migration of Blacks to the South."
            Pp. 59–75 in Stanley D. Brunn and James O. Wheeler (eds.) The American Metropolitan
            System: Present and Future. London: John Wiley and Sons.
Johnston, Ronald J.
    1981   "The state and the study of social geography." Pp. 205–222 in Peter Jackson and Susan J.
            Smith (eds.) Social Interaction and Ethnic Segregation. London: Academic Press.
Kain, John F.
    1968   "The distribution and movement of jobs and industry." Pp. 1–39 in James Q. Wilson (ed.)
            The Metropolitan Enigma: Inquiries into the Nature and Dimension of America's "Urban
            Crisis". Cambridge: Harvard University Press.
Kantrowitz, Nathan
    1973   Ethnic and Racial Segregation in the New York City Metropolis: Racial Patterns Among
            White Ethnic Groups, Blacks and Puerto Ricans. New York: Praeger Publishers.
Levy, Mark R. and Michael S. Kramer
    1972   The Ethnic Factor. New York: Simon and Schuster.

Lieberson, Stanley
    1961   "A societal theory of race and ethnic relations." American Sociological Review 26
            (Dec.):902–910.
    1980   A Piece of the Pie. Berkeley: University of California Press.
Long, Herman and Charles S. Johnson
    1947   People vs. Property: Race Restrictive Covenants in Housing. Nashville, TN: Fisk Univer-
            sity Press.
Los Angeles Times
    1980   "Watts, 1980: 15 Years after the riot." 12 part series from August 10 through August 31.
Marx, Gary T.
    1969   "Religion: opiate or inspiration of civil rights militancy among Negroes." American
            Sociological Review 32(1): 64–72.
Massey, Douglas S.
    1983   "A research note on residential succession: the Hispanic case." Social Forces 61: 825–
            833.
McCone Commission
    1965   Violence in the City—An End or a Beginning?" Report prepared by the Governor's
            Commission on the Los Angeles Riots.
McKenzie, Robert D.
    1967   "The ecological approach to the study of the human community. Pp. 63–79 in R. E. Park
            [1925] and E. W. Burgess (eds.) The City. Chicago: University of Chicago Press.
McWilliams, Carey
    1946   "Culture and society in southern California." The Annals of the American Academy of
            Political and Social Science 248:209–15.
    1951   Brothers Under the Skin. Boston: Little, Brown and Company.
Merton, Robert K.
    1949   "Discrimination and the American creed." Pp. 34–47 in Norman R. Yetman and C. Hoy
            Steele (eds.) Majority and Minority (3rd ed.). Boston: Allyn and Bacon.
Meyer, Rebecca L.
    1983   "Black suburbanization in the Los Angeles SMSA." Unpublished paper, Department of
            Geography, UCLA.
Moore, Joan W.
    1981   "Minorities in the American Class System." Daedalus (Spring):275–299.
Moore, Joan W. with Robert Garcia, Carlos Garcia, Luis Cerda, and Frank Valencia
    1978   Homeboys: Gangs, Drugs, and Prison in the Barrios of Los Angeles. Philadelphia: Temple
            University Press.
Moore, Joan W. with Harry Pachon
    1976   Mexican Americans. Englewoods Cliffs, NJ: Prentice-Hall.
Morrill, Richard
    1965   "The Negro ghetto: problems and alternatives." The Geographical Review 55:339–361.
Myrdal, Gunnar
    1944   An American Dilemma. New York: Harper and Row.
National Advisory Commission on Civil Rights
    1973   "Comparing the immigrant and Negro experiences." Pp. 99–103 in Edgar G. Epps (ed.)
            Race Relations. New York: Winthrop Publishers.
New York Times
    1964   "Anti-rights plan winning on coast: California trend appears to back proposition 14."
            November 14:34.
Noel, Donald L.
    1968   "A theory of the origin of ethnic stratification." Social Problems 16 (Fall): 157–172.

O'Connor, James
  1973 The Fiscal Crisis of the State. New York: St. Martin's Press.
Osofsky, Gilbert
  1963 Harlem: The Making of a Ghetto. New York: Harper and Row Publishers.
Park, Robert
  1975 "The urban community as a spatial pattern and moral order." Pp. 21–31 in C. Peach (ed.) Urban Social Segregation. New York: Longman Group Limited.
Park, Robert and Ernest W. Burgess
  1967 The City. Chicago: University of Chicago Press.
  [1925]
Pearce, Dianna
  1979 "Gatekeepers and housekeepers: institutional patterns in racial steering." Social Problems 26:323–342.
Phillips, Phillip D. and Stanley D. Brunn
  1978 "Slow growth: a new epoch in metropolitan evolution." The Geographical Review 68:274–292.
Portes, Alejandro
  1979 "Illegal immigration and the international system: lessons from recent legal Mexican immigrants to the United States. Social Problems 26(4):425–438.
  1977 "Towards a structural analysis of illegal immigration." International Migration Review 12 (Winter):425–438.
Rose, Harold M.
  1970 "Development of an urban subsystem: the case of the negro ghetto." Annals of the Association of American Geographers 60:1–17.
  1971 The Black Ghetto: A Spatial Behavioral Perspective. New York: McGraw-Hill.
Rose, Harold M. and Charles M. Christian
  1982 "Race and ethnicity: a competitive force in the evolution of American urban systems." Pp. 361–390 in Charles M. Christian and Robert A. Harper (eds.) Modern Metropolitan Systems. Columbus, OH: Charles E. Merrill Publishing Company.
Rosenberg, Terry J. and Robert W. Lake
  1976 "Toward a revised model of residential segregation and succession: Puerto Ricans in New York." American Journal of Sociology 81(5): 1142–50.
Scott, Allen J.
  1982 "Production systems dynamics and metropolitan development." Annals of the Association of American Geographers 72:185–200.
Sheppard, Nathaniel
  1980 "Miami's Blacks have 'nothing to lose'." *New York Times,* May 23, II:4.
Spaulding, Charles B.
  1946 "Housing problems of minority groups in Los Angeles County." The Annals of the American Academy of Political and Social Science 248:220–225.
Sternlieb, George and James W. Hughes
  1975 Post-Industrial America: Metropolitan Decline and Inter-regional Job Shifts. New Brunswick, NJ: Center for Urban Policy Research, Rutgers University.
Squires, Gregory D. and Ruthanne De Wolfe
  1981 "Insurance redlining in minority communities." Review of Black Political Economy 11:347–364.
Tolbert, Emory J.
  1980 The UNIA and Black Los Angeles. Los Angeles: Center for Afro-American Studies.
Taeuber, Karl E. and Alma F. Taeuber
  1970 "The changing character of Negro migration." American Journal of Sociology 70:429–41.
  1965 Negroes in Cities: Residential Segregation and Neighborhood Change. Chicago: Aldine.

Willhelm, Sidney M.
  1970   Who Needs the Negro. Cambridge, MA: Schenkman.
Williams Robin (et al.)
  1964   Strangers Next Door. Englewoods Cliff, New Jersey: Prentice-Hall Inc.
Wilson, Robert A.
  1972   "Anomie in the ghetto: a study of neighborhood type, race, and anomie." American
         Journal of Sociology 77(1):66–88.
Wilson, William J.
  1978   The Declining Significance of Race. Chicago: University of Chicago Press.

HISTORICAL GENERATIONS AND YOUTH MOVEMENTS:
A THEORETICAL PERSPECTIVE

Richard G. Braungart

Young people are marching again throughout Western Europe and the United States with banners and signs reading: EUROSHEIMA NE!, EUROPA ATOM-WAFFEN FREI, RAUS NATO!, NON AUX CENTRALES NUCLEAIRES, NOTTINGHAM FOR NUCLEAR DISARMAMENT, NO NUKES, and PENN-SYLVANIA IS EVERYWHERE. During an October, 1981 peace rally in Bonn, West Germany, more than 250,000 young people gathered to hear American Coretta Scott King (widow of the slain U.S. civil rights leader, Dr. Martin Luther King, Jr.) and singer Harry Belafonte tell the crowd, "Millions of Americans stand by your side," and the entire crowd sang the civil rights hymn "We Shall Overcome" at the close of the rally (Reid, 1981). While the dominant themes in many of these marches and demonstrations have been the political and social implications of nuclear weapons and nuclear technology, contemporary youth movement activity is not limited to the nuclear power issue, nor is it confined to North America and Western Europe. Issues have included racism and unemployment (in London, Johannesburg, Miami), revolutionary insurrection

Research in Social Movements, Conflict and Change, Vol. 6, pages 95–142.
Copyright © 1984 by JAI Press Inc.
All rights of reproduction in any form reserved.
ISBN: 0-89232-311-6

(in Northern Ireland, Colombia, El Salvador, Nicaragua), crime, rowdyism, and youthful rampages (in the Soviet Union, United States, Switzerland), student strikes (in France, Italy, Pakistan, Poland, South Korea, the Philippines), and ideological-religious struggles (in Spain, Turkey, Thailand, Uganda, Afghanistan, Iran, Egypt).

Given the extent of youthful political activity in the last two centuries and the modern explosion of such activity that reached its zenith in the 1960s and continued, albeit to a lesser extent in the 1970s and 1980s, there are surprisingly few theories that explain the historical patterns and generational cycles of youth movement activity. In particular, what remains unclear is the relationship between historical and generational forces that give rise to youth movements, and especially why certain epochs experience dramatic generational rebellions while others do not. In order to address this issue, the present study will explore how and why historical and generational forces interact to produce youth movements. The attempt is made to construct a theoretical model of historical generations and youth movements that is broad, global, and historically applicable. To accomplish these rather ambitious tasks, the following procedures are outlined. First, two theoretical approaches, the historical and the generational, to the study of youth movements are presented and discussed in detail. These theoretical approaches are among the most popular macrosociological theories explaining youth movements.

Second, in order to further explore the theoretical possibilities of the historical and generational theories of youth movements, both approaches are cross-classified to identify four conceptual types. Based on these four types, a model of the convergence of historical and generational forces is proposed. Finally, the theoretical model is compared over the nineteenth and twentieth centuries to show how the convergence of historical and generational factors is able to account for youth movements within its structure. This historical review also identifies four significant historical generations in world time over the last two centuries: the Young Europe, Post-Victorian, Great Depression, and 1960s Generation.

I. HISTORICAL APPROACHES TO THE STUDY OF YOUTH MOVEMENTS

Those who view social movements in general and youth movements in particular from a historical perspective generally assume that such movements arise at certain times, and not at others, because of the particular sociohistorical context. What is critical in studying youth movements is to identify the historical contexts and specify the conditions under which young people are likely to organize and engage in collective action. Two contrasting historical approaches to this task can be distinguished: (1) the social discontinuity or breakdown approach; and (2) the mobilization approach.

A. Social Discontinuity or Breakdown Approach to Youth Movements

The social discontinuity approach to youth movements emphasizes changes or disruptions within the sociopolitical system that threaten its stability and balance. The assumption is that various "breakdowns" open up the system for new forces and movements for social change.

One of the foremost proponents of the breakdown perspective is Neil Smelser (1963, 1968), who defines social movements as an episode of collective behavior by which mobilized participants attempt to reconstitute their sociocultural environment on the basis of a generalized belief. To Smelser, a key to understanding social movements is the process of differentiation such as that brought about by agricultural, industrial, and urban changes. Differentiation is important not only in the changes it brings but also in its pace and unevenness. With fast but uneven change, the resulting discontinuities breed anomie, as disharmonies emerge between life experiences and the normative framework which regulates them (Smelser, 1968). While anomie may be relieved partially by new integrative mechanisms such as unions, voluntary associations, and government regulations, these new integrative devices may well be opposed by the traditional vested interests they threaten. What results is a three-way tug-of-war between the forces of tradition, the forces of differentiation, and new forces of integration, which contains unlimited potentials for group conflict.

Smelser (1968) then argues that when discontinuity exists, there are three classic responses—anxiety, hostility, and fantasy—and if and when these responses become collective, they may crystallize into several types of social movements: peaceful agitation, political violence, millenarianism, nationalism, revolution, and underground subversion. The most likely candidate to join a social movement, according to Smelser, is someone who has been dislodged by the forces of differentiation from old social ties without being integrated into a new social order. As an illustration, Smelser notes that students and adolescents generally have a high rate of participation in various types of collective behavior. This participation arises because youth are in gap between the relatively clearly prescribed roles of childhood and those of adulthood, which provides opportunities to become involved with new and often peripheral forms of behavior.

Another discontinuity theorist is William Kornhauser (1959) who identifies the breakdown in political authority and community that facilitates the rise of extremist social movements. He maintains that youth and other social movements tend to appear when autocratic political authority is being displaced by democratic authority. During these times, traditional authority is vulnerable, particularly if the introduction of democratic values is rapid and there is no strong constitutional tradition—such as occurred when the ancient regime in France was replaced by the Jacobins, followed by a coup d'état, or as in Germany and Italy prior to World War II, when the prevailing governments were replaced with fascist dictators. Kornhauser notes that sharp discontinuities of the sort stressed by Smelser make the emergence of social movements more likely. Arguing along similar lines, Scott Greer (1979) contends that discontinuities between culture and structure coupled with the rapid expansion of society (in areas such as population growth, public education, unemployment, and citizenship), and catastrophes (such as wars, epidemics, defeats, destructive technology) destroy old structures and set the stage for social movements.

S. N. Eisenstadt (1978) emphasizes that social movements are rooted in historically changing social anomalies and inequities. Like Smelser and Kornhauser, Eisenstadt focuses on the discontinuities associated with structural differentiation and modernization but also stresses the importance of basic historic themes of equality, freedom, and solidarity. According to Eisenstadt, the modern student movements that occurred in capitalist societies are attributed to disparities between ideal culture and society: burgeoning bureaucratization, private versus public ownership of resources, the expansion of education, and the rise of new service sectors in the economy. New patterns of conflict are created, moving from class-based to status-based, as more social institutions shift toward greater participation. With the university as a center of cultural, creative life and legitimacy in society, students see themselves both as a new important intellectual status group and as the rightful vanguard of social change.

Joseph Gusfield (1979) focuses attention on the expansion of society and politics as the precursor of social movements. The rise of the nation-state and extension of citizenship have placed increased pressure on the system. Historically, the rebellions, revolts, and protests of earlier times were mainly specific responses to particular grievances, more often directed toward restoration than at changing relationships. By the nineteenth century, however, the social imagination, influenced by rapid industrial change, expanded toward a future society that was "shapable" by planned human actions and the shared notion that social issues are "public" questions. Gusfield also observes that some of the most strident conflicts in modern society are less over issues of class and material welfare than they are over moral and spiritual questions.

Societal breakdown, as Harry Eckstein (1976) sees it, involves unstable and incongruent authority patterns. Stable societies, says Eckstein, exhibit a correspondence between the authority patterns of society and the polity. But if government authority patterns are isolated from other segments of society, if there is an abrupt change in authority patterns in any adjacent sector of society, or if contradictory authority patterns exist, then governments will be unstable. As an example, he cites the Weimar Republic in Germany which was highly incongruent and unstable, having a democratic constitution and parliament but traditional authoritarian family life, education, and social patterns.

Richard Hamilton and James Wright (1975) focus on what they call nonroutine or exceptional occurrences as important in setting the stage for social movements. They discuss the "spillover effects" of intermittent yet highly important events in history, such as wars, depressions, and internal conflicts, which affect "subsequent routines," such as career lines, socialization, ideas, education for individuals and society. For example, they argue that World War I in Germany not only caused four years of military and civilian losses but also influenced at least ten years of subsequent routines in German society. The disruptions were most serious in small towns and rural areas—the same areas where the Nazi's had their strongest support. The Nazi social movement was, in their view, heavily drawn from the ranks of lower-middle-class men, many of whom were ex-soldiers who had directly experienced the defeat in World War I and who lacked occupational security.

Ted Robert Gurr (1970) roots collective violence in relative deprivation, which is "the tension that develops from a discrepancy between the 'ought' and the 'is' of collective value satisfaction . . ." (1970:23). Gurr develops a social psychological model which assumes that relative deprivation is an uncomfortable condition such that in the long run, rebellious men will attempt to adjust their value expectations to their value capabilities. In general, the greater the discrepancy between expectation and achievement, the greater the discontent and potential for collective violence. As Gurr concludes, "Discontent is not a function of the discrepancy between what men want and what they have, but between what they want and what they believe they are capable of attaining" (1970:359).

According to the social discontinuity explanation, the stage appears to be set for the formation of youth movements when young people come up against a disruptive and disappointing set of conditions created by their elders. Social inconsistencies, societal breakdowns, and marked discontinuities influence the cognitive awareness of young people who are receptive to new possibilities and opportunities in a stagnating or contradictory society. The discontinuity explanation specifies some of the societal circumstances that are necessary for the rise of youth movement activity; however, it has been argued that the more significant factor is the mobilization of young people into active movements for social and political change.

B. The Mobilization Approach to Youth Movements

Mobilization theorists differ from those stressing historical disruptions in that they place more emphasis on the role of voluntaristic political activity. This activity can be either attitudinal or behavioral, but the important point is that most proponents of this view see the occurrence of mobilization as problematic in any historical situation, even highly discontinuous ones.

Amitai Etzioni (1968) suggests that historical factors influence the cognitive and affective personality structures of generations, and youth become motivated and activated into generation units. Youth growing up react affectively toward change—they may approve, disapprove, or remain uncommitted over specific issues and problems. The psychosocial tensions created by their cognitive-affective commitments can, but do not necessarily "energize" them into individual or collective actions.

In Etzioni's view, mobilization is not just a by-product or outgrowth of interaction among macro and micro units; it is, in part, deliberately initiated, directed, and terminated. Unlike the historical breakdown theories, external conditions do not determine the level of mobilization in that the extent to which social units submit or react to these conditions is influenced largely by the unit's collective decision and efforts. Thus, youth movements do not represent mere responses to the environment; rather, youth movements are attempts to actively participate in and shape the environment. Etzioni also observes that the actions and drives by one social unit may well trigger counter-mobilization in other units.

One of the strongest challenges to the breakdown or discontinuity approach is offered by Charles Tilly (1975; Tilly, Tilly, and Tilly, 1975), who takes issue with the assumption that some "inefficiency" in the "system" expands the reservoir of discontent which in turn leads to assaults on those in power. Instead, Tilly argues, strains of modernization and industrialization play only a small part in promoting collective action. What the breakdown theorists neglect are the struggles among groups and classes, along with the power blocs which constitute much of political conflict. It is less disorganization and hardship than it is solidarity and articulated interests that account for collective action.

According to Tilly, a group can be said to be mobilizing when it increases its collective control over either normative resources (commitments to ideals, groups, and other people), coercive resources (means of punishing and limiting alternatives), or utilitarian resources (all the rest, especially those things men find rewarding to acquire). Conversely, when collective control over such resources decreases, the group can be said to be demobilizing. The types of collective action that may be undertaken include competitive action (involving claims by rivals or enemies to a resource neither controls), reaction (involving a claim being laid to a resource now or previously under the control of a group being sought by another group), and proaction (involving claims to a resource not previously accorded).

Anthony Oberschall (1973) argues that dislocations result from social changes that establish both support and resistance to change. Some of the structural sources of conflict involve economic and political discontent, but, according to Oberschall, structural conditions vary greatly in terms of predictive ability. While gradual or dramatic changes may or may not produce youth movements, it is mobilization that is both a necessary and sufficient condition for such movements. He argues, for example, that the Nazi success in the 1930s was not only due to the structural condition of unemployment but the politicization and mobilized violence attributed to the resistance offered by socialist workers and communists against Nazi strong-arm tactics. The three years of resulting conflict made the middle class receptive to the promises by the Nazis to restore law-and-order.

What are important, says Oberschall, are the mobilizing functions of secondary associations in a social structure. His basic thesis is that rapid mobilization is more likely to occur among people who are already organized. In his view, leaders, influenced by ideological commitments and peer group approval, are the agents of mobilization and the architects of organization. Oberschall uses the sudden appearance of the Free Speech Movement (FSM) on the University of California, Berkeley campus in 1964 as an illustration of mobilization. The FSM was possible because of the existence of a network of political, civil rights, and special interest groups and their leaders in an already highly politically mobilized and ideologically sophisticated student population. Since almost all student groups, both left and right, felt their interests were threatened by a sudden ban on political campaigning at one of the main entrances to the campus, FSM grew out of an overnight merger of existing campus groups.

The resource mobilization theory offered by Mayer Zald and John McCarthy (1979) concentrates less on social psychological and collective behavior and more on political, social, and economic factors related to the growth, decline, and change of social movements. In their view, historical breakdown and discontent are not sufficient conditions for youth movements. First of all, those who are atomized or alienated without solidarity relations are least likely to be mobilized for collective action. Secondly, merely being discontented is not enough; the discontent must be focused and channeled through group consciousness and the notion that something can be done.

According to the mobilization theorists, it is out of the interplay, competition, and conflict between groups that youth movements gain and sustain their momentum. What neither the historical discontinuity nor mobilization explanations directly address is why certain social movements are largely comprised of the young and represent active generational movements for societal change. It is the generational theorists who deal more explicitly with the propensity of youth to be at odds with the older generation and to divide along generational lines to form active youth movements.

II. GENERATIONAL APPROACHES TO THE STUDY OF YOUTH MOVEMENTS

A. History of Generational Thought

The notion of generations as a force for conflict and change has deep historical roots. Of particular enduring concern has been the issue of "youth" and their relationship to adult society. For example, a 4,000-year-old tablet discovered on the site of the Biblical city of Ur read, "Our civilization is doomed if the unheard-of actions of our younger generation are allowed to continue" (Lauer, 1977:265). Reflecting the view of ancient Greeks that youth was a time of impetuousness, Aristotle remarked that "They overdo everything" (McJeon, 1941:1401). Plato and Herodotus identified generational awareness and strife as a causal mechanism of political change, while Aristotle found political revolutions to be due not only to the conflict between rich and poor but in the struggle between fathers and sons (Feuer, 1969; Nash, 1978; Esler, 1979).

This theme of generational conflict is reflected in numerous other historical reports. However, the beginning of concerns over generational politics and youth movement activity has been dated to the nineteenth century, the groundwork for which was provided by industrialization. The discovery of the stage of life defined as adolescence, according to Gillis (1974), essentially belonged to the middle classes, due in part to the drop in child mortality, a parental attitude favoring low rather than high fertility, and, with the decline of agriculture and the movement of industry away from the home, the reduced economic importance of children and youth. This new care and concern for youth, coupled with the rise of secondary education, extended youth's dependence.

Awareness of the generational phenomenon began to grow. The issue came to be not just the conflict between youth and adults but also the idea emerged that youthful orientations to the world might be quite distinct from those of adults. Goethe, although not concentrating his efforts on the topic, observed that every person's fundamental world view is determined by the experience of his or her youthful formative years, and members of the same generation are linked throughout life by bonds of mutual understanding that set them apart from others. Novelists (Flaubert, Tolstoy, Turgenev, Mann) and philosophers alike (Comte, Rousseau, Locke, Mill) employed the generational theme in their works. The cultural historian Wilhelm Dilthey probably can be credited with the first systematic analysis of the social generation (Esler, 1974). Writing in the 1860s, Dilthey first observed that many of the great romanticists were born within a single decade, which suggested to him the importance of generational placement. A generation, he said, "is constituted of a restricted circle of individuals who are bound together into a homogeneous whole by their dependence on the same great events and transformations that appeared in their age of [maximum] receptivity, despite the variety of other subsequent factors" (Schorske, 1978:121). This perspective, as Mannheim (1952) later commented, shifted the emphasis in the notion of contemporaneousness from "mere chronological datum" to the qualitative importance of shared, subjective historical experiences.

While the ideas of Dilthey suggested later thinking about how history and generations merge, in the short run they were less influential than were the works focusing on the psychological aspects of youth generations. In this tradition, the idea of set "stages" has been important. By the turn of the twentieth century, the middle classes were growing increasingly aware of the psychological turmoil of youth. This view was developed by G. Stanley Hall who, in a 1904 book, characterized adolescence, running from the time of puberty to adulthood, as a time of *Sturm und Drang,* where the emotional life of the adolescent oscillates between contradictory tendencies (Muuss, 1968).

Another stage theorist who described the characteristics of adolescence was Freud, who viewed the behavior, social and emotional changes that occur during adolescence as universal, due largely to their ties to physiological change. Freud's analysis implies the "problem of generations" in that conflicts during adolescence are manifested "at least for a time, in rejection, resentment, and hostility toward parents and other authority" (Muuss, 1968:40). Another important contribution of Freud is his notion of repression and sublimation of biological urges. While Freud did not pay much attention to social factors or history in his psychoanalytic theory, he provided the foundation for subsequent explanations of generational animus and youth movement activity by Erikson, Feuer, and Keniston, popular in the 1960s.

B.   Early Generational Theorists

The concept of social generations begun by Dilthey gained support in the 1920s. Francois Mentre's doctoral dissertation *Les Générations sociales* at the Sorbonne offered the definition of a generation as "a collective state of mind embodied in a group of human beings which extends over a period of time comparable to the duration of a genealogical generation." In his dissertation, Mentre distinguished between familial generations, which represent the continuous succession of grandfathers, fathers, and sons, and social generations, which are characterized by the development of distinct "sentiments and beliefs." However, in contrast to Dilthey, Mentre rejected the notion that social generations are determined by the course of political events, and instead saw them based in intellectual life that develops through opposition, ultimately derived from the struggle between fathers and sons. Mentre assumed that generations possess a regular rhythm, concluding they last about 30 years, since that is about the duration of a man's effective social action. Discontinuity between the generations is the rule and continuity the exception, with the struggle of one generation with another more violent and thus more evident at some times than at others (Esler, 1974; Wohl, 1979).

More widely known are the discussions of generations offered by the philosopher and social critic Jose Ortega y Gasset in *The Modern Theme* (1961) and *Man and Crisis* (1962). Ortega argued that "Age . . . is not a date, but a 'zone of dates'" (Ortega, 1962:47). Like Mentre, Ortega claimed it is less historical events that mold a social generation than it is intellectual thought. Economic and political change, after all, depends upon changes in ideas, taste, and mores (Ortega, 1974). In Ortega's view, members of a generation share "an essential destiny," which he pictures as:

a caravan within which man moves [as] a prisoner, but at the same time, a voluntary one at
heart, and content. He moves within it faithful to the poets of his age, to the political ideas of
his time, to the type of woman triumphant in his youth, and even to the fashion of walking
which he employed at twenty-five (1962:44–45).

Ortega thus portrayed a model of a generation as a social reality that has profound impact on the lives of its members and fundamentally separates them from
other generations formed at different times.

According to Ortega, life for each generation exists in terms of the previous
generation (institutions, ideas, values) and the liberation of its own creative
genius. Interaction between the two age groups of masters and new initiates is
especially important. When they agree on fundamentals, they reinforce each
other, providing a sense of harmony and purpose, which Ortega termed an "age
of accumulation." When they disagree, an age of polemics and rebellion results,
which belongs to the young and represents an "age of elimination" (Ortega,
1962; Esler, 1974; Wohl, 1979).

Around the same time as Ortega, the German sociologist Karl Mannheim
spelled out "The Problem of Generations" in his famous essay published in
1928. Mannheim's special interest was identifying the classes or subgroups in
society that shape one's world view. Mannheim (1952:291) suggested that both
generations and social classes "endow the individuals sharing in them with a
common location in the social and historical process" and restrict individuals
belonging to them to "a specific range of potential experience, and a characteristic type of historically relevant action." A key feature in Mannheim's model
is the suggestion that biological generations are not necessarily sociological
generations until the shared historical experiences produce similar perceptions
and understanding of reality. What is important, Mannheim insisted, is the
process of social change which sets one generation apart from the next. He
argued that "the quicker the tempo of social and cultural change," the more
likely a generation will experience a "concrete nexus" or sense of "participation in a common destiny." Mannheim (1952:310) went on to say that "whether
a new generation style emerges every year, every thirty, every hundred years, or
whether it emerges rhythmically at all, depends entirely on the trigger action of
the social and cultural process." However, Mannheim did qualify his thesis by
stating that periods characterized by war, natural catastrophe, and total political
mobilization rarely develop generational differentiation due to the leveling of
values resulting from fear and/or national solidarity. But, during times of relative
security and protracted institutional growth, the faster the rate of social and
cultural change, the higher the probability that successive generations will develop their own "entelechies" (Braungart, 1974).

Each generation, according to Mannheim, experiences a fresh contact with
traditional values and principles, and when social change is rapid, traditional
ways may appear outdated. The fresh contact of youth—at a time when they are

beginning to reflect on problematical issues and are dramatically aware of the process of destabilization—provides a revitalization process for society. He also realized that the romantic-conservative and liberal-rationalist youth belonged to the same actual generations, yet embraced different ideologies. These different subgroups within the same generation represent "generation units," which are those groups of the same age group which "work up the material of their common experience in different specific ways" (Mannheim, 1952:304). Thus, within a generation there can exist any number of protagonistic or antagonistic generation units competing with one another who exert pressure on their members to conform to partisan points of view.

These early generational theorists viewed generations as more than the biological succession of age groups. The essence of a generation is social, a sharing of attitudes and viewpoints that links together members of the same age group. Youth and young adulthood are considered a formative stage in the life cycle for the development of social awareness and attitudes toward self and society. What gives shape to these youthful, emerging attitudes are the prevailing social, economic, cultural, and political circumstances and intellectual thought that characterize society as its younger members come of age. When change is rapid, young people born around the same time in history often have a different set of historical experiences than their elders and consequently develop their own distinctive style and response to society and politics.

C.   Contemporary Generational Theory

By the mid-1930s, the theory of generations was fairly well developed. While there was not much interest in further expanding the idea of generations per se for several decades, the works of Mentre, Ortega, and Mannheim continued to influence thinking on the subject. Most of the contemporary discussions of generations have focused on the extension of social generations to political generations, the stage of youth as a time in the life cycle when generational confrontation is likely, and the sociology of generations that explains why young people have become an increasingly significant force for social change.

In 1951, when discussing "the problem of political generations," Rudolf Heberle asserts that "the rhythm of changes in political ideas and institutions seems to be closely associated with the rhythm in the change of generations," and that "the generation as a collective mentality tends to become the basis for social groups . . . [and] becomes a valuable tool in the study of social change" (Heberle, 1951:118–119). Crucial to the development of generations are the "decisive experiences" that occur during the "formative period." The politically dominant generation of roughly ages 40–65 tends "to look upon these issues in a way different from that of younger men and women"; hence, the younger generation is likely "to be in opposition." Heberle also presents the notion of differences existing not only between generations but within generations as well (Heberle, 1951:124).

One of the most lucid explanations of political generations can be found in Marvin Rintala's article in the *International Encyclopedia of the Social Sciences* (1968). Rintala (1974:17) states that a political generation represents "a group of individuals who have undergone the same basic historical experiences during their formative years." The implicit assumption is that once established, "the individual's political attitudes do not undergo substantial change during the course of his adult lifetime." Rintala also suggests that the boundaries or limits of a political generation, as well as its distinctiveness from other generations, is a function of "the degree of uniqueness" of the historic events involved in its formation. In keeping with Mannheim, Rintala further notes that those whose formative experiences differ fundamentally cannot be members of the same political generation.

In the 1960s, youth protest activity on college campuses and in the streets spurred a revival of interest in generational politics as a force for social change. Social scientists and historians directed their efforts to the problem of generations and a number of different explanations were offered, many of which were based on early generational theory. For example, from a Freudian or psychoanalytic perspective, Lewis Feuer (1969) bases the heightened youthful political activity in the generational animus that presumably exists between the parent generation and their offspring. To Feuer (1969), generational conflict is a universal theme in history. Ignoring any concrete historical causes of rebellion, such as the Vietnam war and civil rights, Feuer asserts that student movements are rarely materialistic but are derived from the deep unconscious sources of the conflict of generations. Referring to conditions that "made for a breakdown in the 'generational equilibrium' of the society," Feuer (1969:11) defines a student movement as "a combination of students inspired by aims which they try to explicate in a political ideology, and moved by an emotional rebellion in which there is always present a disillusionment with and rejection of the values of the older generation." He further claims that the students in such movements "have the conviction that their generation has a special historical mission to fulfill where the older generation, other elites, and other classes have failed." In specifying the social conditions under which student movements formalize, Feuer suggests there is usually a gerontocratic order, a feeling that the older generation has failed in some way and is "deauthorized," a political apathy and helplessness among the people, and the perception among youth that the political initiative is theirs.

Similarly, Bruno Bettelheim (1963) roots youth rebellion in generational conflict. In modern technological societies, Bettelheim notes, the older and younger generations no longer need each other. Kept on the margins of society and constrained to the role of the "rebel without a cause," young people use the one power resource they have, which is "to be the accuser and judge of the parents' success or failure as parents" (Bettelheim, 1963:75). According to Bettelheim

(1963:89), youth is "happiest when it feels it is fighting to reach goals that were conceived of but not realized by the generation before them."

From a life cycle view of generations, Erik Erikson (1968) modifies Freud's psychosexual theory of development into a psychosocial theory. Erikson sees identity formation as a "generational issue," and the major developmental task or crisis in personality development faced by the adolescent. The older generation provides "those forceful ideals which must antecede identity formation in the next generation—if only so that youth can rebel against a well-defined set of older values" (Erikson, 1968:30). Developing ego strength is a key to healthy personality and Erikson strongly emphasizes the importance of the interaction between the individual and the community. At the core of youth's "most passionate and most erratic striving" is fidelity—a search for something and somebody to be true, which arises "only in the interplay of a life stage with the individuals and the social forces of a true community" (Erikson, 1968:235). The appeal of participation in social movements is in the need for "feeling 'moved' and for feeling essential in moving something along toward an open future" (Erikson, 1968:243). If an ideology can inspire youth, they "will make the predicted history come more than true." This is the way young people authorize their generation—the way they legitimate their own collective strivings.

The sociology of generations can be divided into two distinct models explaining youth movements. The first model is a functionalist one which assumes that society normally operates as an interrelated and integrated system, but that alienation and rebellion occur when the institutional components fail to mesh or are imbalanced. In this model, age acts as a primary characteristic for stratification and integration into society. While youth attempt to link their "personal situation" to sociocultural values, their integration into the society and their attainment of personal identity can be thwarted in modern complex societies because they are an economic liability not an asset, the orientations of an achievement-oriented society are at odds with the nurturance of family life, and additional demands are placed on each succeeding generation to cope with new sets of social problems (Braungart, 1974). When the middle-age group generally holds the power and is the most atavistic and status quo oriented regarding the relinquishing of their social position, then intergenerational cleavage and conflict are likely to occur. Nevertheless, because the conflict is tied to a stage of life, Eisenstadt (1963) argues that youth movements represent little more than temporary or symbolic revolts of the young attempting to gain the status denied them by adult society.

The second sociological model is the generational unit model, drawn largely from Mannheim, which suggests that social change is rooted in the emerging consciousness of generation units at odds with the older generation and with themselves. The crucial factor here is the structuring of consciousness which forms the basis of their intergenerational and intragenerational behavior. The sharing in the same inner dialectic provides the critical experience, "partly

simplifying and abbreviating . . . [and] . . . partly elaborating and filling . . . out" a set of political views and orientations (Mannheim, 1952:306).
The generational unit model predicts that chronological age alone will not determine common generational patterns of behavior, but exposure to select historical, social, and cultural factors in combination with a new psychological consciousness and common destiny will lead to such behavior (Braungart, 1974).

A comparison of the two sociological models indicates that while both models
suggest a theory of generational change, the functionalist argument assumes the
organization of a social system in a fixed or finite sense, and the movement of the
system toward symmetrical order. As a result, the functionalist model of generational change represents a static relationship between its components and system
equilibrium, with youth revolts viewed as attempts to restabilize the system. In
comparison, the generational unit model is more dynamic and open-ended, less
concerned with system equilibrium than with emerging forces and creative syn-
theses that give rise to new patterns of social organization over time. The generational unit model applies to youth movements throughout the world that express
dissatisfaction and disenchantment—on both the left and right—with the status
quo. These youth are pressing for major changes and the radical transformation
of contradicting and imperfect social orders. The generational unit model suggests less that youth are rebelling against society, than they are creating revolutionary new forms of consciousness which are simultaneously the result of biological, social, and cultural forces (Braungart, 1974).

III. HISTORICAL AND GENERATIONAL PERSPECTIVES ON YOUTH MOVEMENTS

Historical forces provide the structure and political conditions that influence the
rise of youth movements. These include not only the rates of social change, degree
of structural differentiation, levels of cultural variation, and mobilization of
human resources but also the effects of unique historical events and other sudden
transformations. Generational forces also influence the rise of youth movements
through the conscious transformation of age cohorts into mobilized generations
and the resulting intergenerational and intragenerational conflict. While these two
theoretical perspectives come from different traditions within sociology, there is
also an affinity between them. That is, each theoretical tradition requires the other
for its completion. Historical discontinuity and mobilization theorists posit within
their discussions the idea of self-conscious groups seeking to make social changes,
although little attention is devoted to the topic of youth movements per se or why
young people as a group periodically rebel against society.

The generational literature, on the other hand, attempts to account for the
formation of youth movements as arising out of a kind of natural conflict that

occurs between the young and the old in the process of generational succession, which at times is so intense that young people unite with each other through their shared mentality and take on the older generation in the political arena. For the generationalists, history plays a role in the development of values and behavior—by influencing the structure of consciousness as one comes of age and providing the issues-of-the-day for contention—but it is of secondary importance relative to generational factors. The consequences imputed to the historical and generational positions are likely to follow from a combination of both traditions, which suggests the need for a more encompassing theoretical framework than is available in either perspective alone.

In order to further explore the theoretical possibilities of these two approaches, theoretical and empirical studies of youth movements can be examined by cross-classifying historical and generational factors. See Figure 1. The result is a four-cell typology in which: Cell 1 represents the perspective that largely ignores both historical and generational explanations and instead focuses on psychological or personal motivations; Cell 2 represents the perspective that concentrates on historical sources of youth movements; Cell 3 represents the emphasis on generational sources in order to explain youth movements; and Cell 4 represents a view that combines historical and generational perspectives to account for youth movements. Studies in the literature on youth movements have arisen within three of these perspectives, as seen in the following discussion.

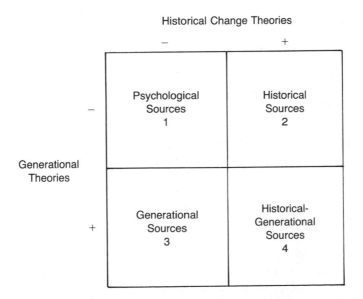

Figure 1.   Typology of Historical and Generational Sources of Youth Movements.

A.   Psychological Perspectives on Youth Movements

The first cell in the typology indicates those examinations of youth movements and youth activists which are essentially ahistorical and nongenerational in that they either ignore or treat as secondary social structural and generational factors. Instead, they typically focus on personal motivational characteristics to account for participation in youth movements. Several different psychological perspectives, including personality traits, emotional needs, perception, and belief-behavior consistency, are represented in these works.

There are a number of psychological studies that attempt to explain youth movement activity by identifying and measuring those personality traits that distinguish youthful activists from nonactivists. Many of the personality studies conducted in the 1960s and 1970s show remarkable consistency, which indicate that activists, when compared to moderates or nonactivists tend to be: (1) spontaneous and impulsive; (2) strong-willed, assertive, rebellious toward authority, nonconforming, and concerned with the manipulation of others; (3) self-confident and self-centered; (4) idealistic, altruistic, romantic, and nonmaterialistic; (5) alienated and distrustful, although not maladjusted psychologically; (6) somewhat more intellectually oriented; and (7) adhering to the intellectual, expressive, humanitarian, and political views of their parents (Braungart, 1980). Some studies also report personality differences between left- versus right-wing activists and male versus female activists (Braungart, 1980). One recent study of 64 revolutionary leaders covering a span of 300 years from 5 continents and 12 countries found that revolutionary leaders tended to be young men, well-educated and left-wing, who visualized politics and the world in Manichaean terms. Their specific personality traits were identified as vain-egotistic-narcissistic, ascetic-puritan-virtuous, with a strong sense of justice-injustice, and a desire to set things right (Rejai and Phillips, 1979).

A second set of studies generally have assumed that certain young people were mobilized for political activity because such activity met or fulfilled their deep psychological and emotional needs. Murphy (1974), having examined a number of youth movements around the world, discounts explanations of youth protest as rooted in aggression and generational conflict; instead, he argues that youth movements involve specific emotional needs. Studies of college students and radical activists have argued that heightened political activity can be an attempt to fend off or defend the self against depression and despair, which the activists have converted into a search for "the oceanic feeling of union with an omnipotent presence" (Duncan, 1980; Hendin, 1975). The young radicals' acute sense of injustice and of being victimized politically is portrayed as being derived from their own personal vicitimization of being unloved or rejected by their parents.

A third psychological perspective, which rests on gestalt or perceptual factors, describes how youthful activists selectively structure and perceive their political environment. It has been found that activists were likely to perceive pronounced discontinuities in society and viewed themselves as active agents of social and political change through self-assertion against the status quo (Bakke and Bakke, 1971; Haan, 1971). In one study of student activists groups in the late 1960s, both the extreme right- and left-wing groups, in contrast to moderate youth political groups, tended to reject more political positions than they accepted, with a tight consensus within their ranks regarding what is and is not acceptable political ideology (Braungart and Braungart, 1980). Similarly, the tendency to distort objective political facts was much greater among extremist youth groups (Braungart, 1979b). These studies suggest that when young persons embrace an extremist political position, whether left or right, perceptual distortion of reality might be expected to allow little diversity of opinion within the ranks of the group and to make compromise with such groups difficult.

A final psychological area of investigation includes those studies that have focused on belief-behavior consistency. Although many young people may share similar attitudes about society and politics, studies have shown that those relative few who took action on the basis of their beliefs came from more harmonious, consistent family backgrounds which offered social support for their views. Students who did not follow through on their beliefs more often came from more conflictful and unhappy family backgrounds (Cowdry, Keniston and Cabin, 1970). Demerath, Marwell and Aiken (1971) found in their study that activist youth sensed a feeling of "specialness" and "duty" which pushed them to a point where they felt that they had to take action to honor their commitments.

These psychological studies see youth movements as the result of individual personality traits, motivational needs, perceptual and interpretative responses, and a striving for consistency between one's attitudes and behavior. Largely ignored are the historical circumstances and generational forces which may impel young people to mobilize for social change.

B.   Historical Perspectives on Youth Movements

One of the major arguments of the historical approach is that rapid changes that transform the community, culture, social structure, and political system produce conditions that frequently precipitate various types and levels of youth unrest. There are a number of social, political, economic, cultural changes and discontinuities which have been associated with the rise of youth movement activity during various periods in history. One factor is simply population growth (Moller, 1972). A sudden increase in the numbers of youth can provide the sheer momentum and power for potential mobilization, which, if activated, can destabilize institutions. For example, one of the largest cohorts in Germany was the 1900–1914 birth group, which came of age in war-torn Germany. After the war this cohort faced economic depression and deteriorating social and political conditions. This was the age group that was keenly receptive to the appeals made by the Nazi Party, swelled its ranks, and provided its victory in the 1930 election which brought Hitler to power (Loewenberg, 1974). It has similarly been argued that the more recent rapid increases in the numbers of youth going to colleges and universities, which have long been centers of criticism and unrest, provided a critical mass of young students responsive to the quick spread of ideas and easily mobilized for social and political change (Weinberg and Walker, 1969; Feuer, 1969; Esler, 1971; Meyer and Rubinson, 1972).

Industrialization, urbanization, secularization, and bureaucratization are social trends that have been credited with providing the seedbeds for youth movements. These forces both inspire young people's aspirations and bring a number of social problems—rural-urban migration, urban poverty, impersonalization, and other dislocations (Gurr, 1970). Another major political factor in the lives of young people has been the drive for nationalism, which spearheaded the first major youth movements in the nineteenth century known as the Young Europe movement and which later became the impetus for the anti-colonial and na-tionalist struggles during the twentieth century in Asia, Latin America, Africa, and the Middle East (Lipset and Altbach, 1969; Snyder, 1982). Similarly, the quest for citizenship, suffrage, and egalitarianism has provided issues and tactics for student activism throughout the world.

The dislocations that result from wars have also been linked to youth move-ments. Wartime defeat appears to result in political and social disorganization as well as loss of national honor. The defeat of Napoleon at Waterloo and the desire for national unity spurred the Young Italy and Young Germany movements in the 1800s. The defeat of Germany after World War I drew young people toward right-wing fascism with its paramilitary appeals and simplistic violent solutions (Loewenberg, 1974; Hamilton and Wright, 1975). Resistance to war has also triggered youth movements, as in the United States in the 1930s and again in the 1960s (Draper, 1967; Starr, 1974).

Debilitating economic conditions, particularly depressions and unemploy-ment, stimulated youth unrest throughout the industrialized world in the 1930s. For example, hard economic times in the United States during that period created a "locked-out generation" of middle-class youth, and "the student movement was in part a result of this declassment" (Draper, 1967:156).

Technological changes too have provided both a direct and indirect impetus for youth movements. Technology was a direct issue in the 1960s, 1970s, and 1980s ecology movements, ban-the-bomb, and anti-nuclear power rallies in the United States, Europe, and Japan. The upsurges in protest in the 1980s were staffed not only by newly active young people but many former student radicals from the 1960s (Braungart and Braungart, 1980). Youth have also reacted against technology by creating countercultural movements, such as the Wander-vögel movement in Germany around the turn of the twentieth century which urged young people to abandon the materialistic values and life styles of their parents and return to a more simple, natural life. This same theme appeared again in the 1950s Beat Generation and 1960s hippie movements.

The tie between the cultural context and youth movement activity appears to be a close one. As historical dislocations and surges in youth population tended to separate youth and adults, young people have reacted against adult values and norms by creating their own culture in opposition to conventional society. Such youth cultures have ranged from romantic notions of "student freedom fighters" in nineteenth century Europe to the mix of music, dress, argot, drugs, and personal style that infused the political anti-war movement in the 1960s. This perspective, consistent with the work of both Mentre and Ortega, suggests that it is intellectual thought and cultural forces that captivate young people's imaginations and play an overriding role in heightening their consciousness and potential for mobilization. During every major period of youth mobilization, there has been an identifiable influence from intellectual and creative works which has inspired the hearts and minds of the young.

C.   Generational Perspectives on Youth Movements

In examining the scattered empirical literature on generations, considerable support exists for a number of the tenents and assumptions asserted earlier by Mentre, Ortega y Gasset, and Mannheim. First, the life-cycle research confirms the notion of the importance of youth as a formative and crucial stage in the development of political awareness, attitudes and behavior, while the cohort studies indicate that these orientations are carried through life (Adelson, 1975; Gallatin, 1980; Hudson and Binstock, 1976). Second, the generation gap concept is supported in a general sense. Research has shown that at any given point in time, younger people as a whole appear more liberal than older adults (Glenn, 1974)—a generalization which lends credence to Feuer's (1969) contention that the conflict of generations is, despite its variations, inevitable and recurrent. Nevertheless, congruence in political direction between parents and their children has also been consistently found. For example, left-wing youthful activists in the 1960s tended to come from homes where the parents were Democrats, liberals, socialists, or held other leftist persuasions, whereas right-wing activist youth were more often from homes where parents were Republicans or conservatives (Flacks, 1971; Westby, 1976; Braungart, 1979a). These findings are more consistent with a "political diaper," as opposed to a generational revolt, explanation of youth politics (Keniston, 1968). Still, the generational revolt theory cannot be dismissed categorically, since, as Flacks' and Keniston's investigations of the family backgrounds of left-wing activists indicated, many of the 1960s activists from politically liberal homes criticized their parents for not taking social and political action based on their beliefs. Thus, these young people, by being actively involved in left-wing politics, appeared to be striving to achieve closer fidelity in their own lives than they felt they had witnessed in the lives of their parents.

Generational analysis can subsume history within its framework—as did Mentre, Ortega, and Mannheim—by positing the importance of historical experiences during youth in formalizing life-long consciousness. In contrast to the pervasive finding that young people are more liberal while older people lean towards conservatism, which is often interpreted as showing that people become more politically conservative as they age (Crittenden, 1962), several studies employing a cohort approach (examining, over time, groups of people born around the same period in history) have found greater differences in the modal responses between cohorts, even as the cohorts age (Bengtson and Cutler, 1976). For example, Inglehart (1977), in a cross-national survey of European nations, discovered that cohorts which came of age prior to 1945 and grew up under conditions of economic insecurity during the depression exhibited ''acquisitive'' values and attitudes, embracing values such as financial security, domestic order, and support for the status quo. On the other hand, the cohorts that came of age after 1945 and were raised under relatively affluent circumstances, held ''post-bourgeois'' values and attitudes, tending to be more concerned with expressive political issues and change. Similarly, Hunt's (1982) analysis of American national election data reveals, among other findings, that the cohorts which grew up after 1948 were much more supportive of political protest and nonconventional political activities as tactics of social and political change.

Examinations of generation units—those groups within the same actual generation that work up the material of their common historical experiences in different ways—have not been numerous, but the findings strongly support Mannheim's notion of intragenerational conflict. For example, Simirenko (1966) studied a Russian ethnic community in Minneapolis and identified two generation units rooted within the same historical generation, each pursuing quite different objectives and life styles. Zeitlin (1966), applying Mannheim's framework, found both intergenerational and intragenerational patterns in responses to the Cuban revolution. Workers who were members of the ''Castro generation,'' the age cohort 28–35, when compared with other generations, were most likely to favor revolution, because of their common frame of reference developed during the anti-Batista struggle. However, two generation units were also apparent within the Cuban revolutionary generation, depending on employment status. Workers who were unemployed or underemployed prior to the revolution formed the procommunist generation unit, as opposed to workers who were regularly employed and exhibited less revolutionary enthusiasm.

More recently, Fendrich (1974) tracked members of a generation unit of former civil rights activists over time and reported that a decade later they retained their distinctive political characteristics. They did not become more moderate or disillusioned with society, as many critics had predicted, but instead maintained a strong political commitment which was highly consistent with their earlier ideological views and political objectives. A study by Braungart and Braungart (1980), which synthesized several follow-up studies of 1960s activists and traced some of the more prominent activist leaders over time, found that both radical activists and leaders tended to remain committed to their previous political goals and were likely to stay active politically, albeit using different tactics and approaches.

The opposing political orientations held by separate generation units within a generation may be partially grounded in differential social location which has limited and influenced the stratification of experience. For example, one of the earliest studies of the 1960s left- and right-wing student activists found that left-wing youth tended to be drawn from upper-middle-class homes, whereas right-wing youth came from working-class backgrounds (Westby and Braungart, 1966). In general, such factors as social status, family environment, and college attendance have been found to be associated with the emergence of different generation units (Braungart, 1976, 1979b).

D.   Historical-Generational Perspectives on Youth Movements

The psychological, historical, and generational approaches have each attempted to account for youth movements. The psychological perspective involves factors "within" the individual, such as personality traits, emotional needs, perceptions, and belief-behavior consistency, which act as personal motivations for participation in youth movements. The historical sources of youth movements stem from forces "outside" the individual, such as social discontinuities, or "among" individuals, such as mobilization, influencing the formation of youth movements. The generational impetus for youth movements comes "from below" and involves the ongoing dynamic relationship between and within age groups in society and history struggling over the definition and control of reality, continuity, and change. Little has been done, however, to bring these various approaches together. In this section, the emphasis is on synthesizing the issues and concerns derived from the historical and generational literatures.

One approach to conceptualizing the covergence of historical and generational forces is suggested by some of the recent works in the area of life-span development. According to the life-course literature, three different dimensions of time are involved in understanding generational attitudes and behavior: (1) life time, which includes the orderly and sequential life-cycle changes that occur within the individual, governed largely by a biological timetable; (2) social time, or the social meaning of age in a given society, involving age norms and roles which impose an expected pattern of behavior on life-cycle development; and (3) historical time, or the events, circumstances, and mentalities of a given period of history which influence the context of social time and, in turn, life time (Elder, 1980). The common location in life time, social time, and historical time for a group of individuals born around the same period in history is represented in a cohort.

During so-called routine historical periods, youth cohorts come and go, reflecting a connection between life-course patterns and social change. Within each successive cohort, processes of socialization and role allocation serve as linkages between the young and social options. Under such times or conditions, youth are incorporated in the adult social structure without major incident. However, significant historical changes can threaten the fragile character of these linkages and disparities may emerge between youth and their elders, as well as within their own youthful age group. Over the last two centuries, numerous historical changes (rapid population growth, expanding higher education, rising nationalism, depressions, and wars) produced periods of social and revolutionary change that were characterized by self-conscious and mobilized age cohorts. Times of heightened political activity by young people represent a convergence of historical, generational, and psychological forces which combine to produce a historical generation having its own particular character and form.

Youth movements are types of collective behavior in which age-conscious groups, or generations, organize and mobilize either to bring about or to resist historical change. Such movements develop out of the specific combinations of generational and historical forces to produce extraordinary volatile periods in world time. These combinations are typically unique and may never be repeated in exactly the same way. Unlike successive cohorts that come of age on a continuous basis and act in harmony with prevailing historical forces, historical generations can, when mobilized and self-conscious, reject existing social and political forms and erupt in a flurry of political and cultural activity. Historical generations represent periods of "moral upsurge" (Mills) or "creedal passion" (Huntington) in world time when cultural ideals clash with social reality. The conflict and tension created by newly formed or perceived ideals and the existing social and political conditions lie at the root of generational movements. Youth movements, believing strongly in the moral superiority and worth of their goals and mission, embrace sets of ideals that appear difficult to fulfill through existing social and political institutional channels.

E.   The Historical-Generational Model

When the historical discontinuity and mobilization theories are compared with generational theories, considerable overlap is evident. Each view includes components of the other in predicting youth movements. These approaches can be combined to form a historical-generational theory which encompasses the predictions of both the historical and generational arguments within a single framework. According to this combined theory, historical generations occur when sociohistorical forces interact with generational mobilization to produce youth movements. These youth movements occur when young people, as an age group, reject the existing order, join together and attempt to redirect the course of human history as their "generational mission." Historical generations involve both intergenerational and intragenerational forms of conflict. That is, while youth movements typically challenge adult society, a number of opposing generation units may emerge to compete vigorously among themselves over certain social and political goals and the means to achieve them. After a limited period of heightened activity, historical generations run their course and decline. The duration and changes brought about as a result of a historical generation's efforts determine its effectiveness and impact on society and history.

Intergenerational conflict takes place when the new generation rejects and/or extends significantly beyond the values, norms, and practices of the dominant older generation. This produces a break in the continuity between the generations and severs the institutional linkages that hold or bind the generations together. Intergenerational conflict creates barriers between the generations such that the values and norms of the older generation cannot be easily transmitted to, or assimilated by, the younger generation. Intergenerational conflict may emerge when historical changes generate inter-age inequality, and when those with conscious interests determine it would be useful to mobilize youth against their elders for social, cultural, and political reasons.

Intergenerational conflict involves two basic processes. The first represents the deauthorization of the adult generation's historical dominance. Deauthorization of the older generation includes the open rejection, attacks, and destruction of the values, norms, and traditions of adult authority and control. The means used to achieve deauthorization may be symbolic or violent. The deauthorization theme has been expressed by the historical change theorists in the discontinuity of authority (Kornhauser), a perceived gap between aspirations and achievement of elites (Gurr), and a lag in the achievements of elites (Hamilton and Wright). Along the same lines, the generational theorists refer to detachment of youth from parents as necessary to achieve independence and autonomy (Freud), rejection of the older generation (Feuer), and disappointment in the search for fidelity (Erikson). The notion of deauthorization also appears in psychological studies of youthful activists as the need for adversaries to build solidarity (Murphy), and the projection of parental rejection and aggression onto other authority figures (Duncan).

The second, and perhaps most important, process involved in intergenerational conflict is authorization of the youth generation to act as the vehicle for social change. Authorization of the youth generation occurs when, in order to legitimize their own goals and means to achieve them, members of the younger generation attempt to vigorously create and validate their own "indigenous" values and norms that are perceived to transcend, supercede, and replace those of the older generation. The struggle to authorize the young generation involves symbolic authorization and radical or violent types of authorization. The historical discontinuity theorists include the idea of seeing oneself or one's group as a vanguard for social change (Eisenstadt), and the belief in the capability of attaining certain goals (Gurr). In contrast, the mobilization theorists' major contention is that social change comes about through active collective solidarity and effort. Simiarly, the generational theorists place considerable emphasis on authorization, such as in the formation of a consciously shared collective destiny (Ortega, Mannheim), the conviction of a generational mission (Feuer), and finding identity through participation and activity (Erikson). The notion of authorization is given attention in many of the psychological studies as well, such as seeking political activity to meet emotional needs (Duncan, Murphy), and taking action on the basis of one's beliefs (Cowdry, Keniston, and Cabin).

Intergenerational conflict enhances the likelihood of intragenerational conflict. Intragenerational conflict is represented by generational units within the same historic generation which compete for the definition and control of reality. With the unstable, destabilized, or discordant breakdown in intergenerational continuity, new forms of intragenerational conflict emerge which may be either spontaneous (arising from youth groups themselves) or sponsored by adult organizations. In the absence of clear lines of institutional authority and socialization created by intergenerational conflict, youth groups or generational units on both sides of the political spectrum compete vigorously with each other over the authorization and legitimation of their particular set of ideological or utopian values and goals.

Intragenerational conflict can be represented by proactive, reactive, and active generation units (Tilly, Mannheim). Proactive or change-oriented generation units favor radical or revolutionary change from the political left, reject the ideological status quo among liberal groups, and embrace more radical or utopian alternatives. They usually precede and may stimulate the emergence of right-wing reactive groups that reject both the idea of change and the ideological status quo among conservative groups in favor of radical utopian solutions to their problems and perhaps the atavistic return to an earlier time in history. The different social and cultural positions of youth and the specific historical changes and problems play a major role in determining the political direction and thrust of intragenerational conflict (Oberschall, Smelser). Active generational units are those that emerge representing centrist ideological positions (e.g., moderate liberal or conservative) in society. Active generation units are typically comprised of groups that are either sponsored or in some way influenced by adult groups in society. The divergent and often opposing generation units do no negate the existence of a historical generation, for beneath the generational diversity lies a generational unity. While each generation unit rejects the adult generation for different, and sometimes similar, reasons, their major point of departure is the way in which they authorize the members of their own generation unit to change the course of history.

Historical generations decline when the historical and mobilizing forces that produced intergenerational and intragenerational conflict lose their potency. Intergenerational conflict comes to an end when: (1) the historical problems that precipitated the conflict lose their saliency and new issues emerge (new wars, post-revolutionary periods, inflation, prosperity); (2) the historical problems are corrected or ameliorated through institutional reforms; (3) generational movements lose their leadership, mobilization, solidarity; (4) adults and youth cooperate and compromise their differences, adults coopt the youth movement, and/or adults crush the youth movement (police or military force); and (5) youth movements succeed in their efforts to overthrow the opposition.

The conflict between generation units (intragenerational conflict subsides when: (1) the historical or ideological issues are resolved or are replaced by new issues or objectives; (2) the competing generational units are unable to sustain momentum (loss of leadership, organization, resources, mobilization, solidarity), so the units tire and give up their cause; (3) competition between generational units continues until one unit emerges victorious (with or without adult support); and (4) a compromise is worked out between the competing units such that they are willing to coexist in a peaceful fashion. Once the historical and generational forces decouple, the historical-generational dynamic loses its momentum, and generational conflict declines.

The extent of change or modification of society brought about by historical-generational movements can be determined by examining the scope and degree of change, along with the longevity of generational conflict. The scope of change includes the breadth of the generational conflict throughout society, and the level (university, local, national, international) of society that is affected by the youth movements. The actual amount or degree of change involves the depth of institutional penetration and adjustment (the degree to which institutions, values, and norms are modified) brought about by generational movements. And finally, the duration of the historical generation affects the ability of social institutions to withstand or resist generational conflict.

The temporal relationship between historical change, generational mobilization, and youth movements is presented in Figure 2. The three variables represented in the model are: historical change, the independent variable; generational mobilization, the intervening variable; and the emergence of youth movements, the dependent variable. Because it is difficult to measure historical changes, particularly in the short-run since societies are continually undergoing change, a crude indication of the long-term amount of change between earlier and later estimates is represented by the two dashed lines. What this expanding fan of historical change suggests, in a very general way, is that historical change is dependent upon the interactions between institutional figures and interest groups within the population. The rate of such change may increase continually over time as the number of such figures and groups increases. Under times of routine or gradual change, historical forms are accepted by age cohorts and the socialization process proceeds without much incident. Generational mobilization does not occur and youth movements do not develop. However, during rapidly changing or contradictory times, age cohorts may become transformed or converted into generational movements and burst through the boundaries of conventional history to produce historical generations, as represented by the solid line in Figure 2. Historical generations are not the passive recipients of history but become active

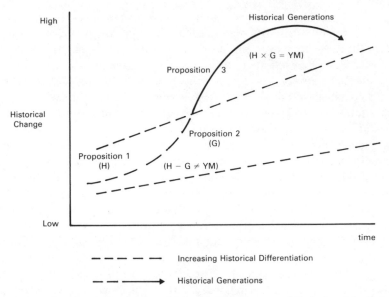

Figure 2. Historical-Generational Model: The Temporal Relationship Between Historical Change (H), Generational Mobilization (G), and Youth Movements (YM)

forces for institutional change. When historical generations arise, generational mobilization interacts with historical forces to produce youth movements. This dynamic process is represented by three propositions.

Proposition 1: Historical changes occur through the development and decline of social, political, economic, and cultural institutions. Population growth is one important component of social change, as the numbers of young people increase and exert pressures on institutions in society. Youth status groups (students, intellectual circles, clubs, delinquent groups) emerge as objective social categories or membership groups—that is, they are not necessarily self-conscious or politically motivated. Youth status groups and cohorts, as they pass through the life cycle, are, under uneventful or gradual conditions of historical change, typically absorbed into and controlled by adult-dominated institutions.

Proposition 2: Generations or generational movements develop out of youth status groups. Generations take form when objective membership group status (the age cohort) becomes transformed into a subjective reference group status (the generation). While influenced by history and reacting to historical circumstances, generational movements are not determined by history. Their origin, dynamic structure, and process represent new or novel forms of social organization and behavior. Generational movements are more likely to occur under

conditions that include: dynamic leadership, collective consciousness or solidarity, the mobilization of power (people, resources, and organization), and
action.

Proposition 3: Historical forces combine and interact with generational
forces to produce youth movements. This dynamic process results in the formation of decisive historical generations, which are mobilized age groups that
attempt to change the course of history. Two major forms of conflict are part of
the historical-generational process: intergenerational and intragenerational conflict. Historical generations influence the course of institutional growth and can
affect the scope, degree, and length of social change. Over time, however,
historical generations lose their force, become unlinked, and return to the status
of age cohorts.

IV. FINDINGS AND DISCUSSION

The purpose of this analysis is both to explore how and why historical-generational forces interact to produce youth movements and to construct a theory of
historical generations that has: (1) the analytic ability to incorporate other existing theories of youth movements within its framework; (2) global scope and
applicability; and (3) the capacity to withstand the test of time.

The prior discussion has both reviewed existing writing on this topic and
shown how the theory developed here integrates a range of other relevant theoretical work. In order to evaluate the scope and applicability of this theory, a
review was conducted of historical data concerning youth movements during the
past 150 years. The results of this review are summarized in Table 1. The data in
Table 1 portray the convergence of historical changes, generational forces, and
youth movements over time and reflect the argument that historical factors interact with generational forces, in the form of mobilizations aimed at deauthorization and authorization, to produce youth movement activity.

While there is no one-to-one relationship or perfect correspondence between
the three dimensions, a number of clearly identifiable patterns exist. As shown in
Table 1, the structural features that produced the Young Europe historical generation in 1815–1848 also occurred when youth movements appeared at later times
in Latin America, the United States, Asia, Africa, and the Middle East. The
proliferation of youth movements over the last 150 years has been dramatic,
beginning with four youth movements in Europe during the 1800s and increasing
to at least 50 nations with youth movements in the 1960s. The same conditions
that gave rise to political activity among nineteenth century European youth were
conducive to similar kinds of political activity among young people throughout
the rest of the world. That is to say, historical changes and discontinuities
interacted with the generational forces in the form of deauthorization and authorization to produce youth movements. In the following sections, brief summaries

Text continues on page 130

Table 1. Young Europe, Post-Victorian, Great Depression, and the 1960s Historical Generations: The Relationship Between Historical Change, Generational Forces, and Youth Movements

Historical Changes	Generational Forces	Youth Movements
1815–1848		
	YOUNG EUROPE HISTORICAL GENERATION	
Western Europe. Industrialization led to the growth of bourgeois wealth, undermined traditional authority and brought realignment of social classes and class conflicts; population growth led to surge in the number of young people; rising problems of unemployment, particularly among the young; university enrollments increased, with students in a marginal status (as cultural and intellectual elite but without economic or political influence). The defeat of Napoleon at Waterloo (1815) ushered in a new age of nationalism with emphases on nation-state unification and national independence. Ideal of liberalism (freedom) and utopian socialism (equality) swept across Europe, raising issues of universal suffrage and rights of citizenship. The Sturm und Drang and French romantics movements depicted the hero as a young outlaw. Political and class conflicts led to revolutionary upheavals in Germany, France, and Italy in 1848.	Germany. Indignation among German youth over the national humiliation of German states by Napoleon; seeing a "new age about to begin," youth rejected the "night of long disgrace" at the hands of French rule and looked to the regeneration of Germany and rallied behind national unity. University-based youth throughout Germany organized the famous Wartburg Festival in 1817. Italy. Following the defeat of Napoleon, youth denounced adult prorestoration elements. The youthful, charismatic Mazzini (1805–1872) emerged as a key mobilizer who championed the legitimacy of youth and the failures of the old order. Mazzini wrote: "Place the young at the head of the insurgent masses; you do not know what strength is latent in those young bands, what magic influence the voices of the young have on the crowd; you will find them a host of apostles for the new religion." France. The French "Generation of 1830" assaulted Orleanist Monarchy, overthrew the last of the Bourbons and revolted against bourgeois liberal thought. The intellectual themes of youth rejected the prevailing political, social, and economic structures and proclaimed the legitimacy of their own visions for France.	A widespread student association, the Burschenschaften Movement, began in 1815. It advocated the idea of a unified German state with representative institutions. Due to its radical activities, the Burschenschaften was forced underground by the Karlsbad Decree in 1819. In Italy, Young Italy organized to fight for the liberation of Italy from foreign oppression and for the overthrow of "traditional authority." Young Italy excluded those over 40 years of age from its ranks. Young France consisted of three separate youth movements: the Young Republicans favored the ideal republic of reason and virtue Robespierre dreamed of in 1790; the Saint Simonian socialists envisioned a technocratic utopia guided by an enlightened new Christianity; the romantic Bohemians withdrew from society and developed the first modern counter culture.

122

Crimean War (1854–1856); War of Italian Unification (1859); Austro-Prussian War (1866); Franco-Prussian War (1870–1871).

Little generational mobilization during the war years.

1860–1890s

Russia. In Russia, which had been one of the most culturally isolated, economically underdeveloped and politically autocratic societies, major changes were forced to occur. The "Czar Emancipator" Alexander II (1856–1881) pushed reforms throughout Russian life (from the courts and the military to local government and the schools—including a large expansion of educational opportunities).

Ideological writings and doctrines surged, including Marx, Herzen, Bakunin, Nechaev, Kropotkin, Dostoyevsky and Nietzsche.

Russia. Widespread intellectual ferment among the young against the autocratic government and economic backwardness of the society; mobilization, especially based on university networks and intellectual groups where students rejected rules that restricted their freedom and bitterly resented surveillance and cruelty; mobilization also based on assassinations and other acts of terrorism. First came the nihilist youth (Russian sons who turned against their fathers); next, came the narodniks (populist socialists who worshiped the narod, the Russian folk), and intellectual circles such as the Petrashevtsy circle.

Young Russia established. Russian students carried on 60 years of rebellion and terrorism that ripped open Russian society; there were 83 reported strikes between 1857 and 1914; thousands of students were expelled from universities, three Ministers of the Interior were assassinated by students; and many students were exiled to Siberia.

1890–1910

Significant population growth in Europe and many other countries; a period of great migrations from Europe to the United States; industrialization and urbanization led to increased unemployment, class po-

POST-VICTORIAN HISTORICAL GENERATION

Germany. German youth criticized the efficiency and rigid formality of life in Wilhelmine Germany but stressed successionist, rather than direct action. At Hohe Meissner (mountain laden with German mythology) a coalition of youth groups united under the name Freideutsche Jugend. Generational activity spread to Switzerland and Austria.

Wandervögel (1896–1919), Ausschus für Schülerfahrten (Wandering birds, Committee for schoolboy rambles) was a countercultural movement of youth who liked to tramp through rural Germany in pictur-

(continued)

Table 1. (Continued)

Historical Changes	Generational Forces	Youth Movements
larization, and class conflict; increasing economic extremes contrasted with the "serene confidence" of the Victorian Era, the Guilded Age, and "Gay 90s" (materialistic, acquisitive). Expanded government expenditures for education and increased numbers of university students in many countries. Last of the great empires (Victorian, Austria-Hungary, Ottoman, Ch'ing) came under attack.		esque costumes, strumming guitars, singing folk songs, and camping outside. Later, Wandervögel members became more politically right-wing, militant and split into the Bünde phase (1919–1933).
	India. Young, educated Indians, often unemployed, protested against British colonial rule. Mobilization also occurred through direct action as youth manufactured bombs, procured arms and assassinated several British officials. Mahatma Gandhi, age 31 in 1900, emerged as a leader for national independence.	India. Young India established: "India for the Indians."
Mass democracy and support for socialism on the rise throughout Europe along with expanded citizenship rights, suffrage, welfare, unions, and universal education. Period of extreme ideological polarization and party politics. Marxist and socialist parties moved Europe to the political left. Nationalism continued to spread throughout Europe and anti-colonialism took root in Asia and the Middle East. Ethnopolitics became popular in Central Europe.	Turkey. During the latter part of the Ottoman Empire (1880–1920), students denounced the Sultans and rejected Turkey's cultural and political backwardness. Western-educated young Turks mobilized through secret societies and other organizations for national independence and reforms in education, women's rights, law, local administration, and economic development.	Turkey. Young Turkey: The Young Turk revolution of 1908 led the way for the establishment of the Turkish Republic; Kemal Ataturk, himself part of the student movement, was age 27 in 1908.
Social Darwinism ("survival of the fittest") and the writings to Nietzsche and Schopenhauer ("will"	Yugoslavia. Inspired by the Russian Revolution of 1905, young Bosnian youth rejected the annexation of Bosnia and Herzegovina by Austria-Hungary in 1908. The goals of Bosnian youth were to "revenge the people." "We, the youngest, have to make a new history. Into our frozen society we have to bring sunshine . . . we the messengers of new generations and new people . . . we shall win." Often favoring assassination politics, one activist murdered the heir to the Austrian throne, the act that precipitated World War I.	Yugoslavia. Young Bosnia ("Mlada Bosna"): youth movement embraced a strong nationalist resentment of the Austro-Hungarian Empire and prepared the way for a new Yugoslav state.

to power") challenged Victorian beliefs that the world was an act of divine creation. Hall wrote *Adolescence* (1904), the first textbook on the problems of youth. Advances in science, technology and communication transformed society; science and new technologies equated with progress. Authority shifted in the direction of the middle classes. International sports movement began with the revival of the ancient Olympic Games.	China. Students, active in the downfall of the Manchu Dynasty, helped spread radical ideas of nationalism, modernization, and democracy; youth were outraged and felt betrayed by the concessions won by foreign powers at Versailles; youth mobilized around anti-imperialist, anti-Japanese and anti-Christian issues. Disenchanted with Western liberalism and wooed by Soviet envoys, young, alienated intellectuals turned to democracy, equality, science, socialism, national self-determination, and Bolshevism.	China. Young China: Chinese student movement was a turning point in modern Chinese history as it drew young Chinese into political struggles (Mao Tse-tung, as a young man of 26 in 1919, was active in these movements).
Latin America. The ideas of the French philosophes and British liberals undermined the legitimacy of the colonial system of education. Narrow scholasticism was rejected in favor of the philosophy of Rousseau, Quesnay, Voltaire, Condillac, and Locke. After independence new governments concerned themselves with higher education, accelerated the tendency toward secular control of universities, and new universities proliferated throughout the hemisphere.	Mexico. In Mexico, revolutionary youth rejected the Diaz regime which was perceived as a government of the privileged and of elderly men who could not resign themselves to giving up power.	Mexico. Mexico's Revolutionary Generation of 1910 led youth revolts against class and age.
	Latin America. In Latin America, vigorous intellectual circles such as the Ateneo de la Juventud (Antheneum of the Young) preached liberation and radical change. At the turn of the 20th century, many Latin American university students, inspired by Enlightenment philosophers, turned their energies to university reform and national political development. The new intellectuals were anti-clerical, anti-imperialistic, and strongly populist; they favored secular education, accused the old leadership of complicity to imperialism and wished to transform the universities into active agents of social and political change. The president of the national Council of University Students in Peru said in 1920: "A vast intellectual renaissance has manifested itself among the students of Latin America, which shows a profound divergence between the thought of the rising generation and the the generation that preceded it. . . . The young are following no master . . ."	Latin America. Latin American student movement began with the First International Congress of American Students, held in Montevideo in 1909 and was attended by students from Argentina, Bolivia, Brazil, Chile, Paraguay, Peru, and Uruguay. The Cordoba Movement, established in 1918, quickly spread to 18 other Latin American nations.
World War I (1914–1918); Russian Civil War (1918–1921)	Little generational deauthorization and authorization during the war years.	

(*continued*)

Table 1. (Continued)

Historical Changes	Generational Forces	Youth Movements
1930–1940s	GREAT DEPRESSION HISTORICAL GENERATION	
Population in Europe and America continued to increase. Worldwide depression produced unprecedented social and political instability; economic collapse led to sharp increases in unemployment with rates even higher for youth. Large increases in university enrollments and in government expenditures on education in Europe and America; small but increasing numbers of youth in the Third World societies obtained college educations. Economic and political malaise in the 1930s weakened centrist governments and parties; the rise of fascist governments in Germany, Italy, and Spain, and fascist movements in other countries. Japan emerged as the industrially dominant and militaristic power in Asia.	Germany. Wartime losses severely damaged generational continuity. Humiliated at Versailles, and with their lives disrupted by the depression, inflation, and unemployment, German youth and youthful veterans who felt "undefeated in the fields," but "stabbed in the back" by the politicians, flocked to join the Freikorps and Hitler Jugend. National Socialism came to power as the party of youth; Hitler courted and cultivated young people: "The future of the German Volk depends on the youth." The Hitler Youth Law transformed the Hitler Youth movement into a compulsory universal state organization in 1936.	Hitler Jugend established in 1926 as part of the Nazi movement; Hitler Jugend incorporated the romantic Volkish style of the Wandervögel and the more militant and strident style of the Bünde.
	In Italy, youthful WWI veterans called for reform: "Down with the old parties! Let us have new talents! Let us have new energy!" Mussolini used the term "youth" to mobilize his leadership.	Italian youth joined Wolf Cubs, Avanguardia Universitaria, Gruppi Universitari Fascisti and other fascist groups.
	In Spain, youth mobilized around right-wing and monarchist issues. Franco seized control of the Falange in 1937 in a bloodless coup and made it the official state party.	Spanish Falange Movement grew based on support by students and young army officers. Fascist youth movements spread quickly through Central and Eastern Europe, Scandinavia, and the British Isles in the 1930s.
	In England, mobilization efforts had a strong generational tone. Sir Oswald Mosley warned that "the enemy is the old gang of our present	Right-wing youth joined Britain's Blackshirts; anti-war youth joined in

political system. . . . The real political division of the present decade is not a division of parties but a division of generations.'' George Orwell noted that the revolutionary feeling in England ''was a revolt of youth versus age . . . everyone under forty was in a bad temper with his elders. . . . The dominance of old men was held to be responsible for every evil known to humanity.''

In the U.S., the strength grew of left-wing radicals who were pro-labor, anti-fascist, and anti-war. New sets of values developed as a revolt against puritanical morals and the cult of progress; the ''Roaring 20s'' with a New Paganism; H.L. Mencken: ''enlightened hedonism is the thinking man's philosophy''; Gertrude Stein to Hemingway: ''You are all a lost generation''; Dadaist movements reflected the revolt against reason.

supporting the Oxford Pledge.

In the United States, youth rejected moderation and favored radicalism. Youth mobilized around issues of pacifism, anti-fascism, university reforms and labor unions. Strong intellectual ferment at colleges mixed with pursuit of the ''fun culture.''

A range of ideological youth movements grew in the U.S.; student strikes against the war steadily escalated and by 1936 over 350,000 college youth participated in the annual anti-war strike; many signed the Oxford Pledge. United Front Movement peaked during the years 1936–1938.

Nationalism spread throughout India, Ceylon, Burma, Malaya, Vietnam, and Indonesia. ''The atmosphere became electric,'' Nehru commented on Wilson's Fourteen Points, ''and most of us young men felt exhilarated and expected big things to come in the near future.''

The Civil Disobedience Movement in India of the 1930s ushered in the most active period of political agitation undertaken by Indian youth in the move toward national independence. Mohammad Ali Jinnah mobilized Islamic youth in India and called for a separate Muslim state. Major mobilization campaigns occurred as thousands of youth went to jail; many left college to work for national independence, the labor movement, and Gandhian social and educational projects.

In India, the All India Students' Federation was created in 1936 which united the student movement; by 1938 it had 50,000 members.

In China, Sun Yat-sen tried to revamp the Kuomintang along

In China, youth were involved in both Kuomintang and communist forces. The failure of the Kuomintang to maintain leadership, pursue

China's student movement moved leftward. In 1936, the pro-commu-

(continued)

Table 1. (Continued)

Historical Changes	Generational Forces	Youth Movements
Leninist lines to form a united front. Chiang Kai-shek split the Chinese Communist Party in 1931. Mao Tse-tung called for a national effort to rid China of Western influence, Japan, warlords, landlords, and capitalism.	reforms, or resist the Japanese invasion of Manchuria contributed to the effectiveness of mobilization by the communists. Mao offered youth a "new democratic China" as opposed to the "old China."	nist National Student Association was founded.
World War II (1939–1945); Korean War (1950–1953)	Little generational mobilization during the war years.	
	THE 1960s GLOBAL HISTORICAL GENERATION	
1960–1970s	Adult society rejected and challenged by youth around the world for not living up to ideals; university, as well as other local, national, and international issues were emphasized in youth mobilizations to deauthorize adult authority. "Never trust anyone over 30" became a global cliché. Generational authorization reflected many familiar themes: "seizing power," France; "creative agitation," West Germany; "democracy," S. Korea; "solidarity," Nigeria; and "freedom," Turkey.	The following countries experienced active youth movements in the 1960s: In Europe: Austria, Czechoslovakia, Denmark, Finland, West Germany, Italy, Netherlands, Norway, Portugal, Spain, Sweden, United Kingdom.
Continuing population increases throughout the world, with greatest increases in the Third World. Sharply increased university enrollments in Europe and the United States. World economic polarization between rich and poor nations (the industrial "North" versus the underdeveloped "South"); increased unemployment in Third World countries, especially among the young. Rise of multinational corporations that dominated world indus-	Commenting on the eve of the 1960s, Sartre noted in his essay entitled "The Kids Take Over," that "Only the young had enough anger and anguish to attempt [the Revolution], enough integrity to succeed."	In Latin America: Argentina, Bolivia, Brazil, Chile, Colombia, Cuba (1959), Dominican Republic, Ecuador, Guatemala, Mexico, Nic-

aragua, Panama, Puerto Rico, Uruguay, Venezuela.

United States, Australia.

In Asia: Burma, China, India, Indonesia, Japan, S. Korea, Malaysia, Philippines, Sri Lanka (1971), S. Vietnam, Thailand.

In Africa: South Africa, Algeria, The Congo, Ghana, Morocco, Nigeria, Tunisia.

In the Middle East: Israel, Iran, Turkey.

In the U.S. concerns over civil rights, the Vietnam war, the environment, and the state of the university were key factors in mobilization. In the U.S. and in Western Europe, there was a principled rejection of the "society of consumption" that was linked to adult society. Elsewhere, youth mobilized against dictorships, ethnic inequities, and political oppression.

In China, Red Guards promoted the Cultural Revolution as a means to overcome what they saw as growing rigidities in their society: ". . . crush the old world into pieces and create a new world in the debris."

Commenting on the ferment of the 1960s, Andrew Hacker wrote: "Youth may best be seen as a separate country, in which young people take out citizenship. That nation has a culture of its own which now reaches every hamlet."

Counterculture appealed to youth all over the world; youth defy adult society and create their own society: similar patterns throughout the world (long hair, "sloppy" dress, jeans, music, drugs, casual sex, admiration of same revolutionary leaders); growing distrust and rejection of liberal, scientific, and "functionally rational" values, for more personal, communal, humanistic, and "substantively rational" values.

tries and markets. Post-World War II world divided into three blocs: East, West, and Third World. Nationalism became a more significant force challenging traditional world order but the proliferation of nation-states led to a trend toward mini-nationalism (regional, tribal, ethnic, religious) and away from macro-nationalism (Pan-Islam, Pan-Slavism, Pan-Germanism). National self-determination and citizenship (freedom and equality) were now part of global political culture. Third World countries struggled to become less "dependent" on powerful, industrial-center nations.

Development and spread of nuclear weapons. Rapid growth in communications, transportation, and other technologies linked the world closer together. Rise of global mass culture; homogenization of values, expectations, and consciousness.

Sources:
Altbach (1974), Backman and Finlay (1973), Bakke and Bakke (1971), Braungart (1980, 1982, 1984), Brax (1981), DeConde (1971), Emmerson (1968), Esler (1971, 1979), Feuer (1969), Gillis (1974), Kearney (1980), Klineberg, Zavalloni, Louis-Guerin and BenBrika (1979), Laqueur (1962, 1969), Larsen, Hagtvet and Mykelbust (1981), Liebman, Walker and Glazer (1972), Lipset (1967), Lipset and Altbach (1969), Mitchell (1976), Moller (1972), Nelkin and Pollak (1981), Simon (1967), Snyder (1982), Statera (1975), Szyliowicz (1972), United Nations (1981), Walker (1967), Wallbank and Taylor (1961), Wohl (1979).

129

of key features of each of these periods are presented. The sources for the information presented in these summaries are listed on Table 1.

One finding that emerges from this historical review is that youth movements were neither random nor constant forms of political behavior but clustered around four periods in world time. These periods are identified as the Young Europe, Post-Victorian, Great Depression, and 1960s Historical Generations. These were times when historical conditions interacted with generational forces in a particular way to produce extraordinary youth movement activity.

A.   Young Europe Historical Generation

The Young Europe movements reflected the growing numbers of youth who had more education than ever before, yet were kept on the margins of society. While considered intellectual elites, they were denied economic and political opportunities and power. These young Europeans were very much caught up with nationalism and political change. The adult generation was deauthorized because they failed to live up to new ideals, particularly the ideals of liberty and equality. Young people were able to authorize their generation primarily through the mobilization of charismatic leaders, through university networks and intellectual circles.

The Young Europe movements, which included the Burschenschaften, Young Italy, Young France, and Young Russia, represented a turning point in modern world time. To begin with, it involved a rejection of absolutism in favor of the modern nation-state. Begun by the German student unions and led by Mazzini and later by Garibaldi's Red Shirts, European youth deauthorized the parent generation over their humiliating defeat at the hands of Napoleon. German and Italian youth reacted vigorously against any possibility of the return or restoration of Europe to the ancient regime. The young republicans and Saint Simonian socialists of France fought for greater liberty, freedom, and participated in the Revolutions of 1848. Inspired by French successes, bomb-throwing Russian students and nihilists led one of the most significant student movements recorded in world history. All across Europe, young people felt a new age was about to begin.

B.   Post-Victorian Historical Generation

The insurrectionary pattern laid down in the mid-nineteenth century was repeated during *fin-de-siècle* Europe. Once again, youth were up in arms, deauthorizing the ''backward world'' of their parents and looking forward to a new modern future. Wandervögel youth reacted against the rigid formalism of Wilhelmine Germany and took to hiking through the romantic countryside. Young revolutionary leaders like Mahatma Gandhi, Kemal Ataturk, and Mao Tse-tung were preparing to lead their countries and young colleagues away from colonialism and despotism to nationalism, modernization, and democracy. It was a young Bosnian youth who shot the heir to the Austrian throne in 1914 which triggered the onset of World War I. In another part of the world, Latin American students were challenging a university system with a tradition that dated back to the Middle Ages. Paradoxically, as European colonialism was at its peak—with English poets writing of "the white Man's burden," Germans speaking of spreading *Kultur* over the globe, and the French describing their *mission civilisatrice*—mass democracy, nationalism and socialism were preparing to replace the "serence confidence" of the Victorian colonial age. Youthful intellectuals, such as the Bloomsbury circle, the revolutionary generation of Lenin, the Fabian socialists, and bohemians in the Paris of Toulouse-Lautrec opposed conservative European society. Young Wales, Young Ireland, youthful Czechs and Poles, and the Spanish Generation of '98 authorized their generation and were caught up in the ferment of youth movements from 1890–1914.

C. The Great Depression Historical Generation

Another turning point in world time occurred during the 1930s. Unhappy with the Versailles Treaty, the faltering global economy, rising unemployment, the Bolshevik revolution, and unstable political systems, young people once again mobilized for change. Generational revolt, mobilized among students, young army officers, demoralized soldiers and other youth, played a prominent role in the emergence of authoritarian and fascist movements. Youthful rejection of established authority in Europe, the United States, and Asia was widespread and intense. In order to redirect these rebellious tendencies, adult-sponsored youth groups like the Hitler Jugend, Mussolini's Sons of the Wolf, and Russian Komsomol were created. These organizations were successful in directing the rebellious utopianism of youth into totalitarian and political service. Fascist-controlled youth groups quickly spread from the core fascist countries of Germany, Italy, and Spain throughout all of noncommunist Europe. During the same time, the United States experienced its first widespread student movement and one of its largest to date. American youth reacted against the depression, fascism in Europe, the threat of another impending world war, and fought for university reform. In Asia, Indian youth in unprecedented numbers participated in the national independence movement and were the most radical in Indian political life during the 1930s. Chinese youth were unhappy over the Japanese invasion of Manchuria and Shanghai, the divided national leadership, and began to look to communism for solutions to their problems.

D. The 1960s Historical Generation

The post-World War II years witnessed an unprecedented growth and spread of youth movements throughout Europe, Latin America, the United States, Asia,

Africa, and the Middle East. Everywhere the signs and symbols of a new global malaise were the same. Youth mobilized over issues ranging from university reform and local problems to national and international issues. Young people were particularly concerned with three major issues: (1) the destruction and reform of the existing regime; (2) unity with workers and the poor; and (3) the formation of an international student movement. The major means youth employed to achieve their goals were demonstrations, riots, strikes, and occupations. The consistency or homogeneity in goals and means of youth movements throughout the world indicated that the world had now become highly politicized with an international political culture. These two themes were reinforced by contemporary global nationalism and the new political culture made possible by modern technology and communications systems. The 1960s represented a watershed in youth movement activity which occurred on every continent around the world. The 1960s historical generation created a precedent for high levels of political activity among youth that has not totally dissipated during the 1970s and 1980s.

Like intergenerational conflict, intragenerational conflict has been global in scope and has increased over time. During each of the periods of heightened youth movement activity, youthful political groups have formed which acted in opposition to each other—representing proactive-reactive generation units. To date, there have been at least 40 pairs of proactive and reactive generation units identified over the four historical-generational periods. Due to space limitations, a full description and discussion of these opposition youth groups is not possible (for further information on the topic, see Braungart, 1982, 1984).

Historical generations represent a rhythmic recurrence of youth movement activity. During so-called cumulative periods in world time, historical forces influence and interact with the aging process in established or conventional ways. New age cohorts are absorbed into existing social institutions on a routine basis and with the usual amount of difficulty and success. During cumulative periods in world time, adult society dominates the general direction of historical development and change, the socialization process of the younger age groups, and the type of politics prevailing at the time.

However, when youth cohorts experience the same historical location as they come of age and perceive inconsistencies in the adult world, they may mobilize to challenge adult hegemony in the form of intergenerational and intragenerational conflict. This is what occurred during the Young Europe, Post-Victorian, Great Depression, and 1960s Historical Generations. See Figure 3. When generations are both influenced by national and international forces through their conscious exposure to historically conditioned structures, processes, and events, and they organize and exert their collective will (whether cultural or political) on existing institutional forms to bring about radical political change, they become historical generations, thereby representing eliminating periods in world time. During eliminating periods, youth movements or historical generations dominate

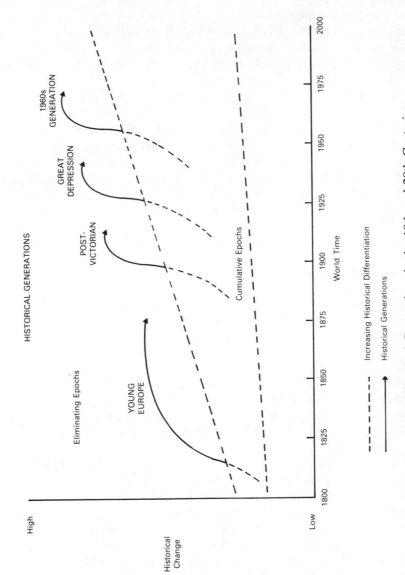

Figure 3. Major Historical Generations in the 19th and 20th Centuries

133

or significantly influence the structure and form of social change, the socialization process, and the style of politics expressed at the time.

During cumulative periods, age cohorts come and go like the ebb and tide of great seas—on a regular and relatively predictable basis. These periods in world time are represented by recurring biological rhythms of birth, aging, and death. However, when historical generations emerge to unleash their destabilizing force and energy on society, they take on the appearance of a tidal wave in the course of world time, breaking through the crust of historical continuity and change and offering a radical transformation and regeneration of the social order.

While we outlined the general pattern of youth movement activity that arose during four periods in history, briefly identified the growth of youth movements throughout the world, and found that youth movements resulted from a combination of historical and generational forces, the question remains: how consistent is the historical-generational model over time? That is, are the historical and generational conditions associated with heightened youth movement activity similar over world time, or did each historical generation arise out of a different set of historical and generational circumstances?

From the historical approach or perspective, it appears that there were similarities in the social and political conditions giving rise to youth movement activity. One common demographic feature was an increase in the youth population ages 16–25 over each of the four historical-generation periods. Higher education was expanded dramatically with most of the participants in youth movements coming from the ranks of university-registered students. Each of the historical generations was a time when large numbers of young people came of age personally and politically and reacted strongly to the conditions of their society. Yet, although many of these young people represented intellectual elites, they were frequently economic nonelites. Not absorbed into adult society—either because of high mobility, educational status, unemployment, or age—the status of youth in the society-at-large was highly tenuous or marginal. This marginality appeared to be a universal characteristic associated with the rise of youth movements.

A second consistent pattern during modern world time is the political drive for nationalism, self-determination, and citizenship, which was a key factor for each historical generation. Nationalism and the desire for freedom and equality have been powerful forces for both mobilization and disruption, particularly by the young. The quest for self-determination in the earliest youth movements centered around the issue of national unification. However, in more recent times there have been a growing number of nationalist-separatist movements based on ethnic rather than political identification.

Third, it appears that during times of great wars, youth movement activity was negligible, but in the periods between wars, youth movements increased. War was also likely to be an issue in the rebellions of youth, either because they were disheartened by the parent generation's failure at war, discontented with the treaties of war, or did not wish to go to war.

A fourth consistent theme over the four periods is the rise of ideological and utopian pursuits, with young people committing themselves to political "isms" such as socialism, communism, or fascism. In general, most historical generations represented a drift to the political left, such as in the Young Europe, Post-Victorian, and 1960s Generation. Yet, in the 1930s in Europe, the political movement among youth was to the right. This right-wing swing, however, took form partly in opposition to the growing left-wing movements following the Bolshevik revolution and among youth who were reacting to unstable political and economic conditions.

While a number of similarities in social and political conditions were exhibited, the economic and cultural factors associated with youth movement activity were less consistent across world time. The economic issue was a complex one. The unemployment theme was one of the major issues of contention for the 1930s Depression Generation, particularly in Europe and the United States, although youth unemployment also was relatively high during the Young Europe and Post-Victorian eras. More often than not, however, over the past 150 years, young people have taken to the streets and mobilized over political issues, such as nationalism and wars, rather than purely economic concerns.

Cultural forces played an increasing role in the rise of youth movements for several reasons. On the one hand, cultural traditions were precipitating factors at times when young people reacted strongly against the dominant bourgeois values of their parents and created their own self-conscious countercultural movements, as in the Young Europe, Post-Victorian, and 1960s Generations. But modern mass culture appeared to be a problem related to youth movements primarily in Europe, Japan, and the United States. Throughout the rest of the world, the dominant issues on the minds of youth were political or social reform and nationalism, not cultural problems per se. On the other hand, culture gained salience relative to other institutional factors in relation to youth movements. The rise in communications technology in particular facilitated the spread and homogenization of mass political culture on a global scale. One of the effects was a worldwide diffusion of the ideals of national self-determination and citizenship, as well as social movement tactics and strategies. This cultural dimension in historical change appears to be gaining momentum, greatly facilitating the growth and spread of youth movements.

In examining each of the four periods of heightened youth movement activity, it became apparent that while there were a number of similarities and some differences in the pattern of historical factors related to youth movements, a common feature of all four periods was the theme of generational conflict. In each case, the younger generation deauthorized the older generation over such issues as defeat in war, colonialism, and lack of economic and political opportunities. At the same time, and perhaps more importantly they authorized their own youthful generation to fight for nationalism, citizenship, or political ideology. In specific areas of the world and during certain times in history, the younger generation also reacted against the stagnant, materialistic culture of the adult generation and created their own spontaneous, more irrational counterculture. The generations have been at odds too over the highly proximal issues of university reform and going to war. The issues of deauthorization and authorization varied, but the generational conflict between the young and their elders appeared to be a constant factor associated with the rise of historical generations and youth movements.

Strong support appears to exist for the argument that mobilization of the young occurs in the form of intergenerational conflict. When the youth generation comes into contact with a disappointing set of historical circumstances which they see as having been created by the older generation, they may take it upon themselves to organize for change. Mobilization appears to take form through a process of the deauthorization of the adult generation and an authorization of the younger generation to work actively to change the course of human history. During times when intergenerational conflict occurs, we can also expect to see the formation of opposing political groups within the younger generation, or intragenerational conflict among groups who disagree and compete openly over the definition and control of reality. These dynamic processes represent important components of the historical-generational theory.

V. CONCLUSION

In many ways this study reflects the struggle in political sociology with the ghosts of Karl Marx and Max Weber. The historical-generational theory represents a compromise between these two positions, although the results of this study appear more supportive of Weber than of Marx. First of all, the concept of historical generations appears to fit Marx's paradigm of revolutionary change, where objective class position is transformed into subjective class consciousness, which culminates in social movements. This logic pertains to historical-generational theory as well. In the present study, it is not class but age-status position that becomes transformed into generational or age consciousness which precedes youth movement activity. Historical generations as revolutionary forces are not the result of economic determinism, as Marx suggested. In fact, economics is not a consistent condition for the rise of historical generations over time. Out of the four historical generations that have emerged over the last 150 years, the economic factor only accounted for massive youth movement activity during the Great Depression Generation.

. More important than economic struggles are the political struggles that have plagued the world, particularly over the last 200 years with the rise of the modern nation-state. Marx neglected the importance of political conflict; to him, the state was just an arena in which economic conflict took place. This does not appear to be the case with the rise of youth movements. Politics, more particularly nationalism and self-determination, is a consistent theme in all four historical-generation periods. This political theme was the centerpiece for the writings of Max Weber, Otto Hintze, and Louis Snyder. Weber emphasized the importance of political conflict over economic conflict in world change; Hintze saw the nation-state as the one great international process among world-historical societies; and Snyder documented the shift away from macronationalism toward the more recent trend of micronationalism.

Aside from politics, another major factor explaining the spread of youth movements is the rise of global political culture. New cultural ideals and culturally transmitted role models have become rapidly diffused throughout the world today, made possible by the revolution in communications technology. Population explosions, increased global consciousness, and rising expectations explain the recent trends in youth movement activity. The new international political culture provides a fertile setting for fermenting historical and generational forces which are waiting for the right opportunity to unite and once again work their will on world time.

ACKNOWLEDGMENTS

This is a revised version of a paper presented at the Meetings of the World Congress of Sociology, Mexico City, August, 1982. I wish to express my thanks to Margaret Braungart for her helpful comments and suggestions.

REFERENCES

Adelson, Joseph
   1975   "The development of ideology in adolescence." Pp. 63–78 in S. E. Dragastin and Glen H. Elder, Jr. (eds.), Adolescence in the Life Cycle. New York: Wiley.
Altbach, Philip G.
   1974   Student Politics in America: A Historical Analysis. New York: McGraw-Hill.
Backman, Earl and David J. Finlay
   1973   "Student protest: a cross national study." Youth and Society 5:3–46.
Bakke, E. Wight and Mary S. Bakke
   1971   Campus Challenge: Student Activism in Perspective. Hamden, CT: Archon Books.
Bengtson, V. L. and N. E. Cutler
   1976   "Generations and intergenerational relations: perspectives on age groups and social change." Pp. 130–159 in R. H. Binstock and E. Shanas (eds.), Handbook of Aging and the Social Sciences. New York: Van Nostrand Reinhold.
Bettelheim, Bruno
   1963   "The problem of generations." Pp. 64–92 in E. H. Erikson (ed.), Youth: Change and Challenge. New York: Basic Books.

Braungart, Richard G.
   1974   "The sociology of generations and student politics: a comparison of the functionalist and generational unit models." Journal of Social Issues 30:31–54.
   1976   "College and noncollege youth politics in 1972: an application of Mannheim's generation unit model." Journal of Youth and Adolescence 5:325–347.
   1979a "Family Status, Socialization and Student Politics." Ann Arbor, MI: University Microfilms International.
   1979b "The utopian and ideological styles of student political activists." Paper presented at the annual meetings of the International Society of Political Psychology, Washington, D.C.
   1980   "Youth movements." Pp. 560–597 in J. Adelson (ed.), Handbook of Adolescent Psychology. New York: Wiley.
   1982   "Historical generations and generation units: a global pattern of youth movements." Paper presented at the annual meetings of the Social Science History Association, Bloomington, IN: Indiana University.
   1984   "Historical and generational patterns of youth movements: a global perspective." Forthcoming in R. F. Tomasson (ed.), Comparative Social Research, Vol. 7. Greenwich, CT: JAI Press.
Braungart, Richard G. and Margaret M. Braungart
   1980   "Political career patterns of radical activists in the 1960s and the 1970s: some historical comparisons." Sociological Focus 13:237–254.
Brax, Ralph S.
   1981   The First Student Movement. Port Washington, NY: Kennikat Press.
Cowdry, R., K. Keniston and S. Cabin
   1970   "The war and military obligations: private attitudes and public action." Journal of Personality 38:525–549.
Crittenden, John
   1962   "Aging and party affiliation." Public Opinion Quarterly 26:648–657.
DeConde, Alexander (ed.)
   1971   Student Activism: Town and Gown in Historical Perspective. New York: Scribner's.
Demerath, N. J., G. Marwell and M. T. Aiken
   1971   Dynamics of Idealism. San Francisco: Jossey-Bass.
Draper, Hal
   1967   "The student movement of the thirties: a political history." Pp. 151–189 in R. J. Simon (ed.), As We Saw the Thirties. Urbana: University of Illinois Press.
Duncan, Martha
   1980   "Radical activism and the defense against despair." Sociological Focus 13:255–263.
Eckstein, Harry
   1976   "A theory of stable democracy." Pp. 142–151 in R. G. Braungart (ed.), Society and Politics. Englewood Cliffs, NJ: Prentice-Hall.
Eisenstadt, S. N.
   1963   "Archetypal patterns of youth." Pp. 24–42 in E. H. Erikson (ed.), Youth: Change and Challenge. New York: Basic Books.
   1978   Revolution and the Transformation of Societies. New York: Free Press.
Elder, Glen H., Jr.
   1980   "Adolescence in historical perspective." Pp. 3–46 in J. Adelson (ed.) Handbook of Adolescent Psychology. New York: Wiley.
Emmerson, Donald K. (ed.)
   1968   Students and Politics in Developing Nations. New York: Praeger.
Erikson, Erik H.
   1968   Identity: Youth and Crisis. New York: Norton.
Esler, Anthony
   1971   Bombs Beards and Barricades: 150 Years of Youth in Revolt. New York: Stein and Day.

1974   The Youth Revolution. (ed.) Lexington, MA: D. C. Heath.

1979   Generational Studies: A Basic Bibliography. Copyrighted, unpublished.

Etzioni, Amitai

1968   The Active Society. New York: Free Press.

Fendrich, James M.

1974   "Activists ten years later: a test of generational unit continuity." Journal of Social Issues 30:95–118.

Feuer, Lewis S.

1969   The Conflict of Generations. New York: Basic Books.

Flacks, Richard

1971   Youth and Social Change. Chicago: Rand McNally.

Gallatin, Judith

1980   "Political thinking in adolescence." Pp. 344–382 in J. Adelson (ed.), Handbook of Adolescent Psychology. New York: Wiley.

Gillis, John R.

1974   Youth and History. New York: Academic Press.

Glenn, Norval D.

1974   "Aging and conservatism." Annals of the American Academy of Political and Social Science 415:176–186.

Greer, Scott

1979   "Discontinuities and fragmentation in societal growth." Pp. 308–316 in A. H. Hawley (ed.), Societal Growth. New York: Free Press.

Gurr, Ted Robert

1970   Why Men Rebel. Princeton, NJ: Princeton University Press.

Gusfield, Joseph

1979   "The modernity of social movements: public roles and private parts." Pp. 290–307 in A. H. Hawley (ed.), Societal Growth. New York: Free Press.

Haan, Norma

1971   "Moral redefinition in families as a critical aspect of the generation gap." Youth and Society 2:259–283.

Hall, G. Stanley

1904   Adolescence. New York: Appleton.

Hamilton, Richard F. and James Wright

1975   New Directions in Political Sociology. Indianapolis: Bobbs-Merrill.

Heberle, Rudolph

1951   Social Movements. New York: Appleton-Century-Crofts.

Hendin, Herbert

1975   The Age of Sensation. New York: W. W. Norton.

Hudson, R. B. and R. H. Binstock

1976   "Political systems and aging." Pp. 369–400 in R. H. Binstock and E. Shanas (eds.), Handbook of Aging and the Social Sciences. New York: Van Nostrand Reinhold.

Hunt, John P.

1982   "Political behavior, political alientation, and the sociology of generations." Sociological Focus 15:93–106.

Inglehart, Ronald

1977   The Silent Revolution. Princeton, NJ: Princeton University Press.

Kearney, Robert N.

1980   "Youth protest in the politics of Sri Lanka." Sociological Focus 13:293–313.

Keniston, Kenneth

1968   Young Radicals. New York: Harcourt Brace and World.

Klineberg, Otto, Marisa Zavalloni, Christiane Louis-Guerin and Jeanne BenBrika

1979   Students, Values, and Politics: A Cross-cultural Comparison. New York: Free Press.

Kornhauser, William
1959   The Politics of Mass Society. Glencoe, IL: Free Press.
Laqueur, Walter
1962   Young Germany: A History of the German Youth Movement. New York: Basic Books.
1969   "Student revolts." Commentary 47:33–41.
Larsen, S. U., B. Hagtvet and J. P. Myklebust (eds.)
1981   Who Were the Fascists: Social Roots of European Fascism. Bergen: Universitetsforlaget.
Lauer, Robert H.
1977   Perspectives on Social Change. Boston: Allyn and Bacon.
Liebman, Arthur, Kenneth N. Walker and Myron Glazer
1972   Latin America University Students: A Six Nation Study. Cambridge: Harvard University Press.
Lipset, Seymour M. (ed.)
1967   Student Politics. New York: Basic Books.
Lipset, Seymour M. and Philip G. Altbach (eds.)
1969   Students in Revolt. Boston: Houghton Mifflin.
Loewenberg, Peter
1974   "A psychohistorical approach: the Nazi generation." Pp. 82–105 in A. Esler (ed.), The Youth Revolution. Lexington, MA: D. C. Heath.
Mannheim, Karl
1952   Essays on the Sociology of Knowledge. London: Routledge and Kegan Paul.
McJeon, Richard (ed.)
1941   The Basic Works of Aristotle. New York: Random House.
Meyer, John M. and Richard Rubinson
1972   "Structural determinants of student political activity: a comparative interpretation." Sociology of Education 45:23–46.
Mitchell, B. R.
1976   European Historical Statistics 1750–1970. New York: Columbia University Press.
Moller, Herbert
1972   "Youth as a force in the modern world." Pp. 215–237 in P. K. Manning and M. Truzzi (eds.), Youth and Sociology. Englewood Cliffs, N.J.: Prentice-Hall.
Murphy, H. B. M.
1974   "Mass youth protest movements in Asia and the West: their common characteristics and psychiatric significance." Pp. 275–296 in W. Lebra (ed.), Youth Socialization and Mental Health. Honolulu: University Press of Hawaii.
Muuss, Rolf E.
1968   Theories of Adolescence, Second Edition. New York: Random House.
Nash, Laura L.
1978   "Concepts of existence: Greek origins of generational thought." Daedalus 107:1–21.
Nelkin, Dorothy and Michael Pollak
1981   The Atom Besieged: Extraparliamentary Dissent in France and Germany. Cambridge: MIT Press.
Ortega y Gasset, Jose
1961   The Modern Theme. New York: Harper and Row.
1962   Man and Crisis. New York: W. W. Norton.
1974   "The importance of generationhood." Pp. 3–6 in A. Esler (ed.), The Youth Revolution. Lexington, MA: D. C. Heath.
Oberschall, Anthony
1973   Social Conflict and Social Movements. Englewood Cliffs, NJ: Prentice-Hall.
Reid, Robert H.
1981   "Thousands protest missiles." Syracuse Herald-American, October 11:A12.
Rejai, Mostafa and Kay Phillips
1979   Leaders of Revolution. Beverly Hills, CA: Sage.

Rintala, Marvin
   1974   "Generations in politics." Pp. 15–20 in A. Esler (ed.), The Youth Revolution. Lexington,
       MA: D. C. Heath.
Schorske, Carl E.
   1978   "Generational tension and cultural change: reflections on the case of Vienna." Daedalus
       107:111–122.
Simirenko, Alex
   1966   "Mannheim's generational analysis and acculturation." British Journal of Sociology
       17:292–299.
Simon, Rita J. (ed.)
   1967   As We Saw the Thirties. Urbana, IL: University of Illinois Press.
Smelser, Neil J.
   1963   Theory of Collective Behavior. New York: Free Press.
   1968   Essays in Sociological Explanation. Englewood Cliffs, NJ: Prentice-Hall.
Snyder, Louis L.
   1982   Global Mini-Nationalisms. Westport, CT.: Greenwood Press.
Starr, Jerold M.
   1974   "The peace and love generation." Journal of Social Issues 30:73–106.
Statera, Gianni
   1975   Death of a Utopia. New York: Oxford University Press.
Szyliowicz, Joseph S.
   1972   A Political Analysis of Student Activism: The Turkish Case. Beverly Hills, CA: Sage.
Tilly, Charles
   1975   "Revolution and collective violence." Pp. 483–555 in F. I. Greenstein and N. W. Polsby
       (eds.), Handbook of Political Science, Vol. 3. Reading, MA: Addison-Wesley.
Tilly, Charles, Louise Tilly and Richard Tilly
   1975   The Rebellious Century, 1830–1930. Cambridge: Harvard University Press.
United Nations
   1981   International Youth Year: Participation, Development, Peace. New York: United Nations
       Publications.
Walker, Kenneth N.
   1967   "A comparison of the university reform movements in Argentina and Colombia." Pp.
       293–317 in S. M. Lipset (ed.), Student Politics. New York: Basic Books.
Wallbank, T. Walter and Alastair M. Taylor
   1961   Civilization: Past and Present, Vol. 2, Fourth Edition. Chicago: Scott Foresman.
Weinberg, Ian and Kenneth N. Walker
   1969   "Student politics and political systems: toward a typology." American Journal of So-
       ciology 75:77–96.
Westby, David L.
   1976   The Clouded Vision: The Student Movement in the United States in the 1960s. Lewisburg,
       PA.: Bucknell University Press.
Westby, David L. and Richard G. Braungart
   1966   "Class and politics in the family backgrounds of student political activists." American
       Sociological Review 31:690–692.
Wohl, Robert
   1979   The Generation of 1914. Cambridge: Cambridge University Press.
Zald, Mayer N. and John D. McCarthy (eds.)
   1979   The Dynamics of Social Movements. Cambridge: Winthrop.
Zeitlin, Maurice
   1966   "Political generations in the Cuban working class." American Journal of Sociology
       71:493–508.

TAYLORED WORK GROUPS:
MANAGERIAL RECOLLECTIVIZATION AND CLASS CONFLICT IN THE WORKPLACE

Gerard J. Grzyb

The past decade was marked by an explosion of managerial and scholarly interest in various "work humanization" proposals. A concern with work groups that are established through managerial initiatives has been a central feature of most of these proposals, and the importance of such groups has been suggested in a broad range of literature in recent years. For example, in the influential *Work in America* report (1973), there is a list of work humanization case studies in which terms like "autonomous work groups" or "teams" frequently appear in the descriptions of the particular techniques involved. Similarly, Jenkins (1974:170) asserts that those theorists and practitioners who have been most successful in harmonizing individual and organizational goals (a major aim of work humanization) are those whose ideas and actions have been concentrated upon work groups. In an extensive review of work redesign studies conducted by Porras and Berg (1978), the construction of work teams was found to be the single most common feature among the studies. Finally, in a special report on "the new industrial relations" presented by *Business Week* (1981), every example of the

Research in Social Movements, Conflict and Change, Vol. 6, pages 143–166.
Copyright © 1984 by JAI Press Inc.
All rights of reproduction in any form reserved.
ISBN: 0-89232-311-6

techniques said to increase worker involvement in organizations includes some type of work group.

The advocates of managerially-constructed work groups typically link their proposals to concerns over worker productivity and the need for American industry to improve its competitive position in the international market. Discussions of the implications of their proposals for class relationships in the workplace are usually absent. A central contention of this essay, however, is that those proposals represent attempts by management not only to boost productivity, but also to erect new structures of control over the workforce and the labor process without by any means abandoning older methods for achieving such domination. The proposals are also clearly shaped by worker responses to the older methods. As such, work humanization or redesign efforts centered on the managerial creation of work groups constitute a relatively new managerial thrust in the dialectic of class confrontation in the workplace, with as yet largely-unexplored implications for the future of that conflict. Workers, union officials, and even managers themselves still openly wonder about both short- and long-term effects.[1]

The aim of this essay is to provide a framework within which to analyze both general theories and specific examples of the construction of work groups by managers, a phenomenon that has been termed "managerial recollectivization" (Grzyb, 1981). I will begin with a consideration of the antecedent decollectivization of the workplace in order to provide something of a context for an exploration of recollectivization. The context will be completed through a review of the reasons for heightened managerial interest in recollectivization at this point in history. A description and analysis of four major approaches to managerial recollectivization will follow. The article concludes with a discussion that emphasizes the similarities among the approaches and considers the range of likely worker responses.

I.   THE DECOLLECTIVIZATION OF THE WORKPLACE

Informal work groups are the most powerful means employed by workers to demand and exercise some control over their daily lives on the job. The products of such groups, as Weir (1973, 1974) discovered, are work cultures that consist of evolving sets of responses to the problems of working life. With these cultures, workers have been able to develop and enforce some of their own conceptions of the proper organization and procedures of work.[2]

Managers have historically had an ambivalent, but generally hostile, orientation towards informal work groups. From the firmly-established standpoint of Taylorism, with its assumption of an inherent manager/worker conflict of interests, such groups and their cultures are thought to be normally used to resist managerial control of work and workers (i.e., the worker conceptions mentioned previously are assumed to run counter to those espoused by management). However, the legendary Hawthorne experiments seemed to show that with careful interventions, management can use work groups to further managerial interests.

While managerial theorists have paid much attention to the supposed lessons of Hawthorne, it is fair to say that in the actual history of modern managerial practice worker collectivities have been seen as problems to overcome. A diverse number of observers (those cited include Marxists, human relationists, and even a practicing line manager) have concluded that the workplace has been progessively decollectivized in the modern era. Informal work groups have been destroyed, they say, through the installation of modern (or "automated," or "rationalized") technology (Seligman, 1966:370; Friedmann, 1964:43; Blumberg, 1973:60ff; Ehrenreich and Ehrenreich, 1976:13; Battersby, 1976). The most common explanations offered are that technology limits or even eliminates the possibilities for interaction among workers during the course of their work, and that it reduces or obviates the need for cooperation among workers during the work performance.

As I have argued elsewhere, the decollectivizing effect of modern technology is also accounted for by its deskilling effect (Grzyb, 1981). A technology that demands skill is one that calls for active and creative interventions from workers who cope with the uncertainties or variable elements of the work process. Such a process presents workers with an array of problems to be solved—problems that may change in character from day to day or even minute to minute, and that may never have "one best solution." Consequently, the exercise of skill virtually impels workers to put their heads together in informal work groups to search for common solutions to common problems.

What the exercise of skill provides, then, is a powerful work-based motive for workers to develop the bonds with one another that will facilitate the collective maintenance and refinement of skill. A technology that did not require as much skill would provide that much less of a motive. Other problems that might benefit from collective solution-seeking are likely to remain (e.g., overbearing supervision, unsafe working conditions), but a major source of problems that inspire horizontal ties will have been diminished. While Kusterer (1978) is certainly correct that few if any jobs have been totally deskilled, even a relative deskilling will likely contribute to a reduction in group cohesiveness, especially if the other decollectivizing aspects of modern technology mentioned earlier are also involved. The uses of modern technology do, of course, lead to the creation of some highly-skilled jobs in which workers are drawn into informal groups and networks. Nevertheless, there is a fairly strong consensus among most observers that the number of such jobs is small in comparison with the number of new, lower-skilled jobs involving "high tech." The available evidence clearly suggests that the design and implementation of modern technology has had, on the average, a substantial decollectivizing effect.

Questions of managerial choice and intentionality in the design and implementation of technology do not yet have firm answers, although the orthodoxy of technological determinism is clearly under attack. Some recent analyses (e.g., Marglin, 1974; Braverman, 1974) suggest that managers have tended to choose those technologies that fragment work and the workforce, thus facilitating the development of direct managerial control of the labor process. Indeed, one of the approaches to recollectivization discussed at length in this essay (the sociotechnical approach) is founded on the notion that management incorporates *social* system design choices into the designs of technical systems of production. Adherents argue that these choices affecting the existence of work groups and networks must be conscientiously made if efficiency and productivity are to be maximized. But whether or not managers have consciously sought to decollectivize the workplace, there is no earlier record of their anxiety over that result of their actions. Even if decollectivization was unintended, it was not undesired.

It has not been the aim here to argue that decollectivization can be accounted for entirely in terms of the effects of technology, but only to underscore one of the ways in which technological innovation has had such a result. One can readily think of a number of other managerial choices that may have furthered decollectivization (e.g., piecework payment schemes), as well as decollectivizing factors beyond managerial control. Neither will I claim that managerial recollectivization is only undertaken in response to the effects of decollectivization. In some instances, recollectivization might well be intended to supplant existing informal work groups. Nonetheless, one cannot be familiar with a range of American workplaces and yet claim that decollectivization is the exception rather than the rule.

II.   THE MOTIVES FOR MANAGERIAL RECOLLECTIVIZATION

If the workplace has been decollectivized, and if that has even been in substantial part the conscious intention of managers, why would American managers even consider recollectivization? Managerial domination of the work process in the United States, after all, is arguably more firmly established than in many other capitalist nations. And why *now,* given that proponents of recollectivization stretch all the way back to Elton Mayo, without any seeming to have had a long-lasting impact? The answers are to be found in the changing economic situation of American capitalism, the emergence of a different set of attitudes toward work and leisure among some workers, the characteristics of modern technology, the contradictions of traditional managerial theory and practice, and the continuing development of social engineering techniques for the design and control of work groups. In short, the answers come from both the objective realm of material production and distribution, and the subjective realm of ideas.

Among the factors just mentioned, changing economic conditions are by far the most important. Two changes seem to be of primary significance. The first is that in recent years many American firms have found their world market dominance undercut by foreign competition. As a result, the trade position of the U.S. has been seriously weakened, and the country has become a net importer of many finished goods (Blumberg, 1980). Analyses of why the U.S. has become uncompetitive typically cite evidence of a relatively low productivity growth rate among American workers, and stress that improved productivity is essential for the recovery of American industry.

The second economic change is that the logic of capitalist accumulation no longer provides strong encouragement for managers to invest in expensive productivity-boosting technology (Goldman and Van Houten, 1980; Blumberg, 1980). Mergers and expanded foreign operations are increasingly seen as better uses of capital in the pursuit of more capital. While these uses may not serve the purpose of long-term growth as well as new investments in technology might, they also limit the ability of U.S. industry to increase productivity through the purchase of new technologies. The result, in any case, is a decline in the rate of technology-based productivity growth that can only be countered by inducing workers to increase their own productivity.

The American worker and the composition of the workforce have also changed (Yankelovich, 1979), in ways that challenge the deskilling and decollectivizing thrusts of modern management. Among the salient characteristics are a higher level of education, an increased leisure/consumption orientation, a greater demand for meaningful and challenging work, and a lower average age. In dealing with this changed workforce, managers found themselves facing workers who demanded jobs that made use of their education, and jobs that were at least as interesting as their leisure (how many modern jobs lack the challenge and involvement of an ordinary video game?).

Certain characteristics of modern technology serve as important motives for recollectivization. The two most important characteristics mentioned in this context are a technological necessity for cooperation among workers and a technological requirement for the development of highly specialized work behaviors. The latter is typically associated with a corresponding decrease in managerial knowledge of the specific job activities of the managed. At first glance, the two characteristics seem to contradict earlier assertions about the decollectivizing effects of modern technology. The possibility raised here, however, is that while modern technology may have been used to enforce decollectivization, maximum efficiency will not be achieved with that technology unless at least a partial recollectivization takes place. That is to say, the very technology which is used to destroy informal work groups might also require some kind of work groups for its successful operation. This possibility is given serious consideration by some of the recollectivization proponents, and their reasoning will be outlined in the discussion of their respective approaches in this essay.

There are contradictions in established managerial theory and practice, and they have become notably apparent as managers sought to wring more productivity from their employees in recent years. The first stems from the capitalist assault on the populist view of labor, and its displacement by a managerial view in the early decades of this century. In this latter view, labor is just another production factor, and not a very important one at that. This view constitutes an attack on "the workingman's perception of his self-worth" (Zimbalist, 1975:44) and, as such, is hardly likely to heighten a worker's commitment to work as an activity in which personal fulfillment can be found.

At the level of practice, Zimbalist (1975:40) notes that shortly after F. W. Taylor's death in 1915, efficiency experts began to realize that Taylorist rationalization led to a loss of managerially-needed worker creativity. The decollectivization of the workplace has had the same kind of effect. Now virtually every proponent of recollectivization argues that the "right kind" of work group would yield both the creative solutions to work process problems and the higher productivity sometimes associated with cohesive work groups. In short, managers were urged to destroy work groups because their creativity in solving workplace problems and their ability to enforce a stable level of output were often turned against managerial interests, but managers are now told that they need to channel rather than destroy groups because they need that very same creativity and ability in order to reestablish the international competitive position of American industry. The irony seems obvious.

The final factor in an explanation of increased managerial interest in recollectivization is the continuing development of theory and practice for the creation of managerially-dominated work groups. This decades-long development is usually traced back to the Hawthorne experiments and the prescriptions of Elton Mayo, but the spirit of recollectivization is present in Durkheim's proposals for reducing the disintegrative effects of the modern division of labor. Between Mayo and today's recollectivization theorists, one finds antecedents of recent practice in the Scanlon plans and the Work Simplification movement of the World War II era (Fein, 1976:481f). Lewin's studies of group dynamics, and an oft-cited experiment wherein worker participation was used by management to gain acceptance of a new piecerate (Coch and French, 1948), were also influential developments in that period.

The approaches to recollectivization that will be examined in this article encompass the major modern developments in recollectivization theory and practice. Perhaps the most noteworthy development has been the Japanese version of recollectivization, especially as interpreted by William Ouchi for American managers. Japan's success in the world market has been connected, at least in the minds of many American practitioners, to its extensive use of small groups in the workplace. Regardless of the validity of that connection, it currently provides a noticeable stimulus for recollectivization in America.

It is apparent, therefore, that changing economic conditions, plus changes in technology and in the workforce, brought about by American capitalist development after World War II, have served to make the contradictions of decollectivization quite visible in the past quarter-century or so. An existing body of theory and research has been further refined in an attempt to resolve the contradictions.

III. THE MODERN THEORY AND PRACTICE OF RECOLLECTIVIZATION

Four approaches to recollectivization have received the bulk of the attention in managerial journals and textbooks: (1) the System 4 approach of Rensis Likert; (2) the sociotechnical systems approach advanced by members of the Tavistock Institute and others; (3) the Japanese approach, epitomized by Quality Control Circles; and (4) the Theory Z modification of the Japanese approach, espoused by William Ouchi. In the following section, each of these approaches will be examined in some detail.

A. System 4

Rensis Likert presented the System 4 theory of recollectivization in two classic, and widely used, management textbooks: *New Patterns of Management* (1961) and *The Human Organization* (1967). Through these texts alone, System 4 is known to countless thousands of organizational theorists and practicing managers.

In justifying his approach, Likert mentions most of the factors cited in the preceding section: a new system of management is needed because of worldwide competition, changing worker values, increased worker educational levels, concerns about workers' mental health and growth, the apparent disutility of older theories, and the requirement of new technologies for specialized worker behaviors that are not well-known to managers (1961:1f). Likert also observes that workers have always made decisions about their work, but sometimes did so without giving primacy to organizational objectives or knowing all the "facts" (1961:211f). Furthermore, the competition that has been engendered among workers by older systems of management has discouraged workers from helping or goading each other into raising productivity (1967:74). While Likert does not directly discuss decollectivization, his stress on competition among workers and on the failures of older management systems (i.e., scientific management) seem to point in a similar direction.

Likert's solution consists of an elaborate recollectivization of the entire work organization, for he finds "restriction and waste" at all organizational levels (1961:29). His review of the literature finds a "low positive" relationship between high work group cohesiveness and pride in collective producing ability on the one hand, and high productivity on the other (1961:29). Higher productivity in groups characterized by loyalty and pride is said to result from greater cooperation, more efficient work-sharing, and lower absenteeism. With these claims in hand, Likert proposes that all employees be made members of small work groups.

One of the primary features of Likert's groups is that they mix personal contact among workers with an emphasis on maintaining and reinforcing existing hierarchies of authority. In each of the groups, one would find employees who share a particular function and hierarchical level in an organization, with their supervisor serving as the group leader. In turn, the supervisor would be a member of a group in which his or her supervisor was the group leader. Within such a structure, each group leader/supervisor is to play a "linking-pin" function by channeling influence and ideas both up and down the hierarchy.

The supervisor is charged with the task of making each group "highly effective" by utilizing a variety of group leadership techniques and by continuously applying "the principle of supportive relations." Among the techniques are: respecting subordinates' ideas, meeting frequently with the group, treating members as whole human beings, identifying with them as well as with the company, and giving group rather than individual assignments. The principle of supportive relations specifies that all experiences of life on the job should enhance each worker's "sense of personal worth and importance" (1961:103).

The supervisor also plays the key role in harmonizing individual goals and organizational objectives. This is to be done by using noneconomic motives such as status needs ("personal worth"), as well as economic motives, to establish high performance objectives (1961:36; 1967:52, 64). Likert's conviction that workers' economic and noneconomic needs are best served by boosting their output is strong—so strong that he argues that an absence of high performance objectives might mean that workers have not been able to exercise sufficient influence to get their needs met.

A similar argument underlies Likert's strongest statement regarding the possibility of groups turning their collective power against the organization. He notes that workers bring values and goals from nonwork groups into the workplace, and that these are likely to "reflect the constructive values and goals of their society" (1961:177). If the values and goals of work groups conflict with those societal values and goals, workers will seek to bring the former into line with the latter, and they will more readily accomplish this in "highly effective" work groups. For Likert, then, the solution to problems of collective restriction of output and the like is simply to maximize member influence in work groups. The causal chain can be summarized as follows: group-oriented supervision maximizes group effectiveness, which maximizes the influence of every individual member, which reduces the chances for deviant individuals with "bad"(i.e., short-term, selfish) goals to dominate the group.

While Likert seems to be claiming that his system of recollectivization maximizes societal democratic control of work organizations, high productivity is not to be simply left to processes of democratic influence in work groups. In his view, organizational members who share goals and confront the same facts—the "hard, objective realities" (1961:213)—will make the same decisions. If the "facts" are gathered and confronted in a group context, individuals will not be likely to push for purely self-interested solutions. Consequently, Likert stresses that organizational members should be taught how to apply and interpret measurement techniques. Then they will all see what must be done in a given situation, and the experience of hierarchy will fade as facts, rather than superiors, give orders.

What is perhaps most notable for the present discussion is that some of the central features of Likert's approach to recollectivization are not all that different from those of the more recently popular approaches. The aim of System 4 is to construct a multitude of overlapping groups in such a way that the hierarchical distribution of power is reinforced while the subjective experience of hierarchy is muted. The underlying assumption is classically Mayoist: groups are the most significant factor in accounting for behavior within organizations. If the power of informal groups to achieve goals opposed to those of management is to be broken once and for all, formal groups under subtle hierarchical control must be created to displace them. In effect, Likert's system seems to be a means of recollectivization under managerial control that has the intended effect of the decollectivization of worker-controlled groups where necessary. Likert also goes beyond specifying the *form* of work groups and their interrelationships. The collective fact-gathering he proposes constitutes an attempt to prescribe the *content* of group activity as well.

Nearly two decades after System 4 was introduced, Likert was still promoting the same ideas (International Management, 1979). The actual current impact of those ideas is in dispute. Despite earlier claims of considerable currency for his system (Bucklow, 1966), his basic formulation has been attacked by prominent theorists (Hall, 1982:311f; Tausky, 1978:51f; and esp. Perrow, 1979:114–128), and some studies have questioned the claimed effectiveness of the system (Tausky, 1978:52). Likert has recently advocated Management By Group Objectives (MBGO), a System 4-like attempt to develop group participation in objective-setting, to counter the negative impact of the interpersonal competition said to be engendered by Management By Objectives (MBO) schemes (Likert and Fisher, 1977). But Likert also has indicated that he is impressed by various experiments involving autonomous work groups, and seems increasingly convinced that groups need not be as hierarchically controlled and structured into the formal organization as he proposed in System 4. In consequence, he has recently spoken of System 5 (Reilly, 1978). But if System 5 is to be centered on autonomous work groups, it will only incorporate what adherents of the sociotechnical approach have been pushing for decades.

B.   Sociotechnical Systems

The central tenet of the sociotechnical approach to recollectivization is that all work takes place within both a technical system and a social system (Davis and Trist, 1974:247). While the two systems are analytically distinct, they are indissolubly wedded in actual work processes. The technical system consists of those things that are sometimes referred to as the "physical technology" of work (machines, raw materials, etc.). The social system consists of the spatial arrangement and social organization of workers in relation to the physical technology, or what is sometimes called the "social technology" of work.

The perceived problem said to call for sociotechnical recollectivization is the failure of managers to design the proper social system features into the technical system, "intentionally or . . . accidentally, either casually or as the result of some omission in planning" (Davis and Taylor, 1976:380). In the famous long-wall mining study (Trist and Bamforth, 1951), improper managerial choices in bringing in a new technology that deskilled miners led to decollectivization, which in turn led to a dramatic drop in productivity. Recollectivization, in the form of autonomous work groups, solved the problem.

Autonomous work groups have the following features: (1) each group is responsible for a whole task; (2) group members are multiskilled in relation to the task; (3) the group exercises discretion over the choice of work techniques, the sequential arrangement of task components, and the distribution of task responsibilities among group members; and (4) the group is rewarded and given performance feedback on a group basis (Cummings, 1978:625; Bucklow, 1966:68f; Davis and Taylor, 1976:402f). The unifying concept often used to characterize the situation of these groups is "responsible autonomy."

It is claimed that changes in worker values mean that social system considerations must be given attention even in the design of highly routinized work, lest workers "become even more unreliable than originally assumed" (Davis and Taylor, 1976:385), and that sociotechnical recollectivization is appropriate for all types of work (Davis and Trist, 1974). However, the recent emphasis in this approach has often been on workers employed in advanced technological processes, and changed technology is often seen as the most important reason for recollectivization from the sociotechnical standpoint.

Modern technology is said to make it difficult to impose external controls over work (e.g., written rules) because the relationship between worker actions and desired outputs is either unknown to managers, or hard to observe and decipher (Davis and Taylor, 1976:404). Given this dependence upon workers, managers must enhance workers' ability to "reduce variance from goal attainment" (Cummings, 1978:627). Managers can monitor the quality and quantity of outputs, but need to leave many of the details of actual work procedures to the discretion of workers in autonomous work groups.

One emphasis in the sociotechnical approach is on careful design and control of the new social system; the desired system will not occur automatically. Adherents argue that "the group structure . . . must be consciously installed if it is to succeed"[11] (Davis and Taylor, 1976:403). This involves such techniques as employing group facilitators trained in group dynamics, developing group-based financial incentives, providing feedback on group performance results, making group membership a matter of worker choice, minimizing the turnover of group members, and stabilizing groups through sufficient wage and job security (Cummings, 1978).

Where autonomous work groups are brought into being, the supervisor's role is no longer dominated by the requirements of directly supervising worker behavior. Instead, the supervisor is to function as one who maintains group boundaries (e.g., through external relations and supply functions), facilitates the development of group processes, and serves as a communications link to other parts of the organization (Davis and Taylor, 1976:399, 403; Cummings, 1978:631f).

With properly designed and supervised autonomous work groups, a certain causal sequence is expected to result. Autonomy yields high levels of worker commitment, which in turn enhances workers' desire to make the appropriate "nonprogrammable interventions" to "stochastic events." Such responses lead to a properly functioning production process, and that means that the economic objectives of the firm will be met (Davis and Taylor, 1976:389). Modern technology is characterized by its generation of stochastic events, and managers are dependent upon workers to deal with that work process uncertainty.

Sociotechnical thinkers also argue that the autonomy and commitment which yield maximum efficiency with modern technology are also just what is needed to meet the social and psychological needs of workers, especially as expressed in rising demands for meaning and satisfaction in work. Thus, they claim, both modern technology and the extraorganizational social milieu support the development of autonomous work groups (Davis and Taylor, 1976:405; Cummings, 1978:629). As for the possibility that groups might exercise their collective strength against their employers' goals, Cummings (1978:630) simply says that it will not happen if the social aspect of the sociotechnical system has been properly designed. Indeed, Davis and Trist (1974:257) speak of the possibility that effective design will lead to a unity of worker and manager interests in the minds of workers.

Some claims to the contrary (e.g., Bucklow, 1966:65), the sociotechnical approach, like System 4, involves less of an alteration in the actual distribution of power and control in the workplace than in the manner in which they are exercised. The real aim of the "primary work group reorganization" (Davis and Trist, 1974:248) advocated by sociotechnicalists is to incorporate the software of group processes into the hardware of production systems such that groups will function in a reliable manner in response to unpredictable events. This goal represents a response to the realization that insofar as modern technology requires some specialized or even skilled workers, managers are dependent upon those workers and had better find a way of controlling them and the informal work groups that they might otherwise form.

There is, however, one important difference between the sociotechnical approach and the others treated herein. The approach specifies much about the form of recollectivization, but prescribes comparatively less in terms of content. While the "reorganized" work groups are to be limited in their decision-making to some facets of the immediate work situation, not much is said about the ways in which the decisions will be made. The supervisory role also seems to be less central in these groups than it is in other recollectivization schemes. Perhaps more than other schemes, then, the sociotechnical approach requires a certain managerial trust that worker decisions about the immediate work process will support managerial objectives, and a belief that such decisions may strengthen or at least not erode management's control over the making of broader decisions.

While there have been a very few experiments involving autonomous work groups in America (e.g., the legendary Topeka dog-food plant experiment described in detail in *Work In America,* 1973), the sociotechnical approach has not found widespread acceptance in that country. Bucklow (1966:74) claims that this lack of acceptance has been because American managers are steeped in the ideology of scientific management. A hallmark of scientific management, of course, is the belief that workers are basically lazy and *not* to be trusted with even the smallest decisions concerning work process details (Zimbalist, 1975:36f). In contrast, says Ouchi (1981a), trust is at the heart of the Japanese work organization.

C.   Quality Control Circles

The Japanese now offer us the very model of a modern recollectivization effort, and the results seem quite impressive. The description of their system offered here draws heavily upon Cole's (1979) recent study, which appears to be more analytical then the somewhat idealized accounts offered by Ouchi (1981a) and others.

Recollectivization is extensive in Japan. Cole (1979:134) reports that some seventy percent of Japanese firms use some form of small group participation. Recollectivization was a response to many of the same conditions mentioned in other approaches (increased worker educational levels, changing worker values, increasingly sophisticated technology) plus a tight labor market (particularly in blue-collar jobs) that developed in the late 1960s and early 1970s, in part because of those conditions. According to Cole, the focus on "small-groupism" began in the early 1960s, and involved a blending of Western techniques with Japanese traditions.

The Quality Control Circle (QCC) is an example of such an amalgam, and it also epitomizes Japanese recollectivization. A QCC consists of a group of workers within a work unit who meet to find ways of improving the quality and quantity of production. Cole observes that while its Western originators intended it for use at the middle management level, it was a Japanese innovation to apply it at all organizational levels.

Several features serve to distinguish the QCC from other forms of recollectivization. Perhaps the most obvious is that QCC members are given training in statistical quality control methods to use in solving production problems (Yager, 1981:103; Werther, 1981:15). This restricts the activities of QCCs in one way, but in addition, Cole reports that (contrary to the claims of some Western commentators) managers in Japan do select many of the problem areas for QCC study. But in marked contrast to the common Western conviction that workers "hold back" their working knowledge for fear of having it turned against them, the Japanese assume that neither managers nor workers know the solutions or even all of the problems beforehand.

Other distinguishing features of the QCC include its voluntary nature (although Cole finds that managerial pressures to participate are not unknown), the fact that its members receive very little financial reward for their production improvement suggestions, and the fact that QCC meetings are often held outside of normal working hours. All of these features are supported by a strong worker identification with organizational goals, the source of which will be considered when Ouchi's Theory Z approach is considered. A final distinguishing characteristic is that QCC meetings are fairly infrequent; Cole reports that only 20% of the QCCs he surveyed met 3 or more times per month. This does not mean that work takes place in a decollectivized atmosphere, however, for both Cole's and Ouchi's descriptions show the Japanese workplace to be populated with a variety of work groups.

The role of the supervisor or foreman in the QCC is considerably more like that prescribed in other recollectivization schemes. The foreman receives intensive training in both the statistical techniques mentioned earlier and in leadership and group dynamics (Werther, 1981:18; Hutchins, 1981:30). He will either serve as the QCC leader (most often the case), or will be responsible for selecting a senior worker with leadership abilities for that position.[3] The purpose of these policies is to see to it that workers perceive their foremen or other QCC leaders as technically competent "natural leaders" (Nosow, 1981:20; Cole, 1979: 137f, 245). The effect is a diminution of the experience of hierarchical domination in group activities.

As with other recollectivization schemes, the ideology of QCC creation also includes the claim that workers will personally benefit from QCC activities. Benefits include the development of their leadership abilities, skills, satisfaction, motivation, and cooperative powers. QCC activity is also an area in which workers can attempt to demonstrate their supervisory potential.

The claims that the major benefits of QCCs for management are cost saving or improved productivity have been questioned. The seemingly small improvements made by workers through QCCs do add up to significant economic gains for their employers in some cases. Nonetheless, Cole argues that the "company success and its attribution, in part, to QC-circle activity becomes part of management ideology designed to legitimate management power" (1979:166). Another of his interesting observations, not found yet in most Western accounts, is that QCCs seem to require regular revitalization (e.g., through meetings with QCCs from other firms, membership rotation, etc.). Worker apathy is said to be a common problem, and when the novelty of a technique such as the QCC wears off, workers are more likely to see them "more as a policy imposed by management than as spontaneous worker-initiated behavior" (Cole, 1979:41). Some Japanese managers try to solve this problem by hurling a series of recollectivization schemes and other work humanization techniques at their workers in more or less regular succession. These efforts suggest that Japanese success may result in part from making the inherently temporary "Hawthorne effect" into a permanent phenomenon. It would appear that workers—even Japanese workers with their much-discussed social traditions of collectivism—cannot be permanently manipulated into active participation in recollectivization schemes.

Japanese managers, however, seem little worried that workers will turn the managerially-created groups against their designers. Management thoroughly dominates QCCs and similar groups. Managers set improvement suggestion quotas, restrict the range of group activities to production-improvement areas, control QCC training as well as job rotation and the career patterns of their members, enforce hierarchical control through the use of foremen or foremen-selected workers as group leaders, and constantly infuse the organization with the ideology of the identity of managerial and worker goals. In consequence, Cole notes that "many Japanese scholars . . . see QCCs as a device to break worker collective resistance and rebuild group solidarity on the basis of management goals" (1979:203).

QCCs do seem to represent the most successful attempt, from a managerial standpoint, to recollectivize the workplace without reintroducing managerial dependence on the autonomous functioning of informal work groups. The organizational hierarchy is *strengthened* rather than threatened by this "high penetration" of "primary-group relationships" (Cole, 1979:243). Perhaps this maintenance of hierarchical control accounts for the fact that the theory and practice of the QCC have spread much more rapidly in the U.S. than either System 4 or the sociotechnical approach ever did. Lockheed was the first American firm to introduce QCCs (in 1974), and there are now thousands of them in operation. In 1981, Honeywell led all other firms with its total of 251 functioning circles (Training and Development Journal, 1981). In contrast to the Japanese model, American QCCs typically meet on company time (for an hour per week or so), and receive significantly greater financial rewards for productivity improvement suggestions. A modification of Japanese efforts is also at the heart of Theory Z.

D. Theory Z

William G. Ouchi has espoused Theory Z, a mixture of Japanese and American managerial techniques and orientations, in a bestselling book (1981a). The underlying analysis and philosophy, however, are more apparent in a series of articles that appeared in leading journals of organizational theory (Ouchi, 1977, 1978, 1979, 1980, 1981b; Ouchi and Jaeger, 1978; Ouchi and Johnson, 1978; Ouchi and Price, 1978; Ouchi and Maguire, 1975; and Johnson and Ouchi, 1974). Ouchi is not so directly concerned with the details of recollectivized group structure and process as he is with the product of groups. For him, the critical product is the culture they produce. The control of that product and the process by which it is created is the aim of all recollectivization. The underlying assumption in all of the schemes reviewed herein is that properly-designed, and managerially-dominated, work groups will not produce an oppositional culture. In fact, their members may well be led to see managerial values and goals as identical to their own.

The erasure of the distinction between manager and worker goals, without substantively altering the former, is the Holy Grail of recollectivization. But Ouchi, noting that recollectivization has not produced consistent success, argues that the merger of goals must take place *before* new work groups are formed. He even suggests that "small groups are the results, rather than the cause, of organizational success" (Ouchi and Price, 1978:26). In other words, to prevent the emergence of an oppositional culture based on alternative worker goals, it is essential to make sure that workers do not have oppositional goals as they enter the recollectivized workplace. And that is to be accomplished through "cultural management" (Ouchi and Price, 1978:44).

Ouchi argues for the managerial control of culture in terms of both an organizational problem (Ouchi, 1980, 1979) and a societal problem (Ouchi and Jaeger, 1978; Ouchi and Johnson, 1978). The organizational problem, similar to that perceived by sociotechnical theorists, is that certain technologies make it difficult to assess an individual worker's contribution to production and to ensure that he or she is working in accordance with managerial objectives. The solution offered to this problem is the development of a subtle, implicit type of control that Ouchi calls "the clan." Clan control is accomplished through extensive and intensive socialization of clan members, such as that said to be characteristic of the Japanese organization. The end result is an internalization of organizational values and goals by members, or *goal congruence* (Ouchi, 1980:132; Ouchi and Price, 1978:36). Worker behavior is then guided not by bureaucratic rules or market forces, but rather by an "implicit philosophy" or "theory about how that organization should work." Given such internalization a worker can deduce "an appropriate rule to govern any possible decision, thus producing *a very elegant and complete form of control*" (Ouchi, 1980:139) (Italics mine). Clan control thus makes explicit performance evaluations and detailed monitoring of worker behavior unnecessary; the implicit evaluations central to clan control are attuned to values and objectives evidenced by workers, not specific work behaviors (Ouchi, 1979:845).

Ouchi remarks that clans are to organizations as cultures are to societies (1979:837). His recollectivization, then, can be adequately conceptualized as *cultural control*. Theory Z, a response to an America in which Ouchi assumes that the total cultural control of the clan would be resisted by workers and managers alike because of a national heritage of individualist values, is simply a mixture of clan, bureaucratic, and market controls. Or, as Ouchi and Price put it, Theory Z equals "hierarchical clans" (1978:25).

Ouchi also proposes clan control as a solution to a societal problem. Ouchi and Jaeger (1978:305f), observing that traditional groups such as family, church, and community have been weakened by industrialization, offer the avowedly Durk-heimian solution of making the workplace the center of belonging. Clan control, by meeting affiliative needs that are no longer met in traditional groups, will produce happier and mentally healthier individuals (Ouchi and Jaeger, 1978:312). But Ouchi and Jaeger do not mourn the passing of traditional groups, for those groups posed a "threat to the efficiency of the organization" (1978: 307).

Techniques which facilitate clan control include slow promotion (which spurs acculturation), slow evaluation (which diminishes the experience of hierarchical subordination), and the discouragement of career specialization (which might otherwise lead to an orientation toward professional rather than organizational goals, and to excessive interfirm mobility that hinders acculturation) (Ouchi and Jaeger, 1978:308f). Above all, lifetime employment or a reasonable facsimile thereof, which Ouchi (1981a:17–25) asserts is at the heart of Japanese organizational success, is essential for clan control (Ouchi, 1980:138). These organizational features are said to distinguish Ouchi's approach from the human relations tradition of Mayo and Likert—theorists with whom he otherwise feels a close kinship (Ouchi and Johnson, 1978:311f).

Some have openly worried about the swallowing of the individual by such organizations (e.g., W. R. Scott, 1981:298f; W. G. Scott and Hart, 1979). Ouchi dismisses the worries with the rather untenable suggestion that most organizations will "maintain an essentially democratic power structure" (Ouchi, 1979:842f) and the further reassurance that "most Theory Z companies are thoroughly integrated into the values of the larger society" and have only "a very limited capacity to infuse . . . philosophy into . . . employees" (Ouchi, 1981b:40). Thus, it is claimed, "no one will have to be 'brainwashed' " (Ouchi and Price, 1978:43). But if, as Ouchi himself claims, societal values have been weakened by industrialization, it may well be that work organizations have become major *creators* of the "values of the larger society." Salaman (1979: Section IV) argues that this creation involves both explicitly developed and disseminated ideology, and the incorporation of organizational values into the design and control of work itself. Ouchi's reassurances, then, are not convincing.

Theory Z is now presented in book, film, and videotape form. Reflecting the managerial interest in his ideas, Ouchi's consulting fee, according to an administrator at my institution, has reached as high as $10,000 per day. In the book and in the visual presentations, Ouchi describes several firms that are already doing Z-like things. But the actual impact of his ideas has been very little researched and is hard to judge. Doubtless, the current fascination with—and fear of— things Japanese has spurred the popularity of Ouchi and Theory Z in the U.S.

IV. DISCUSSION

In pursuing the Tayloristic rationalization of work, with its attendant deskilling and fragmentation, management has significantly decollectivized the workplace. Whether by intention or accident, the design of modern production technology aided in achieving that result. But decollectivization also meant that the creativity of work groups and their ability to enforce work norms was lost to the service of managerial goals as well as to those of workers, even while management's direct control of the labor process was strengthened.

Increased competition in the international market combined with negative worker reactions to Taylorized work (epitomized by the alienation of younger, more educated workers) to force the issue. But is is interesting to note that modern technology itself may also have played a part. While this technology may have been actively designed, through the deskilling and fragmentation of work tasks, to discourage the creation of informal work groups, work groups are seeming still required if maximum productivity is to be obtained with the technology. As Kusterer (1978) contends, few if any workers are wholly unskilled, and managers are always dependent upon them for an appropriate application of their "working knowledge." In the literature reviewed for this essay, proponents of at least three of the recollectivization schemes have made a similar point, and suggested that modern technology may have even amplified the dependence. It seems, then, that managers may have fallen into the trap of believing, as did Taylor, that their rationalization of the work process could be so complete as to eliminate any dependence whatsoever.

The proposals for escape, however, have not involved a wholesale abandonment of Taylor's fundamental prescriptions. That much is apparent in reviewing the similarities of the recollectivization schemes. One of the most important similarities is that all of the schemes contain detailed procedures for rationalizing the *form* of primary work groups. All prescribe limits for group activities, and two of them (System 4 and QCCs) advocate a more specific rationalization of the *content* of group activities by prescribing measurements and statistical analyses to help workers see the "facts" for themselves.

Each scheme includes an attempt to ensure the hierarchical domination of work groups through a rationalization of supervision beyond that described by Edwards (1979). The "linking pin" of System 4 and the "natural leader" of the QCC are the most obvious examples, but all schemes share the advice that the supervisor be conscientiously trained as a communicator, coordinator, group developer, corridor for external contacts, and all-around "nice guy" (the last via "supportive relations," "wholistic concerns," and such). Through this rationalization of supervision, the worker's subjective experience of hierarchy is softened while the objective reality of hierarchy is strengthened.

A final similarity is that all of the schemes purport to serve worker interests such as "status needs," "mental health," and above all, "personal worth." The irony is that, having consciously sought to destroy the image of labor as the heart of production, management now finds it necessary to claim to be restoring the sense of self-worth through recollectivization. Thus, the recollectivization schemes attend to the matter of worker legitimation of managerial initiative as well as to managerial capital accumulation motives.

What the recollectivization schemes do *not* advocate is a full-scale retreat from the pursuit of direct control via Taylorist principles. The technological and organizational arrangements based on these principles are to be left largely or even entirely intact. That is not to say, however, that managerial recollectivization is simply an extension or refinement of Taylorism. In terms of their respective views of the trustworthiness of workers in serving managerial goals, of the possibility of managerial domination of work groups, and of the feasibility of absolute direct control, Taylor and the recollectivizationists are at odds. Certainly Taylor would have choked on such notions as "responsible autonomy."

But in a curious way, recollectivization is not unrelated to Taylorism, much less antithetical to it, and it is also inappropriate to conceive of recollectivization as simply a reaction to or even a reversal of Taylorism. The study of work group processes and leadership, with the aim of rationalizing and controlling them, is really not so different from time-motion studies. Neither is the specification of group problem-solving techniques so different from the specification of detailed work procedures. As Taylor urged managers to study and control workers' laboring actions, so Ouchi asserts that the "informal social system" must be treated not as "an anomaly or an epiphenomenon," but rather as "the subject of analysis central to the problem of organization" (1979:837). A similar spirit pervades both Taylorism and recollectivization, for neither is less concerned with extending managerial control than the other. Thus, while Taylor aimed to further managerial control by preventing *any* work groups from forming (Tausky, 1978:184), it is meaningful to speak of "Taylored work groups" in describing the current efforts to use work groups to achieve greater control through managerial recollectivization. One of the crucial, but often overlooked, aspects of the current recollectivization innovations has been the goal of completing the Taylorist project by rationalizing aspects of the labor process that Taylor, quite incorrectly, thought could be eliminated.

Managerial recollectivization, in this light, represents an advance in the managerial domination of the forces of production. Assuming that it does yield the higher productivity of more efficient control that its proponents claim, and given a continuingly competitive world market situation, it must then become general among all firms that intend to survive or thrive in the competition. The voices of American managers as they regard Japan in the pages of their periodicals clearly envision such an inevitable trend.

The concept of managerial recollectivization also suggests modifications of Edwards' (1979) historical analysis of the development of control in the capitalist workplace. Edwards argues that "bureaucratic control" (control through written rules and company policies) represents the current state-of-the-art in control. While his use of that concept is fairly similar to that of Ouchi, he also notes that the internalization of appropriate values among employees is essential if bureaucratic control is to be fully effective. Career ladders (in many ways the functional equivalent of Japan's lifetime employment system) will facilitate internalization. But what I have termed "cultural control" needs to be analytically separated from bureaucratic control. Control via rules derived from an internalized corporate culture is qualitatively different from control via detailed rules in policy manuals.

That difference can be highlighted by considering what cultural control aims to accomplish. The written rules of bureaucratic control can be circumvented or even turned against managerial objectives, and workers might decide just how to do this in their informal work groups. But the processes of decollectivization and recollectivization take the groups that have been the basis for resistance out of the hands of workers, and return them with a managerially-designed form and content. As such, those processes will hinder workers in struggling for their own class interests in workplace conflicts.

Ouchi understands that hindrance very well, and his work constitutes the most direct statement of the philosophy of managerial recollectivization. While others talk of the details of group design and function, he goes right to the crux of the matter: if you want to control the culture produced by work groups, control the culture in which the groups are produced. His ideas are based on the notion that people more readily identify with little groups than with big groups (organizations), but that cultural management can transform loyalty to the former into loyalty to the latter. Again, this is the aim of all recollectivization: to end the conflict that F. W. Taylor had assumed to be without end—the conflict between individual and organizational goals.

But will it really work? Can the direct control orientation of Taylorism blend with seemingly participatory techniques, such as Ouchi prescribes with Theory Z? One factor that is typically not taken into account by Ouchi and others is the possible response of workers to recollectivization efforts. Such responses could be determinant of the ultimate outcomes of these efforts.

It is of course, possible that workers might decide to wholeheartedly embrace managerial means and ends. There are already reports of QCC members suggesting that unproductive workers be fired (*Business Week,* 1981:98) or that their own jobs be eventually eliminated (Murray, 1981:69). Even short of such actions, it seems that workers in recollectivized groups do find many ways to cut costs or increase profits, often by improving the efficiency of their work. Nonetheless, Cole's analysis of Japan hardly suggests that the wholehearted embrace would be permanent. Moreover, it is not at all clear that workers, in meeting managerial objectives, are necessarily indicating their adoption of managerial values. Instead, they may be acting in a cynical fashion, appearing to pursue managerial objectives in hopes of fulfilling their own (e.g., gaining a promotion). Apathy or resistance would likely set in the minute the pursuit of the former is perceived to block, or at least be irrelevant to, the latter.

But another possibility, sometimes called the "domino effect," has been advanced by a few radical academics. Among the abandoned experiments in recollectivization are those that seemed to have failed because they demonstrated the collective power of work groups to workers (Jenkins, 1974:35; Edwards, 1979:156; Bucklow, 1966:65f). Management cancelled the projects when the recollectivized workers began to challenge management. As both Goldman and Van Houten (1980:86) and Clegg and Dunkerley (1980:517) have observed, the danger to management is that recollectivized work groups might give workers a glimpse of what an alternative organization of production—one without bosses— might be like. Cole (1979:202) also hints at such a transformation, in which incremental quantitative changes in worker participation might lead to a qualitative change, a real transformation of workplace power relations.

Wrenn (1982:33) counters that "workers have shown no ability, and, in most cases, no interest in pushing management to humanize work further or to yield more control to workers." Their challenges have not extended to fundamental managerial prerogatives. But while Wrenn provides a useful corrective to those whose analyses may have been colored by wishful thinking, his own analysis overlooks an important point. Recollectivization brings together workers who might otherwise have remained isolated from one another, and demands that they talk about *work* with one another. While these new relationships are in many ways unlike those of informal work groups, and are heavily burdened with managerial prescriptions concerning their content, it is still impossible to entirely specify and enforce that content. The new relationships and any new sense of unity they help produce may well prove useful to workers should they decide to mount a collective challenge to managerial authority. That workers currently show little sign of mounting such a challenge is perhaps not so important (or of as much concern to some of the many managers who have rejected recollectivization out of hand) as the fact that they might one day do so, and may be assisted in doing so by their experience with recollectivized groups.

The managerial moth has now danced before the flame of the work group for several decades. The dance is more precise and controlled now, and the confidence of the moth has been bolstered by many consultants and theorists. But, like its predecessors, cultural control is not complete, and all of the managerial science in the world cannot yet separate the flame from the heat.

ACKNOWLEDGEMENT

Research for this paper was funded in part by the School of Arts, Humanities, and Social Sciences and the School of Administrative Science at The University of Alabama in Huntsville. Some of the ideas contained in it were first presented at the 1982 meetings of The Society for the Study of Social Problems (San Francisco). The author wishes to express his thanks to Nancy DiTomaso for her comments on an earlier draft.

NOTES

1. While this paper is primarily concerned with developments in capitalist societies, many of its arguments are equally applicable to nominally socialist societies such as China and Yugoslavia. The phenomena described in this paper differ somewhat from country to country, and are introduced within different ideological frameworks. Such differences should be explored in future research.

2. My understanding of informal work groups has been heavily influenced by Stan Weir, both through his written work (cited in the text) and through extensive personal communication.

3. At the Toyota Auto Body facility in Cole's study, workers resented the hierarchical dominance implied by the supervisory leadership of QCCs, and a shift to senior workers as leaders was underway. My own conversations with production workers at a microelectronics assembly plant revealed that the feature of QCCs they spotted first and suspected most was the use of supervisors at QCC leaders.

REFERENCES

Battersby, A. J.
    1976   "What about the workers?" Management Today 1:66–69.
Blumberg, P.
    1973   Industrial Democracy: The Sociology of Participation. New York: Schocken.
    1980   Inequality in an Age of Decline. New York: Oxford.
Braverman, H.
    1974   Labor and Monopoly Capital: The Degradation of Work in the Twentieth Century. New York: Monthly Review.
Bucklow, M.
    1966   "A new role for the work group." Administrative Science Quarterly 11:59–78.
Business Week
    1981   "The new industrial relations." May 11:84–98.

Clegg, S., and D. Dunkerley
   1980   Organisation, Class and Control. London: Routledge.
Coch, L., and J. R. P. French
   1948   "Overcoming resistance to change." Human Relations 1(4):512–32.
Cole, R. E.
   1979   Work, Mobility, and Participation: A Comparative Study of American and Japanese Indus-
          try. Berkeley: University of California.
Cummings, T. G.
   1978   "Self-regulating work groups: a socio-technical synthesis." Academy of Management
          Review 3(3):625–34.
Davis, L. E., and J. C. Taylor
   1976   "Technology, organization and job structure." Pp. 379–419 in R. Dubin (ed.), Handbook
          of Work, Organization, and Society. Chicago: Rand McNally.
Davis, L. E., and E. L. Trist
   1974   "Improving the quality of work life: sociotechnical case studies." Pp. 246–80 in J.
          O'Toole (ed.), Work and the Quality of Life: Resource Papers for Work in America.
          Cambridge, Mass.: MIT.
Edwards, R.
   1979   Contested Terrain: The Transformation of the Workplace in the Twentieth Century. New
          York: Basic.
Ehrenreich, J., and B. Ehrenreich
   1976   "Work and consciousness." Monthly Review 28(3):10–18.
Fein, M.
   1976   "Motivation for work." Pp. 465–530 in R. Dubin (ed.), Handbook of Work, Organiza-
          tion, and Society. Chicago: Rand McNally.
Friedmann, G.
   1964   The Anatomy of Work: Labor, Leisure, and the Implications of Automation. New York:
          Free Press.
Goldman, P., and D. R. Van Houten
   1980   "Uncertainty, conflict, and labor relations in the modern firm I: productivity and cap-
          italism's 'human face'." Economic and Industrial Democracy 1(1):63–98.
Grzyb, G. J.
   1981   "Decollectivization and recollectivization in the workplace: the impact of technology on
          informal work groups and work culture." Economic and Industrial Democracy 2(4):455–
          82.
Hall, R. H.
   1982   Organizations: Structure and Process. (3rd ed.) Englewood Cliffs: Prentice-Hall.
Hutchins, D.
   1981   "How quality goes round in circles." Management Today (January): 27–32.
International Management
   1979   "No manager is an island." 34(1):22–4.
Jenkins, D.
   1974   Job Power: Blue and White Collar Democracy. New York: Penguin.
Johnson, R. T., and W. G. Ouchi
   1974   "Made in America (under Japanese management)." Harvard Business Review 52(5):61–9.
Kusterer, K.
   1978   Know-How on the Job: The Important Working Knowledge of "Unskilled" Workers.
          Boulder, Colo.: Westview.
Likert, R.
   1961   New Patterns of Management. New York: McGraw-Hill.
   1967   The Human Organization: Its Management and Value. New York: McGraw-Hill.

Likert, R., and M. S. Fisher
1977 "MBGO: putting some team spirit into MBO." Personnel 54(1):40–7.
Marglin, S. A.
1974 "What do bosses do? The origins and functions of hierarchy in capitalist production." The Review of Radical Political Economics 6(2):60–112.
Murray, T. J.
1981 "The rise of the productivity manager." Dun's Review 117(1):64–5, 69.
Nosow, S.
1981 "The first-line supervisor, the linchpin in the Japanese Quality Control Circle." Industrial Management 23(1):19–23.
Ouchi, W. G.
1977 "The relationship between organizational structure and organizational control." Administrative Science Quarterly 22:95–113.
1978 "The transmission of control through organizational hierarchy." Academy of Management Journal 21(2):173–92.
1979 "A conceptual framework for the design of organizational control mechanisms." Management Science 25(9):833–48.
1980 "Markets, bureaucracies, and clans." Administrative Science Quarterly 25:129–141.
1981a Theory Z: How American Business Can Meet the Japanese Challenge. Reading, Mass.: Addison-Wesley.
1981b "Organizational paradigms: a commentary on Japanese management and Theory Z organizations." Organizational Dynamics 9(4):36–43.
Ouchi, W. G., and A. M. Jaeger
1978 "Type Z organization: stability in the midst of mobility." Academy of Management Review 3(2):305–14.
Ouchi, W. G., and J. B. Johnson
1978 "Types of organizational control and their relationship to emotional well being." Administrative Science Quarterly 23:293–317.
Ouchi, W. G., and M. A. Maguire
1975 "Organizational control: two functions." Administrative Science Quarterly 20:559–69.
Ouchi, W. G., and R. L. Price
1978 "Hierarchies, clans, and Theory Z: a new perspective on organizational development." Organizational Dynamics 7(2):25–44.
Perrow, C.
1979 Complex Organizations: A Critical Essay. (2nd ed.) Glenview, Ill.: Scott, Foresman.
Porras, J., and P. O. Berg
1978 "The impact of organizational development." The Academy of Management Review 3(2):249–66.
Reilly, A. J.
1978 "Interview." Group and Organization Studies 3(1):11–23.
Salaman, G.
1979 Work Organisations: Resistance and Control. London: Longman.
Scott, W. G., and D. K. Hart
1979 Organizational America: Can Individual Freedom Survive Within The Security It Promises? Boston: Houghton Mifflin.
Scott, W. R.
1981 Organizations: Rational, Natural, and Open Systems. Englewood Cliffs: Prentice-Hall.
Seligman, B. B.
1966 Most Notorious Victory. New York: Free Press.
Tausky, C.
1978 Work Organizations: Major Theoretical Perspectives. Itasca, Ill.: Peacock.

Training and Development Journal
   1981   "Quality circles growth increases at Honeywell." 35(7):6–7.
Trist, E. L., and K. W. Bamforth
   1951   "Some social and psychological consequences of the longwall method of coal-getting."
          Human Relations 4(1):3–38.
Weir, S. L.
   1973   "The informal work group." Pp. 179–200 in A. Lynd and S. Lynd (eds.), Rank and File:
          Personal Histories by Working-Class Organizers. Boston: Beacon.
   1974   "A study of the work culture of San Francisco longshoremen." Unpublished Master's
          thesis, University of Illinois.
Werther, W. B., Jr.
   1981   "Productivity improvement through people." Arizona Business 28(2):14–9.
Work In America
   1973   Report of a Special Task Force to the Secretary of Health, Education, and Welfare.
          Cambridge, Mass.: MIT.
Wrenn, R.
   1982   "Management and work humanization." The Insurgent Sociologist 11(3):23–38.
Yager, E. G.
   1981   "The quality control circle explosion." Training and Development Journal 35(4):98–105.
Yankelovich, D.
   1979   "Work, values, and the new breed." Pp. 3–26 in C. Kerr and J. M. Rosow (eds.), Work
          in America: The Decade Ahead. New York: Van Nostrand.
Zimbalist, A.
   1975   "The limits of work humanization." The Review of Radical Political Economics 7(2):50–9.

WORKER OWNERSHIP:

COLLECTIVE RESPONSE TO AN

ELITE-GENERATED CRISIS

Joyce Rothschild-Whitt

I.   INTRODUCTION

The worker ownership phenomenon, while it has been spreading very rapidly in the U.S. over the past five years, is still in its early stages of development. Its future is not set in concrete. It contains within it, I believe, the potential to move in several different, if not contradictory, directions. It is the thesis of this paper that the direction toward which worker-ownership turns in the future, and which groups will come to benefit from it, will depend upon which of several competing constituencies prevails in its efforts to define and control the worker ownership issue.

Surely this is no typical social movement like the anti-war movement or the civil rights movement, where the activists associated with the movement shared a basic unity of values. When we look at who has been actively involved in the passage of national legislation favorable to worker ownership, we see that it

Research in Social Movements, Conflict and Change, Vol. 6, pages 167–194.
Copyright © 1984 by JAI Press Inc.
All rights of reproduction in any form reserved.
ISBN: 0-89232-311-6

includes some of the most liberal members of the U.S. Congress along with some of the most conservative. When we examine who is involved in the actual worker buy-outs of existing plants or in the establishment of new worker-owned facilities, we see that leadership has come variously from managements, owners, unions, workers, city officials, and even sometimes social scientists. Indeed, what is so intriguing about the worker ownership movement in the U.S., is that different groups are able to read into it so many different meanings. For example, some of those in the U.S. who have been instrumental in advancing worker ownership have seen in it a way to save or reinvigorate capitalism; others have seen in it a way to bring economic justice to the society; and still others have seen it as the first step toward democratic socialism. Yet others bring to their efforts no conscious ideology at all, seeing it merely as an available financing mechanism to save businesses and jobs.

It is a premise of this paper that worker ownership is inherently ambiguous in the class interests it serves. It can be made to serve any number of competing class interests and its ideological justifications can be altered accordingly. Thus, little can be learned from normative statements about what worker ownership "should" or "must" do. The future of worker ownership will not be predicted; it will be made.

The outcomes of worker-ownership as a social movement—whether it brings democratic control of production or whether it simply ushers in a new form of elite control—will be determined by the outcome of collective actions and struggles that are presently undertaken. In time the interests of some of the groups that are presently involved in developing the worker ownership option will win out over the others, and this will determine the future form that worker ownership takes in the U.S. It is incumbent upon us, therefore, to understand the competing visions and actions that the different classes in the U.S. bring to this movement in its present form. From a sociology of knowledge perspective, this paper will attempt to examine how each class sees the issue, how they justify it, and what they hope to materially gain from it. The competition to define and control this issue then will be set in the context of a class analysis of what's at stake.

The push for worker ownership, in as much as it is an organized, collective effort to bring about a social change, in this case a change in the ownership and possibly the control of productive facilities, meets the basic qualification of a social movement. But, I will argue, it is an unusual and complex social movement, whose examination will allow us to shed light on several issues of long-standing concern in the field of social movements.

First, there is considerable debate in the field on the question of why social movements form. Traditionally, collective behavior has viewed movements as a response to newly-found grievances. The resource mobilization theorists, on the other hand, have tended to view the existence of grievances as relatively constant (Jenkins and Perrow, 1977). Here the formation of a movement depends chiefly upon the availability of resources and people for the collective action. The grievances themselves are secondary, and may be manufactured or at least orchestrated by the movement's entrepreneurs (McCarthy and Zald, 1973). In the first section of this paper I try to identify the contextual factors that have given rise to worker ownership, arguing that the flight of capital has caused severe economic dislocation in American communities, generating in its wake not just "grievances," but financial ruin for an ever widening circle of workers, local managers and even small business owners. This is the basis of the worker ownership movement.

Once the contextual groundwork has been laid for a social movement, the next major issue raised in the literature is *how* the emergent social movement will access the resources it needs to attain its ends. Zald and McCarthy have shown that in the 1960s and 1970s there was a rise in the number of professional social movement organizations whose professional staffs were adept at raising outside contributions and at coopting mainstream institutional resources. For the work ownership movement I raise the issue from the opposite direction, asking whether their dependence on outside institutional resources—and in this case bank loans are absolutely necessary—will coopt the worker buy-outs.

If people in worker ownership drives want instead to mobilize their internal constituencies of workers and others who would be directly affected by the buy-out, then they must face Mancur Olson's (1968) famous dilemma of collective action. The second section of this paper examines the nature and magnitudes of the worker ownership movement, asking how they balance, if they do, their dual need for external support and internal involvement.

A third set of issues in the field of social movements has to do with the strategies and incentives that any social movement must devise. Most people probably think of social movements as employing rather non-institutional methods such as riots, demonstrations or consumer boycotts. However, as Ash (1972) points out, it is not always clear which means are legitimate and which are not. Sometimes grassroots activism gives rise to government bureaus or laws (as with the Civil Rights Act, Morris, 1981; McAdam, 1982); at other times elite sponsorship of government bureaus or programs feeds grassroots action (as with the National Welfare Rights Organizations [Bailis, 1974]). On the whole, the resource mobilization perspective has tended to stress the growing institutionalization of social movement methods, and the rationality of social movement actors.

In the case of worker ownership, virtually all of its spread in the U.S. since the mid-1970s came about as a result of its success at gaining institutional support in the way of favorable state and national legislation, government loan guarantees and private bank loans. Conspicuously absent were any type of protest grassroots actions such as worker sit-ins, although direct worker actions of this kind have been used in recent years in Europe and in Canada to achieve worker buy-outs of industrial plants. Such methods also have been used in previous periods of American history to create worker cooperatives.

A separate issue in the field, related to the question of strategy, is the extent to which social movements are expressive as opposed to instrumental in nature. Those with a background in collective behavior would search for the seed of social movements in the sentiments and ideologies of their members, or for the conversion experience of participants who join for non-ideological reasons (Turner and Killian, 1972). On the other hand, those with a resource mobilization perspective would tend to view social movements as a more instrumental, even opportunistic response to available resources, with the outcome determined largely by how well leaders can mobilize such resources in behalf of their cause (McCarthy and Zald, 1973; 1977).

All social movements have aspects of instrumentalism as well as aspects of ideology in them in varying degrees, and both conceptions are well developed in the social movements literature. The third section of this paper, on actors' motivations, will attempt to assess the *relationship* between ideology and instrumentalism, and specifically, which comes prior. Does the availability of resources for an instrumental activity call up its own ideology? Or is the reverse true: do people with a deeply-felt cause go about finding or creating the resources that can solve their problem? In section three I look at each of the groups of actors who have been involved in worker ownership efforts—politicians, owners and managers, and workers and union leaders. In it I try to identify the particular mix of ideological and material incentives that attracted each group to worker ownership. As we shall see, they each see in worker ownership very different things, they speak in different vocabularies of motive, and each would shape it to suit their own interests. In the end, the shape that worker ownership takes in the U.S. and who it benefits will depend upon which of the interested constituencies prevails.

II. THE CONTEXT OF WORKER OWNERSHIP: ELITE-GENERATED CAPITAL FLIGHT

In the mid-nineteenth century we were still a nation of small entrepreneurs, independent craftsmen, and small farmers: more than half the working people were self-employed. By 1970 the situation had reversed: 91% of our workforce worked for a wage, and only 9% were self-employed. Not only was the opportunity for self-employment lost this century, but with the growing specialization of work throughout the twentieth century, work became less skilled; supervision became closer; and workers became more easily replaced (Braverman, 1974). The specialization process was reinforced by the geometrically expanding size of organizations, both public and private, again rendering control more remote from the individual. This loss of worker autonomy, of control over the process and product of work, is the chief background variable to an understanding in essence of any movement toward worker ownership or control.

The development of worker ownership is related to the growing concentration in the U.S. economy, especially since World War II. In 1950 the largest 200 U.S. corporations held 47.7% of the nation's manufacturing assets, by 1972 they held 60%. Today 80% of the nation's manufacturing assets are controlled by 500 corporations, leaving 300,000 small businesses to carve up the other 20% (Report of the House Committee on Small Business, 1980: 19).

Yet, new jobs have not come from this concentrated pool of capital. In fact, for the years 1969-76 the 1000 top corporations in America created only eight-tenths of one percent of all of the jobs added to the economy (Congressman Breckenridge, Congressional Record, March 8, 1978). A recent study by David Birch (1979) reveals how this can be possible: he finds that ⅔ of the new jobs created over the last decade in the U.S. have been created by small businesses, while the other ⅓ of the jobs have been created by government. Virtually none of the job creation has come from the large corporations.

To understand the paradox of growing corporate giants that do not create jobs, one must turn to the conglomerate merger and acquisition practices of the 1960s and 1970s. The conglomerate merger movement is considered to have reached its peak during the 1967-69 period, with over 3500 mergers annually, but the practice has continued and subsequent mergers have been of larger and larger size. For instance, in 1975 $15 billion was spent by U.S. corporations to buy other corporations. By 1980 the amount mushroomed to $40 billion, by 1981 it reached an annual rate of $70 billion, representing nearly a 500% increase in six years. These enormous capital resources have gone into rearranging the ownership of existing properties rather than building new production facilities or adding to employment.

The result of this merger activity has been an equally prolific conglomerate divestiture movement. An exhaustive study by Birch (1979) that followed 6400 firms that were acquired during 1972-74, compared their growth rates (both before and after the acquisition) with the rates for 1.3 million firms that were not acquired, indicated the following pattern: conglomerates tend to acquire fast-growing, profitable, well-managed businesses, contrary to the theory that they seek out poorly-managed, inefficient firms. The acquisition, however, does not speed up the acquired firm's growth. In fact, firms that remain independent grow faster than acquired firms. In addition, rates of job creation, productivity, and innovation all tend to slow down after independent companies are absorbed into large conglomerates (House Report on Conglomerate Mergers, 1980: 33-34). Anti-trust laws, as they are presently written, can do little to inhibit this merger activity because they are written to regulate horizontal and vertical integration, not conglomerate acquisitions in unrelated industries.

The net effect is that there are numerous shut-downs of what once were and what might again be, healthy productive facilities. Bluestone and his associates (1982) have found that plant closings eliminated nearly a million jobs in the New England states alone from 1969 to 1976. Nationwide Bluestone estimates, and this has been confirmed by an independent Brookings Institution study, that some 32 millions jobs were lost to plant shut downs during the decade of the 1970s. That is, roughly one-third of all of the nation's jobs that existed in 1969 were gone ten years later. It is here that fertile soil for the employee-owned firms has developed.

When a firm is closing because its market is shrinking or because its capital equipment is obsolete, there is not much that a change in ownership can do to "save" the firm. However, as the Bluestone (1980) and the Cornell studies have found, shut-downs sometimes occur in firms that have a long record of profitability but where their new-found conglomerate owners do not find the level of profit high enough, or where they have badly mismanaged the firm since taking it over, or where they have decided to "milk" it for investment elsewhere in their empire, or where they decide that it simply no longer fits with their overall corporate strategy. In these cases worker-ownership does have a chance where conglomerate ownership failed. Thus, paradoxically, it is the growing concentration in the economy that gave rise to the massive disinvestment practices observable today and that, in turn, sets the stage for the worker-ownership option.

When a conglomerate decides to shut-down a subsidiary plant, whether they have mismanaged it or whether they simply have an opportunity to earn a higher return on their equity elsewhere, they go. Unlike many other nations, to date, we have no statutes in the U.S. that would inhibit a corporation from moving operations to Brazil or Sri Lanka, or wherever. But, while capital is internationally mobile, communities and workers are not. Capital flight leaves in its wake not just job loss for the directly affected employees. Depending upon the size of the community, each job lost in the shut-down will have a "ripple effect," resulting in a multiplier of as many as seven jobs lost in the community for each job lost in the shut-down plant. The sudden loss of a major payroll cannot help but produce sharply lower consumption in the town and tax revenues, resulting in the bankruptcy of other businesses, job loss for their employees, and sharply reduced public services at a time when they are most needed.

Studies of long-term unemployment show unequivocally that it leads to heightened incidence of heart attacks, increased blood pressure, ulcers and a host of other stress-related diseases, children of the unemployed begin to do worse in school, marital disruption goes up, alcohol and drug dependencies increase, problems of depression and anxiety become legion, and suicides are not unknown. Dr. Harvey Brenner (1976) finds that each one percent increase in the unemployment rate nationwide over a six year period corresponds to 37,000 additional deaths, 20,000 of which are due to cardiovascular disease, 920 suicides, 650 homicides, 4000 mental hospital submissions, and 3300 state prison admissions.

In addition to the above, protracted unemployment can be devastating financially. Bluestone and his associates find that the job loss that results from shut-downs is of longer duration on average than the unemployment that results from other causes. In order to find another job, the average shut-out workers will have to take a 25% loss in wages (Bluestone and Harrison, 1982: 55-61). As a general rule, the higher one is on the occupational ladder to start, the steeper will be the decline, known among economists as "skidding." A skilled steelworker, for example, can expect to take a 46% cut in the first two years after being laid-off, and the same rule applies to professional and managerial personnel. Even if they find work eventually, these workers will experience downward mobility, and in their entire lifetimes they cannot expect to fully recoup the financial loss.

In short, capital flight has a profound effect on the life of communities and on the unfortunate people who happen to live in them. It alters the entire way of life of the population. Directly affected workers and their families will find that everything has been disrupted: their closest personal relationships, their familial ties, their institutional affiliations, their standard of living, their mental outlook and even their physical health. They can also see that they did not do anything to produce this devastation. Capital mobility is an elite decision, and as we have argued, it is often an avoidable decision. As often as not, the corporate officers making the decision are located thousands of miles from the community in question. It is not meant to be anything personal, but its effects are felt very personally.

The sense of injustice that results may conceivably lead to a popular questioning of the rights and responsibilities of elites, but this has not yet been studied. From a social movements point of view, this is an example of how an elite-generated crisis can set the stage for a social movement (Useem, 1980; Walsh, 1981). The raw material of social movement formation is here; movement entrepreneurs do not have to go about manufacturing "grievances." But it is important to note that not every community that faces an unnecessary shut-down mobilizes community and worker support for a worker buy-out. Collective action along this line presupposes the existence of local leaders who can articulate the problem and organize the solution. As the worker ownership option gets more publicity and familiarity around the country, its consideration appears to be spreading. More to the point, because the economic dislocation has been caused by the decisions of multi-national capital, leaving local plant managers, local business and city fathers in the "same boat" as local workers, the worker ownership option inherits the possbliity of an unusual inter-class coalescence.

III. THE NATURE AND MAGNITUDES OF WORKER OWNERSHIP: MOBILIZATION FROM WITHOUT AND WITHIN

Since tax incentives for Employee Stock Ownership Plans (ESOPs) were passed into law in the mid-1970s, there has been a burgeoning of this type of organization in the U.S. Today there are an estimated 5000 firms that are to some degree employee-owned, involving an estimated 3 to 4 million employees. Before one gets carried away with that statistic, however, it is important to bear in mind that in many of these firms the percentage of ownership may be small. The potential for worker *control* exists only in that subset of firms where there is *substantial* worker-ownership of the *voting* stock. Given the possible dispersion of non-worker-held stock, a numerical majority may not be needed for effective control. Nevertheless, recent surveys number majority worker-ownership situations at 500, with a mean size of 680 workers each (National Center for Employee Ownership, personal communication).

In addition to the development of worker-ownership, two other trends toward work democratization have developed over the last five years. Quality of work life programs (QWL) try to give workers greater voice in the work process, while not extending ownership to workers. Walton (1979) estimates that one-third of the *Fortune* 500 firms have instituted some form of worker participation or QWL and a recent survey by the New York Stock Exchange (1982) indicates that only 3% of corporate managers believe that this current trend toward worker participation will prove to be a fad. Another, analytically quite separate, trend in the development of workplace democracy lies in the scores of grassroots collectives and cooperatives that have arisen in many communities in the U.S. in the past decade. These three forms of democratization each constitute a separate movement at this point in time, with their own separate leaders, social networks, conferences, ideologies, publications and organizations. This paper will address only the worker ownership phenomena, as distinct from the grassroots collectives and worker participation efforts.[1]

The legislative history of employee stock ownership in the U.S. goes back to 1921 when Congress first gave special tax exemptions to profit-sharing and stock bonus trusts. The Tax Revision Act of 1942 further served to induce business to institute tax-sheltered retirement plans. These laws set the stage, but it was not until the IRS' Revenue Ruling 46, enacted in 1953, that a qualified trust (such as an ESOP) was permitted to borrow money for the purpose of purchasing stock. One year later, the country's first leveraged ESOP was born, the Peninsula Newspapers, and it is still thriving today as an employee-owned firm. However, the major impetus for ESOPs and their proliferation did not really begin until ERISA (The Employee Retirement Income Security Act) was signed into law in 1974 and the Tax Reduction Act in 1975. These laws detail the procedures for setting up an ESOP and provide various tax incentives for doing so. Over the last few years of the Carter Administration, several pieces of legislation were passed which enabled and encouraged various federal agencies to make loan guarantees to employee-owned firms.

In brief, an Employee Stock Ownership Plan (ESOP) provides a legal mechanism for the transfer of stock equity to the hands of employees without requiring any contribution other than labor. The ESOP sets up an Employee Stock Ownership Trust (ESOT) which borrows money for the purpose of purchasing stock. The company's stock is held in the ESOT, and is voted by the trustees. Each year, as the company repays its ESOP loan, the corresponding number of shares are released from the ESOT and credited to individual employee accounts. When the entire ESOP loan has been repaid, all of the shares in the ESOT will have been released to the employees. These shares may or may not be voting shares. To service its ESOP debt, the company may contribute annually up to 25% of its total covered payroll cost, and this is done in pre-tax dollars. In other words, the company is allowed a tax deduction of up to 25% of its payroll cost for the purpose of repaying its ESOP loan. Herein lies the main tax advantage of ESOPs. Although ESOPs are governed by some of the same IRS provisions that cover pension and profit sharing plans, *only* ESOTs are permitted to borrow money to acquire employer stock and to pay back the principal on such loans with pre-tax dollars. It is this feature that makes the ESOP attractive as a means of debt finance and capital formation as well as deferred compensation.

The tax laws and IRS rulings covering ESOPs are key to an understanding of the nature of worker ownership as a movement, and also for understanding some of its chief limitations. The ESOP, as it is structured by law, is a finance mechanism by which equity ownership can be gradually transferred from private hands to the employees of a firm. To buy the stock from the private owners, so that it can be slowly allocated to the employees, a bank loan is often necessary. These cases are called "leveraged ESOPs." In the first few years of ESOP creation (the mid and late 1970s), this fact confronted the local organizers of worker buy-outs with the question of how to access private bank capital or secure a federal loan guarantee. The latter was often necessary in order to produce the former. In the last few years, however, word of the success of ESOPs has become widespread and articles extolling the virtues of ESOPs have been placed even in banking industry magazines. The National Center for Employee Ownership reports that it is now relatively easy to convince banks to make loans to fledging ESOPs (personal communication).

From the Zald and McCarthy perspective, we would have to conclude that worker ownership advocates and entrepreneurs have been very adept at accessing institutional resources for their movement. But I would argue, this may not be a case of a movement coopting institutional resources. More likely, dependence on external resources makes the worker-owned organizations highly vulnerable to finance capital control.

For example, when the workers in a large asbestos mine in Vermont, following a massive community-worker grassroots mobilization, managed to prepare an offer to buy the plant from GAF, the multi-national firm that had scheduled the operation for shut-down, they naturally needed a bank loan. The new worker-owned entity, Vermont Asbestos Group, gots its loan, but with it came the restriction that the bank would appoint the new president of the firm. The bank imported another banker for the job rather than anyone with any local knowledge or asbestos experience. The insensitivity of this person to worker input and the growing disenchantment of the workforce with this person's decisions and management style, soured the whole enterprise and eventually led the workers to sell what turned out to be a very good investment to a local entrepreneur in whose management skill they at least had more confidence. Studies have not yet been done indicating in how many of these cases dependence on bank loans leads to finance capital control.

Organizers of worker-owned firms, like leaders of any movement, need to mobilize the active participation of directly-involved constituents as well as bringing in outside institutional resources. The worker ownership drives that we studied at Cornell, involved both these aspects. Especially where the buy-out was seen as an emergency to replace a scheduled shut-down, city officials, branch plant managers and worker leaders all typically cooperated to achieve the shared goal. The mobilization of the community and the workforce was often rapid and intense.

The frequent success of these mobilization efforts was due, first, I believe to the sudden capital flight and subsequent economic dislocation that threatens the way of life of workers, families, and whole communities. This becomes the raw material to which the mobilization organizers can readily appeal. Second, at least in a small or medium-size community where many of these conversions take place, individuals can see that their contributions are important to the worker-ownership drive, and that its eventual success will bring them major benefits. In Olson's (1968) terms, the worker ownership movement gives out "selective benefits" to the individual. This is because ESOPs are legally structure to provide for *individual* employee ownership, not *collective* ownership. It is my impression that these drives are able to elicit considerably more community solidarity and vigorous support where the community is relatively small, confirming Olson's hypothesis about the relationship of size to the distribution of selective benefits. In this case, since the actual ripple effect of the potential shut-down will be greater in a smaller community than in a large city, individual decisions to contribute to the worker ownership drive are rational.

IV.   THE ACTORS: IDEOLOGICAL AND MATERIAL INCENTIVES MAKE FOR STRANGE PARTNERSHIPS

One of the most intriguing aspects of the worker ownership movement is that it has attracted people to its banner from all parts of the social system. Politically, people who would otherwise describe themselves as left, right or moderate, have come to support worker ownership. Economically, workers and unions as well as certain business elements, have been drawn to the idea. This section will seek to identify what I believe is an extraordinary range of incentives that worker ownership has to offer, arguing that the breadth of its appeal derives from this characteristic.

The social movements field has long been concerned with the extent to which movement participation is expressive or ideological at root versus the extent to which it is instrumental, or even opportunistic, in character. The resource mobilization perspective has tended to stress the growing instutionalization of social movement methods, and the rationality of social movement actors. In this section I examine each of the groups who have been involved in worker ownership efforts—politicians, owners and managers, and unions and workers, identifying the particular mix of ideological and material incentives that brought each to the worker ownership issue.

I will attempt to show that worker ownership, in itself, is ambiguous in the class interests it serves. It can be made to serve any number of competing class interests, and the ideological justifications for it can be modified accordingly. I will attempt to demonstrate that the different groups that today support worker ownership see in the issue different, sometimes diametrically opposed, political means and economic opportunities. Each group is trying to shape it to suit their own ideological and material interests. The outcome for worker ownership— whether it will bring more democratic control of production or merely a new form of elite control—will depend upon the outcome of collective actions that are presently being undertaken by the interested groups.

V.   ACTORS IN LEGISLATIVE ARENAS

The political meaning attributed to worker ownership depends to a great extent on whom you talk to. Some of the leaders in the worker ownership movement today look to Johann Henrich Von Thunen, a nineteenth century economist in Germany who fathered "marginal productivity" theory, for the origination of the idea of an ESOP. A contemporary of Karl Marx, Von Thunen agreed with Marx that capital was capturing all of the surplus generated by the production process. But, he argued, the way to deal with this concentration of wealth was not to expropriate it and put it in the hands of the state, "but rather turn the coin over and find ways to make everyone a capitalist." It is reported that Von Thunen applied his ideas of employee ownership and profit sharing on his own farm, with considerable success (Metzger, 1978:2–4).

This idea of broadening the ownership of the means of production, is an idea that is subject to varying interpretations. President Reagan has described ESOPs in this way:

An ever-increasing number of citizens would have two sources of income—a paycheck and a share of the profits. Could there be a better answer to the stupidity of Karl Marx than millions of workers individually sharing in the ownership of the means of production? (reported in Frisch, 1982: V).

What Mr. Reagan's understanding is of the theories of Marx, I do not profess to know, but ESOPs get his support because of their apparent opposition to such theories.

On the other side of the political spectrum, Derek Shearer and Martin Carnoy have written a whole book outlining the rationale and programs that would constitute *Economic Democracy* (1982), and Tom Hayden made this a central part of his platform in his California bid for the Senate. For these architects of the New Left and others of their generation, the distinguishing feature of the New Left—and where it departed from the views of the Old Left—was the primacy it gave to democracy: It was actually a short distance from insisting on the rights of the Vietnamese to self-determination to insisting on the same for Blacks, for gays, for women, and so forth. The demand for self-determination, or in the words of the liberation movements of the 1960s, for control over the conditions that effect one's life, is similar to the claims made in the 1980s for "economic democracy." It is the same desire for control, this time applied to the workplace. It is my impression that the issue of *process* (who controls and how) has over the last 20 years greatly overshadowed the earlier left concern for redistribution. Yet, many on the left would argue that a more decentralized and democratic process of control, especially over workplace and financial decisions, would lead to more equitable outcomes.[2]

To the extent that leftists might tend to assume, consistent with the theory of Marx, that ownership of capital confers control, they may well be drawn to any mechanism that promises to extend ownership to workers. In this sense, ESOPs can be interpreted as falling squarely in the territory of the left. When all of the philosophizing is done, worker ownership (via ESOPs, coops, whatever) is one of the only concrete proposals on the political agenda in the U.S. that holds even the promise of greater worker control in a capitalist society.

Despite this potential, other leftists in the U.S. have opposed the development of ESOPs and coops, arguing that "no diffusion of power is possible unless the means of production are publicly owned." (Wallis, 1983: 15). That is to say, the long-standing debate among the left in the U.S. remains between those who would support a centralized state control model of socialism versus those who would support a decentralized, local control model. The claims of worker ownership appeal chiefly to the latter group.

Moreover, the claim that people are entitled to democratic control over the organizations that effect their lives appears to have spread far beyond the left. Applying this principal to the workplace, a poll conducted by Hart Associates and reported in Rifkin (1977: 45-57) asked citizens in which of three types of systems they would personally prefer to work. Only 8% opted for a government agency, and surprisingly, only 20% would choose to work in a private investor owned corporation, the now dominant form of employment. The majority, 66%, opted for companies owned and controlled by their employees.

So the popular support, at least at a passive level, is there for worker-ownership and possibly control of industries. But, to be sure, there is no mobilized public protest on the streets for greater worker self-management, nor is there a political lobby for this cause in Washington. There is no organized consumer preference for worker-owned forms nor a boycott against the products of disinvesting conglomerates, though some worker coops have found that worker-ownership can be a significant marketing advantage.[3]

Yet even in the absence of the sort of popular protest activity that is often associated with social movements, the worker ownership effort has been incredibly effective at securing favorable national and state legislation. This legislative support, and especially the tax advantages contained in it, has been critical to the proliferation of ESOPs. How did it come about?

In 1958 Louis Kelso, a corporate consultant and attorney, and Mortimer Adler, editor of the *Encyclopaedia Britannica,* authored *The Capitalist Manifesto,* urging broadened ownership of capital as essential to the vitality of the capitalist system. The ideology of Kelso's next book was telegraphed in its colorful title: *How to Turn Eighty Million Workers into Capitalists on Borrowed Money* (1967). The ideas in these works captured the attention of Senator Russell Long, conservative head of the Senate Finance Committee, and one of the most powerful members of the Senate. Senator Long made ESOPs one of his top priorities. Senator Long was instrumental in the success of the ESOP tax provisions contained in 1974-75 laws discussed earlier and in the legislation to follow.

During the spring of 1977 an unusual relationship began to develop between academic professors who had been doing research on worker ownership and several young progressive members of Congress who were searching for new ideas that could effectively deal with the problems of shut-downs and job loss. On the academic side, William Foote Whyte, head of the New Systems of Work and Participation Program at Cornell University (on which this author served as a faculty member) and Joseph Blasi, head of the Project on Kibbutz Studies at Harvard University, took the lead. They drew liberally on the research findings from those two programs and others to feed information and ideas to the staff members of three involved Congressmen, Representatives Stanley Lundine and Mathew McHugh of New York and Representiative Peter Kostmayer of Philadelphia. With the university people providing suggestions based on research, and the Congressional staff people providing the legislative expertise, the Voluntary Job Preservation and Community Stablization Act was designed and written.[4]

The effectiveness of this University-Congress alliance suggests a more aggressive role for academics than is typically pursued. When academics speak of "policy research" they generally refer to the evaluation of the results of social policies of which they played no part in the creation. In this case, academics took a pro-active role, seeking to shape the policy outcomes of a social movement phenomenon. They did not start out to do "applied" research. This was basic, exploratory research, the practical implications of which were then drawn out for policy makers. This example suggests the need to rethink the usual dichotomy between "basic" and "applied research," and the role that university researchers can play in the public policy process.

In sum, the worker ownership legislation was to have three unique advantages: it had the serious commitment of several members of the House and Senate who, while supporting it for very different reasons, were willing to vigorously work for it. Second, it had no sustained opposition, as it is difficult for anyone to oppose a measure that creates or sustains jobs through worker-community initiative. Third, it was on a subject about which substantial academic research had been done, the preliminary findings augured well for the prospects of the firms and the university people were willing to "get their hands dirty" by contributing directly to the public policy process. With these advantages, but without traditional social movement agitation for this measure, how did the worker-ownership legislation fare?

On March 1, 1978, Representatives Kostmayer, Lundine and McHugh introduced the Voluntary Job Preservation and Community Stablization Act, a name carefully phrased to garner support and minimize opposition. The bill, to be administered by the Economic Development Administration (EDA), was designed to provide loan capital to workers to buy firms threatened with shut-down. In addition, it required that an economic feasibility study be done before such conversions took place and that technical assistance be provided to help workers learn what their options are regarding different forms of organization available under the law. With the aid of only one small lobby group, the Catholic Sisters of Network, a religious lobby for social justice, the bill quickly picked up approximately 70 co-sponsors. The list of co-sponsors included some of the most liberal and some of the most conservative members of the House. Most of this bill subsequently became part of Title II of the National Public Works and Economic Development Act of 1979 which passed the House by a vote of 300 to 99, and the Senate by a lessor margin. This bill was the reauthorization act for the whole EDA and would have opened up all of the EDA's programs (e.g., loans, technical assistance and demonstration programs) to employee-owned firms. However, because of disputes in the conference committee (having nothing to do with the worker ownership provisions) the bill never became law.

Shortly thereafter, Representatives Kostmayer and Nowak and Senators Stewart and Long introduced the Small Business Employee Ownership Act which directed the SBA to make loans and loan guarantees to worker buy-outs as well as to worker-owned start-ups. This passed the Senate by unanimous consent, and later became Title V of the Small Business Development Act of 1980 which passed both Houses and was signed into law by President Carter on July 3, 1980.

On August 12, 1982 the National Development Investment Act passed the House by a three-to-one margin. This bill would reauthorize the EDA, an agency the Reagan administration has tried to dismantle. Stan Lundine, one of the Congressmen originally involved with the Cornell group, drafted language in the bill that gives the EDA specific statutory authority to support employee-owned firms, and gives grant and loan priority to firms that are majority worker-owned. In addition, it requires of these firms that they grant full voting rights on the ESOP stock and that they review employee paraticipation in management. Though this bill is still pending, the EDA is operating in the interim and it is actively supporting worker-owned firms in this manner.

This attention and enthusiasm for employee-ownership in Congress has not been lost on the States. Beginning in 1979 with the legislatures of the States of Maryland and Michigan, eight states have now passed laws facilitating worker-ownership, and others are considering them. Although States are not in a position to offer the kind of tax incentives that the federal government can, they can take other steps to promote worker-owned firms. Some states, like Maryland and Delaware, have declared broadened ownership to be state policy and have directed every state agency involved in economic development to issue an annual report stating what they have done to promote worker-owned firms. States have taken other steps to provide information by putting out brochures on how worker ownership works, holding workshops around the state or developing a technical assistance capacity through state small business centers. While many buy-outs are financed privately and often with difficulty, some states, like Illinois and Michigan, have helped on the finance side by issuing state bonds to finance ESOP loans below the prime rate. Many other states are following the lead of Illinois and Michigan in proposing similar bond issues and loans for ESOPs, including New Jersey, Pennsylvania, California, New York, Wisconsin, and Connecticut. Other states have begun to scrutinize and change their state laws that impede employee-owned firms. For instance, California exempted leveraged ESOPs from state securities laws because a previous law had blocked the employee takeover of Continental Airlines. Massachusetts recently developed a statute that facilitates the incorporation of worker cooperatives.

Finally, in addition to all of these legislative successes at the state and federal levels, it is clear that worker ownership is emerging as a centerpiece of a comprehensive national policy on capital flight and the need for reindustrialization. In Pennsylvania, Governor Thornburgh has recently embraced ESOPs as part of his state economic recovery plan in his highly-touted "Advanced Technologies Policies" statement. At the national level the new House Democratic Caucus Report on economic policy, developed as an alternative to Reaganomics, lists "employee participation in management and ownership" as the first precondition for economic growth. A recent fundraising letter from the emerging progressive leadership in the Democratic Party, called "Congressional Agenda '80s," lists employee ownership and control as a key issue, (this was signed by Representatives Gephart, Pat Schroeder, Tom Downey, Tim Wirth, among others). At this stage, the issue seems likely to become a major plank of the 1984 presidential platform on the Democratic side.

So there we have the ideal policial issue. Even in the relative absence of vigorous lobbying or social movement protest activity, worker ownership has managed to attract a broad constituency of political actors. The degree of legislative success of the worker ownership issue came as a surprise to even the academic researchers who were involved from the start. Blasi writes of the process:

> A variety of worker-owned firms, unions and community groups expressed some interest, but as a close reading of the extensive hearings on the subject indicates, it was the members from the House and Senate themselves—people of all stripes—who were excited by the idea and evidence of its success around the country. (Blasi, 1981:12).

To the conservatives, this was "people's capitalism;" to the left, it was "democratic socialism;" and as we shall see, many of the participants did not care what it was, so long as it meant jobs.

VI.   OWNERS AND MANAGERS

The stance that private owners and top management take toward worker ownership cannot help but effect the opportunities that this new form has to spread. Case studies show that under some conditions owners and managers have been very receptive to worker ownership; under other circumstances they have bitterly opposed it. In what circumstances can we expect owners and managers to support, or conversely, to try to block worker-ownership?

In some cases consideration of the ESOP option arises because a parent company is shutting down a local plant whose chief product they are continuing to make in other locations. In these cases the parent company has little interest in allowing any competition from an employee-run firm in its same product line. So it does what it can to scuttle the idea. For instance, when International Paper was approached by an employee group regarding the purchase of a plant being shut down in North Tonawanda, New York, they simply refused to provide the group with any financial or operating information. By keeping its records closed, a company can make it all but impossible for an employee buy-out to occur.

In cases where a conglomerate may be shutting down a subsidiary plant that is not in its same line of business and therefore not in a competitive position, the employee buy-out has a better chance of succeeding.[5] In fact, in such cases *local* management may be enthusiastic about the idea and instrumental in its implementation. The reason is that the employee-ownership plan may allow local management to be promoted or at least retained in their positions, with considerably more autonomy than they had under conglomerate ownership and freed of the "profit hurdles" that had previously been imposed from above. For example, when Sperry Rand, chiefly in the electronics business, decided to shut down its sole library furniture plant in Herkimer, New York, top management in the plant knew they faced a choice between accepting a move to a different part of the country and trying to learn the electronics business from scratch or being out of a job. It is no surprise that they choose the option—in this case a blend of worker and community ownership—that allowed them to stay put and to build on the decades of expertise in the furniture business that they already had. In this case, local management became instrumental in the employee acquisition, providing among other things immediate access to the necessary financial records. At Bates Fabrics, too, it was because the parent company had moved into the energy business that they were willing to sell the last of their textile operation to the employees in a 100% ESOP. This type of circumstance then, where the parent company is in one line of business and the would-be ESOP is in another, provides a fertile opportunity for employee-ownership because (1) these firms are often quite viable enterprises, even if their profit margins are not high enough to please the parent company; (2) local management often have as much incentive to save these firms as do the workers and so their cooperation can be enlisted; and (3) the parent company, while it may have little to gain from a worker buy-out, has little reason to resist, and the public relations advantage of selling to the employee group, as opposed to an outright shut-down, is not lost on them.

Actually, the majority of ESOPs do not arise out of impending shut-downs, even of the type described above. A recent survey of 98 majority employee-owned firms was conducted by the National Center for Employee Ownership. Only 18.5% of these firms originated as buy-outs of endangered companies; another 17% were started as employee-owned.[6] Today we are seeing the use of ESOPs in an increasing number of start-ups of high-growth firms. Peoples Express, a new airline providing low-cost service, is one example of a firm that was started by its investors and managers as a 33% ESOP. The broad employee-ownership of stock and the participatory management that followed were partly credited with giving this company the lowest cost structure in the business according to Wall Street analysts, and since the stock went public last year, its price has tripled. As managers and investors become alert to the financial and tax advantages that leveraged ESOPs offer and to the motivation and productivity advantages that ESOPs are believed to bring, we can expect ESOPs to spread, as indeed they already are, in highly profitable firms.

Another circumstance where owners and managers sometimes become active initiators of employee-ownership is in the successful, long-standing family-owned (or closely-held) corporation where the owner wishes to retire. According to the Center's survey, transfers of ownership from a retiring owner account for almost 30% of the majority employee-owned firms. As the entrepreneur approaches retirement, especially if there is no heir apparent to manage the firm, a transfer of ownership to the employees may well serve the owners' needs. For the retiring owner of a substantial firm, the only way he can get his equity out of the firm is to find an outside buyer for his shares, which is often quite difficult, or to redeem his stock (sell it back to the corporation) in which case the sale would be taxed as ordinary income. With the invention of ESOPs, the owner can sell to an internal market—the employees—and the gain on the sale of stock to the ESOT will be taxed at the much lower long-term capital gains rate. In addition to the relative ease in finding a buyer (i.e., the employees) and the tax advantage in selling to an ESOP, many entrepreneurs probably feel better choosing this option. They are doing more to ensure the community that the firm will continue to operate and grow, and they are doing more to protect the well-being of their long-time employees. Selling to an outside conglomerate makes the future of the firm more uncertain, and even if it were assured, many entrepreneurs who have built a successful business do not wish to see the integrity of that business lost as it becomes a small subsidiary in a large conglomerate. So there are motivations aplenty for the successful entrepreneur to go in the direction of ESOPs too. Because ESOPs by their very nature create a market for a firm and allow the owner to sell his equity on terms that are tax-advantaged and determined by an independent third party appraisal, they solve an important problem for the independent businessman, and 3 out of 4 of the national organizations representing small business testified in favor of the Small Business Employee Ownership Act.

In a similar vein, Jack Curtis, a well-known attorney specializing in employee-ownership, has suggested that venture capitalists may begin to turn to ESOPs as an investment partner, since the ESOP can effectively purchase the stock when the venture capitalist wants to cash out his earlier investment.

Yet another type of circumstance that may in the future get management and owners behind employee-ownership is the increasing frequency of unfriendly take-over attempts, as conglomerate acquisition activity comes to touch ever larger economic units. About a year ago Continental Airlines tried to resist an unfriendly takeover bid by Texas International Airlines through a proposal to create an employee stock ownership trust which would own and control 51% of the total stock outstanding. The employees and management were joined in this effort, but due to peculiarities in California state law, the effort failed. Nonetheless, it demonstrates to other companies that are similarly threatened a new defense strategy against conglomerate takeover. Dan River, a textile maker with over 14,000 employees, recently succeeded in establishing an ESOP to prevent a takeover by the Icahn Group.

As knowledge of employee-ownership as a legal mechanism becomes more widely-known, we can expect this form of ownership to spread rapidly, and to be picked up by investors and managers for all of the reasons cited above. Those managers who have experience with ESOPs already report quite favorable attitudes: a recent survey by the ESOP Association of 213 companies found 70% of the managers reporting that the ESOP had improved employee motivation and productivity. Similarly, in the National Center's recent survey of majority-owned companies, 71% of the managers of democratic ESOPs and 100% of the coops reported satisfaction with worker ownership.

The specific legal and tax aspects of ESOPs are important to an understanding of the conditions of capital's support for worker ownership. It should be evident from this discussion that capital's support did not for the most part arise out of ideological conviction. People with a philosophical belief in broadened ownership succeeded in translating that value orientation into concrete legal, financial and tax incentives for making the transition. Capital's interest in the scheme arose and has been sustained by these demonstrated material advantages. Is the same true for labor?

VII.   UNION AND WORKER VIEWS

The view that labor takes toward worker ownership will greatly influence how this phenomenon unfolds. Labor's view, like capital's view, cannot be said to be either unified or static. It depends on the circumstances in which they find themselves and the degree of experience that they have with employee ownership. It also depends upon whether we are talking about rank and file workers, local union leaders, or national union leaders.

In the early days of employee ownership the union position could best be described as ambivalent. Worker ownership was not the unions' issue. It was not conceived, designed or even anticipated by the unions. As detailed earlier, it was conceived by conservatives who believed that broadened ownership could re-vitalize and stabilize capitalism, and was translated into a set of legal advantages designed to make business stop and take note. But in the mid and late 1970s, as industrial shut-downs spread, particularly in unionized firms, the Cornell studies found that where the idea of worker ownership was known, it quickly won the support of both management and labor. Under the cloud of threatened job loss, issues of job security naturally move to the fore, and worker ownership had *prima facie* appeal to workers who would otherwise lose their jobs. After the appropriate feasibility studies indicated that an operation could be viable if reorganized under the terms of an ESOP, we witnessed numerous cases where local management and working people worked intensively and cooperatively to mobilize the necessary financial and community support to "save" the plant. This process, at least for the time being, brought management and labor together in a unified cause, but what did it do for workers and unions?

In the mid-1970s, international union leaders had some difficulty formulating a stance on worker ownership. On the one hand, it would be rather unseemly for union leaders to oppose an effort that stood a chance of preserving jobs. On the other hand, they had at least four good reasons to suspect the whole idea. First, some trade unionists recalled that unions had supported the formation of worker cooperatives in the nineteenth century and that their relatively short life spans were regarded as a failure. Second, national union leaders feared that locals that survived by way of an ESOP would be forced to take substantial pay reductions which could undercut workers elsewhere and possibly undermine the wages and benefits generally prevailing in an industry. Third, ESOP plans had sometimes entailed the dropping of hard-won pension plans. The substitution of ESOP stock in a possibly shaky employer for a more diversified set of pension investments struck many trade unionists as risky. Beyond these concerns about the conditions of employment in the new ESOP firms and whether these cases would be used to force worker sacrifices elsewhere, trade union leaders worried that the union might have no place in the employee-owned firm. This was expressed in the often repeated statement, "you can't bargain with yourself."

Ironically, then, as economic conditions and structural incentives set the stage for the explosive development of employee-ownership, unions were caught without a policy and without any in-depth information on the subject. The national unions could not help but be concerned about job preservation, but the apparent contradiction between collective bargaining and worker ownership left them so immobilized that they were generally of little help to local unions in formulating ESOPs. This left the initiative in the hands of local managers, who were soon followed by local workers and community leaders. The fact of management initiative then became another reason for suspicion by the international unions. The notion that the traditional adversarial relationship might be suspended in favor of cooperation understandably brought fears that management would use this as an opportunity for productivity initiatives, without sharing the productivity gains with the workers.

The reservations about employee ownership show up on a 1977 survey of national union leaders conducted by Stern and O'Brien.[7] Asked for a general assessment of employee ownership, three-quarters of those surveyed were "basically negative." However, three years later, a survey of trade union leaders on the same subject reveals a sharp change in attitude. By 1980, only 29% of the surveyed union officers were negative to employee ownership. Moreover, there was a marked difference between those international officers whose locals had had some experience with employee ownership and those who had not, with virtually none of the respondents who had observed employee ownership (in one or more of their own locals) expressing disapproval. Overall, the studies suggest that as trade unionists accumulate more direct experience with employee ownership, their attitudes toward it are getting more positive because their experiences with ESOPs have not for the most part justified their earlier fears. They are coming to realize that if they take an active role in the formation of the ESOP, they can shape it to meet their concerns and to further worker interests.

There are at least two fundamental ways in which the ESOP form of ownership can be used to advance worker interests. It can be used to enhance the material well-being and job security of the worker. And it can be used to extend the sphere of worker influence or control over the workplace. After an initial delay in recognizing these opportunities, some unions are now beginning to investigate and to exploit the opportunities inherent in the ESOP form.

First, there are the cases, widespread during a recession, where management demands wage concessions from the workforce, with the threat that without them they will be forced to reduce the workforce or close down. In the past, unions could either give in or they could refuse the concessions and learn later whether or not management was bluffing. Either way, the possible losses were high.

With the advent of ESOPs, unions have a new bargaining strategy available to them. If they are convinced that the company is genuinely in dire condition, they do not have to choose between permanent wage cuts or job loss. They can agree to negotiate wage cuts, provided stock is issued to the workers through an ESOP arrangement to make up for some or all of the value of the cuts.

This bargaining strategy has already been used successfully at several of the airlines. Pan American led the way a couple of years ago. On the brink of financial collapse, managements' claim for the necessity of wage reductions was credible, but the union leaders countered by demanding stock in exchange. Ultimately the workers negotiated a 12% voting interest in Pan Am, receiving $3 worth of stock for every $9 sacrificed in pay. Now that Pan Am is solvent and profitable again, the stock is worth $6. So the employees have made back two-thirds of their original pay cut, and Dick Phenneger, who led the union bargaining effort, reports that the employees are using their 12% interest in Pan Am to influence corporate policy. Inspired by the Pan Am example, employees at Western Airlines insisted on stock in return for a pay cut they would have had to take. They won an 18% share of the company, with full voting rights. Similarly, employees at Eastern will soon reveive a 25% ESOP. At Hawaiian Airlines an employee demand for stock in return for salary reductions was not acceptable to management. Nevertheless, the extent to which this strategy has spread throughout the airline industry in less than two years is indicative of its potential.

The UAW has been the first major national union to suggest worker ownership in its contract talks. Arising again in a time of crisis, the Chrysler Loan Guarantee Act provided Chrysler employees with 15-20% of the total company stock, building on the argument in Congress that if the government is going to make loans to private corporations, the cost to the taxpayers is at least more justified if the benefits of the loan are spread more broadly to the workers rather than concentrating only on the investors. Over 1981-82, $81 million worth of Chrysler stock was allocated to the employees. That stock has more than quadrupled in value, and now holds a valuation of approximately $400 million, the total value of the sizeable concessions that the workers made.[8] In addition, Doug Fraser, former president of the UAW, was put on the Board at Chrysler. The experience with Chrysler may well set a precedent for UAW contract negotiations with GM and Ford. Since there is no reason to believe that contract concessions in the auto or airline industry would have been any smaller had the workers *not* got stock in return, the unions' insistence that companies match any wage concessions with stock has been a plus for workers and a very important new bargaining strategy.

The other way in which unions are just beginning to use ESOPs to further worker interests is in recent attempts to establish "democratic ESOPs." The pioneering case of this kind, and one that is receiving a great deal of attention in both union and business circles, is Rath Packing Co. in Waterloo, Iowa. After a long corporate decline and substantial worker sacrifices in wages during the 1970s, the company asked the workers to take even deeper cuts in 1979. The union leaders, representing the United Food and Commercial Workers, refused, unless a transfer of ownership and change in management could be got in return. This case differs from many others in that it was the local union that took the initiative. After extensive negotiations a complex plan was worked out whereby the workers would deduct $20 per week from their pay to receive 60% of the Rath stock, with 50–50 profit sharing between the company and the workers, and the company to receive a $4.6 million UDAG loan for necessary capital investments. What makes this plan the first of its kind is the provision that workers elect their Board members on a one-worker-one-vote basis, *not* on the basis of number of shares owned. The previous Board was expanded from 6 to 16 in order to give the union slate ten seats on the Board. Final approval of the ESOP came in December of 1980, and since then, following significant management changes, the union and the management have worked together to effect major changes in labor-management relations, from the shop floor to the boardroom. With the assistance of researchers from Cornell University, "action-research teams" were set up in many departments, and after training in group-process and problem-solving skills, many of these teams have made impressive productivity improvements in their departments, without which the company could not have survived. Groups have been involved in everything from strategic planning, to the types of new machines that should be bought, to safety issues. Arising out of a truly desperate situation (where employee ownership would not ordinarily be counselled), the involvement of the workers in the ownership and decision-making at Rath is credited with substantial productivity gains, but whether this will be enough to put the company, which has recently suffered financial setbacks, in the black is still an open question.

Following the lead at Rath in setting up a democratic ESOP, the UAW Local 726 organized a $53 million buy-out of a bearing plant from GM. The 100% worker-owned company, now called Hyatt Clark Industries, was established in October, 1981. Workers put up $100 each to hire an outside consultant to do a feasibility study. Based on the results of the study, the workers agreed to a 100% ESOP, with a 30% reduction in wages, about half of which is expected to be made up the first year through a profit-sharing plan. What makes this plan unusual is that the shares are *not* allocated differentially according to wages. Everyone gets an equal share of stock, and therefore, an equal voting right (although they cannot vote the stock until 1990). The initial Board has 3 union representatives, but over time (recall that ESOPs only gradually transfer ownership) workers will elect the whole Board. It is interesting that the International UAW kept a neutral stance in this case, especially in light of a growing number of union leader statements that give qualified support to the ESOP form and a recent AFL-CIO questionnaire evaluating the voting records of members of Congress that assessed a positive rating if they were for certain worker-ownership provisions.

The brand new "O & O" stores in Philadelphia (so named because they are worker-owned and operated) represent yet another unprecedented scheme for democratic worker ownership, arising out of adversity. In this case, when A & P announced that they would shut down many of their stores in Philadelphia, the United Food and Commercial Workers representing 2000 members who would have lost their jobs, actively put together and ultimately ratified a collective bargaining agreement whereby A & P will contribute 1% of gross sales at its Super Fresh stores to a union-controlled trust to be used to finance worker cooperatives. The union has options on a number of A & P properties and is determining which would be most viable, and has rights-of-first-refusal on the leases of remaining stores, should the company decide to sell or franchise them in the future. In October, 1982, the union opened up the first couple of stores. They are set up as worker cooperatives with ownership as a condition of employment, one-worker-one-vote, and full participation in policy and planning. Although workers must make an investment of $5000 in the coop (these are not ESOPs) worker interest in joining is very high, and sales are reportedly good.

Finally, in the most ambitious example to date, the heads of 13 unions representing the employees of Conrail are acting in concert to put together a proposal for a worker buy-out of Conrail. Last year the government announced that it would sell Conrail by the end of 1984. If the union-sponsored bid is accepted, this will be the largest case of its kind, with some 40,000 employees, and it will be the first case where the heads of national unions have initiated a bid to buy a company that is not failing.

All four of these cases, started between 1980 and 1982, contrast sharply with the sorts of cases we saw in the mid to late 1970s. They were initiated and actively organized by local unions, not by management. The internationals assisted or took a neutral stance, unlike a case like South Bend Lathe in the mid-1970s, where the international was hostile to the conditions of the ESOP and the local's role in it. These four recent cases were union-sponsored, and as a result, the worker-ownership brought with it worker voice in company affairs, access to information so that workers could oversee their investment, formal positions on the Board, and democratic voting rights.

It is crystal clear that when worker-ownership is actively formulated by working people and their union leaders, it will have organizational outcomes very different than when it is initiated and planned by management. The vast majority of ESOP cases initiated by capital do not even extend formal voting rights to workers, much less democratic participation. Even the ESOP cases that do provide for majority worker-ownership of voting stock seldom consider larger changes in the social organization of the workplace. The Cornell studies found that in the management-initiated cases, managers were ordinarily so preoccupied with legal, financial and technical concerns, that they failed to consider what social and organizational changes the new ownership structure might imply. The National Center's March 1983 survey estimates that perhaps 50% of the majority worker-owned firms provide for full voting rights, but that still refers to voting one's stock which is nearly always unequally distributed. Another survey done earlier of 299 ESOPs established between1975-76 found that in only 3% of the cases were the ESOP trustees selected by the employees! They found that only 21% of the companies gave the ESOP participants full voting rights (voting rights requirements were strengthened in 1980). Asking these respondent (managers) why they had instituted the ESOP, 51% wanted to improve productivity, 35% wanted to finance company growth, and 8% admitted to wanting to avoid unionization.[9]

VIII.   CONCLUSION: WHO WILL BENEFIT?

There is no question that the surveys and the case studies reveal missed opportunities (from a worker control point of view) in many of the management-initiated ESOPs. Nonetheless, it would be premature to dismiss ESOPs as "cooptation." The potentialities of worker ownership are still fluid. Like most important social inventions in their early stages of development, worker ownership could move in a number of different directions in the U.S., depending upon which of its constituencies manages to shape the issue. Management-oriented ESOPs dominated the first stage, but now we appear to be entering a second stage, and unions are coming to realize that they can shape the ESOP instrument toward worker ends.

In the long run, worker ownership cannot help but bring major changes in the relationship between workers and management. Recall that the transfer of ownership in the ESOP is gradual. As the principal on the loan is repaid, the shares are allocated to the employees. It would not be unusual, for example, for it to take 18 years for 51% of the stock to be released in this fashion and 25 years for 100% of the stock to be allocated, as is the case at Bates, a 100% ESOP. We found in the Cornell studies that workers in the 1970s tended to go into ESOPs with vague expectations of more say and more respect in the firm and that management tended to go into it thinking that it would give them a more motivated or compliant workforce. Without either side making specific plans and structures to accommodate these rather incoate expectations, hopes got dashed, and industrial relations deteriorated. In the absence of any special avenues for participation, workers at Saratoga Knitting Mill, as at other partial worker-owned firms, did not feel like "owners" any more than did non-owning workers. Nevertheless, as the ESOP mechanism distributes stock slowly, workers have a long time before they become majority owners, and over time workers may come to recognize that ownership and voting rights are an opportunity to mobilize for greater information and greater voice in the workplace. The specific structures they may evolve to effect greater worker control cannot be determined in advance, but all is not lost if some of these firms start off without such structures. As management and workers come to mutually recognize that they cannot realize many of the potential advantages of worker ownership within the traditional hierarchical arrangement, they are likely to begin altering the social organization of the workplace.

Management and small business owners were quick to grasp ESOPs, as were workers who were facing job loss. The unions took a few more years. Slowly but surely, however, they too are coming around to worker ownership, not out of some a priori ideological commitment, but out of the practical opportunities it offers for job preservation, for getting shares of stock in return for concessions that would be exacted anyway, and for advancing democratic control of the workplace. The outcomes in the individual firms that are started or converted to worker ownership, and the outcomes for this movement as a whole, depend to a great extent on who stays involved in bringing the changes about.

If workers and their union representatives continue to take the initiative in planning and developing ESOPs, as they did in the four post-1980 cases discussed in this paper, we can expect to see more majority (51% to 100%) worker-owned firms, with more worker control over the shop floor, more access to corporate information, and more avenues for worker voice at higher levels, including the Board room. Following the pioneering example of Rath Meat Packing, we will see the development of more "democratic ESOPs," utilizing the cooperative principle of "one worker-one vote." On the other hand, if capital continues to dominate the planning of ESOPs, we can expect to see more ESOPs with minority worker ownerships takes, devoid of voting rights and without any special avenues for worker participation. In this case, the ESOP will come to be seen by all concerned as a simple supplement to wages, like a profit sharing plan or a pension, signifying no essential alteration in the social relations to production.

There is a well-known Latin proverb that says that "necessity is the mother of invention." This paper has examined an important invention in the social organization of the workplace. ESOPs are changing the ownership of the means of production in the firms that they touch, and as such, they have the potential to alter control over the means of production, or what a Marxist would call the social relations to production. In tracing the evolution and political development of this invention, it becomes clear that ESOPs were dreamed up by people who liked the idea on ideological grounds, but who also were successful at translating it into a set of concrete legal and material incentives. ESOPs owe their widespread proliferation to these structural incentives. Management, workers, and small business owners all see different things in worker ownership and hope to gain from it in different ways. They are all trying to create ESOPs that will serve their own interests. Because in different ways, employee ownership serves the practical everyday needs of so many different classes, it has developed a constituency in the U.S. that is as broad as it is odd. The future of worker ownership will depend on which constituencies prevail in their efforts to define and control the issue.

ACKNOWLEDGMENT

Information in this paper is partly drawn from the author's participation in the New Systems of Work and Participation Program at Cornell University, ILR School, which was supported by a grant from the National Institute of Mental Health.

I wish to thank Scott Cummings, Cory Rosen, Bernard Wilpert, and Allen Whitt for their comments and suggestions on an earlier version.

NOTES

1. In other work I have analyzed the organizational inventiveness of the grassroots collectives (Rothschild-Whitt, 1979), and the ideological origins and sense of mission that characterize this movement (forthcoming).

2. Indeed, worker-run cooperatives from around the world have been very egalitarian in the distribution of rewards. See Rothschild-Whitt (1979) for examples.

3. See, for example, the worker coop, *Citizen's Voice,* and how it captured the market from its previous employer, the conglomerate-owned newspaper in Wilkes-Barre, PA. (Keil, 1982). Similarly, Peoples Express, a new airlines, advertises that when you fly it, people serving you will be owners.

4. For a more detailed description of the development of this and other pieces of employee ownership legislation, see "Worker Ownership and Public Policy" by J. Blasi and W.F. Whyte, and "From Research to Legislation on Employee Ownership" by Whyte and Blasi.

5. See, Stern and Hammer (1978) for an analysis of this and other factors that influence the success of employee buy-out attempts.

6. Survey results are reported in Employee Ownership, Vol. III, No. 1, March 1983: 1-2.

7. The 1977 survey of union leaders' attitudes toward worker ownership was conducted by Bob Stern and Ray Ann O'Brien at Cornell University. Surveys were mailed to 140 international union presidents or research directors, and the survey reports 49 responses. Many of the negative attitudes discussed above are based on the Stern-O'Brien work. The 1980 survey was conducted by Joseph Blasi, Doug Kruse and Eric Asard at Harvard University, and received responses from 42 union officers.

8. Market stock prices quoted in this paper are as of May 27, 1983.

9. This survey by Thomas Marsh and Dale McAllister is reported in Employee Ownership, Vol. I, No. 3, December 1981, p. 5-6.

REFERENCES

Ash, Roberta
1972   Social Movements in America. Chicago: Markham Publishing Co.
Bailis, L.
1974   Bread or Justice. Lexington, MA: Heath.

Birch, David
    1979   "The job creation process." Cambridge, MA. MIT Program on Neighborhood Regional
        Change.
Blasi, Joseph and William Foote Whyte
    1981   "Worker ownership & public policy." Presented at International Conference on Producer
        Cooperatives, Copenhagen Denmark, May 31-June 4.
Bluestone, Barry and Bennett Harrison
    1980   "Why corporations close profitable plants." Working Papers for a New Society 8
        (May/June): 15-23.
Bluestone, Barry, and Bennett Harrison
    1982   The Deindustrialization of America. New York: Basic Books.
Braverman, Harry
    1974   Labor & Monopoly Capital. New York Monthly Review Press.
Committee on Small Business, U.S. House Representatives
    1980   "Conglomerate mergers—their effects on small business and local communities." Wash-
        ington, D.C.: U.S. Government Printing Office (House Document No. 96-343): October 2,
        1980.
Frisch, Robert
    1982   ESOP for the '80s. Rockville Centre, NY: Farnsworth Publishing Co.
Jenkins, Craig and Charles Perrow
    1977   "The insurgency of the powerless." American Sociological Review 42:249-268.
Keil, Thomas
    1983   "Community factors in the emergence and stabilization of a producer cooperative." In-
        stitute for New Enterprise Development. Cambridge, MA.
McAdam, D.
    1982   Political Process and the Development of Black Insurgency. Chicago: University of Chi-
        cago Press.
McCarthy, John and Mayer Zald
    1973   "The trend of social movements in America: professionalization and resource mobiliza-
        tion." Morristown, NJ: General Learning Press.
McCarthy, John and Mayer Zald
    1977   "Resource mobilization and social movements: a partial theory." American Journal of
        Sociology 82:1212-1241.
Metzger, Bert
    1978   "Achieving motitavion through employee stock ownership." Paper prepared for the an-
        nual conference of the ESOP Council of America.
Morris, A.
    1981   "Black southern student sit-in movement." American Sociological Review 46:744-767.
New York Stock Exchange
    1982   People and Productivity: A Challenge to Corporate America. New York Stock Exchange.
Olson, Mancur
    1968   The Logic of Collective Action. New York: Schocken Books.
Rifkin, Jeremy
    1977   Own Your Own Job. New York: Bantam Books.
Rothschild-Whitt, Joyce
    1979   "The Collectivist Organization: An Alternative to Rational-Bureaucratic Models." Ameri-
        can Sociological Review 44 (August):509-527.
Rothschild-Whitt, Joyce and Allen Whitt
    1984   Work without Bosses: Conditions and Dilemmas of Organizational Democracy in
        Grassroots Co-operatives. Forthcoming.

Shearer, Derek and Martin Carnoy
  1980   Economic Democracy. White Plains, NY: M.E. Sharpe.
Stern, Robert and Tove Helland Hammer.
  1978   "Buying you job: factors affecting the success or failure of employee acquisition attempt."
          Human Relations, 753-763.
Turner, Ralph and Lewis Killian
  1972   Collective Behavior, second edition. Englewood Cliffs, NJ: Prentice-Hall.
Useem, B.
  1980   "Solidarity Model, breakdown model, and the Boston anti-bussing movement." American
          Sociological Review 45:357-369.
Wallis, Victor
  1983   "Democracy through public ownership." Workplace Democracy 10 (Winter):15.
Walsh, E. J.
  1981   "Resource mobilization and citizen protest in communities around Three Mile Island."
          Social Problems 26:1-21.
Walton, Richard
  1979   "Work innovations in the United States." Harvard Business Review (July-August):88-98.
Whyte, William Foote and Joseph Blasi
  1980   "From Research to Legislation on Employee Ownership." Economic and Industrial De-
          mocracy 1:395-415.

POWER, INSURGENCY, AND STATE INTERVENTION:

FARM LABOR MOVEMENTS IN CALIFORNIA

Theo J. Majka and Linda C. Majka

I. INTRODUCTION

A social history of agricultural labor in California from 1870 to the present establishes several patterns in the relationship among agricultural workers, the agricultural landowners or growers, and what will be defined as the state. These patterns relate to the repeated attempts by farm workers to organize, the prominence of certain kinds of "control" issues in their demands, the weakness of most organizing efforts as reflected in either defeats or merely temporary gains, the intransigence of most growers, and shifts in government policies and actions. These patterns have set the context within which the United Farm Workers, AFL-CIO (UFW), under the leadership of Cesar Chavez, has attempted to organize agricultural workers in California during the 1960s, 1970s, and early 1980s.

Research in Social Movements, Conflict and Change, Vol. 6, pages 195–224.
Copyright © 1984 by JAI Press Inc.
All rights of reproduction in any form reserved.
ISBN: 0-89232-311-6

II.   THE FARM LABOR MARKET

Large-scale production has dominated California agriculture virtually since statehood. Variously described during the past century as the "grower-shipper interests," the "farm factories," and most recently "corporate agriculture" and "agribusiness," these operations have become increasingly concentrated. Concurrently, there has been a decline in the number of farms, especially small farms.[1] Many large growers have had various formal connections with corporations related to agribusiness, such as banks, processors, and shippers. In addition, corporate involvement in agricultural production has increased to the point that by 1970 one-fourth to one-third of cropland production came from corporate farms. Forty-six percent of California corporate farms have operations in two or more states. Moreover, half of the acreage of corporate farms is held by corporations engaged in businesses other than agricultural production (Fellmeth, 1973:78–79, Day, 1971:37).

Corporations involved in agricultural production are of three types. First there are family corporations engaged in farming. Some of these are quite extensive. Bruce Chruch, Inc., for example, is a wholly-owned family corporation growing lettuce, celery, cantaloupes, broccoli, spinach, carrots, tomatoes, cotton, alfalfa, and feed grains on 20,000 acres in California and Arizona (Sosnick, 1978:18). Other large agricultural operations are publicly owned corporations primarily engaged in food processing or distribution. Some prominent examples are Del Monte, Libby McNeil and Libby, H. J. Heinz, Coca Cola, Ralston-Purina, Green Giant, DiGiorgio, Great Western Sugar, Heublein, Safeway Stores, and United Brands. Finally, there are publicly owned corporations that have substantial investments in agriculture but whose main operations are in nonfood areas. Tenneco, for example, whose operations have extended from petroleum to pipelines, chemicals, shipbuilding, and farm machinery, has farm operations covering 35,000 acres and has become the nation's largest shipper of fresh fruits and vegetables. Other prominent corporations that have invested in agriculture include Dow Chemical, Purex, Standard Oil of California, Gulf and Western, Boeing, Getty Oil, Goodyear Tire and Rubber, Union Carbide, Sterling Precision, Prudential Insurance, Kaiser Alumninum, Penn-Central, and Southern Pacific (Sosnick, 1978:19).

Large agricultural operations have been the employers of an increasing proportion of seasonal farm workers. California, the leader in employment of both migrant and nonmigrant seasonal farm labor, appears to have a fairly constant number of field workers. The average annual employment of seasonal workers in 1975 was 117,000. Of this number 17,000 were classified as intrastate migrants, 13,000 as interstate migrants and 87,000 as locals, that is, workers who commute from their homes to jobs in the vicinity. These figures exclude farmers and unpaid family members (70,000) and year-round permanent employees (99,000). The average number of seasonal farm workers in California in 1975 actually represented a slight increase from a low of 110,000 in 1972 and was similar to the average from 1966–69 (Sosnick, 1978:7).

Large-scale agricultural operations have provided the primary source of employment for farm labor in California. The California food-producing industry has undergone considerable change within the last hundred years in terms of concentration of ownership, size, corporate involvement, technology of production, and crops harvested. Nevertheless, agricultural growers' desire for certain kinds of workers has remained remarkably constant. Growers have sought a labor force that is essentially passive, powerless, tractable, and unorganized, and as a whole they have vehemently resisted the numerous agricultural unionization attempts marking the history of California agriculture. The growth of corporate-owned operations has not appeared to alter this pattern. As a result of their successes, growers have been able to keep labor costs down and in the process render agricultural workers one of the lowest-paid segments of the working class.[2]

In order to secure a labor force with the preferred characteristics, the growers have employed a succession of nonwhite minorities excluded from the predominantly white, urban-based labor union movement. From 1870 to the present, Chinese, Japanese, Mexicans, and Filipinos, to mention only the most numerous groups, have at different times dominated the agricultural labor force. Each of these groups, at its first introduction into the fields, served as a controllable work force. Contrary to their employers' expectations, however, when a homogeneous minority group became the dominant labor supply in certain types of harvest work, it began to organize, demand wage and other concessions, challenge the growers' control of working and employment conditions, and strike if it met grower intransigence. The Chinese alone were excluded from this pattern and remained basically compliant with the terms of their employment, in large part because they were subjected to an exceptional campaign of discrimination and suppression throughout the West. When labor unrest and organization became widespread and the group no longer was the source of low-wage, powerless labor, the large agricultural landowners attempted to undermine its dominant position in the agricultural labor force and hire another group to undercut the organized. Some members of the previous group still remained to compete with the newer workers on terms set by the growers, but with little of their former power. Ethnic diversity has been a further insurance against successful organization, for rivalries and distrust among ethnic factions have hindered collective actions. Gradually obstacles were overcome, organizational efforts increased, and strikes were called. Then growers would look elsewhere in the chronically oversupplied agricultural labor market for a source of low-wage, unorganized workers, and the cycle would be repeated.

The California farm workers' struggle to organize throughout this century is a remarkable passage in working class history. The struggles varied in intensity, organization, tactics, duration, specific grievances, leadership, and extent of mass involvement. Farm worker poverty and the overwhelming strength of their opponents made agricultural labor organizations extremely vulnerable. Given this historical vulnerability in which the vast majority of past farm labor associations had only a brief existence, the survival and growth of the United Farm Workers Union under the leadership of Cesar Chavez during the past twenty years are extraordinary.

We have selected several major focal points around which to organize our presentation of historical evidence and analysis of its most significant patterns. Three are critical. First, contrary to typical portrayals of only limited labor struggles in agriculture, throughout the history of agricultural labor conflict in California a significant number of organizational attempts and strikes went beyond seeking wage concessions and raised demands for changes in hiring practices and greater control by labor over employment and conditions of work. Second, until the UFW's most recent drives, agricultural workers have been unable to implement permanent improvements in these conditions. That this weakness has remained for each group of workers, despite the variety of strategies, organizational structures, and leadership styles, suggests that factors other than the workers' own abilities and inclinations to engage in struggles have been crucial. Finally, the state has played critical roles in determining the characteristics of the farm labor force and the chance of success of each wave of farm worker unionization attempts. The centrality of state responses in this history indicates that the role of the state merits careful examination. In this analysis we will consider each of these three points in order to develop a more comprehensive analysis of the changing patterns of capital-labor struggles in California agriculture.

III.   FARM WORKER PROTEST
AND CONTROL ISSUES

Many of the more prolonged periods of insurgency involved demands for unionization and concurrent alterations in the method of labor recruitment and hiring. Farm workers have consistently sought guarantees of stable employment and changes in existing work practices as well as increased wages. These control objectives have the potential to transform the established methods of agricultural labor recruitment and hiring to the advantage of labor. The practice of direct grower hiring or the traditional hiring through labor contractors has functioned to place control over the labor force with the employers. Workers have been exposed to severe forms of exploitation with little countervailing power except the ability to disrupt production.

Control issues challenge the prevailing patterns of the utilization of labor and the conditions of work. They are aimed at adapting the production process to worker needs, narrowing the area of management's arbitrary power, and incorporating worker representatives into decision-making processes within the company (Gorz, 1964:35–41; Montgomery, 1979:1–7, 98–99). Nearly all analysts of worker movements and objectives do not interpret control issues as relevant for the "unskilled" segments of the labor force within which agricultural workers would be conventionally included. In fact, the traditional paradigm of U.S. labor relations, as represented by Commons and Perlman, sees workers primarily concerned with wage or "bread-and-butter" issues. Workers are portrayed as trimming their aspirations to an evolutionary accommodation to the structure of American capitalism and as threatening little encroachment upon the prerogatives of management (Perlman and Taft, 1935; Kerr et al., 1960:208–216). While authorities do focus on control issues, these demands are considered only as they are defined by workers in advanced sectors of production (Gorz, 1964; Montgomery, 1979:91–112; Mallet, 1975). Low-paid and low-skilled workers in nonunionized sectors of production are absorbed by the need to defend their existing standard of living, and are believed to be almost exclusively concerned with wage issues.

These assumptions about unskilled workers are clearly contradicted by the history of agricultural workers in California. Besides the recruitment issue, agricultural workers have repeatedly fought for union recognition, improvements in health and safety conditions in the fields, the creation of tolerable living conditions in labor camps, the limitation of working hours, the elimination of excessive charges for meals in the camps and at the work site, and the rehiring of strikers without discrimination. The legacy of such organizing in California is extensive: the agricultural movement of ethnic clubs and unions, activity by the Industrial Workers of the World (IWW or Wobblies) from 1913 to 1917, strikes by the Cannery and Agricultural Workers Industrial Union (CAWIU) from 1932 to 1934, organizing efforts by the United Cannery, Agricultural, Packing and Allied Workers of America (UCAPAWA) from 1937 to 1940, union opposition to the bracero programs, and, most notably, current UFW efforts (Majka, 1981). Before the UFW, many of these control issues were articulated and demanded but were not institutionalized since no union or worker organization had sufficiently established itself to be able to pursue the implementation of these demands. Nevertheless, the prevalence of control issues in farm labor protests over time indicates a realization that before long-term qualitative improvement in the circumstances of farm workers could take place, it would be necessary to challenge the growers' unilateral control over conditions of employment and work as well as to alter the prevailing norms for exploitation.

Of those who have analyzed control issues in the labor movement, David Montgomery and Serge Mallet have provided the most useful approaches. Montgomery (1979: esp. Chapters 4 and 5) regards as control struggles strikes involving such issues as union recognition, the dismissal of unpopular foremen or the retention of popular ones, the enforcement of work rules, the regulation of layoffs or dismissals, the eight-hour day, and expressions of sympathy or solidarity with other groups of workers. Mallet's (1975:87, 102–4) definition encompasses struggles for control over employment and hiring, work conditions (especially health and safety), job classification, and work organization and hours. The issues from farm worker strikes that most closely parallel Montgomery's and Mallet's definitions are those concerned with abolishing the labor contractor system, improving job safety, regulating hiring and seniority, improving meals and sanitary conditions in the labor camps, and eliminating the bonus system. During the UFW era control issues have been elaborated to an unprecedented extent. Along with seeking wage gains, the UFW has specifically attempted to gain union recognition and contracts, eliminate the labor contractor system and establish a union hiring hall, institute a seniority system through the hiring hall, end illegal child labor, control pesticide use, establish ranch committees of workers to handle problems with employers, and regulate the mechanization of agriculture in order to prevent a massive displacement of workers. Farm worker demands are control issues because they oppose the arbitrary power of the employer and the prevailing norms of exploitation in agriculture. Although the strike issues of farm workers stop short of managerial control, they still represent attempts to gain a necessary qualitative improvement in the balance of power with the growers, and have not been compromised for wages. The history of strikes by rural laborers in California gives evidence that *unskilled* workers and workers who have been very poor throughout this century have organized around control issues: both wage and nonwage control issues proved capable of mobilizing agricultural labor.

The importance of control issues is explained in part by Harry Braverman in *Labor and Monopoly Capital*. Control over the labor process has always been central from the point of view of employers. For the sake of expanding profits, capitalists had to remove control over the labor process from the workers and retain it themselves. Historically the transition from control by the worker to control by the capitalist was experienced by the worker as a progressive alienation from the process of production. For capitalists this was the problem of "management" (Braverman, 1974:53–59; Montgomery, 1979:1–44). The same method of reordering the labor process to centralize control in the hands of employers was applied to a wide variety of occupations. First, the labor process was disassociated from workers' skills so that it became independent of tradition, craft, and worker knowledge. Then all possible conceptual work was removed from the point of production. Finally, employers used their monopoly over knowledge of work to control each aspect of the labor process and the manner of execution (Braverman, 1974:113–119).

The result was a transformation of working people into factors of production and instruments of capital (Braverman, 1974:113–119; Brody, 1980:9–14; Montgomery, 1979:101–103). Both Montgomery and Braverman assert that this was a condition repugnant to its victims, no matter what their level of skill or pay. It violated the human conditions of work, not because laborers were destroyed as human beings, but because they were utilized in inhuman ways. At the same time, each new generation of workers had to be habituated to the capitalist mode of production. Workers were acclimatized through the destruction of any other way of living (a result of the evolution of capitalism), powerful economic forces, and corporate employment and bargaining policies (Braverman, 1974:139–151).

The centralization of control in agriculture has resulted in largely successful attempts to remove skills from agricultural work, which in turn produced chaotic patterns of employment and ways of life for farm workers and their families. Growers have used their control over the labor force to insist upon a plentiful supply of labor at low wages. This has been accomplished at different times by the manipulation of immigration policy, repression of unionization attempts with the help of the state, access to contract labor from Mexico. and cooperation with a labor contractor system that promised to leave intact the pattern of employer control and exploitation of the work force. Farm workers have responded with control demands that have become more sharply defined in each succeeding period of mass insurgency. The early California ethnic clubs sought to gain some order in the hiring process to the point of enforcing closed shop conditions whenever possible. IWW militancy focused on the effects of exploitative conditions in the everyday lives of farm workers. A succession of unionization efforts in the 1930s generated demands for the abolition of the labor contractor system and wide-ranging issues related to the day-to-day experience of making a living as a farm worker: protests over housing, sanitary conditions, discrimination, the length of the work day, medical services, transportation, and work implements.

More than any previous unionization effort, the UFW has been able to move beyond wage demands in favor of objectives oriented toward control over the labor process. It has insisted on the hiring hall in an attempt to gain control over hiring and in order to include seniority rights and exclude child labor, remove the arbitrary control over the work force embodied in the labor contractor system, and insure a correspondence between the number of workers needed for a job and the number supplied. All of these functions of the hiring hall are aimed at narrowing the sphere of management's arbitrary power and adapting the system of production to the needs of workers. Pesticide control clauses in UFW contracts have attempted to modify the technique of production and to challenge employers' prerogatives where the health and safety of field laborers and consumers were concerned. Both pesticide limitations and the hiring hall have been crucial issues of contention between growers and the UFW.

Given the large numbers of individual contracts and differences in crops, size of ranch operations, requirements for packing, stages of mechanization, types of pesticide usage, and even composition of the labor supply, administration from a central union headquarters is very difficult. Most UFW officials were convinced that if the organization is to follow up on the enforcement of its contracts, the most effective way is to delegate authority to the ranch committees. Locally elected, autonomously functioning ranch committees would have the authority to enforce contracts, negotiate over the implementation of contract provisions, and settle grievances. Despite their apparent advantages such committees have proved difficult to establish on a permanent basis. Problems arise largely because of grower noncooperation and resistance but also because of continued uncertainty within the union of the kind of balance between the authority of top union officials and that delegated to ranch committees. Nevertheless, a number of effective ranch committees have been firmly established for several years.

The pattern of growers' opposition to UFW demands has shown the extent to which hiring and pesticide use were regarded as major prerogatives of the employer. Growers would informally cede to lower management and even labor contractors the power associated with the hiring hall, but growers vehemently resisted granting them in any contract to the union because the formal surrender of these powers challenged management's ultimate authority over workers. Growers have been willing to make concessions on wage demands, the traditional bread-and-butter issues, but not on control, because the cost of wage increases may be passed on to the consumer, whereas control concessions have a different kind of "cost."

As organizing objectives, the effective pursuit of the hiring hall and pesticide issues have been attainable only by mass worker involvement and support. The focus on such issues has stimulated political awareness around such concerns as child labor, the premature aging and disability of farm workers, political participation and permanent community residence, and consumer protection, as well as other areas of control over the labor process. Pursuit of control issues has placed farm workers in an offensive rather than defensive position; it has raised consciousness and increased worker competence and knowledge of the agribusiness system. The struggle for pesticide restrictions, the hiring hall, and the elimination of the labor contractor has not aimed to gain ownership, abolish profits, or give political control to the working class. Where successfully implemented, however, increased worker control over some aspects of the labor process has provided a meaningful link between the union's daily actions and the goals of reducing exploitation, guaranteeing stable employment, elevating the standard of living, and eroding the domination of grower profit over the human needs of workers (Majka, 1978).

IV.   RESOURCE MOBILIZATION
AND FARM WORKER MOVEMENTS

Sociologists and social historians who analyze social movements have tended to explain their rise and logic in terms of such factors as structural strains and dislocations, rising expectations, rapid social change, generalized beliefs, relative and absolute deprivation, and class antagonism. These approaches attempt to understand why collective actions and social movements occur at specific points in history or in the development of a particular society. Much attention is paid to analyzing the conditions most conducive to the emergence of collective protest. While these are certainly valid questions, the frequency of farm labor protests in California throughout this century suggests that more relevant concerns would be the ability of such movements to elicit concessions from growers or, more significantly, alterations in agricultural capital-labor relations.

In order to evaluate the successes and failures of farm worker struggles, it is necessary to examine the factors that contribute to the strength and effectiveness of collective protests and social movements. As an alternative to the approaches concerned with the origins of social movements, the "resource mobilization" approach is more relevant to a practical understanding of what facilitates or inhibits such movements. Though varied in content and emphasis in its different applications, this approach focuses on the same kinds of questions that have concerned social movement leaders and practical theorists. The relevant issues are how people can organize, pool their resources, and wield power effectively. In particular, this approach examines the variety of resources that must be mobilized in order to achieve success. Resources may come from the constituents of the movement or from sympathetic supporters external to it (Zald and McCarthy, 1979:1–5; Oberschall, 1973; Tilly, 1978; Jenkins, 1983). The mobilization of resources creates a source of power for those who seek to influence or change the policies of a political system (Bachrach and Baratz, 1970:54). Viewed in this way, social movements are best analyzed as extensions of normal forms of political participation.

Questions relevant to mobilization involve two distinct kinds of resources. The first involves the collectivity upon which the movement is based: how a constituency can be mobilized; what issues or events might activate it; what are the best targets or goals; what are the most effective structures, leadership, and divisions of labor; and what strategies can best achieve gains and minimize the adverse effects of social control. Resources within the collectivity include the time people have available to spend on movement activities, the presence of a common culture and heritage, the similarity of people's understanding of their common situation, the possession of technical skills and goods within the collectivity, the availability of money, and the proclivity of the movement's constituency to engage in cooperative, collective endeavors. These can be referred to as "internal resources."

Other resources can be mobilized that are in the strict sense external to the collectivity. The important questions here concern how outside individuals, organizations, and structures can be mobilized to contribute to the success of the movement. How might a political alliance with other groups and organizations be initiated and sustained? How might a large, diffuse sympathetic public be created? In what ways can the media be used to the movement's advantage? How can political leaders and elites be persuaded to support it? How can external support be used to neutralize the social control policies of authorities? The kinds of assistance that sources outside the collectivity can provide a social movement can be called "external resources."

Our research on agricultural labor unionization attempts in California has led us to make several generalizations concerning variables critical to the success of these efforts. The predominance of failures and only short-term gains is not due to the unwillingness of farm workers to engage in struggles. The internal resources of agricultural workers have been repeatedly mobilized, as indicated by the numerous instances of strike activity and unionization attempts. Farm labor organizations have been quite diverse in their kinds of leadership, size and structure, ideologies, strategies, tactics, and specific goals. Ethnic homogeneity and shared cultural traditions have often created unusually high levels of worker solidarity. Farm workers have shared the recognition of collective oppression and selected common targets to oppose. They have displayed a willingness to endure repression from authorities and sacrifice their meager resources in the hope of improved future conditions. However, despite the presence of internal resources and the impressive early strengths of worker protests, significant successes have been infrequent, and concessions, when won, have been only temporary. Typically, concessions are withdrawn after the threat of strikes and disruption of the harvest has passed. The ability of farm labor by itself to successfully assert its interests is weak—a factor shared with other segments of the poor. Under ordinary circumstances farm workers lack the leverage necessary for the long-term survival of their organizations and of the concessions ceded during periods of labor defiance (Majka, 1980).

What has been critically lacking during most strikes and unionization attempts is the mobilization of external resources. The success of a movement is related to the ability of its leaders to gain external support, promote alliances with other movements and organizations, legitimate the movement through the media, enlist elites in the cause, and obtain concrete gains through political channels. The problem for farm workers has been that few of these kinds of resources have been available. The possibility of assembling external support simply has not existed for farm labor for most of its history.

There are two related reasons for this failure to mobilize external resources: the pervasiveness of racial and ethnic divisions and the separation between agricultural and urban labor. Since agricultural labor has been predominantly nonwhite (we include Mexicans and Mexican-Americans in this category), historically its demands for better conditions have not been sympathetically received by both government officials and the public, and the support of the relatively few sympathizers during most periods has been overshadowed by the power of the interests that benefited from the existing pattern of labor exploitation. Political leaders and the media tended either to ignore the labor conditions prevailing in agriculture or to be hostile to suggestions for change. During earlier periods urban-based labor unions, logically farm labor's most suitable allies, offered little support to the several attempts to establish agricultural labor unions under the American Federation of Labor. There is ample evidence that earlier in this century organized labor in general took little interest in the unionization of nonwhites. Segregationist beliefs dominated labor ideology, especially at the national level. For a significant portion of its history, organized labor promoted policies of racial exclusion. In California, white-dominated unions, which held considerable political power during the late 1880s, were primary proponents of discriminatory legislation aimed primarily at Chinese and Japanese immigrants and often excluded them and other minorities from union membership.

In fact, before the late 1950s (when unions agreed to support the antibracero movement), urban-based labor unions offered significant support for agricultural labor demands only when the farm workers involved were predominantly white. For example, such support came during the 1913–17 insurgency, led by the Industrial Workers of the World, of mostly white hop- and wheat-field workers, and during the attempts to organize whites from the Dust Bowl region who had migrated to the California fields in the latter part of the Depression. Support for other organizing attempts, if forthcoming at all, was brief, meager, noncommital, and inconsequential.

As a result, racial and ethnic divisions and the hesitancy of white labor to provide support for nonwhites combined to strengthen the already established separation between agricultural and urban labor. Historically there has been little mobility between the agricultural sector and skilled urban occupations. Agriculture was simply outside the occupational areas that labor unions were concerned with organizing. The segmentation of occupations produced what several researchers have termed a "dual labor market." Markets for nonwhite manual workers have been disproportionately centered in agriculture and low-skilled, low-wage urban jobs, while markets for white manual workers have included the higher-skilled, better-paying industrial, manufacturing, and craft occupations. These two labor markets drew from different sources of labor, had their own mechanisms for recruitment and training, and produced barriers to block mobility for the less privileged. This separation, enhanced by racial and ethnic divisions, prompted the more privileged, predominantly white labor force to view advancements by nonwhites as threats to their living standards and occupational security. The option of incorporating nonwhite agricultural workers into existing labor federations like the AFL did not prevail until relatively recently.

Urban union organizers regarded agricultural workers as unorganizable. This attitude was based in part on unsupported assumptions regarding various nonwhite ethnic groups and their cultures. But the belief also prevailed among union organizers that the migratory patterns associated with much agricultural work did not provide a stable base for unionization. This opinion became self-fulfilling. Social historians have noted that successful protest movements among agricultural workers and other rural peoples throughout the world typically have received urban-based support for mobilization, and this support has been a critical factor in achieving gains (Oberschall, 1973:140). Until fairly recently, however, this kind of support was not widely available for nonwhite farm workers. Only after significant changes in race relations, largely initiated by the civil rights movement, did it become possible for the UFW to forge alliances with urban groups and mobilize resources external to the farm worker population.

These external resources were critical for the successes achieved by the UFW. Massive public support of a consumer boycott of table grapes resulted in union contracts covering 85 percent of California's table grapes in 1970. More importantly, the success of a renewed table grape boycott in 1973 and a contemporaneous boycott of head lettuce and Gallo wines helped create a crisis within California's agricultural industry which resulted in the passage of the California Agricultural Labor Relations Act (ALRA) in 1975.

V.   FARM WORKERS AND STATE CONTROL

The most critical result of the lack of external resources has been the inability of farm worker movements and organizations to channel or influence government reactions and policies. Despite several exceptions, most notably the present period, agricultural labor historically has simply lacked the leverage on government agencies and officials necessary for the institutionalization of the changes it has sought. In contrast, agricultural employers have had lines of political influence that have been both numerous and influential. Consequently the effects of government actions and policies throughout this history have been overwhelmingly in direct support of the interests of the large growers.

The necessity of governmental intervention is evidenced by the fact that the growers, either as individuals or through their organizations, have been unable by themselves to regulate the agricultural labor supply completely to their own advantage. This has been the case despite the frequent successes of agribusiness in recruiting from both inside and outside the United States a labor force with what growers considered desirable characteristics. Many of the forces that channeled groups into the agricultural labor market, such as changes in immigration laws and their enforcement, economic hardships, racial and ethnic discrimination, migration patterns, and conditions prevailing in other countries, operate largely outside the growers' control. The state, that is, government in the broad sense including both the federal and other levels, has, therefore, periodically intervened to regulate and manipulate the agricultural labor supply. Its shifting policies and practices have been a crucial determinant of the kinds of capital-labor relationships that have been characteristic of agriculture.

Agricultural workers have been particularly vulnerable to state power. They have in the past lacked sufficient contervailing power to offset grower pressure on the state, and as nonwhites they have often been subjected to discrimination, which prevented them from building a political power base and otherwise exercising electoral power commensurate with their numbers. During most periods state intervention has served the immediate interests of the large growers by helping maintain grower control over the work force. Changes in immigration laws and their enforcement, opposition to, and sometimes repression of, farm worker unionization efforts, discriminatory legislation that altered the labor status of nonwhites, and the government-directed bracero programs are the most outstanding examples of state regulation of the agricultural labor supply. In agricultural areas themselves, law enforcement officials and local courts routinely have taken the side of growers in labor disputes and cooperated with attempts to recruit strikebreakers and limit strike activity. Many state actions have had the effect of either eliminating unionization efforts altogether or undermining the position of influence that an organized and militant group has established within the labor force.

State intervention has played a major role in the periodic shifts in the composition of the agricultural labor force in California. These shifts have predominantly benefited employers. Japanese immigrants were initially welcomed by the growers early in this century. But grower sentiment changed when effective organization and labor tactics by Japanese farm workers evoked grower concessions making the Japanese the highest paid segment of the agricultural labor supply. At this point, the growers jointed anti-Japanese forces and helped pressure the federal government into arranging a suspension of Japanese immigration in 1907. Several years later, Japanese workers began to combine their savings to purchase or lease agricultural land and compete successfully as producers with large growers. Once again the growers used their collective power to pressure government to preserve their class interests. This time they were instrumental in achieving passage of the California Alien Lands Acts of 1913 and 1920 which forbade Japanese ownership of agricultural land and placed stringent restrictions upon Japanese leasing of farm acreage (Majka and Majka, 1982:37–50). The initial large-scale immigration of Mexican farm workers during World War I was welcomed by the growers and helped replace the higher paid and better organized Japanese workers. But by the early 1930s when harvest strikes and unionization efforts by Mexican farm workers began to win them concessions, the U.S. government tightened enforcement of immigration regulations and conducted a series of deportation raids. Filipino farm workers were encouraged to immigrate to offset gains made by Mexican workers, but Filipino immigration itself was suspended in 1934 when Filipinos also had begun to organize effectively (Majka and Majka, 1982:61–73).

State actions have also been directed against farm labor leaders and farm worker unions. After strikes, boycotts, and other forms of agitation primarily led by the IWW resulted in significant improvements in wages and working conditions for many field workers, the federal government arrested over one thousand IWW leaders and members in 1917 for violations of the Espionage Act. Gains won through collective worker defiance were quickly erased (Majka and Majka,

1982:51–61). Also, less than a year after CAWIU had led the 1933 cotton strike, the largest farm labor strike to that point in U.S. history, and had been successful in winning grower concessions for farm workers during the preceding two years, virtually the union's entire leadership was arrested by California officials and charged with criminal syndicalism. Again, improvements were rapidly eliminated (Majka and Majka, 1982:74–87). The bracero programs, a series of "guest worker" agreements from 1942–1964 which permitted large numbers of Mexican nationals to work in Southwestern agriculture, secured under federal supervision a farm labor force on terms effectively dictated by large growers and their organizations. Federal, state, and local officials routinely ignored abuses of bracero workers and violations of the terms of the agreements, and bracero labor was often used (illegally) to replace striking domestic workers. Utilization of braceros dominated the relationship between agricultural capital and labor. The impact for domestic workers was uncertainty of employment, worsening of working conditions with little bargaining power, an erosion of residential stability with an increase in migrancy to find work, and, for a substantial number, a displacement from agricultural work altogether (Majka and Majka, 1982: 136–58).

Such state intervention helped secure for growers a labor force that was in each case initially powerless, controllable, inexpensive, and unorganized. Yet it did not prevent attempts at organization by nearly every group engaged in agriculture for any considerable length of time. Confronted with an increasingly organized and militant agricultural work force, the state response typically has been to help promote the migration or immigration of a replacement labor supply, setting the stage for the following period of labor insurgency.

More complex, and perhaps ultimately more significant, are interventions by the state aimed at mediating agricultural conflicts by attempting to provide certain guarantees to labor. Mediation efforts are exceptions to the predominant pattern of governmental response and have been undertaken largely over the opposition of the growers. During two relatively brief periods—the late 1930s and the era beginning in 1975 and continuing until at least the early 1980s—the California state government has provided support for efforts aimed at unionizing California's agricultural labor force. These interventions led not only to vital wage gains for farm workers, but also created the potential for alterations in the balance of power between agricultural capital and labor. Also important are the implications of state mediation: the limitations it imposes upon insurgent organizations, its power to channel militancy in certain directions, and its effects on future labor insurgency, unionization, and alliances with sympathetic individuals and organizations.

State mediation has the potential to alter the relationship between farm labor and capital. Control over hiring procedures, job seniority, the terms of employment, and the work process itself may be shifted toward labor. Because of this potential, we treat government efforts that provide the framework for unionization as historically significant events rather than ameliorative reform measures that leave class relationships unchanged.

VI.   THEORETICAL PERSPECTIVES ON STATE MEDIATION

To interpret these contrasting state responses to farm labor insurgency, we have utilized elements from several recent attempts to develop an analysis of state policies and functions that differs from both pluralist political theory and classical Marxism. Pluralist analysis sees the state as an independent locus of power, possessing, in theory, clear autonomy from class groups but also responsive to, and influenced by, those groups that mobilize in their own interests. The state then acts not as a representative of certain interests or as an agent in reproducing prevailing class relations but rather as a neutral mediator that does not consistently give advantage to any one segment of the population. Reforms undertaken by the state are analyzed as complex responses to conflicting social demands. Claims upon the state are manifested by election preferences, political pressure, and organized interests, all generated from outside the state itself. In positing that reforms stem from the kind of representative process to which most groups have access, pluralist analysis tends to ignore the ways in which the institutional context can limit the potential impact of reforms; for example, constraints imposed within Western societies by the necessity of maintaining markets, profits, and capital accumulation in the private sector exceedingly limits reform.

The second approach, that of classical Marxism, is the one most often associated with the Leninist tradition. State actions are interpreted as simply functioning to insure the domination of a capitalist class. The very institutional structures of the state have been organized in ways that insure bourgeois interests. A corollary of this view is the idea that reforms under capitalism are something of a sham, designed primarily to preempt growing discontent and curb radicalization. Certainly any attempt to apply a Marxian analysis to the study of political crises and state actions has to focus on the state's bias in favor of capital, but there is a strong tendency in this approach to ignore ways in which state actions can also serve a more diverse range of interests.

Several alternatives to both pluralism and the Leninist tradition have been developed during the past 15 years. These approaches, representing neo-Marxist theories of "the capitalist state," provide useful analytical issues for understanding periods of institutional change. Especially salient is their recognition that there is no singular state purpose or function and, consequently, their awareness of differences among the various state responses to conflicts and crises.

In contrast to viewing the state solely as an instrument of class domination, one such approach examines "contradictions" within state policies and government interventions. The modern state performs a number of functions related to insuring the continued viability of a social system containing specific relations of dominance and subordination, including work relations. Some of these functions may conflict with others under certain conditions. For example, both economic and social stability may be difficult to obtain by the state simply because state action seeking the maintenance of one can be detrimental to the achievement of the other.

As a representative of this approach, James O'Connor analyzes the capitalist state in terms of its function of creating and maintaining the conditions for profitable capital accumulation and its simultaneous role of preserving social harmony through winning mass acceptance for its programs and policies. The dual functions of accumulation and legitimation are conceived of as contradictory since it must aid the specific interests of capital while also appearing to pursue the interests of society as a whole. For example, the state's use of coercive powers to maintain or rationalize private accumulation may deprive it of legitimation and support for its policies (O'Connor, 1974:5–6; See also Offe, 1974a; Offe 1974b; Offe, 1976; Offe and Ronge, 1979:345–56). These related but potentially contradictory processes, both critical to the functioning of the capitalist state, place state intervention within a particular historical context and demonstrate the limits imposed on its possible actions. While contradictory demands on the state can, in times of crisis, lead to a consideration of government policies that are at odds with the immediate interests of capital accumulation, O'Connor and others do not argue that the state ever undertakes any truly anti-capitalist solutions.

These issues have been most thoroughly explored by what has been called the "structuralist" approach in Marxist theory. According to the structuralists, state actions do not stem from the power and interventions of specific individuals, groups, or classes inside or outside government, but rather they reflect the functions the state must perform to reproduce capitalist society as a whole. The works of Nicos Poulantzas contain perhaps the most developed example of a structuralist approach to the capitalist state (See Poulantzas, 1973; Poulantzas, 1975; Poulantzas, 1969; and Poulantzas, 1979). The fundamental issue is how the state reproduces class relations in ways that enhance the interests of the dominant classes, even when faced with substantial pressures from the working class. It is to his credit that Poulantzas places "class struggles" at the center of the dynamics by which state-sponsored reforms are undertaken. Implicit in his approach is the assumption that political class struggle contains the potential to transform class relationships. The stage attempts to insure that this transformation does not occur by sustaining the conditions for a viable capitalist economy.

Poulantzas argues that the state, which plays a decisive role in the reproduction and accumulation of capital, represents the political interests of the dominant classes as a whole (the entire bourgeoisie) rather than the specific economic interests of particular segments of capital. In contrast to those who portray the state as controlled by a cohesive and dominant class, Poulantzas sees the capitalist class as too segmented into unequal class fractions, each concerned with divergent, parochial interests and none able to represent adequately the class's general political interests. As a consequence, the state must be able to free itself from direction or manipulation by segments or fractions of capital if it is to represent the long-term political interests of the capitalist class: a position defined as "relative autonomy."

Given a position of "relative autonomy" from the interests of capital, the state is capable of protecting certain economic interests of subordinate classes even when to do so is contrary to the short-term interests of the capitalist class in terms of profit maximization and control over the labor force. However, even when forced by political and economic struggle to grant reforms beneficial to subordinate classes, the state also attempts to undermine their political strength and potential to win further concessions. Such containment is accomplished by short-circuiting their political organization, reinforcing their internal divisions, depoliticizing their struggles, and absorbing class conflicts into state structures that appear to represent the interests of society as a whole (Poulantzas, 1973). The emphasis, then, of structural Marxists, and especially Poulantzas, is on the ways that mediation by the state maintains the long-term viability of a capitalist mode of production with its accompanying class relationships even when oppositional groups are able to translate their insurgency into concrete concessions.

A number of writers have responded critically to structuralist Marxism. A common point in these criticisms is that the structural analysis of the state ignores the possibility that the state might promote solutions that actually erode the political and economic dominance of capital. Theda Skocpol (1980) labels this position "political functionalism" and argues that its analysis sees the capitalist state basically as a vehicle of system maintenance.[3] In its extreme form, the structuralist position sets up a deterministic model whereby a system called capitalism absorbs all challenges to its hegemony short of revolutionary transformation.

The general criticism contains two more specific arguments. First, structuralists, while regarding the state as a condensation of class relations, slight the possibility that the state might be unable under certain circumstances to reproduce class relations. Several critics argue that class struggles shape the state as much as the state limits class struggles (Wolfe, 1974; Gold et al., 1975:38; Esping-Anderson et al., 1976:189–90; Reich and Edwards, 1978). The state may be analyzed as a constantly shifting entity whose position at any moment depends on the strengths of the particular forces brought to bear upon it. For example, specific personnel within the state, such as elected officials and specific agencies or structures of the state, become important elements within the political class struggle and cannot be dismissed as mere instruments channeling insurgency by subordinate classes in directions that minimize its effect.

Second, implicit within structural Marxism is the idea that the state has a crisis-management function, but the full implications of this have not been developed. In particular, crisis-management might give the state itself an interest in resolving intense conflicts in ways that insure stability, independent in theory from the entire class structure or mode of production. While there are compelling reasons why state managers ordinarily pursue pro-capitalist policies, such as the dependence of the state apparatus (as well as political careers) on economic growth, the state's fundamental interest in maintaining order may during crisis periods lead it to enforce concessions that shift power toward subordinate classes (Skocpol, 1979; Frankel, 1979; Block, 1977).

Fred Block attempts to develop an approach that recognizes such concessions to subordinate classes but also one that analyzes the political and class dynamics that compel the state to orient its policies and structures to accommodate the imperatives imposed by capital accumulation. Block argues that there are structural reasons why even in the absence of ruling-class pressures, state managers generally do not pursue anti-capitalist policies. The basic idea underlying his formulation is that there is a key division between capitalists and what he calls managers of the state apparatus, i.e., "leading figures of both the legislative and executive branches" including "highest-ranking civil servants, as well as elected and appointed politicians" (Block, 1977:8). The structural relationships among state managers, capitalists, and the working class produce state policies that overwhelmingly contain pro-capitalist biases. The reason is that state managers and the power of the state itself are dependent on profitable capital investments by the private sector to facilitate economic growth and well-being. The growth of the state apparatus as well as the administrative and political careers of state managers themselves rest on a continued healthy economy. Not only does the state facilitate profitable private investments but it also must insure business confidence in investment by creating and maintaining social stability. Block argues that this structural relationship between state managers and capitalists (or the state and capitalism) insures that the state has a pronounced tendency not only to disregard anti-capitalist policy options but also to pursue explicitly pro-capitalist ones (Block, 1977:6–21). Block's logic is based on the assumption that subordinate classes themselves will not re-elect politicians who undertake anti-capitalist policies since these changes will undermine business confidence and lead to worsening economic prospects.

Demands by the working class have the function of expanding the role of the state. But, once state structures come into existence to deal with insurgency through concessions and reforms, state managers ordinarily will attempt to channel these structures in ways that contribute to the smooth flow of capital investments. Also, reforms judged detrimental to the interests of capital may be neutralized or revoked. Class conflict and subsequent reforms stimulate the state to discover new ways of overcoming economic contradictions and facilitating the integration of insurgent groups and the working class in general. As a result, reforms and the extensions of state power that were initially won by insurgency or other pressures from below eventually become functional for capitalism and accepted by capitalists who often initially opposed the changes. However, Block does admit that these processes may occur with a great deal of friction and conflict. State managers do not automatically know how to rationalize capitalism and instead grope toward solutions. Mistakes can occur, including excessive concessions to the working class. As a result, outcomes other than pro-capitalist ones remain a possibility despite these structural relationships (Block, 1977: 20–26).

Block's analysis moves away from the determinism of Poulantzas, but it is still not sufficient. Even while recognizing that state interventions do not guarantee long-term state policies and structures supportive of, or at least not unfavorable to, capitalism, his analysis emphasizes that state policies are a crucial aspect of reproducing class relations, especially during periods of crisis. As a result, his theory remains within the Marxian "functionalist" orientation of Poulantzas. While acknowledging the insight of such an approach, more consideration should be given to the autonomous influences of state agencies and officials, political parties and leaders, and the strength, organization, and goals of subordinate groups. For example, it may not simply be a "mistake" that during periods of crisis certain political leaders actively pursue changes that cut into the privileges of capital. Rather, politicians may attempt such changes to gain the support of insurgent groups and expand or solidify their own power base and electoral constituency. Also, there may be structural reasons why reforms that are *not* in the long-term interest of capital in fact become institutionalized, such as the evolution of state agencies whose explicit mandates are to guarantee the interests of subordinate groups.

VII.   STATE MEDIATION AND FARM LABOR INSURGENCY

Several analysts have observed that discussion of the capitalist state has taken place primarily at an abstract level. Relatively few attempts have been made to bring these theories "down to earth" by applying them empirically. Drawing on both the theories of the capitalist state literature and our own research on the history of farm worker insurgency in California, we have developed a framework useful in the analysis of state interventions with respect to agricultural labor which we will summarize here.

The capitalist state is involved in the dual functions of stimulating capitalist accumulation in the private sector and legitimating its policies by appearing to pursue the general interests of the entire society. These potentially contradictory functions contain opportunities for subordinate groups to force government concessions. Short-term gains, however, are not synonymous with alterations in the balance of power between dominant and subordinate groups. While mediating conflicts, and especially during periods of crisis, the state may force reforms over the opposition of powerful segments of capital. However, by such means as absorbing class conflicts into government agencies and regulating them through bureaucratic structures, the state will attempt to depoliticize and circumscribe conflict and otherwise strive to preserve the general political interests of the dominant class.

The ability of the state to use these processes effectively to reproduce class domination is, nevertheless, limited by the strength of class struggle and the interests of state officials in mediating crises successfully. The functions of the state are not determined only by structural relationships between the state and the economy and between the state and class relations; state structures are also objects of class struggle. Democratic processes provide mechanisms of influence that can sometimes be effectively used by groups demanding major reforms. As a result, the internal structure of the state as well as policy choices emanating from it are "simultaneously a *product,* an *object* and a *determinant* of class conflict" (Esping-Anderson et al., 1976:191, emphasis in original).

Politicians and state officials are also not fully accountable to capital. Their autonomous relationship to the economic sphere makes it possible for political leaders and state agencies to serve as resources for insurgent groups. While constrained by limits imposed by capitalist structures, the political interests of some officials might motivate them to extend or strengthen their bases of support among subordinate groups. Moreover, they do not necessarily know how to mediate conflicts in ways that reproduce class relationships and insure the long-term interests of capital.

To the extent that reforms do not alter the underlying causes of conflict and that the state is politically unable to neutralize the segments of the working class making demands, state intervention may create a situation in which subsequent demands are more directly concerned with restructuring basic class relationships. This possibility depends on the long-term results and implementation of mediation attempts and how these affect future class struggles. In other words, class struggles translated into the political arena shape the historical development of reforms and the state agencies designed to facilitate mediation. When class struggles come to dominate the development of state structures and begin to win the kinds of concessions that actually shift power toward subordinate classes, state interventions can occur that are best described as "nonreformist reforms."

The problem of interpreting periods of infrequent, but significant agricultural labor reforms has led us to our theoretical position. State mediation that facilitates the establishment of farm labor unions contains the potential to shift the power relationship between agricultural capital and labor more to the advantage of labor. Successful pursuit of control issues by farm labor represents such a shift in class relations.

Such changes are markedly different from those government-sponsored reforms that do not support the emergence of an independent power base for labor.

Similar to grower concessions forced primarily by short-term insurgency, reforms solely sponsored and implemented by government may quickly be eroded after the crisis that produced them disappears. When the beneficiaries of reforms are not structurally located to fight against reversals of government policy, there is little to prevent the state from reverting to past patterns of government accommodation to the interests of capital.

Government reforms stimulated by IWW-led insurgency during the years immediately prior to U.S. entry into World War I provide a good example. The Wobblies were instrumental in promoting strikes and even worker boycotts of certain growers in protest of deplorable conditions for field workers and in reaction to the conviction of two IWW leaders of second-degree murder charges. The latter issue arose out of a confrontation between workers and the local sheriff's department during a hop-pickers strike near Wheatland in 1913. As worker defiance was substantial and threatened to continue, the California government passed legislation improving working conditions and setting standards for grower-owned camps for migrant workers (Foner, 1965:261–267; Daniel, 1978; Majka and Majka, 1982:51–57). But such reforms also coincided with government attempts to eliminate the IWW as an effective force. After U.S. entry into World War I, Wobbly leaders were arrested nationwide and charged with criminal syndicalism under the recently passed Espionage Act. In California, much of the IWW leadership was imprisoned and the Department of Justice even opened an office in Fresno and asked all growers with labor trouble to make reports to it. The threat of IWW-led insurgency was eliminated and government-sponsored reforms disappeared almost immediately. Wages were drastically reduced; working conditions deteriorated; and migrant camps returned to their previous neglected state. New sources of compliant labor were recruited, including young workers from public schools and others from special volunteer "patriotic" organizations. As a result, profits for agricultural landowners increased considerably over previous levels (Foner, 1965:277–278; Brissenden, 1957:282; Perlman and Taft, 1935:420, 432; Majka and Majka, 1982:57–61).

We have provided a detailed description and analysis of the two most substantial mediation attempts by the state elsewhere, so they will only be briefly summarized here (Majka and Majka, 1982:97–135, 224–276, 293–300). Both of these attempts, first in the 1930s and then in the 1970s were undertaken after nearly a decade of intense farm labor unrest, including widespread farm worker strikes, continuous unionization efforts, a drastic transformation of much of the farm worker population from passivity to militancy, widespread support from and alliances with liberal and labor organizations and, in the latest effort, the effective utilization of the consumer boycott. Together, these factors produced a crisis in agricultural production that seriously threatened agribusiness interests.

Farm labor activism did not disappear after the elimination of CAWIU in 1934. However, for several years the activism became more localized, predominantly under the direction of smaller, independent, ethnically-constituted farm labor unions. Also, from 1935 to 1938 the massive migration to California of displaced small farmers, tenant farmers, and sharecroppers from the "Dust Bowl" region thrust prevailing conditions for field workers into the national spotlight, especially after the publication of John Steinbeck's *The Grapes of Wrath* in March 1939. Later during the decade, much of the union activity was connected with the newly-formed, CIO-affiliated United Cannery, Agricultural, Packing, and Allied Workers of America (UCAPAWA). UCAPAWA offered the potential for unprecedented leverage for farm worker unionization efforts. The strategy was for the permanently employed and better-paid cannery and packing workers to provide a stable financial base for the union. Additionally, UCAPAWA's ties to the industrial unionization movement through its affiliation with the CIO could bring monetary assistance, political alliances, publicity, and other external support, resources that had been noticeably lacking during previous farm worker unionization efforts. Farm worker defiance and organizing efforts increased, and some of the agricultural strikes during the late 1930s approached the scale of the 1933 cotton strike. Polarization was extreme, and with the help of armed vigilante groups and the local police, growers continued to resist efforts by UCAPAWA to negotiate concessions and union contracts.

Within this context both the California and federal governments began to provide support for agricultural labor reforms and unionization attempts. Migrant camps were established by the federal Farm Security Administration (FSA), and these were supervised by government employees. This freed many migrant workers from constant surveillance by growers since many workers previously lived in employer-owned housing out of necessity. The managers of the FSA camps often implicitly or directly encouraged union participation by the camp's residents.

Farm workers gained leverage not only through continued insurgency but also with the election of a reform-minded administration that attempted to assist unionization. Democrat Culbert Olson was elected as governor in 1938, and many of the priorities of his administration were an outgrowth of the prevailing political climate in California during the 1930s. Olson himself had political roots in the EPIC (End Poverty In California) campaign earlier during the decade which reached a culmination in Upton Sinclair's campaign for governor in 1934. Even though Sinclair lost to the conservative Republican Frank Merriam, a number of candidates with EPIC ties, including Olson, were elected statewide that year. The 1938 elections produced a sweep for left-liberal Democratic Party candidates in California for the positions of governor, lieutenant governor, and U.S. senator, and many officials in the Olson administration represented this left wing of the New Deal. Regarding agrarian issues, officials in Olson's administration, including Carey McWilliams, author of *Factories in the Field* (1939), proposed substantial reforms in farm labor laws, offered government relief to strikers, and supported inclusion of agricultural labor under the National Labor Relations Act (the NLRA or Wagner Act had been passed in 1935 but applied only to industrial workers).

Also, the Olson administration prodded a reluctant U.S. Congress and Roosevelt administration to become more actively involved in agricultural labor reform efforts. The result was extensive investigations by two Congressional committees, the House Committee on the Interstate Migration of Destitute Citizens headed by Representative John Tolan of Oakland, California, and the Senate Subcommittee to Investigate Violations of Free Spreech and Assembly and Interference with the Right of Labor to Organize and Bargain Collectively headed by Senator Robert M. La Follette, Jr., of Wisconsin. Seen in retrospect, these committees' findings and recommendations might have served as the foundation of substantial reforms had not the political and economic climate suddenly changed.

Both the La Follette and Tolan Congressional Committees made thorough studies of different aspects of the agricultural situation and recommended substantial changes in federal policy. Additionally, the La Follette committee exposed, publicized, and delegitimated vigilante and sometimes terrorist tactics used by growers and their supporters to intimidate farm workers, repress agricultural labor strikes and undermine unionization efforts. The Committee also placed inclusion of agricultural labor under the NLRA at the center of its recommended reforms.

As a result of continued farm labor activism and sympathetic public response, momentum was building toward changes in agricultural capital–labor relations similar to changes precipitated by the industrial union movement and the passage of the NLRA which led to the unionization of industrial workers during the 1930s and 1940s. However, an historic opportunity was lost. Before any substantial reforms became institutionalized, World War II intervened, the migrant surplus was siphoned off into war-related industries or the armed forces, unionization efforts abruptly ceased, and Mexican workers began to be imported on terms extremely favorable to agribusiness. A similar opportunity for reform would not occur for another 35 years.

Present mediation efforts beginning in 1975 were preceded by ten years of strikes and UFW-promoted consumer boycotts. Together these produced recurrent crises in California's agricultural industry. Renewed farm worker insurgency began in 1965 with the Delano-area table grape strike. The resultant consumer boycott of table grapes seriously eroded the regular market outlets and substantially reduced grape sales by 1970. This economic pressure resulted in the UFW signing labor contracts covering 85 percent of California's table grape industry. UFW successes precipitated anti-UFW state intervention by both the Nixon administration in Washington and the Reagan administration in California. Because of the Nixon administration's support of a grower-Teamster union alliance, the UFW was unable to institutionalize concessions the union had won in its contracts. However, such efforts to weaken and perhaps eliminate the UFW failed. The 1973 table grape strike was the largest agricultural labor strike to that point in U.S. history. The UFW also cemented its alliances with labor, religious, and citizens' action organizations and mounted a consumer boycott of table grapes, head lettuce, and Gallo brand wines. According to a Louis Harris public opinion poll released in October 1975, these boycotts were the most effective union boycott of any product in U.S. history. Union-sponsored strikes also continued, although on a much smaller scale. As a result, both the production and distribution ends of a substantial proportion of California's agricultural industry became unstable, and there was little to suggest that this crisis could be overcome by a continuation of past agribusiness and government policies.

The UFW's strategy became to promote this crisis as a resource for securing agricultural labor legislation in California that would allow government-supervised farm worker unionization elections. In the past, there had been little hope of passing a UFW-endorsed farm labor bill over the certainty of a veto by Governor Reagan. The election of Jerry Brown as governor in November 1974 removed the obstacle of an intensely pro-agribusiness administration. Also, Democratic majorities in both houses of the California legislature were strengthened by the 1974 election.

Similar to reform attempts during the late 1930s, prolonged agricultural labor insurgency combined with the election of a liberal administration to produce a political climate favorable to state mediation. Brown successfully sought UFW endorsement for his candidacy, and the union actively campaigned on his behalf. Brown also sought electoral support from UFW sympathizers in metropolitan areas, and a major campaign issue was his repeated statements that one of his first legislative priorities would be an attempt to resolve the farm labor issue. In fact, Brown would later be remarkably successful in mobilizing UFW supporters in his efforts to expand his political power base. Meanwhile, when faced with the dramatically changed priorities of the state government, grower representatives indicated a new willingness by agribusiness to compromise its hardline stance and cooperate with attempts to find a legislative solution to the grower–UFW stalement.

The result was the California Agricultural Labor Relations Act of 1975 (ALRA), worked out through negotiations among UFW officials, agribusiness representatives, and officials of the Brown administration. Since its passage, the law has been used successfully by the UFW to gain a more permanent basis for unionization than was the case for previous UFW union contracts. UFW election victories helped eliminate (for the present, at least) the Teamster union as a competitor whose positions and policies were often closer to those of agribusiness than to those of the UFW. Also, union contracts under the ALRA have preserved, with modification in some cases, union hiring halls and have continued enforcement of pesticide regulations. The most recent series of contracts has given workers input over mechanization and changes in work routine, and stipulated stronger grievance procedures and contract enforcement. Additionally, under rulings by the Agricultural Labor Relations Board (ALRB), individual growers are now threatened with substantial financial penalties for failure to comply with the law or obstructing its implementation.

The ALRA's effectiveness is allowing the UFW to become more permanently established and to pursue alternations in the balance of power between agricultural capital and labor has led to repeated attempts by agribusiness to substantially alter both the law and the pattern of its enforcement. For example, Governor Brown vetoed three grower-supported alterations of the ALRA intended to erode the UFW's ability to determine what constitutes "good standing" within the union's membership. Other spot bills have been prepared that, if passed, would amend the ALRA in ways that would effectively eliminate the ability of the ALRB to penalize financially individual growers found guilty of bad-faith bargaining and alter union decertification procedures, the definition of bargaining units, election procedures, and the determination of union seniority, all to the advantage of agribusiness. Another legislative proposal seeks to repeal the ALRA and replace it with an "Agricultural Labor-Management Act," which conforms to NLRA provisions including the Taft-Hartley Amendment. Agribusiness strategy seems to be to keep pushing such amendments and proposals until political forces in California allow their passage (Majka and Majka, 1982:270).

Also, the ALRA has not been without its restrictive aspects for farm labor unions. Tactical options have been reduced, mainly through restrictions on the legal use of the secondary boycott (storewide boycott, as opposed to product boycott) and recognition strikes. When the secondary boycott was in effect, the union had been engaged in a struggle not only with a specific segment of growers, but with much of the food industry, including supermarket chains. It focused attention on the entire food-for-profit system with its mutually sustaining elements. The conflict now involves only the growers and the union. Although the UFW threw its full weight behind the compromise which produced the final version of the ALRA, Governor Brown's initial proposal of the law undermined UFW-backed legislation that was given a good chance of passage and that contained few restrictions on farm labor unions. The UFW was prevented from doing what agribusiness routinely has done until recently: use the state as a vehicle for the pursuit of its own interests.

In addition, the mechanisms of farm labor elections and labor contract negotiations have proven to be cumbersome and time-consuming, and tend to monopolize the UFW's attention. The time needed to secure labor contracts encourages the union to confine its activities to California. Other agricultural unions patterned after the UFW have arisen in Ohio, Arizona, and Texas. Although in some cases their organizers are former UFW officials, the UFW has not yet established formal linkages.

Perhaps more significantly, the UFW must defend itself against future restrictions and changes in the law detrimental to its interests. With the decline of produce boycotts and the emergence of an election mechanism, the network of support groups the union relied upon in the past has been eroded. Whether it can be recreated if needed in the future is problematic.

David Montgomery's analysis of the effects of the NLRA of 1935 raises issues relevant to the future of the present farm worker movement. Activity by the federal government in support of unionization during the Depression was simultaneously liberating and cooptive for workers. Labor struggles and government response lifted the burden of absolute managerial control from the work force. In addition to securing wage gains, union contracts won workers power on the job. Management was obliged to deal with workers' elected representatives, and the workers were accorded some degree of protection against company favoritism and arbitrary dismissals. But institutionalization also created processes through which the rank and file could be disciplined and brought under tighter control and labor organizing constrained from threatening the prevailing market and profit mechanisms. Additionally, industrial unions were subjected to more rigid legal and political controls. Management, once it accepted the existence of unions, encouraged the development of union structures and policies most adaptable to corporate goals. And the process of seeking advantageous rulings from government agencies strengthened the importance of union officials relative to union members (Montgomery, 1979:163–166).

Thus, institutionalization may move the UFW into a more defensive position. Indeed, there are compelling reasons why the UFW should pursue more defensive strategies. Agribusiness has not completely accepted the existence of either the union or the ALRA, and the organized growers have attempted to use the resources at their disposal, including their political allies in the California legislature, to undermine the law's effectiveness through alterations of strategic provisions or limitations on the law's jurisdiction. Ironically, the UFW now finds itself in the position of defending a state structure while agribusiness fights for change.

It is not difficult to imagine a situation in which the UFW's power to win elections would be seriously undermined and the union effectively prevented from expanding. Although UFW-led strikes and boycotts continue, there is no longer a crisis in agribusiness operations. The political climate that produced the ALRA has now changed, and the California governor elected in November 1982, Republican George Deukmejian, has proven to be much less sympathetic to the UFW than Governor Brown was.

The contrasts between the actions of Governors Brown and Deukmejian could hardly be more dramatic. During his gubernatorial campaign, Deukmejian received considerable financial support from agribusiness and purposefully made the ALRA a major issue by repeatedly charging that the administration of the law was biased in favor of the UFW, a contention that echoed grower sentiments. Once in office, he appointed a former Republican Assemblyman, David Sterling, as the ALRB's general counsel. While in the Assembly, Sterling voted in favor of several amendments to the ALRA that would increase restrictions on farm labor unions. Once in the ALRB position, Sterling centralized more of the agency's powers into his office, leading to charges by members of the Board that Deukmejian was trying to convert the ALRB into a pro-grower agency.

Additionally, Deukmejian is currently attempting to reduce the operating budget of the ALRB by 25 percent from its 1982–83 level of $8.9 million. Also, the governor is seeking to eliminate 50 positions, including 17 attorneys, from the ALRB, the largest cut proposed for any single government agency. At present, a decision on a challenge or suit often takes 1–2 years, and reduction in staff would likely lengthen this period. Opponents of the cuts charged that the governor is attempting to render the agency ineffective.

With support from the governor, agribusiness may begin to prevail in its attempts to alter the ALRA, and an amended law may restrict rather than facilitate agricultural unionization. Also, a "guest worker" program has been proposed. If undertaken by the Reagan administration, its effects will most likely be similar to those of the 1942–64 bracero programs: worker demoralization, the displacement of domestic workers, a decline in living and working standards, and the defeat of unionization efforts.

However, the specific outcomes of state mediation are not predetermined, but rather are a result of pressures upon and within the state. The future of the ALRA has now become more important for farm worker unionization than any conflict between the UFW or any other agricultural labor union and a particular segment of agribusiness. The agricultural class struggle has become absorbed into a state structure, but the results will depend upon the strengths of conflicting classes and their allies.

VIII. CONCLUSION

We have argued that farm worker unionization movements have historically included attempts to substantially alter the relationship between agribusiness and the agricultural labor force. This theme has been especially prevalent during the last two decades of UFW organizing. The predominance of "control issues" explains the vehement resistance by agribusiness to farm labor unionism. It also indicates why governmental attempts to facilitate unionization cannot be dismissed as merely empty reformism. Substantial interests are at stake, epitomized by grower hostility to the implementation of the ALRA and the attempts by agribusiness to alter or eliminate the law.

Success for farm labor organizing has been associated with substantial support from non-agrarian segments of the population. These external resources have been utilized by organizers to help offset the enormous institutional advantages enjoyed by agribusiness. Farm labor movements have been most effective during periods of social discontent and decline in the legitimacy of economic elites, most notably the 1930s and the late 1960s and much of the 1970s. During such periods, agricultural labor has been able to pressure effectively for governmental reforms, although the permanence as well as long term effects of changes remains in doubt.

Since state responses to farm labor insurgency have been a critical determinant of the outcome of agricultural capital-labor conflicts, we have employed a synthesized model of state action using several theoretical approaches to the capitalist state. This has been necessary since in our judgement none of the current theories give sufficient emphasis to the possibility that during periods of crises state managers may accommodate the interests of insurgents in order to broaden their own power base and to insure a politically popular resolution of conflicts. Also, such resolutions, especially those involving the creation of a separate state structure (such as the ALRB), may shift power toward noncapitalists in ways that make it difficult for capital to utilize new relationships and state structures to its advantage.

This suggests that a shift in emphasis is necessary in attempts to apply theories of the capitalist state to specific historical instances. While taking seriously both the "structural" and "class-struggles" approaches, it is also desirable to assign a potentially independent explanatory role to the actions of political leaders, state officials, and state structures. As Theda Skocpol (1980:199–201) has argued, political leaders, political parties, and state structures have their own independent histories, and these are not completely determined by socioeconomic changes, dominant class interests, or class struggles. Rather, they have their own autonomous interests and internal conflicts, and these in turn have an independent impact. Incorporating this latter emphasis into our synthesized capitalist state theory has been necessary in order to analyze adequately the two periods in California's agricultural labor history when the state turned from its traditional overwhelming support for the interests of agribusiness to attempts to mediate the agrarian class struggle in ways that shifted the advantage toward the agricultural working class.

NOTES

1. For example, between 1930 and 1954 the size of the average farm in California increased 37 percent; between 1954 and 1969, over 100 percent. The number of small farms in California has declined from 135,676 in 1930 to 80,848 in 1964 (See Fellmeth, 1973:79).

2. For example, Department of Agriculture statistics from the early 1970s listed the average annual income of year-round farm workers in the United States as $4,358. Migrant seasonal farm workers had an average income of 3,350 a year. While the average income of agricultural labor in California has been slightly higher than the national average, by 1975 the California average hourly wage for agricultural labor was slightly less than half the average hourly wage of the state's manufacturing workers. According to the U.S. Census, in 1969, agricultural workers had the lowest median income for male workers in all but three California counties (See Hayes, 1979:13, 96–99).

3. In his later works, Poulantzas moved toward a class-struggle approach, something his critics seldom recognize (See Weber, 1978). Nevertheless, his primary impact has been in developing the kind of structuralist theory of the capitalist state referred to here.

REFERENCES

Bachrach, Peter and Morton Baratz
1970   Power and Poverty: Theory and Practice. New York: Oxford University Press.

Block, Fred
  1977 "The ruling class does not rule: notes on the Marxist theory of the state." Socialist Revolution 33:6–28.
Braverman, Harry
  1974 Labor and Monopoly Capital: The Degradation of Work in the Twentieth Century. New York: Monthly Review.
Brissenden, Paul F.
  1957 The IWW: A Study of American Syndicalism. New York: Russell and Russell.
Brody, David
  1980 Workers in Industrial America. New York: Oxford University Press.
Daniel, Cletus E.
  1978 "In defense of the Wheatland Wobblies: a critical analysis of the IWW in California." Labor History 19:485–509.
Day, Mark
  1971 Forty Acres: Cesar Chavez and the Farm Workers. New York: Praeger.
Esping-Anderson, Gosta, Roger Friedland and Erik Olin Wright
  1976 "Modes of class struggle and the capitalist state." Kapitalistate 4–5:186–220.
Fellmeth, Robert C.
  1973 Politics of Land. New York: Grossman.
Foner, Philip S.
  1965 History of the Labor Movement in the United States. New York: International Publishers.'
Frankel, Boris
  1979 "On the state of the state: Marxist theories of the state after Leninism." Theory and Society 7:204–211.
Friedland, William H., Amy E. Barton and Robert J. Thomas
  1981 Manufacturing Green Gold: Capital, Labor and Technology in the Lettuce Industry. New York: Cambridge University Press.
Gold, David A., Clarence Y. H. Lo and Erik Olin Wright
  1975 "Recent developments in Marxist theories of the capitalist state." Monthly Review 27(5–6):38–50.
Gorz, Andre
  1964 Strategy for Labor: A Radical Proposal. Boston: Beacon Press.
Hayes, Sue Eileen
  1979 Industrial response to Agricultural Labor Relations Act. Austin, Texas: Center for the Study of Human Resources, University of Texas.
Jenkins, J. Craig
  1983 "Resource mobilization theory and the study of social movements." Annual Review of Sociology 9:527–553.
Kerr, Clark, John T. Dunlop, Frederick H. Harbison and Charles A. Myers
  1960 Industrialism and Industrial Man. Cambridge, Massachusetts: Harvard University Press.
Majka, Linda
  1978 Farm workers, labor unionism and argarian capitalism." Ph.D. dissertation, University of California, Santa Barbara.
  1981 "Labor militancy among farm workers and the strategy of protest: 1900–1979." Social Problems 28:536–544.
Majka, Theo J.
  1980 "Poor peoples' movements and farm labor insurgency." Contemporary Crises 4:283–308.
Majka, Linda C. and Theo J. Majka
  1982 Farm Workers, Agribusiness and the State. Philadelphia: Temple University Press.
Montgomery, David
  1979 Workers' Control in America. New York: Cambridge University Press.

Mallet, Serge
   1975   Essays on the New Working Class. St. Louis: Telos.
Oberschall, Anthony
   1973   Social Conflict and Social Movements. Englewood Cliffs, NJ: Prentice Hall.
O'Connor, James
   1974   The Fiscal Crisis of the State. New York: St. Martin's Press.
Offe, Claus
   1975a "The theory of the capitalist state and the problem of policy formation." Pp. 125–144 in
          Leon Lindberg, Robert Alford, Colin Crouch and Claus Offe (eds.), Stress and Contradic-
          tion in Modern Capitalism. Lexington, MA: D. C. Heath.
   1975b "Introduction to legitimacy versus efficiency." Pp. 245–259 in Leon Lindberg, Robert
          Alford, Colin Crouch and Claus Offe (eds.), Stress and Contradiction in Modern Cap-
          italism. Lexington, MA: D.C. Heath.
   1976   "Political authority and class structure." Pp. 388–421 in Paul Connaton (ed.) Critical
          Sociology. London: Penguin Books.
Offe, Claus and Volker Ronge
   1979   "Theses on the theory of the state." In J. W. Freiberg (ed.), Critical Sociology: European
          Perspectives. New York: Irvington Publishers.
Perlman, Selig and Philip Taft
   1935   Labor Movements. vol. 4 of History of Labor in the United States, 1896–1932. John R.
          Commons (ed.), New York: Macmillan.
Poulantzas, Nicos
   1969   "The problem of the capitalist state." New Left Review 58:67–78.
   1973   Political Power and Social Classes. London: New Left Books.
   1975   Classes in Contemporary Capitalism. London: New Left Books.
   1979   "The political crisis and the crisis of the state." In J. W. Freiberg (ed.), Critical Sociology:
          European Perspectives. New York: Irvington Publishers.
Reich, Michael and Richard Edwards
   1978   "Political parties and class conflict in the United States." Socialist Review 39:38–42.
Skocpol, Theda
   1979   "State and revolution: old regimes and revolutionary crises." Theory and Society 7:7–15.
   1980   "Political response to capitalist crisis: neomarxist theories of the state and the case of the
          New Deal." Politics and Society 10:169–181.
Sosnick, Stephen
   1978   Hired Hands: Seasonal Farm Workers in the United States. Santa Barbara: McNally and
          Loftin, West.
Tilly, Charles
   1978   From Mobilization to Revolution. Reading, MA: Addison-Wesley.
Weber, Henri
   1978   "The state and the transition to socialism." Socialist Review 38:9–36.
Wolfe, Alan
   1974   "New directions in the Marxist theory of politics." Politics and Society 4:140–153.
Zald, Mayer and John D. McCarthy (eds.)
   1979   The Dynamics of Social Movements. Cambridge, MA: Winthrop.

PLANT CLOSINGS AND THE CONFLICT BETWEEN CAPITAL AND LABOR

John F. Zipp

Whether it is a textile mill in Massachusetts, a steel factory in Pittsburgh or an auto plant in Detroit, plant closings are becoming a more common phenomenon in all of the older industrialized areas of the United States. Although plant closings have occurred throughout the history of industrialized capitalism, what is new in the U.S. is the frequency and scale of such closings in some regions and the resulting public awareness that they represent a threat to the economic and social well-being of these affected areas. Serious public discussions are now heard regarding the absolute decline, and even the "deindustralization", of what once were the most properous regions of the country.

This paper will discuss the implications of plant closings on society but with an emphasis that differs considerably from most of the scholarly work that has considered the topic. Most typically, analyses of plant closings have emphasized either the personal and economic impacts on workers who lose their jobs or the economic effects on the communities or regions that lose plants. Although some of these studies will be reviewed here, the primary concern in this analysis is

Research in Social Movements, Conflict and Change, Vol. 6, pages 225–248.
Copyright © 1984 by JAI Press Inc.
All rights of reproduction in any form reserved.
ISBN: 0-89232-311-6

with how plant closings represent a newly important aspect of the struggle between labor and management over the pay workers will receive and over issues of control in the workplace.

The major amount of social scientific research devoted to plant closings has taken a "social problems" approach, centering on the economic, social, psychological and physical health effects of plant closings primarily on displaced workers and somewhat less frequently on their communities. Although these effects are quite serious and although many of these studies are well-conceived and executed, such approaches largely have failed to recognize that, especially in the last decade or so, the context in which plant closing decisions are made has changed dramatically. Social scientists studying plant closings have shown less awareness of how plant closings, and even the threat of plant closings, have emerged as a major tactic or resource of managements' efforts to restructure the relationship between capital and labor.

The purpose of this chapter is both: (1) to look at some of the broad range of research that has considered plant closings; and (2) to focus on issues concerning plant closings as an aspect of managements' efforts to control labor. We have divided this chapter into three main sections. First, in order to place our analysis in context, we shall present a brief, selective review of the major findings on the effects of plant closings. There will be no attempt to review all this research, as there are good reviews elsewhere (e.g., C and R Associates, 1978; Gordus, et al., 1981; Haber, et al., 1963). We primarily are interested in demonstrating that, although this work raises important issues, it also exhibits a rather narrow focus. Section II contains an analysis of why plant closings have developed as a factor in the relations between labor and management. Finally, in the third section we present a brief analysis of a case study illustrating how research based on this idea might be done, along with sketching some suggestions for future research.

I. PREVIOUS RESEARCH

Research concerned with the impact of plant closings dates back 50 years (e.g., Clague, et al., 1934; Myers, 1929). And, although the scope and the methodological sophistication of this research have increased, most research efforts have limited their concerns to the direct effects of such closings on the affected workers. At the risk of some oversimplification, what social scientists know about plant closings can be grouped into three areas: economic effects; social and psychological effects; and physical health effects.

A. Economic Effects

The major economic effects associated with plant closings are: unemployment and problems involved in the transition to new jobs; loss of income with the concomitant cuts in savings and expenditures; and loss of benefits such as pension rights and health insurance. Most studies of the unemployment caused by plant closings have focused on the individual workers who have been displaced. There are two major conclusions of this research. First, there is substantial variation in the length of unemployment, primarily due to the economic context in which the plant closing takes place and the differing characteristics (age, skill, etc.) of the workforce (Aiken, et al., 1968; Aronson and McKersie, 1980; Cobb and Kasl, 1977; Dorsey, 1967; Ferman, 1963; Gordus, et al., 1981: 91-2; Parnes and King, 1977: Wilcock and Franke, 1963; Young, 1963). For example, in their study of the 1956 closing of a Packard plant, Aiken, et al. (1968), found that 23% of the displaced workers had never been employed fully two years after the shutdown. Furthermore, even those who had been reemployed after the shutdown and who were still working two years later (45% of the sample) averaged over 5 months of unemployment. Second, despite differences among the studies, the economic effects of unemployment generally are quite severe. Recent Department of Labor estimates indicate that about 40% of displaced workers remain unemployed for two years (Blumberg, 1980:166).

The findings on income loss are similar to those for unemployment. Obviously, displaced workers who remain without work suffer a serious reduction in income. In addition, a significant portion of workers, even when they do find jobs, must take a cut in pay (Claque, et al., 1934; Ferman, 1963; Stern, 1972; Wilcock and Franke, 1963). Concomitant with this loss in earnings comes a drop in savings and a reduction in expenditures (e.g., Gordus, et al., 1981). And, finally, with respect to benefits, (a) although the retention of pension rights has been improved by the passage of ERISA in 1974, it is still a problem; and (b) a study done by Mathematica in the mid-1970's found that 38% of the displaced workers in Massachusetts that they studied lost their health insurance at some point during their initial period of unemployment (cited in Bluestone and Harrison, 1980:70). The overall conclusion of work in this area is that for a large proportion of workers who lose their jobs, plant closings cause severe economic problems.

B. Social and Psychological Effects

Much of the recent research on plant closings has been interested in the "mental health" of the displaced workers. This research has been guided by the conceptual assumption that workers thrown out of jobs by shutdowns are generally representative of "normal" workers, with no more prior personal problems or training limitations than most groups of continuing workers. In contrast, one concern with cross-sectional groups of the unemployed is that, quite possibly, many of them might have personal characteristics which have contributed to their being out of work. With workers displaced by closings it is assumed that the effects of job loss on personal well-being can be studied in a relatively uncontaminated context.

This being said, recent research has focused on the relationship between relative economic deprivation and a host of mental health indicators, theorizing that the inadequacy of economic resources is the essential link between labor market outcomes and attitudes and behavior. Economic deprivation has been found to be associated with anomie, lowered life satisfaction, reduced social participation with friends and relatives, and low morale (Aiken, et al., 1968; Ferman and Gardner, 1979; Cobb and Kasl, 1977; Kasl and Cobb, 1979).[1] Furthermore, there is evidence that the ill effects of job loss on mental health can hinder the chances of finding future re-employment (C and R Associates, 1978). Thus, there is a bit of a catch-22: job loss produces poorer mental health and those with poorer mental health have a harder time finding a job to replace the one lost.

C. Effects on Physical Health

Compared to the aforementioned topics, there has been very little done on the effects of job displacement on physical health. The most complete information on physical health, however, comes from the work of Kasl, Cobb, and their associates. In a series of papers (Cobb and Kasl, 1977; Kasl and Cobb, 1970; Kasl, Cobb, and Brooks, 1968; Kasl, Gore, and Cobb, 1975), they have reported that job displacement is associated with increased hypertension and abnormally high levels of cholesterol, blood sugar and swollen joints. The symptoms exhibited by workers led Cobb and Kasl (1977) to expect that an excess of peptic ulcers, diabetes, and gout might appear. In addition, they found that while job loss caused these physical problems, health status—especially as measured by interviewer (trained nurses) ratings of health—had a solid effect on the number of weeks of unemployment after the shutdown (Cobb and Kasl, 1977: 168-9). Again we find a reciprocal relationship of sorts between job loss and health: job loss leads to decline in physical health which in turn leads to longer unemployment.

It is clear that this research has documented the serious economic, social, psychological, and physical health effects of job loss on displaced workers. Without trying to downplay the magnitude of these problems, we maintain that social scientists have had a rather unbalanced focus on the "problems" without looking at their causes and without giving serious attention to the context in which plant closings occur. Most of the existing research has suggested that the various serious problems caused for workers by plant closings are unintended consequences of larger, impersonal economic forces over which management, as well as workers, have little control. The implied, if not stated, policy recommendations of most of this research has been that government agencies should attempt to mitigate the adverse effects of plant closings on workers.

The problem with this perspective is that it does not consider that management decisions to close plants, or even to suggest publicly the possibility of a shut-down, might be motivated by plans to reshape existing relations beween management and labor. The argument being put forth here is not that management sets out to cause mental or physical problems among workers. Rather, we are contending that it is important to consider that the substantial increase in plant closings in the recent past is to some considerable degree one aspect of an effort by management both to limit the cost of labor, and thereby the incomes received by workers, and to increase control over workers in the workplace.

In this paper we shall maintain that (1) even when focusing only on the negative personal effects of plant closings, these problems are rendered more significant when they are found to be imbedded in and resulting from a management strategy to control labor; and (2) conceptualizing them as part of the struggle between management and labor raises an entire set of additional concerns—as important as the ones mentioned already—which largely have been ignored by social scientists. In the next two sections we address some of these concerns, as we document why plant closings can be seen as a way that management attempts to discipline labor.

II. PLANT CLOSINGS AND THE CONFLICT BETWEEN CAPITAL AND LABOR

In line with a substantial amount of recent literature drawing on Marx (e.g., Braverman, 1974; Burawoy, 1979; Edwards, 1979; Marglin, 1974; Stone, 1974; Zimbalist, 1979), we see capital and labor engaged in a constant struggle for control over the workplace and the return to workers for their labor. This struggle has taken different forms historically, and the most immediate key to understanding it today is to focus on the changing economic, social and political conditions in the post World War II era. In the modern period, this struggle has numerous aspects. For example, Goldman and Van Houten (1980) have identified four principal tactics which are used by management to control labor: preventive labor relations (e.g., avoiding unions by paying workers well); strike tactics (e.g., attempts to keep production going during a strike); political activities (e.g., lobbying to reduce health and safety standards); and plant closings. In our discussion we shall attempt to portray some of the ways in which plant closings have become an integral aspect of management's attempt to discipline labor.

What is important to note is that, in general, the character of plant closings has changed in the last decade over what was common previously. In prior decades, it was more typical for management to close a plant because it was going out of business or, at least leaving an entire line of business. Currently, it is more typical for a plant to be closed by a generally profitable corporation that is nonetheless trying to lower labor costs. It is one thing to close Packard plant because no one is buying Packards, and yet another to close a plant because management can get nonunion or lower-priced labor, or just a more disciplined workforce to produce the same product somewhere else.

Essentially alone among those studying plant closings, Bluestone and Harrison (1982) have presented an insightful and provocative analysis that looks at capital mobility as an aspect of some of the major economic changes since World War II. Their argument in brief is as follows. Due to a variety of factors, U.S. corporations enjoyed a period of unprecedented growth from 1946-1970. During this time, as the proverbial economic pie was growing, management was willing to offer workers considerable raises in income and benefits in return for increased control over the workplace. The keys to this economic expansion were: the emergence after World War II of the U.S. as the dominant power in the world; government policy to underwrite the costs of suburban expansion; the release of the pent-up demand for consumer goods; the introduction of cost-saving technology which allowed higher wages through productivity growth; U.S. military and foreign aid policy which greatly fostered more profitable overseas production; and increased centralization of economic activities at home which provided the financial and administrative means for the expansion. As long as the economy was growing, both management and at least a portion of labor could prosper.

However, since the late 1960s, the U.S. and other capitalist economies stopped expanding as rapidly as they had in the previous twenty years. The capitalist world-system entered another "accumulation crisis," similar in some respects to ones which have characterized and plagued capitalism in the past (e.g., the crises of 1873-1895 and 1913-1940; Frank, 1980:20). This most recent crisis was marked by a declining rate of profit, excessive productive capacity, and increased labor militancy. The real rate of return for all non-financial corporations in the U.S. fell from 15.5% (1963-66) to 9.7% (1975-78) (Holland and Myers, 1980). Capacity utilization in U.S. manufacturing has fallen from over 90% in the mid-1960s to less than 75% at the close of 1970s (Frank, 1980:75). Finally, labor, perhaps buoyed by its impressive wage gains in the post World War II period, became increasingly militant. In fact, Weisskopf (1979) has suggested that this labor militancy was at least partially responsible for declining profit rates.

Both the state and capital employed various strategies to cope with this crisis. Andre Gunder Frank (1980) summarized two of the state's major actions. First, the state attempted to postpone or, in some sectors, prevent the crisis totally by increasing the amount of money in circulation. Perhaps the most dramatic example of this was the U.S. military buildup during the Vietnam War which both delayed for a short time some of the worst aspects of the crisis and fueled worldwide inflation. Second, with this policy failing, the state embarked on various "austerity" programs which cut spending on social welfare programs. Inflation was deemed public enemy number one and the prime causes of it were said to be government spending and high wages. Austerity programs both reduced government spending and increased unemployment.

For its part, business had two ways to increase the rate of profit: identify new, more profitable uses for capital; and/or cut production costs in current endeavors

(Bluestone and Harrison, 1982). Corporations did both and each strategy brought an increase in the number of plant closings. For example, it made no sense to operate a plant with a 10% rate of return when one could get almost twice that in other spheres. Also, borrowing rates substantially greater than expected profits reduced new investment in production. Finally, one very attractive way to cut production costs was to cut the cost of labor—and a prime way to do this was to relocate production facilities in low wage areas.

Bluestone and Harrison (1982) have asserted that if the main impetus for plant closings is profits or capital accumulation, then decision on where to relocate mainly depends on two other factors: unionization and the "business climate." Each of these affects profitability, but just as importantly, each influences the ability of management to control their workforce as they desire. Although Bluestone and Harrison began their book by asserting that management closes plants to discipline labor, in their argument they appear to assign only a secondary role to controlling labor as a reason for capital mobility.[2] Clearly, *ceteris paribus,* the ability to control labor influences capital accumulation and vice versa. For example, with greater control over a workforce, management is more able to rationalize the work process in ways which increase its available capital. Similarly a sizeable amount of capital on hand places management in a better position to weather long-term strikes, which takes away one of labor's strongest weapons. Thus, while capital accumulation and controlling labor are analytically distinct, they interact with each other and often it is difficult to separate them in practice.[3] In fact, in the last decade—at time when management has been particularly aggressive—average weekly wages (in constant dollars) in the U.S. have fallen.

It is thus safe to say, given the current accumulation crisis in capitalism and the relationship between capital accumulation and the control of labor, that a major reason for plant closings may very well be management's quest for greater control over workers and for decreasing the cost of labor. Even if this is not what prompts the closing, the closing itself has important implications for the workplace struggle between capital and labor. Neither Bluestone and Harrison (1982), despite their seminal analyses, nor anyone else has attempted to address these implications in any detail. In the next section, we shall present an outline of such analyses.

III.   SUGGESTIONS FOR A RESEARCH AGENDA

We have outlined both the major research findings of social scientists who have studied the impact of plant closings and the reasons why plant closings need to be considered in light of the battle between capital and labor for control over the workplace. In this section we will present suggestions for future research on plant closings which will be based on seeing them as part of this struggle between capital and labor.

We have organized our suggestions for a research agenda around two dimensions: the types of plant closing *actions* and the types of *actors* who are affected by these different actions. We shall consider three types of actions: threats to close plants; actual closings without the relocation of workers; and closings with substantial relocations of workers. There are three classes of actors who are affected by these actions: workers; unions; and "communities" (including states and nations).

These three actions engender quite different responses from the various actors involved. In a sense, all of the actions place workers, unions and communities on the defensive and give capital more of an upper hand in its battle with labor. *Threats* to close a plant often can lead to some *concessions* by workers, unions and communities to attempt to keep the plant open. Actual *closings* cause substantial economic, social/psychological, and physical health problems for workers along with losses of revenue and strength by unions and local communities. Responses usually include attempts by union and civic leaders to *compensate* for the loss through such mechanisms as severance pay, extended unemployment benefits, counseling and job training and placement services, along with additional industry to provide new jobs and new tax revenue. Closings in which existing workers are *relocated* have a similar impact as a closing on the home community but affect workers, unions and the new community differently. Workers and unions (and corporations) attempt to *establish* themselves and *re-create* their patterns of existence in the new communities. The new communities, on the other hand, have to *adjust* to the presence of additional workers and to other political-economic actors (the company and the union). The impact of the adjustment, of course, depends on the size of both the company and the community. Each of these actions and response can be seen in light of the struggle between capital and labor. We shall briefly sketch out a few issues worthy of research with respect to the responses to threats to close plants and actual plant closings, along with presenting a more detailed examination of one case study of a plant relocation.

A.   The Threat to Close

It is safe to say that there probably are more threats to close plants than are there actual plant closings. And, even where plants do eventually close, there is evidence that there were threats to close for quite some time before the actual closing. In Slote's (1969) study of the Baker plant closing, the local union representative admitted that "everytime you go up against a company they threaten you with a plant closing. Companies always make that threat when they feel that you are pushing them too hard at the bargaining table" (p.72). In the late 1970s, U.S. Steel threatened to close several of its plants unless workers agreed to a three-year freeze on wages (Blumberg, 1980:119). Drawing on a number of examples Bluestone and Harrison (1982:179) have remarked:

> Even where unions thought themselves to be safely entrenched, many companies have begun
> to openly threaten plant shutdowns unless the unions will agree to re-open contracts and take
> wage freezes, or even provide the company with givebacks. This has now occurred so
> often . . . that it has taken on epidemic proportions.

The essential point is that the threat to close a plant is an important weapon in management's arsenal and that we know little of its effects on workers, unions, and communities.

There are several areas of potentially fruitful research with respect to the concessions given by workers, unions, and/or communities. Reports from various cases have indicated some of these concessions. When the Millars Fall Company announced in 1976 that it was considering relocating outside Massachusetts, the state, the union and the workers all made major moves to keep it there. The state provided $285,000 to help secure an additional $775,000 from the EDA for a new building site, while a nearby town offered the company 30 acres and its help to raise 1 million dollars for a new plant. The company asked for pay cuts of $1.50 per hour, along with other givebacks from its workers. After months of struggle, the union agreed to some givebacks along with a four year contract with no wage increases (Goodman, 1979:62-63). Similarly, after the announcement that the Baker plant would close in two years, workers—even though they thought the company was bluffing—increased productivity dramatically. The workers were trying to alter the situation, trying to convince the company that Baker was a profitable plant (Slote, 1969). These two examples illustrate the fundamental bargaining power a company has when it can make a credible threat to close a plant. Thus, these threats to close often can evoke concessions from workers, unions and communities and the granting of them can give management an even stronger hand in its relations with workers. This observation is not to be interpreted as implying that there will be concessions in every case, since recently various unions (e.g., UAW, OCAW, UE) have balked at such attempts. The point is rather that the threat to close a plant not only can elicit a set of immediate concessions by workers and their unions (e.g., wage freezes, productivity increases, declines in the filing and winning of grievances, etc.) and by communities (e.g., tax relief, cheap land) but also can re-assert and strengthen the ongoing dominance of the company over their workforce. As such, systematic analyses of the use and results of threats to close plants can increase our understanding of another aspect of the struggle for control between capital and labor.

B. Plant Closings

Although a considerable amount of research has been concerned with actual plant closings (see Section I), this research has been rather narrow in its focus. A substantial amount of displaced workers clearly suffer in economic, social, psychological and physical terms and unions and communities both lose revenues (dues and taxes, respectively) and strength, but we are most concerned with the connections among plant closings, the various *compensating* strategies by workers, unions, and communities, and the conflict between capital and labor.

We can illustrate the relevance of examining compensating strategies with respect to workers, unions and communities. First, plant closings and rising unemployment in older industrial communities may make employers more aggressive in their dealings with workers. For example, in early 1982 a soft drink bottling company located in St. Louis refused the demands of its workers for a raise to what equivalent workers were making in other companies and instead countered with a contract which included a substantial cut in wages. When the workers went on strike, the company had no trouble hiring strike breakers, and in a television interview, a company spokesperson said, in a clear reference to economic times and the woes of the city, that a "few years ago we never would have tried this." Furthermore, in a May, 1982 survey of 400 corporate executives done for *Business Week,* 19% of those polled agreed that they were taking advantage of the *bargaining climate* even though their companies did not need concessions (26% said that they did need them) (*Business Week* 1982:19; emphasis added). Additionally, in a community where unemployment has risen and where employers have begun to act more aggressively, workers are more restricted in the demands they can make in the labor market. This weakened position of workers was reflected in the response two Cincinnati newspapers received recently when they invited people to place "job wanted" ads free of charge. Not only did 7,522 people place ads, but also the gist of many messages was that the person placing the ad "will do any type of work" (*St. Louis Post Dispatch,* 1982). This effect of a reserve army of the unemployed on relations between workers and employers also has been recognized by *Business Week.* In a 1978 editorial they openly argued for maintaining artificially high unemployment rates, since to allow lower unemployment rates would "intensify the shortages of qualified workers and heighten the pressure for wage increases" (*Business Week* 1978:48). Thus, again we see rather candid admissions that specific actions by business that increase unemployment (one of which is plant closings) can be beneficial to business. Finally, in one of the upstate New York communities studied by Aronson and McKersie (1980:69), local union leadership believed that the additional 1100 unemployed workers who were displaced by a plant closing severely hindered the unions' ability to strike successfully. In-depth studies can reveal if, and if so, the process by which, those with jobs moderate their demands, avoid striking and otherwise be more conciliatory with management, knowing that a willing and able replacement workforce waits at the factory gates. Should this change in workers' relations with employers be confirmed by additional research, it would be a clear indication that plant closings affect labor-management relations in yet another way.

Second, communities which suffer plant closings lose jobs and tax revenues both directly and indirectly connected to the closed plant. For example, in 1980 when GM announced that they were closing their huge St. Louis Assembly plant, the city of St. Louis stood to lose one-tenth of its industrial base and one-third of its revenue from its merchants and manufacturers tax. In addition, plant closings have sizeable indirect effects. The U.S. Chamber of Commerce has estimated that for every three jobs lost in manufacturing there is a loss of two service sector jobs (Bluestone and Harrison, 1982:69). Finally, at the same time, communities often need to increase their spending on social services due to higher levels of unemployment.

The two major ways that communities compensate are by raising taxes on those currently living there and by trying to entice other industry there. In the wake of the Youngstown Sheet and Tube closing, the city of Youngstown had to increase taxes by 11 million dollars, along with securing loans in order to meet its obligations (Bluestone and Harrison, 1982:74). Goodman (1979:12) reported that the number of states offering tax exemptions for new equipment and state financing for expansion approximately doubled (to 27) between 1966 and 1975. Despite pressure to cutback spending on education, almost every state now provides business, at no or low cost to the latter, various vocational education programs for training workers. This new "war between the states" continues despite substantial evidence that tax concessions, educational training programs, etc. have little bearing on where business relocates (Bluestone and Harrison, 1982; Goodman, 1979). The gist, however, is that scarce resources—which could be going to maintain the social programs that constitute the "social wage" of workers—instead are diverted to attracting business. Thus, the compensations that communities make to provide a good business climate strengthen the position of business and weaken the positions of other taxpayers and labor in general. The dimensions of what communities do and who bears the brunt of these efforts needs to be examined.

Third, there are indications that plant closings and increased confrontations between employers and unionized workers over concessions have undermined public support for unions. Aronson and McKersie (1980) found that the plant closings in Cortland County (N.Y.) caused considerable anti-union sentiment as there was widespread belief that the unrealistic demands of the union precipitated the closings. As they said, "it was rumored that the pall cast over other negotiations by this anti-union sentiment and the fear of job loss had induced other unions bargaining with local firms to settle negotiations quickly" (Aronson and McKersie, 1980:71). The public perception that unions cause plants to leave has led to public policies based on the corollary notion that plants will relocate in areas with weak or non-existent unions. Goodman (1979:35-40) noted that it is not uncommon for states to publicize their low levels of "unionization" or "work stoppages" in trying to attract industry. This almost defacto weakens labor and strengthens management and has important implications on many factors, especially on the ability of capital and labor to use the state to their own advantage (e.g., right to work laws vs. restrictive plant closing legislation).

C.   Plant Relocations

Because the largest share of research energy has been devoted to plant closings in which all or almost all workers lose their jobs, we know little about plant relocations in which sizeable numbers of workers take jobs in the new plant. Our own work has examined this situation and merits discussion here. In this examination we focus on the ways in which management increased its control over workers and the union as a result of this relocation. We also discuss the adjustment that communities need to make in the wake of the arrival of a new plant.

One qualification should be noted at the outset. A number of studies have indicated that very few workers, especially blue collar ones, are likely to accept transfers outside their home communities (e.g., Dorsey, 1967; Foltman, 1968; Sheppard, et al., 1960; Smith and Fowler, 1964). In fact, Gordus, et al. (1981:102) surmised that unless all costs of the transfer are absorbed by management, only about 20% of displaced workers are likely to transfer. However, this conclusion appears to be based on studies of closings which occurred 20 years ago in a very different economic climate. Prior to the last decade workers probably were more likely to be influenced by beliefs that things were getting better economically and that replacement jobs could be found in the local community. Given the changed economic climate, it is not unrealistic to expect that greater numbers of workers will avail themselves of the opportunity to hold onto their jobs, even if they have to leave their communities. As we note below, in the case that we studied a substantial proportion of the workers seemed quite willing to relocate.

1.   Background of the Relocation

The relocation that we studied was the 1980–1981 move of General Motors' Corvette assembly plant from St. Louis to Bowling Green, Kentucky, a town of 50,000 located between Nashville and Louisville. As part of the 1979 International Agreement between GM and the UAW, St. Louis workers had transfer rights to Bowling Green. Workers in the skilled trades began reporting to Bowling Green as early as December, 1980, while the bulk were notified to report in April or May, 1981. The St. Louis plant employed approximately 1500 workers on two shifts, but due to various changes only 1035 were employed on one shift at the new plant. All of these workers (936), except for some skilled trades, transferred from St. Louis. Full production began in June, 1981.

Labor-management relations at the St. Louis plant gave GM good reasons to want to make some significant changes. This can be seen in several ways. First, the union local (Local 25) was one of the oldest and most powerful in the country, with over 10,000 members working three different lines (Chevrolets, trucks, and Corvettes) as recently as 1979. This multi-line membership afforded the union a considerable degree of power, as all the lines would shut down if the union had trouble with the company on any one of the lines. With Corvettes generally selling very well, threatening to stop production of them practically insured that any union demand would be met. A worker with 28 years seniority recalled the "fix" that GM was in:

> They had to tolerate the passenger line because they needed trucks and Corvettes so badly. GM is changing all these plants around to have one product lines, so they won't be stuck like that again.

Second, union officials conceded that Local 25 was perhaps the most troublesome GM local in the country. Local 25 had one of the highest absenteeism rates and a mind-boggling backlog of grievances. Additionally, the plant was the scene of racial tensions. In 1971, the local's Black Caucus organized a demonstration alleging racial discrimination in GM's hiring and job classification procedures. GM filmed the demonstration and fired 26 demonstrators and suspended 90 others. Because all those disciplined were black (whites also took part in the protest), several of the workers sued both GM and the UAW (for not handling the grievances fairly) on the grounds of racial discrimination. In 1980, the court exonerated the UAW, but found against GM, ordering it to pay a financial settlement to the workers. Thus, given all the above, it is not hard to see why GM might want to break-up the St. Louis facility.

We collected various data on the relocation during the first part of 1982. First, an associate of the author conducted fifty in-depth interviews with a systematic sample of relocated workers. All of these interviews except one took place in the homes of the workers. Although there was no set order to the topics discussed, all interviews covered the worker's personal situation, changes in the new plant, and attitudes toward the company, the union, and the community. All of those interviewed were men (only 3 women transferred), with an average seniority of 17 years in the St. Louis plant.

Second, we conducted various interviews in Bowling Green with city officials, employment agencies, plant and union officials, local retailers, news reporters and other "informed" observers of the local scene. Third, we had access to various company and union documents concerning the St. Louis plant, the Bowling Green plant, and the transfer between them. Information gleaned from all the above was integrated to provide a more coherent analysis of the entire relocation process.

We have analyzed these data in more depth elsewhere (Zipp and Lane, 1983). Here we shall focus on two of the issues to be considered in seeing plant relocations as part of the relations between capital and labor: changes between St. Louis and Bowling Green within the plant and in the strength of the union. As noted, with a new plant workers, their union, and management all try to establish certain modes of existence regarding various aspects of industrial life. What is attempted, how it is attempted and its success can provide useful insights on the labor-management conflict. Finally, we shall suggest important topics of research which tap the effects of plant relocations on the communities where they relocate.

2.   The New Plant

There are numberous ways to see how capital uses a plant relocation to discipline labor by comparing the old and new facilities. In relocations without a transfer of workers, the two major ways that we would expect management to attempt this would be through lower wages/benefits and through trying to prevent unionization. Since the GM-UAW International Agreement called for a worker transfer, these are not relevant here. However, even in an industry with what many believe to be the union which historically has had the best contracts for its members, there are other ways in which management attempts to increase its power. Some of the key factors to consider are: the pace of work; rules governing shop floor behavior; and "rationalization" of the work process. We shall present data on the first two of these to illustrate how such research might illuminate the struggle for control in the workplace.

The first major change concerns the pace of work. GM took advantage of the move to increase the speed of the line by 70%. The St. Louis plant produced 10 cars per hour, the Bowling Green one builds 17. Since the jobs generally are set up in the same way in both plants, workers now have a lot less time to do them. According to a twenty-three year veteran:

> If you mess up one screw, you don't have time to fix it. You gotta hope that a repairman down the line will re-do something if it was done improperly. Now the line is so fast that it is constant pressure to keep up.

In addition, GM reduced the length of the hoses of tools that workers use by several feet. A management official told us that GM didn't want workers from "working back down the line," a common practice in assembly-line work to create spare time. The faster pace of work and shorter hoses have left workers with less time to do their jobs, a reduced ability to create spare time, and thus put them under greater pressure all day. Workers reported virtually no leisure and very little contact with their fellow workers except on breaks. Workers are both worked harder and made more isolated in Bowling Green.

A second coercive tactic used by GM at the new plant concerns the in-plant rules or by-laws. These are the rules governing particular in-plant behavior, especially having to do with the penalties associated with different transgressions (e.g., absenteeism, fighting on the job, etc.) A comparison of these rules in the St. Louis and Bowling Green plants reveals the increased power of management and the form that it takes.

In the St. Louis plant workers possessed a detailed booklet entitled "Plant Rules and Regulations" outlining precise penalties for specific offenses. This booklet told workers exactly where they stood and what they could expect under the progressive disciplinary system. In Bowling Green, in contrast, there are no set plant rules, but rather a "Code of Conduct" which is worth quoting in its entirety:

> It is expected that employes (sic) will act in a manner that concurs with our Plant Philosophy, respecting the rights of others, the product we build, and the property on which we work. Employes dedicated to the objective of building a high quality Corvette deserve a non-disruptive work environment. Individual responsibility is the key to accomplishing this objective.
>
> Occupational disturbances such as possession of intoxicants, illegal narcotics, weapons, theft, assault or abusive or intimidating behavior, sabotage, misuse of company property, disregard of safety regulations, careless workmanship or actions resulting in loss of production, will be considered reasons to implement corrective measures.

The Plant Philosophy referred to in the first sentence reads simply:

> The dedicated objective of the Corvette organization is to provide a work environment and quality of work life in an atmosphere of trust and open communication that will result in product pride, recognition of individual involvement and accomplishment, community responsibility, high quality and competitive cost.

The only other document pertaining to the plant rules is the "Implementation Procedure of the Code of Conduct." This statement outlines a progressive-stage procedure consisting of five levels, each increasing in severity. Level 1 is equivalent to a verbal reprimand by management. Level 2 involves a formal interview, with the next level involving a formal interview and a notation on one's record. Disciplinary action at level 4 equals a 30 day layoff, and level 5 means a discharge. Although not too formidable in written form, the catch is that if "circumstances (are) sufficiently severe" an employee may skip levels and receive an instant disciplinary layoff of 30 days. Furthermore, with no precedents as yet established in the new plant, it would naturally be to the company's advantage to skip employees up levels and to penalize as severely as possible, to gain an initial strong hand. Over time certain penalties will become acceptable for certain offences as precedents are set, but initially the company would want to "start out tough," as one worker phrased it.

This "starting it out tough" can be seen with respect to the rules against absenteeism, which, by consensus, are the toughest of all. This is no accident, since both company records and union officials indicated that absenteeism was a major problem at the St. Louis plant.

The system works on a fault/no fault basis. For unexcused absences, a worker quickly progresses up the five levels of corrective measures, with the ultimate penalty of discharge. For no fault or excused absences, those for which the worker has his foreman's permission, the employee has only slightly more leeway. "Excessive excused absenteeism," as the company terms it, is subject to a sliding scale of disciplinary measures. After a certain number of excused hours, an employee is reprimanded. If excused absences continue, the worker may be "released."[4]

These changes in plant rules touched a responsive chord.

> If you miss 16 hours of work, you go up a level. The only way not to have it (an absence) against us is if it is a life-threatening situation, if you are lying in the hospital dying, or if you ask beforehand. How can you ask before you break a leg? That's not life-threatening, so they'd get you for it."

Changes in these rules seemed to have had some benefits for GM, as according to GM's records, absenteeism is much lower in Bowling Green than in St. Louis. It was obvious that the workers understood full well that these vague rules strengthened management's hand.

3. The Weaker Union

Plant relocations can involve changes from a unionized workforce to a nonunionized one. However, even in cases like this one in which the union also moves, the plant relocation can be expected to weaken the power of the union in a number of ways. First, new union locals, generally with smaller memberships, are not going to be as strong as older, more established ones. Compounding this are two additional factors: (1) any in-plant changes which increase the pace of work or tighten shop discipline leave the union with less latitude; and (2) the union's role in a transfer is usually limited to *reacting* to the plans of management rather than initiating any action. Fourth, since relocations tend to be away from the heavily-unionized frostbelt and to the less-unionized sunbelt, unions often find that they have to establish themselves in an area that is not only largely nonunion but also often actively hostile to unions. This certainly was the case with the Corvette relocation. As one skilled tradesman observed, "The city fathers were very upset when they found out that the union came with the shop. This is a very anti-union area."

All of these factors can be utilized to determine how plant relocations affect the relative strength of management and unions. Dimensions on which to examine them include comparing the new plant with the old in terms of the local agreements, the filing and winning of grievances, the perceived strength of the union, and so on. However, although all are important, we are going to present an additional aspect of the management-union relationship which is likely to occur in new plants: the introduction and/or expansion of various "quality of worklife" programs (QWL).

There are thousands of enterprises now engaging in some form of these programs. GM, for example, has committed $43 billion for building new plants and improving old ones from 1980-85, with QWL being implemented in some form in every one of these plants. Although unions traditionally have been opposed to

QWL programs, the UAW has been an exception. In 1973 the UAW signed an agreement with GM to explore new ways of dealing with QWL. Former UAW International Vice-President Irving Bluestone remarked:

> Too often QWL is written up as the workers cooperating with management to do something for management. It's quite the contrary. It's management moving toward the workers and surrendering certain prerogatives which management has historically enjoyed. (The Harvard Crimson, 1979: 3).

Similarly, a GM spokesperson described QWL as "workers restructuring the job." The examples provided included, "putting a bolt here instead of there to improve efficiency. (In this way) they can redesign the assembly line. They can get better lighting. If they want, they can even get their machine painted blue."

At the Bowling Green plant, QWL meetings are held weekly and workers receive overtime pay for attending them. The usual justification for QWL programs is that they are for the joint benefit of workers and management. Supposedly, with QWL, plants become more efficient and workers more productive. However, there also are indications that QWL programs have been used by management to help reshape relations with labor. For example, QWL meetings, such as those at the Bowling Green plant, can be seen as having two favorable effects for management: (1) they increase the employees' belief that they have real choices in the workplace (e.g., "workers restructuring the job"); and (2) they undermine the power of the union (see also, Parker and Hansen, 1983). With respect to the first, it is instructive to note the examples of "restructuring" provided by the GM spokesperson: a bolt here, better lighting, blue machines. This was not a case of the GM official not being aware of what was being done or of being unwilling to tell the full story. On the contrary, those workers who thought that the awareness meetings were beneficial offered similar changes as evidence:

> Instead of going through the union, and through the safety commission, you can get things done. Like in welding, we got some rubber mats to walk on, and we'd have had to go through safety, and that'd've taken forever.
> You can bring up whatever you want to talk about, and the majority of the time they (GM) will fix things. They've given us a baseball diamond, a horshoe area, and a basketball (court) . . .

A second potential benefit to management of awareness meetings is that the meetings can decrease workers' reliance on the union and increase it on management. An effective QWL program can convince workers that the way to get what they want is to ask the company directly rather than going through union channels. Over time workers may realize that management is not so bad and that the confrontational stance of the union is counter-productive to their own needs. Relatedly, as Parker and Hansen (1983) noted, a successful QWL program can convince workers that their own security is tied to the success of the company rather than the union. Parker and Hansen cited an instance where this attitude resulted in weakening solidarity among union members: the president of a Buick local boasted that a QWL program allowed his division to underbid fellow UAW members in a Pontiac division (presumably for work on a common component). Ultimately, workers may wonder why they are giving up an hour or two's salary every month for a union which really does not do much for them.

Union officials felt that the QWL program was instituted in the Bowling Green facilities as a measure to bypass and subvert collective bargaining. (At the time of our interviews, the local agreement was still being negotiated.) After discussing the issue at one union meeting, the union body voted to discontinue QWL meetings at least until the local agreement was negotiated. All union members were asked to stop attending the meetings, and for a while the meetings were stopped. After a few months, however, people started going back to the meetings. The local neither called for a re-vote nor urged members not to attend. As a result, while the "good union men" did not attend the meetings and therefore lost the time and a half overtime once a week, others did attend.

Even though most who did go indicated that they went only for the money (e.g., "after busting' your ass all day at $12 an hour, it is nice to get paid $18 just to sit there"), their mere attendence was divisive. For one, loyal unionists lost money and were not pleased about it. "It ain't fair that the good union men would have to suffer, financially for sticking with their convictions," exclaimed one worker. "We are all hard up."

The money was not the only issue. The shroud of being "company man" or an informant hung heavily on the heads of those who attended the meetings. "There has been a lot of trouble about it," a worker confided, "cause the union says guys are going and ratting on others, and that creates worker-to-worker problems." Workers clearly were in a bind. Strapped financially by the move, they could net an extra $40 a month for just sitting in these meetings once a week. Despite this, the union and their fellow workers urged them not to attend. Being a good union man clearly had some conflicts with being a good family man and breadwinner. Management was paying the piper and calling the tune: the QWL meetings caused a fair amount of distrust among the workers. In such an atmosphere, solidarity would not be as likely.

GM's ability to introduce and run a somewhat successful QWL program was conditioned to some degree on the relocation. Thus, even in an industry with a strong union, where a company could not take advantage of a relocation to avoid the union or to lower wage rates, the relocation and the accompanying re-creation of the work rules and procedures has provided an opening for management to begin to restructure its control over labor.

4. The New Community

The tremendous growth and success of the Sun Belt are now common knowledge. Texas, and Houston in particular, are symbols of the benefits of a pro-business climate. On almost all social and economic indicators—employment, sales, per capita income, population—cities like Houston are leading the way. Scenes of unemployed workers in Detroit lining up to buy Houston newspapers just for the want ads are testimony to the shared belief in the success of Houston and communities like it.

Although it would be hard to argue that prosperity hasn't helped some in Houston, there is another side to the saga. Bluestone and Harrison (1982: Ch. 4), calling Houston the "quintessential boomtown," presented some of this "downside": highway congestion, air pollution, high murder rates and a housing crisis marked by prices that have tripled in a few years. In addition, the lack of jobs and/or the presence only of low wage ones has led to frustration among these new migrants. The city's overtaxed services has caused its civic leaders publicly to advise the unemployed not to come to Houston. Clearly here and almost certainly elsewhere, the influx of capital has not come empty-handed.

In general, the prevailing wisdom is that it is worth providing a favorable business climate because businesses bring jobs (both directly and indirectly) and pay taxes. There is research, however, which outlines the rather narrow limits of these benefits. Summers and his colleagues (1976) have found that due to transfers, in-migration, the small multiplier effect on other jobs, etc., plant relocations have very little effect on reducing local unemployment rates. And, although studies which systematically assess the changes in tax revenues accompanying plant relocations need to be done, there is some agreement that relocations increase the costs of basic public services—especially water and sewage (Bluestone and Harrison, 1982).

In the Corvette case, the most dramatic price increases were in housing. Although a local judge described this as a "natural" phenomenon when there is substantial immigration, it meant that both the incoming Corvette workers and some Bowling Green residents had to pay sharply inflated prices for new housing and that those who either owned substantial amounts of housing or land reaped huge dividends. Thus, given: (1) the tax benefits accruing to the corporation; (2) the increase in the costs of basic public services (which are more costly to lower income groups); (3) the minor effect on the unemployment rate; and (4) the increased real estate prices with some land owners profitting while most suffer, we would speculate that relocations may very well widen the gap between the haves and the have-nots.[5]

Additionally, when a large corporation relocates in a relatively small town, the corporation is in a position to have a great deal of political power. For one, in most cases the corporation already has received some tax or other benefits for relocating there. Two, the fact that the corporation moved there is evidence that it can move somewhere else if conditions do not suit it. RCA, for instance, closed its unionized plant in Cincinnati in the 1960s and moved to a nonunion one in Memphis. When there was a threat of unionization in Memphis, RCA moved to Taiwan (Bluestone and Harrison, 1980; Goodman, 1979). Thus, it will not be surprising if the town fathers do their best to accomodate the new plant by maintaining a favorable business climate.

Three, there may be great expectations surrounding the arrival of the new firm. In the Corvette case, 35,000 people toured the plant two months after it was opened—this in a town of 50,000. This may leave the firm in a good position to sway public opinion. Again in the Corvette case, before the production workers arrived GM publicized that its workers were paid $20 per hour. Not only was this not true, but also it led to a perception on the part of the Bowling Green locals that the Corvette workers were quite well-off, able to afford high-priced homes, etc. Additionally, it fueled the hesistancy of local employers to hire "GM wives." As the wives of GM workers heard constantly, "Why do you need to work? Your husband's making $40,000." In such a situation, there would be little impetus for the townspeople to be anything but eager to keep GM there and to work for it someday soon.

In sum, research which addresses some of these issues—the gap between the haves and have-nots, the increased pressure to keep the firm there resulting in the maintenance of a pro-business climate, and so on—should help to understand the changes which impinge on the battle between capital and labor that occur in communities in the wake of relocations.

IV.   CONCLUSION

Plant closings cause considerable problems for individuals and communities. A sizeable body of scholarly literature, reviewed above, clearly documents a good portion of these. We have contended, however, that this "social problems" approach is not sufficient for analyzing the impact of plant closings. Focusing only on these social problems inplicitly assumes that impersonal economic forces, ones are beyond consideration, cause plant closings. We do not see these forces as exogenous to our understanding plant closings; in fact, our brief review of the changing economic context since WW II established why plant closings are part of the overall strategy by management to re-structure the relations between it and labor. The crisis of accumulation in the capitalist world-system has given management a reason to try new ways both to cut labor costs and to discipline labor further.

In practice, however, it will be at least extremely difficult and most likely nearly impossible to establish definitively that management intended to close a particular plant largely in order to achieve these kinds of goals. Even if one cannot do this, we feel that it is sufficient to examine the *effects* of the closing on the relationship between labor and management. If the closing substantially alters the balance of power in management's favor, this will be evidence of the need to see plant closings in the larger context of the struggle between capital and labor.

Finally, our case study of the transfer of the Corvette plant and workers from St. Louis to Bowling Green has demonstrated some ways in which the conflict between capital and labor is played out in a plant relocation in which there is a substantial transfer of workers. Studies of plant closings, threats to close, and relocations without transfers need to be conducted along these lines in order to assess the many ways that capital mobility is a tactic used by management to increase its power in the workplace. The research agenda that we have put forth is not intended to be exhaustive but rather to be a first step toward identifying and conceptualizing areas for future study. Sad as it is to say, there are enough instances of closings to examine. Hopefully, systematic analysis of plant closings along the lines suggested will help widen the narrow set of issues which social scientists have focused on thus far.

ACKNOWLEDGMENT

I would like to thank Jan Yoder and Steve Deutsch for their helpful comments and Kathy Lane for research assistance. All interpretations are my own.

NOTES

1. It should be noted that Cobb and Kasl (1977) used a slightly different measure of relative economic deprivation than did the other authors cited here.
2. This is somewhat analogous to the debate over whether or not certain new forms of work organization, technology, etc., were more the result of management's search for efficiency or for greater control over workers (e.g., Marglin, 1974; Noble, 1977; Stone, 1974).
3. There have been reported instances in which capital mobility was more of an attempt to discipline workers than to accumulate profits. Conway (1979), for example, noted that a southern textile manufacturer, when threatened with unionization at one of his plants, simply closed the plant down and sold it piece by piece.
4. As one worker put it, "They try to coat it with pretty words here. You get 'released.' Don't ask me what the difference is between 'released' and 'fired'."
5. Indeed, although they did not directly test this notion, Bluestone and Harrison (1982:87) reported that in the Sunbelt, the richest 5% receives a greater share of total income than does the richest 5% in any other region, with the opposite being true for the poorest 20% of the population.

REFERENCES

Aiken, Michael, Louis A. Ferman, and Harold L. Sheppard
  1968 Economic Failure, Alienation, and Extremism Ann Arbor: University of Michigan Press.
Aronson, Robert L. and Robert B. McKensie
  1980 Economic Consequences of Plant Shutdowns in New York State. New York State School of Industrial and Labor Relations, Cornell University.
Bluestone, Barry and Bennett Harrison
  1982 The Deindustrialization of America. New York: Basic Books.
  1980 Capital and Communities. Washington, D.C.: The Progressive Alliance.

Blumberg, Paul
  1980   Inequality in an Age of Decline. New York: Harper Row.
Braverman, Harry
  1974   Labor and Monopoly Capital. New York: Monthly Review.
Burawoy, Michael
  1979   Manufacturing Consent. Chicago: University of Chicago Press.
Business Week
  1982   "A management split over labor relations." June 14:19.
  1978   "When jobs go begging" June 5:48-49.
C and R Associates
  1978   "Community costs of plant closings: bibliography and survey of the literature." Report
         prepared for the Federal Trade Commission, (July).
Claque, Ewan, Walter J. Couper, and E. Wight Bakke.
  1934   After the Shutdown. New Haven: Yale University Press.
Cobb, Sidney, and Stanislav V. Kasl
  1977   Termination: The Consequences of Job Loss. Washington, D.C. National Institute of
         Occupational Safety and Health.
Conway, Mimi
  1979   Rise Gonna Rise: A Portrait of Southern Textile Workers. Garden City,: Anchor.
Dorsey, John W.
  1967   "The mack case: A study in unemployment." Pp. 175-248 in Otto Eckstein (ed.), Studies
         in the Economics of Income Maintenance. Washington, D.C.: Brookings, 1967.
Edwards, Richard
  1979   Contested Terrain: The Transformation of the Workplace in the Twentieth Century. New
         York: Basic Books.
Ferman, Louis A.
  1963   Death of a Newspaper. Kalamazoo, MI: Upjohn.
Ferman, Louis A., and John Gardner
  1979   Economic Deprivation, Social Mobility, and Mental Health". Pp. 193-224 in L.A. Ferman
         & Jeanne P. Gordus, Mental Health and the Economy. Kalamazoo, MI: Upjohn.
Foltman, Felician F.
  1968   White and Blue-Collars in a Mill Shutdown. Ithaca, N.Y.: N.Y. State School of Industrial
         and Labor Relations.
Frank, Andre Gunder
  1980   Crisis: In the World Economy. New York: Holmes and Meier.
Goldman, Paul, and Donald R. Van Houten
  1980   "Uncertainty, conflict, and labor relations in the modern firm II: the war on labor."
         Economic and Industrial Democracy, 1:263-287.
Goodman, Robert
  1979   The Last Entrepreneurs. New York: Simon and Schuster.
Gordus, Jeanne Prial, Paul Jarley and Louis A. Ferman
  1981   Plant Closings and Economic Dislocation. Kalamazoo, MI: Upjohn.
Haber, William, Louis A. Ferman, and J.P. Hudson
  1963   The Impact of Technological Change: The American Experience. Kalamazoo, Michigan:
         Upjohn Institute.
Harvard Crimson
  1979   "UAW—Lossening the Chains: an interview with Irving Bluestone." February 21:3.
Holland, Daniel and Steward Myers
  1980   "Profitability and capital costs for manufacturing corporations." American Economic
         Review, 70 (May):320-325.

Kasl, Stanislav V., and Sidney Cobb
  1979   "Some Mental Health Consequences of Plant Closing and Job Loss." Pp. 255-300 in
         Louis A. Ferman and Jeanne P. Gordus (eds.), Mental Health and the Economy. Kal-
         amazoo, MI: Upjohn.
Kasl, Stanislav V. and Sidney Cobb.
  1970   "Blood pressure changes in men undergoing job loss: a preliminary report". Psychosomat-
         ic Medicine v. 32:19-38.
Kasl, Stanislav V., Sidney Cobb, and G.W. Brooks
  1968   "Changes in serum uric acid and cholesterol levels in men undergoing job loss". Journal
         of the American Medical Association v. 206:1500-1507.
Kasl, Stanislav V., Susan Gore and Sidney Cobb
  1975   "The experience of losing a job: reported changes in health, symptoms, and illness behav-
         ior". Psychosomatic Medicine, V. 37:106-22.
Marglin, Steven A.
  1974   "What do bosses do? The origins and functions of hierarchy in capitalist production."
         Review of Radical Political Economics 6 (Summer):60-112.
Myers, Robert J.
  1929   "Occupational readjustment of displaced skilled workmen." Journal of Political Economy
         37 (August):473-89.
Noble, David
  1977   America By Design. New York: Oxford University Press.
Parker, Mike and Dwight Hansen
  1983   "The Circle Game." The Progressive 47 (June):32-35.
Parnes, Herbert S., and Randy King
  1977   "Middle-aged Job Losers'. Industrial Gerontology, 4, 2 (Spring):77-95.
St. Louis Post-Dispatch
  1982   "Free ads for jobs draw desperate pleas for work." October 20th: 8A.
Sheppard, Harold, Louis A. Ferman, and Seymour Faber
  1960   Too Old to Work, Too Young to Retire. Washington, D.C.: Government Printing Office.
Slote, Alfred
  1969   Termination: The Closing at Baker Plant Indianapolis: Bobbs-Merrill.
Smith, Luke, and Irving A. Fowler
  1964   "Plant relocation and worker migration". Pp. 491-97 in Arthur B. Shostalk and William
         Gomberg (eds.), Blue-Collar World. Englewood Cliffs, N.J.: Prentice-Hall.
Stern, James L.
  1972   "Consequences of plant closure." Journal of Human Resources 7 (January):1-25.
  1969   "Evolution of private manpower planning in Armour's plant closings." Monthly Labor
         Review. (December):21-28.
Stillman, Don
  1980   "The devastating impact of plant relocations". Pp. 72-88 in M. Green and R. Massie, Jr.
         (eds.), The Big Business Reader. New York: Pilgrim Press.
Stone, Katherine
  1974   "The origins of job structures in the steel industry". Review of Radical Political Econom-
         ics 6 (Summer):113-173.
Summers, Gene F., et al.
  1976   Industrial Invasion of Non-metropolitan America. New York: Praeger.
Weisskopf, Thomas
  1979   "Marxian crisis theory and the rate of profit in the postwar U.S. economy." Cambridge
         Journal of Economics 3 December:
Wilcock, Richard and Walter France
  1963   Unwanted Workers. Glencoe, II: Free Press.

Young, Edwin
   1963   "The armour experience: A case study in plant shutdown". Pp. 144-158 in Gerald G.
          Somers, Edward L. Cushman, and Nat Weinberg (eds.), Adjusting to Technological
          Change. NY: Harper & Row.
Zimbalist, Andrew (ed.)
   1979   Case Studies on the Labor Process: New York: Monthly Review Press.
Zipp, John F. and Katherine E. Lane
   1983   "Plant closings and control over the workplace: a case study." Unpublished manuscript,
          Department of Sociology, Washington University.

MAJORITY AND ORGANIZED OPPOSITION:

ON EFFECTS OF SOCIAL MOVEMENTS

Herman Turk and Lynne G. Zucker

I. PROBLEM AND EMPIRICAL SETTING

A. Contrasting Models and a Specifying Proposition

The extent to which social movements can simply effect social change through mass or collective behavior has become a major theoretical issue. Current versions of the traditional collective behavior model still rest on the premise that social movements rely on spontaneous action by numbers of like-interested persons, undampened by formality, especially when but a single objective is pursued (Piven and Cloward, 1971, 1977:passim; Garner, 1977:12, 112, 118). But the organizational model posits organization and organizational links to be necessary for any kind of social change, placing into question thereby the utility of the very concept of social movement (Oberschall, 1973; Turk, 1977b:86–92; McCarthy and Zald, 1977; Jenkins and Perrow, 1977).

Research in Social Movements, Conflict and Change, Vol. 6, pages 249–269.
Copyright © 1984 by JAI Press Inc.
All rights of reproduction in any form reserved.
ISBN: 0-89232-311-6

Since there is published evidence on behalf of both views, our task is to *specify conditions* under which the traditional collective behavior model applies; for that there are organizational effects on social change is widely accepted as given. We make here the elementary assumption that organization with respect to either side of an issue places that side at an advantage. From this follows our condition-specifying proposition:

> The extent to which any particular change is effected by a widely supported but unorganized social movement varies inversely with the degree of organized opposition to such change.

B.   Natural Quasi-Experiment

We are specifically concerned with the effects of a statewide social movement upon changes in California law as well as with consequent effects upon local budgetary restrictions among 43 California counties, which experienced common, abrupt, and nontrivial changes in their external social, political, and economic environments.

Overwhelming passage in 1978 of the statewide initiative against high taxes and government spending called Proposition 13, the manifestation of a single-issue social movement, was followed by legislation that nearly halved the major revenue source for local government, the local property tax. Apparently in response to minority opposition that supported a social responsibility ethic of social welfare and public employment—such opposition might indeed have constituted a second [minority] movement—the same legislation provided the counties with temporary financial relief and included mandates against certain reductions in local spending, to be described.

This quasi-experimental "treatment," whose short-term impact on 43 local budgets is to be reported, was sudden and unaccompanied by other changes. Hence, we can, with reasonable safety, attribute the changes observed between the 1977–78 and 1978–79 fiscal years to the varying effects of Proposition 13. Here the basic empirical question is how and to what degree were those public political documents called local budgets affected by these statewide events as well as by local support of the movement and locally organized opposition.

The dependent variables are changes in such documentary decision outcomes, which are ubiquitous to modern societies. Constituting records of how governments decide publicly among conflicting interests, budgets are major means through which local implementation of the movement and local responses to organized opposition may be assessed. Local budgetary *violations* of nonlocal law are especially dramatic, given the nonsecret and public nature of the offending documents.

II. STATE RESPONSES TO THE MOVEMENT AND ITS OPPONENTS: THE "EXPERIMENTAL TREATMENT" FOR LOCALITIES

A. The Movement

The public history of Proposition 13 as it appeared in newspaper headlines, in published voter surveys, and in reports of state and local responses to the initiative's outcome has been described elsewhere (Turk, 1979). In brief, it was depicted as a mass movement that protested escalating property taxes and rising expenditures by government but supported the retention of current levels of sanitation and public protection (police and fire). We find that the 1970 rates of owner-occupancy one-family housing units ranged from 48.5 percent to 69.4 percent in the 43 counties (mean of 60.9 percent; source: U.S. Bureau of the Census, 1977). Home ownership, together with severe tax rises based on escalating property values, was the main reason given for the property tax initiative's passage with a nearly two to one majority (64.9 percent).[1] Yet published voter surveys (summarized by Turk, 1979) suggested that the vote also signified sharply rising national distrust of government (see trends reported by Miller, 1974 and Institute for Social Research, 1979) and sentiments that favored reduced government spending. The governor, who had opposed the initiative, and various other state officials publicly defined the vote as a clear call to reduce taxes as well as to reduce government spending.

B. Organized Opposition to the Movement

Still, the same survey reports portrayed opposition to service cutbacks in police, fire, and sanitation; and a majority of the voters were reported as finding some form of public assistance necessary—not to be provided locally, however, but by the state. How they felt about local health care for the poor had not been assessed. The surveys also provided the state's elected officials with information not only about the dominant majority but also about opposition to the initiative by persons, mainly deprived minorities, renters, or government workers and their families, considered likely to suffer from it or not to benefit. Some advocacy organizations for ethnic minorities, such as the Urban League, and a few associations of public employees even published their opposition.

The state's executive and legislative branches were portrayed as responsive both to majority will and to its apparent contradictions, responding also thereby to the initiative's opposition by the voting minority. One might suspect this last response to have been influenced by organized interest groups—representing perhaps another, more organized movement (toward social responsibility) supported by disadvantaged subpopulations, public employees, and nonconservatives—given the heavy emphasis on lobbies in California state politics (Ziegler, 1974). The legislation that enabled the initiative (SB154 1978) reflected this portrayal (1) by having the state assume full responsibility for certain services to which localities had previously contributed (e.g., public assistance) (2) by making a state surplus—called "bailout"—available to local governments on [at the time of study] a one-time basis, in order to prevent immediate reduction in essential services, and (3) by prohibiting (a) reductions in local expenditures for police and fire protection and (b) disproportionate reductions in ones for public health and delivery of health services to the poor. This last provision determined one of our dependent variables.

III.   OVERALL EFFECTS OF MOVEMENT AND LEGAL OPPOSITION: LOCAL UNITS OF ANALYSIS AND LOCAL VARIABLES

A.   Units of Analysis

Forty-six counties had supported general hospital services during the fiscal year before Proposition 13 was passed (1977–78). Since expenditures for these services constitute our main dependent variable, the units of analysis are those 43 counties that had submitted complete budgets to the state government by our cutoff of five months after the initiative's enabling legislation, two months beyond the state's deadline.

B.   Dependent Variables

Two county budget items were selected that—unlike any of their alternatives—allowed comparability of measurement, since they reflected services provided solely at the county level, but yielded variability in outcome from county to county. The first, already suggested above, is the extent to which budgeted expenditures were greater or less than expected, on the basis of expenditures during the pre-Proposition 13 year, for delivery by hospitals of short-term inpatient services to the poor. Though disproportionate reductions were prohibited by legal mandate that accompanied implementation of Proposition 13 and were subject to state prosecution—one form of organized opposition to the movement's thrust—, that mandate failed to be carried out in every county. Its local observance, it will be shown, depended on locally organized opposition to the Proposition 13 movement. The second budget item, constructed the same way, is nonmandated budget excess or shortfall, after Proposition 13, in expenditure for the county government's own main decision body: Its board of supervisors, which actually enacted the budget. This expenditure was not subject to state law, no locally organized opposition to its reduction could be found, and such reduction was indeed "in the spirit of Proposition 13."

Organizationally Affected Local Budget Decision and Indicator Validity

Inpatient services to the poor were explicitly protected by legal machinery in the form of legislation and its enforcement:

> It is the intent of the legislature to maintain essential county health services.. . . A county shall not make a disproportionate reduction in county costs for health services in public health services, outpatient health services or inpatient health services which will be detrimental to the health needs of the public in the case of public health services or the health care needs of the indigent in the case of outpatient or inpatient health services. . . (SB154 1978:53–55)[2]

There was a clear risk of legal sanction—in the form of withholding state bailout funds—to those counties which were defined as violators of the above inpatient mandate. Conformity to or departure from mandate is measured by change in the county budget: i.e., excess in nonrecoverable inpatient money for indigents over the amount to be expected on the basis of the pre-Proposition 13 year's expenditures.[3]

That change in the inpatient budget is a valid indicator of conformity to law vs. risk of sanction is supported by nearly perfect association between post-Proposition 13 shortfall in these budgeted expenditures and whether or not the county was one of nine listed by the state government as facing legal action. Our measure of budgeted change reduced error in predicting this dichotomous event by nearly 100 percent (gamma = $-.99$).[4] Seven of the nine counties provided budgets that were more than one dollar per resident below expectation. Only one county that had a shortfall of more than one dollar (in this case only slightly more) failed to be cited. The remaining two counties facing legal action belonged to a set of seven that failed to meet expectation by less than one dollar. The law allowed disproportionate reductions in funds provided that service delivery did not suffer. Its application, however, has proven to vary directly with the amount of reduction.

Inpatient health care is also unique in providing variables of theoretical interest and others useful for statistical control: (1) A fairly well-defined clientele (the poor) whose number varied from county to county; (2) likely variability in voter support (not asked in voter surveys, but we know that retention of fire and police expenditures received almost unanimous support: Turk, 1979) and in the organization of this support into local opposition to Proposition 13; and (3) the prominence of the service-delivering organizations (hospitals). Finally, unlike police and fire protection, health services had initially been scheduled for large reductions immediately following passage of Proposition 13. One county, for example, had planned a 37 percent reduction in all health services in contrast to 5–20 percent in its other service areas (Zucker, 1982). That nonlocal legislation contradicted this tendency not only provides a demanding test for the effect of law but also makes that effect easier to separate from other forces against reduction that a different effect might simply have reinforced.

Organizationally Unaffected Local Budget Decision and Indicator Validity

Change in the county board of supervisors budget relative to the previous year's expenditures was measured identically to its inpatient counterpart.[5] All of the supervisory boards had five members and similar responsibilities, and there was no mandate to prevent their restricting the amounts available for their own expenses. Nor could any organized interests be identified that supported these expenditures. Shortfall in this item after the anti-tax initiative provides a conservative comparison with inpatient shortfall, since it would run counter to the immediate self-interest of the county's decision body and was under its own control.

Shortfall in the board of supervisor's budget validly mirrors compliance with the Proposition 13 movement through general reductions in nonmandated activities at the county level. Strikingly, the budget shortfall explained 53 percent of the variation (gamma) among counties of a Guttman scale (developed by Turk, 1979) that summarized newspaper reports of how drastically each county reduced *all kinds of* programs, personnel, and service levels. The level of explanation is high, considering that these reports appeared from two to four unstable months before each budget was submitted (also see note 8, to follow). Moreover, no such association occurred in the case of the inpatient budget (direction insignificantly the reverse).

C. Independent Variables

The nonlocal independent variables of statewide vote and consequent legal machinery—i.e., of expression of the movement and of organized opposition—have already been described. Variables pertaining to local expression through voting patterns and local organization will be identified, on the pages that follow, in conjunction with the analyses in which they were employed.

D. Overall Local Effects of Movement and Nonlocally Organized Opposition

If the one budget category responded to the movement and its implementation while the other responded to organized opposition, at least partly taking the form of legal machinery, the amount budgeted for the county board of supervisors after the tax initiative should be less, relative to the amount spent during the year before, than in the case of money allocated to hospital care. The mean amount for inpatient services was reported to be $5.67 per county resident in the 1977–78 fiscal year and actually rose to a budgeted $6.59 in 1978–79. In contrast, the amount budgeted for boards of supervisors fell from a reported $3.69 per resident to a budgeted \$3.08.[6] This change differs significantly from its inpatient counterpart. The more expensive item, be it noted, went up at a time of fiscal crisis, while the less expensive one went down.[7] It would appear that organized opposition took precedence over the movement or consequent fiscal constraint in affecting budget retention, but that the latter variables overshadowed immediate self-interest in making organizationally unopposed political decisions. These general effects of the anti-tax initiative, the altered fiscal environment, and the legal mandate upon the dependent variables were anticipated by our specifying proposition. They also lend validity to the overall research design.

IV. EFFECTS OF LOCAL SUPPORT AND LOCALLY ORGANIZED OPPOSITION

According to visible signs, the Proposition 13 movement approximated single-issue collective behavior. Not as with many other issues (Janowitz, 1978: 529–545), the public was clearly informed and clearly divided. And there is no evidence that the initiative was steered by highly organized interests (Turk, 1979). Certain individuals and small groups, mainly some landlords and realtors leaning toward the political right, did seek to influence via the mass media, forming loose coalitions for that purpose. However, the corporate sector was described as either having opposed the anti-tax initiative or having remained neutral. Even real estate and construction firms seem to have been divided on the issue, and the state's main newspaper (*Los Angeles Times*) explicitly opposed Proposition 13. Pitted against these ambiguities, it will be recalled, were mass rates (mean of 61 percent) of owner-occupancy (taxpayer status) within the counties and the consequent possibility that local mass behavior affected both dependent variables directly—i.e., without organizational intervention. This has *not* proven to be the case.

Our earlier investigation (Turk, 1979) did indeed convey the picture of appreciable association between the percent who voted yes to Proposition 13 in each of California's 58 counties and the aforementioned scaling of subsequent cuts by that county in programs, personnel, or service levels. (Notably missing from these reported reductions, however, were the legally mandated health and public protection services.) Further, not only retention of the organizationally (legally) unaffected board of supervisors budget but even retention of the inpatient budget proved to vary inversely with the percentage of the entire county's electorate which favored Proposition 13—legal mandate against indiscriminate cutting notwithstanding ($r = -.31$ and $-.33$, respectively[8]). It would appear on the surface that the collective behavior model applied to both legally mandated and nonmandated decisions. However, disaggregating the vote belied this.

According to the collective behavior model of social movements, the undifferentiated rate at which the entire county voted yes to Proposition 13 should have affected both kinds of budget shortfalls. According to our specification of this model, locally organized and organizationally supported opposition are expected to dampen this effect. The actual findings, to be described, support our specifying proposition. Reduction in the local board of supervisors budget was subject to local majority accord with the Proposition 13 movement. However, reduction of the local inpatient budget not only responded to overall opposition by the state electorate or by the state's legal machinery but also to opposition by a locally organized, and organizationally linked, minority.

A. Effects of Local Movement Support and Locally Organized Opposition on the Two Budget Decisions

Recall that voters who opposed Proposition 13 tended not to find the movement personally beneficial. The organization of such opposition through political concentration and consequent political representation could be assessed. In California, each county supervisor is elected by district. There are five supervisors in each county, thus five election districts. We have scored each county according to the percent who opposed Proposition 13 in that one of its districts which had the *lowest* (fifth highest) yes-rate. The vote in this least favorable district accounted for a modest 60 percent of variability in outcome of the entire county's vote ($r = .78$). Thus, it is not as though each county's decision about the initiative reflected the action of a homogeneous electorate. A high no-rate in the district least favorable to Proposition 13 meant concentration of the initiative's opponents—including disproportionate numbers of potential inpatients—into a political (here a supervisory) district and the consequent political (i.e., organized) representation of the opponents' interests (here, by the supervisor from that district).

Contrary to the collective behavior model, it was found, first, that conformity to mandated retention of inpatient expenditures for the poor depended upon whether the opponents of Proposition 13—often those same poor—were politically concentrated and represented, quite apart from whether the proponents were also represented. For correlation of the no-rate in the least favorable district with our inpatient variable is $r = .46$. *Moreover, the rate in this district explains the effect of the entire county's yes-vote!* Supplanting the previously reported zero order coefficient of $-.33$ between the county's overall yes-vote for Proposition 13 and the retention of inpatient expenditures for the poor was an insignificant partial correlation coefficient of $+.08$.

This might be taken to mean that a minority of one—here the single county supervisor, reflecting his/her district's opposition to inpatient reductions—can prevail in the decision process, possibly only when the issue is conformity to law. Whether it is the threat of legal sanction or appeal to civic responsibility that would enable this is moot. Regardless, this general interpretation would suggest an extension to interest group theory that accounts for the influence of lobbyists, special petitioners, or legislative minorities. It might also explain the survival of legally prescribed structures, such as government in general, in spite of mass discontent.

The effects of voting are quite different for change in the nonmandated and otherwise organizationally unaffected comparison item, decision about retaining funds for the board of supervisors. The effect of the yes-rate in the district most opposed to Proposition 13 is insignificant ($r = -.14$), but recall the significant effect ($r = -.31$) of the county's overall yes–vote. Once this last is taken into account, even that district's small effect disappears (partial $r = +.16$); and the overall effect remains (partial $r = -.32$). This provides additional support for our assertion that mass sentiment can influence government action, in a single issue movement, where such action is not subject to organized opposition.

In sum, local change that took the form of governmental decision was affected by a relatively unorganized social movement only to the extent that it failed to be countered by organized opposition taking the twin forms of external legal machinery and the representation of politically concentrated local voters. This was anticipated by one part of our proposition: the movement's effect on change varied inversely with the degree of organized opposition to change.

B. Organizational Links and Intensified Effects of Local Voter Opposition

The remainder of the proposition has to do with the availability of links—concrete as well as symbolic—between the movement's organized opponents and relevant formal organizations. We expected such links to operate multiplicatively with opposition to Proposition 13 in preventing shortfall of the inpatient budget. That this occurred will be shown, but not exactly in the manner expected.

Links with Affected Organizations

Relevant organizations can intensify the effects of opposition to social movements on governmental decisions. These decisions have even been viewed as outcomes of coalitions among the affected nongovernmental and/or governmental organizations (Sayre and Kaufman, 1960; Turk, 1973:passim.; Wamsley and Zald, 1976:26–33). Such an effect can be shown in the case of inpatient decisions, but—having found neither interested voting blocs nor variably affected organizations—not in case of the board of supervisors alternative. Thus, the remaining analysis emphasized the effects of organized opposition on the retention of impatient funds, while continuing to consider the effect of the majority on restricting board of supervisors funds simply for purposes of control.

Some counties provided the poor with inpatient services through hospitals that they themselves owned and operated, others did this through contracts with private and other noncounty hospitals, while still others did both. The indicator used to describe type of service is the proportion of all hospital beds in the county that were in county hospitals.[9] Signifying low hospital prestige (Elling and Halebsky, 1961), distrust in government institutions (Miller, 1974 and Institute for Social Research, 1979), and greater expense to the county ($r = .76$ here with inpatient expenditures during the pre-Proposition 13 fiscal year), this variable might have had a negative effect on retention of the inpatient budget, according to conventional wisdom. The reverse proved to be the case. The direct effect of the county hospital indicator is retention of the inpatient budget, once the effect of urbanization on the number of noncounty hospitals is taken into account (partial $r = .33$). Even more striking, however, is the part played by county hospitals in intensifying the observed effect of political concentration on such retention.

County hospitals are likely to have constituted interest groups, not only as organizations seeking to survive but also because local government employees and their families tended to oppose Proposition 13 (Turk, 1979) and thus could strengthen opposition to budget cuts through alliance with other, politically concentrated opponents. However, they also were linked to other interests, first, by providing visible symbols of health care for the poor as well as symbols of expense for the economy-seekers. Indeed, shortly before the legal mandate, Los Angeles County cancelled plans to close some of its hospitals in the light of demonstrations and other organized protest against closure. Second, county hospitals, directly connected to government as they were, could transmit positions taken by the movement's local opponents directly to the county's decision-makers.

The top portion of Figure 1 graphs the effect we have already reported, for all 43 counties, of opposition to Proposition 13 in the district least favorable (low percentages on the horizontal axis) upon budgeted meeting or exceeding expected inpatient expenditures after the initiative (nonnegative dollars per capita on the vertical axis). Note that large shortfalls tended to occur only where more than half the district favored the initiative.

Contrast this result, however, with the much more pronounced association plotted in the middle of Figure 1. The effect of politically concentrated opposition to Proposition 13 upon undiminished health expenditures is sharply increased among counties with prominent county hospitals.[10] Clearly, county hospitals increased the impact of organized minority sentiment upon the budget, further supporting thereby the first proposition.

Links Provided by Large and Diversified Government

Further, since Lineberry and Fowler's seminal work (1967: also see Turk, 1973, 1977b; and Liebert, 1976), political responsiveness has been defined as

Figure 1. Increase in Inpatient Budget over the Previous Fiscal Year, by Voter Support of Proposition 13 in the Least Favorable District

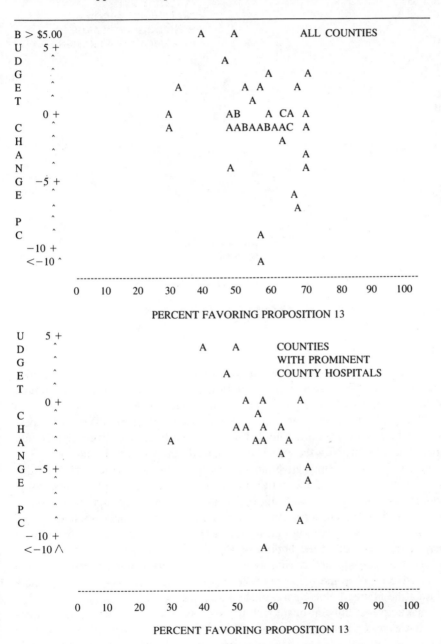

Figure 1. (Continued)

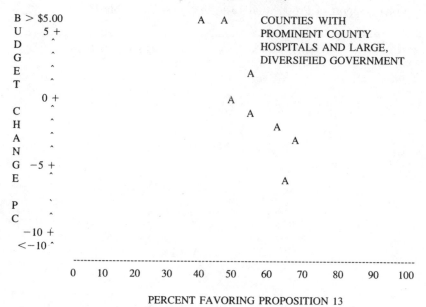

PERCENT FAVORING PROPOSITION 13

N = 43 COUNTIES, WITH A = 1 COUNTY, B = 2 COUNTIES, C = 3 COUNTIES,
ETC.

the closeness of association between governmental decisions and citizen preferences or needs. This association has, in turn, been found to vary with the number
of large agencies of local government that provide multiple channels through
which organized interests can gain access to decision-makers (Turk, 1973:pas-
sim; Liebert, 1976:passim). This led us to expect large and diversified county
government to intensify the effect of organized opposition to Proposition 13.[11]

Whether or not county government was large and diversified made no difference in the effect of the entire county's vote on the board of supervisors
budget. This is in accord with our expectation that majority support of a social
movement is sufficient for social change where organized opposition has failed
to occur. Clearly supporting our argument concerning organized opposition, it
may farther be seen at the bottom of Figure 1 that counties having large and
diversified governments as well as prominent county hospitals were the most
responsive of all to the organized vote that opposed Proposition 13. Note how
closely the plotted points approximate a straight line.

Unanticipated, but consonant with the substance of our argument, is the finding that even the politically organized minority was effective *only insofar* as it
was organizationally linked. The main effect of the no-vote in the least favorable

district disappears once the parts played by county hospitals and type of county government are taken into account. This becomes apparent once the top graph of Figure 1 is reexamined, this time ignoring all of the plotted points that also appear in the center graph. Except for the lowest outlier, the remaining points approximate a no-correlation circle. Taken in its entirety, Figure 1 provides compelling evidence of the effect of organized and organizationally linked opposition even to a powerful social movement.[12]

Formal verification was provided by multiplying the organized minority vote by the county hospital dichotomy (0, 1) and later again by the government dichotomy (also 0, 1) and examining the effects of the joint terms. (The simple product of government times vote proved to have no effect.) The first of these products, together with the direct effect of county hospitals, explained the overall association at the top of Figure 1. The partial correlation coefficient between the district's unspecified no-vote and retention of the inpatient budget is .07, compared to .40 for the product. The second product, involving both the county hospital and the government variable, had an independent effect (partial $r = .26$) but did not eliminate the effect of the first (partial $r = .51$).[13] (Visual verification is provided by Figure 1: Note that ignoring those plotted points which also appear on the bottom graph does not remove all association in the center graph.)

C. Effects of Support, Opposition, and Links Independently of Other Influences

Clearly, influences other than mass sentiment or interest group mobilization can affect political decisions. It has been found, however, that both the effect of organizationally linked minority concentration on mandated decision and that of the majority on nonmandated decision remained when reexamined simultaneously (through multiple regression analysis) with all of these additional factors.

First, the county's urbanization (percent residing in cities) is a global variable which is not only associated with poverty (negatively in California), but also signifies high levels of social and political organization by municipalities, distribution of responsibilities between city and county, types and magnitudes of county revenues and expenditures, and (inversely) the size and complexity of county government. All of these characteristics can affect budgets. Second, overall fiscal strain—whose potential effect on budgeting is obvious—was measured by the magnitude, reduction, and uncertainty (latter, percent of all revenues from what at the time was announced as the one-time "bailout" grant of each county's overall revenues after Proposition 13). Third, potential client demand for inpatient service within each county—this too could have affected budget retention—was measured by the county's poverty rate.[14] Fourth, the size and diversification of county government could either have served to mediate external expectation (Turk, 1973) or could have signified competition for funds among large and equally strong agencies under conditions of fiscal strain.

The results just reported, which supported and extended our two propositions, were not affected by these potentially confounding influences. The direct effect of prominent county hospitals, together with their intensification of organized voter opposition—further intensified by large and diversified government—all remained high, yielding a multiple-partial correlation coefficient of .60[15] with nonreduction of the mandated inpatient budget (.57 for the two multiplicative voter effects alone). Moreover, the results shown on Figure 1 proved to remain undisturbed[16] in 10 separate analyses under the respective conditions of high and low urbanization, high and low overall revenue, high and low revenue reduction, high and low revenue uncertainty, and high and low poverty. And, by way of controlled comparison, the effect on nonreduction in the supervisors budget of the entire county's yes-vote remains undisturbed upon repetition of the same multiple regression analysis (partial r = −.33; please reread Note 8). This last result also proved to be robust when specified, in 11 additional analyses, by size/diversification of government as well as by the 10 levels (just named) based on urbanization, three measures of fiscal strain, and poverty.

V. SUMMARY AND CONCLUSIONS

Guiding our general thought about local-nonlocal relations has been the combination of local decision-making models that emphasize local choice (e.g., Clark, 1968; Laumann, et al., 1973, 1974; Galaskiewicz, 1979a; Clark and Ferguson, 1980) with ones that emphasize nonlocal determination of local actions by the broader institutional environment (e.g., Warren, et al., 1974; Meyer and Rowan, 1977; Zucker, 1977; Zeitlin, 1980). This combination (Turk, 1973, 1977b—called "input-throughput-output" by Galaskiewicz, 1979b) posits the decision *possibilities* to be nonlocally determined, while selection among them is the result of local structure and local process. In the present case, a statewide movement and its effects on state law established the possibilities, but which possibilities materialized as local decisions depended upon local organization and local collective behavior.

In accord with an overall proposition, changes were instituted as a result of a numerically strong, essentially middle-class social movement (a statewide voter initiative supported almost two-to-one, mainly by property owners) to the extent that organized opposition was lacking. At the nonlocal (State of California) level, this meant legislation requiring reduction in local property taxes; at the local level (within each California county) revenues from these taxes were materially affected. The movement's goal of reduced spending by local government was also realized, but not for every expenditure. Neither lobbies nor the resulting nonlocal legislation opposed reductions in local government expenditures for decision-making and administration (for the county board of supervisors); these expenditures were indeed reduced at the local level. However, organized opposition to other effects of the movement was established in the form of legal machinery to protect other local expenditures (for hospital services to the poor), which were significant to the movement's rejection by the voting minority and, it would seem, were supported by various organized representatives of that minority. The protected expenditures actually rose at the local level.

The overall pattern of change in the absence of organized opposition to the movement was replicated within the localities (California counties). Local governments did not uniformly institute the organizationally unaffected expenditure reductions demanded by the movement's voting majority, nor did they uniformly refrain from those reductions that were organizationally opposed in the form of nonlocal legal machinery. Again in accord with the overall proposition, the level at which the entire county's electorate supported the movement affected unopposed reduction (in the board of supervisors budget). But this simple majority had no effect on expenditure reductions that were organizationally opposed in the form of legal machinery (budget items for hospital services to the poor), once locally organized voter opposition to the movement and the organizational links of such opposition were taken into account. The extent to which these expenditure levels were retained varied directly with the salience of affected organizational entities (of county owned hospitals), as well as with the product of such salience times the extent of organization of the movement's voting opponents through their concentration into a political district represented by a local decision maker (one of the five county supervisors). Retention of these expenditures was further influenced by this same product multiplied by the number of large government agencies available as channels to the decision-makers (size and diversification of county government).

The immediate empirical results present participatory and assimilation-oriented democracy with a policy paradox—not unrelated to the issue of at-large versus by-district election of local leaders. Political *influence* is geographically organized—even in systems that do not depend on the immediate expression of citizen preferences—into wards, districts, cities, counties, and regions. (Even if they are externally appointed, local officials must, at least to some degree, take local sentiment into account.) But political *interests* are not always geographically organized, depending as they do on occupation, ethnicity, gender, age, party membership, etc. Still our data suggest that the degree to which interests are met—especially ones in the minority—depends in part upon their concentration within political jurisdictions. The paradox is this: as long as geography defines concentrations of political influence, *segregation,* not integration, is a main device that assures representation of minority interests in the local decision process.

The general findings both support the collective behavior model of social movements—at least under conditions, such as elections, that permit their translation into social change—and specify its limits of applicability. Organized opposition to a social movement, even by a numerical minority of nonelites, can counter some of its effects.[17] The collective behavior model of social movements seemed to apply to governmental decisions not subject to organized opposition. There majority sentiment appears to have prevailed without any elaborate organizational superstructure, and minority sentiments had no effect. But at least where conformity to nonlocal law is at issue, opponents can, it would seem, influence governmental decision, provided that they are politically represented through geographic concentration and can rally about and form links with an appropriate organization, especially where they also have multiple links available to local government. Further, if opposition to Proposition 13 were to be conceived as an anticonservative countermovement based on goals of economic equity, these findings would speak directly to the organizational model of social movements, here of a minority movement.

Underlying the investigation is the premise that decisions subject to organized opposition are shaped by different processes than are decisions free of this constraint. Certain details of such process await further research. However, our actual findings do suggest (but cannot establish) how otherwise powerless sectors of the society may exercise power. They might do so by invoking rules, whose violation is subject to collective outrage or organizational sanction. Law provides small or powerless groups with the capacity to affect decisions by organized appeals to legitimacy or by the threat of sanction. In contrast, such groups have no effective base when the decisions are unattended by legal mandate; there only the elite or large masses have the power needed to influence. Here political representatives of the nonelite were able to influence governmental decision possibly by invoking external (state) mandate. This argument is likely to generalize to other cases.

That locally organized groups which exert limited influence without external mandate can become effective pressure groups when they have legal or moral sanctions as their weapons may also be seen elsewhere. Subject to national law, local issues with respect to Swedish land development (no social movements seem to have been involved) have, for example, been seen to follow such a course (Floderus, 1981 and conversation with the author). Locally elected officials are, on the one hand, responsive to the local voting majority, but their credibility rests upon impartial application of external mandate—a dualism which, it would appear, can be affected even by minority invocation of that mandate. An analogous situation also occurs in the microcosm when lower administrators—say, nurses in an American hospital—can gain ascendency over basically more powerful persons—say, physicians who are there only part of the time—by knowing and therefore being more able to invoke bureaucratic rules (i.e., hierarchical mandates).

Generalizing to an abstract level that transcends our data, the present findings might, further, help to explain why the general but unorganized unpopularity of certain social institutions, such as government (Miller, 1974 and Institute for Social Research, 1979), does not automatically bring about their demise. They continue to exist to the extent that they are subject both to legal mandate and to support by organized and organizationally linked minorities. This observation has implications for theories of social stability as well as ones of social change: it provides one reason why old institutional forms tend to reappear, even after sweeping revolutions.

ACKNOWLEDGMENTS

Partly based on papers presented in Portland, Oregon at the 1981 Annual Meetings of the Pacific Sociological Association and in Essen, Germany at the European Conference on Urban Research, October 2–5, 1981. The data were assembled under grant HS 03405 from the National Center for Health Services Research to the University of California, Los Angeles, which included a contract with the University of Southern California.

NOTES

1.   All election data were obtained from Eu (1978).

2.   The same law also prohibited *any* reduction in funds for police and fire protection. However—unlike these other services, which are provided by cities, counties, and/or special districts—in California local hospital services to the poor are supported exclusively by the county. (Outpatient services and public health had not been uniformly defined by different counties or implemented.)

3.   Following Bohrnstedt (1969), change is in per capita dollars budgeted, residualized upon per capita dollars expended the previous year (source: a mimeographed listing published in 1979 by the California Department of Health Services). Sharp acceleration in inpatient service monies had been reported for the years before Proposition 13 (Zucker, 1982). This, coupled with the legal mandate discussed, should mean that low values of the dependent variable can as readily reflect deceleration as decrease in the inpatient budget. That this variable is sensitive to the legal mandate just described will be shown immediately. That its unmandated board of supervisors counterpart (source: data tapes provided by the Office of the Comptroller, California State Department of Finance) reflected state-wide voter sentiment favoring government reductions will also be shown.

4.   Very highly significant. Unless explicitly stated otherwise all findings reported are statistically significant at at least the .05 level adopted for this research. Association designated either as small or as not significant failed even to approach the .10 level.

5.   Budget items having to do with airports, museums, parks and recreation departments, libraries, departments of public ways and facilities, were not comparable from county to county (since cities and special districts also provided service in some counties, and the degree of support varied widely before Proposition 13 was implemented). Hence, these could not provide the nonmandated contrast to mandated retention of the inpatient budget.

6.   See Note 2 for data sources.

7.   Critics of research exploring the effects of Proposition 13 have been quick to point out that the actual loss of revenues was small. Indeed, use of the state surplus ("bailout") and alternate sources of county revenue, such as user fees, meant reduction in the overall mean dollar revenues reported by the 43 counties of only 2.8 percent below the previous year, state payments for public assistance included (source: data tapes published by the Comptroller's Office of California's Department of Finance). However, the rate of inflation probably meant a mean reduction of 10 to 15 percent in real

dollars—thereby requiring some cutbacks. Moreover, to be explained in more detail later, reliance on the one-time bailout increased uncertainty about each county's overall resources.

8.   Variables based on the aforementioned Comptroller's tapes showed consistently lower association with other variables (not reported here) than did ones based on data from more specialized state offices (e.g., Department of Health Services), which used some of the Comptroller's data but removed the effects of reporting conventions that produced some variability among counties. Thus, the −.31 correlation coefficient is to be taken as attenuated by unreliability. And the 53 percent validation of the board of supervisors indicator (reported above) is all the more persuasive.

9.   Source: a special publication in 1978 by the California Department of Health Services. Reliability is claimed on the basis of correlations of r = .99 with per capita number of county hospital beds and .73 with total number of county hospitals (14 of the 43 counties had none—i.e., awarded contracts to private or other noncounty hospitals for health services to the poor).

10.   Above the median in percent of hospital beds in county hospitals.

11.   In large-scale political economies, such as nations or the California counties studied here, the agencies and officials of government are the main actors in the decision process (Sayre and Kaufman, 1960:passim.; Banfield, 1961; Greer, 1962; Gilbert, 1968; Turk, 1977b:54–55, 123; Zeitlin, 1980:22–28). But the modern county—or, for that matter, any large and complex setting—with its varied array of large organizations defies coordination by governmental imperative.

Rather, government acts by mediating among diverse interests and providing links for issue-specific coalitions (Sayre and Kaufman, 1960:passim.; Dahl, 1961:passim.; Sayre and Polsby, 1965; Turk, 1973:9–28; Polsby, 1980:122–138). It has been argued, based on a composite of political and organizational theory (Turk, 1973:9–28), that government has the potential for providing a mulitplicity of such links to the extent that it is both diversified—broad in the scope of its activities— and large. That governmental diversification is associated with various kinds of binding action by localities has been reported by Lincoln (1976), Liebert (1976), and—also taking size of government into account—by Turk (1977a, 1977b:136–184).

We approximated the measure used for large cities by Turk (1973, 1977b) and Lincoln (1976), which is closely associated with Liebert's (1976) measure of governmental scope and has the same effects on the wide-ranging set of 30 urban variables from Turk's most recent book (1977b:261– 262). All of California's 58 county governments were first dichotomized about the median according to relative size, their total numbers of employees per resident. The 58 governments were then ranked separately according to each of the following numbers of employees per resident: general administration, public protection, public ways and facilities, health and sanitation, public assistance, culture and recreation (source: tapes published by the Comptroller's Office of California's State Department of Finance). The degree of similarity among these seven rankings (computed using the variance-related formula provided by Gibbs and Martin, 1962) signifies how diversified the government is. The diversification score for California's 58 counties was also dichotomized about its median. The county governments above both medians—there are 13 among the present 43—are classified as large in scale and diversified to constitute a dummy variable (0, 1). Encouraging the present analysis, the municipal version of this index has already been found to intensify the effects of externally defined local interests upon local decision (Turk, 1973, 1977b).

12.   Another unanticipaed outcome is the linearity of association shown on Figure 1. We did expect the finding that prominent county hospitals or large/diversified government increased the effect of organized opposition to the anti–tax initiative upon budget retention. We did not expect the additional finding that the presence of these organizations also increased the effect of *the absence of* organized opposition on budget *shortfall*. One might speculate that county hospitals not only constituted visible symbols for the supporters of inpatient expenditures but also visible targets for others. And large, diversified government might just be universally responsive to voter sentiment, responsive even to a majority that tended to oppose the nonlocal legal mandate where—as in the case of county hospitals—the expense in question was high but organized support of mandate was weak.

13.   Removal of the outliers from each graph had virtually no effect on these values.

14. Sources: percent urban, U.S. Bureau of the Census (1977); revenues, comptroller's tapes (Footnote 7) and archives of the Office of the Legislative Analyst, California State Senate's Committee on Finance; percent of families with incomes less than 125% of the national poverty rate (California's cost of living is high), U.S. Bureau of the Census (1977). Reduction in overall revenues was computed by the residual method referred to in Note 3.

15. Variables were routinely transformed throughout the investigation whenever skewness or heteroscedasticity biased regression results.

16. Except for one correlation coefficient based on n = 2.

17. Certain caveats are in order. First, present findings refer to the unusual instance (Janowitz, 1978:491–545) of a single issue-movement whose implications for proponents and opponents appeared to be both clear and zero-sum. As such, they have served to generate at least one ideal type of movement against which quite different movements can be compared. Second, we are less certain that the mass or collective behavior model of a social movement did apply to effects upon the nonmandated board of supervisors variable than we are that it *did not* apply to effects upon its mandated inpatient counterpart. There could have been organized opposition from the political right in certain counties to the funding of such boards—symbolizing "big government" as they did—which might have explained away the effect of the entire county's vote, had appropriate indicators been found. Any such hypothetical findings would have meant that *nowhere* had we found the mass or collective behavior model to apply, even under these ideal-typical conditions of an uncomplicated single issue with a one-sided outcome.

REFERENCES

Banfield, Edward C.
1961 Political Influence. New York: Free Press.

Bohrnstedt, George W.
1969 "Observations on the measurement of change." Pp. 113–133 in E. F. Borgatta (ed.), Sociological Methodology. San Francisco: Jossey-Bass.

California Department of Health
1978 Health Care Costs and Services in California Counties. Sacramento.

Clark, Terry N.
1968 "Community structure, decision-making, budget expenditures, and urban renewal in 51 American communities." American Sociological Review 33:576–593. Slightly revised for C. M. Bonjean, T. N. Clark, and R. L. Lineberry (eds.), Community Politics, A Behavorial Approach. New York: Free Press.

Clark, Terry N. and Lorna C. Ferguson
1980 Political Process and Urban Fiscal Strain. Draft manuscript, Chicago: University of Chicago.

Dahl, Robert A.
1961 Who Governs? Democracy and Power in an American City. New Haven: Yale University Press.

Elling, Ray H. and Sandor Halebsky
1961 "Organizational differentiation and support." Administrative Science Quarterly 6:185–209.

Eu, March Fong
1978 Statement of Vote and Supplement: Primary Election June 6, 1978. Sacramento: Office of the Secretary of State.

Floderus, Asel
1982 "Negotiating for development or change of urban land use." Pp. 361–371 In H. Wollman

and G. M. Helstern (eds.), Applications of Urban Research. Bonn: Institute for Regional Research and Planning, German Federal Republic.

Galaskiewicz, Joseph
    1979a Exchange Networks and Community Politics. Beverly Hills, Cal.: Sage.
    1979b "Directions for an organizational analysis of cities." Contemporary Sociology 8:234–36.

Garner, Roberta Ash
    1977   Social Movements in America. Chicago: Rand McNally.

Gibbs, Jack P. and Walter T. Martin
    1962   "Urbanization, technology, and the division of labor: interactional patterns." American Sociological Review 27:667–677.

Gilbert, Claire
    1968   "The study of community power: a summary and a test." Pp. 222–243 in S. Greer, D. L. McElrath, D. W. Minar, and P. W. Orleans (eds.), The New Urbanization. New York: St. Martin's.

Greer, Scott
    1961   Governing the Metropolis. New York: Wiley.

Institute for Social Research
    1979   "Deepening distrust of political leaders is jarring public's faith in institutions." ISR Newsletter 7:4–5.

Janowitz, Morris
    1978   The Last Half Century: Societal Change and Politics in America. Chicago: University of Chicago Press.

Jenkins, J. Craig and Charles Perrow
    1977   "Insurgency of the powerless: farm workers movements (1946–1972)." American Sociological Review 42:249–268.

Laumann, Edward and Franz Pappi
    1973   "New directions in the study of community elites." American Sociological Review 38:212–230.

Laumann, Edward, Lois Verbrugge, and Franz Pappi
    1974   "Approach to the suudy of a community elite's influence structure." American Sociological Review 39:162–174.

Liebert, Roland
    1976   Disintegration and Political Action: The Changing Functions of City Government in America. New York: Academic Press.

Lincoln, James R.
    1976   "Power and mobilization in the urban community: reconsideration of the ecological approach." American Sociological Review 41:1–15.

Lineberry, Robert L. and Edmund P. Fowler
    1967   "Reformism and public policies in American cities." American Political Science Review 61:701–716.

McCarthy, James D. and Mayer H. Zald
    1977   "Resource mobilization and social movements: A partial theory." American Journal of Sociology 82:1212–1241.

Meyer, John W. and Brian Rowan
    1977   "Institutionalized organizations: formal structure as myth and ceremony." American Journal of Sociology 83:340–363.

Miller, Arthur H.
    1974   "Public policy and political cynicism: 1964–1970." Pp. 453–477 in N. R. Luttbeg (ed.), Public Opinion and Public Policy. Homewood, IL: Dorsey.

Oberschall, Anthony
    1973   Social Conflict and Social Movements. Englewood Cliffs, NJ: Prentice-Hall.

Piven, Francis Fox and Richard A. Cloward
  1971   Regulating the Poor: the Function of Social Welfare. New York: Pantheon.
  1977   Poor People's Movements: Why They Succeed, How They Fail. New York: Pantheon.
Polsby, Nelson W.
  1980   Community Power and Political Theory. New Haven: Yale University Press.
Sayre, Wallace S. and Herbert Kaufman
  1960   Governing New York City: Politics in the Metropolis. New York: Russell-Sage.
Sayre, Wallace S. and Nelson W. Polsby
  1965   "American political science and the study of urbanization." Pp. 114–156 in P. M. Hauser
          and L. F. Schnore (eds.), The Study of Urbanization. New York: Wiley.
Turk, Herman
  1973   Interorganizational Activation in Urban Communities: Deduction from the Concept of
          System. Washington, D.C.: Arnold and Caroline Rose Monograph Series of the American
          Sociological Association.
  1977a "An interorganizational view of pluralism elitism, conflict, and policy outputs in large
          communities." Pp. 51–77 in Roland J. Liebert and Allen W. Imershein (eds.), Power,
          Paradigms, and Community Research. London and Beverly Hills: Sage.
  1977b Organizations in Modern Life: Cities and Other Large Networks. San Francisco: Jossey-
          Bass.
  1979   "Imageries of social control: on the publicized birth and early life of Proposition 13."
          Urban Life 8 (Speical Issue on Social Control):335–358.
U.S. Bureau of the Census
  1977   County and City Data Book. Washington, D. C.: U.S. Government Printing Office.
Wamsley, Gary L. and Mayer N. Zald
  1976   The Political Economy of Public Organizations: A Critique and Approach to the Study of
          Public Administration. Bloomington, Indiana: Indiana University Press.
Warren, Roland L., Stephen M. Rose and Ann F. Bergunder
  1974   The Structure of Urban Reform. Lexington, MA: D. C. Heath.
Ziegler, Harmon
  1974   "The effects of lobbying: a comparative assessment." Pp. 225–251 in N. R. Luttbeg
          (ed.), Public Opinion and Public Policy. Homewood, IL: Dorsey.
Zeitlin, Maurice (ed.)
  1980   Classes, Class Conflict, and the State. Cambridge, MA: Winthrop.
Zucker, Lynne G.
  1977   "The role of institutionalization in cultural persistence." American Sociological Review
          42:726–743.
  1982   "The early impact of Proposition 13 on public funding and services for education and
          health in California." Berkeley, Calif.: California Policy Seminar Monograph Series.

CENTER-PERIPHERY CONFLICT:
ELITE AND POPULAR INVOLVEMENT IN THE BOSTON ANTI-BUSING MOVEMENT

Bert Useem

WELCOME TO BOSTON

The City is Occupied
The Boycott Exists
A Tyrant Reigns
Law is by Decree—Sign at anti-busing rally
Isn't it strange that in this sad state of Massachusetts,
Rapists have "rights."
Grape pickers have "rights."
Wild-life has "rights."
Lettuce pickers have "rights."
Draft-dodgers have "rights."
Minority groups have "rights."
Welfare demonstrators have "rights."
Abortion supporters have "rights."
Anti-American groups have "rights."
Pro-pornography groups have "rights."
Libbers and lovers and lepers have "rights."
Suburbanities have "rights."
But the parents of Boston public school children have none?
      Dick Sinnot, *South Boston Tribune,* March 28, 1974

Research in Social Movements, Conflict and Change, Vol. 6, pages 271–291.
Copyright © 1984 by JAI Press Inc.
All rights of reproduction in any form reserved.
ISBN: 0-89232-311-6

This paper formulates a center-periphery model of social movements. The model postulates that many social movements can be seen as efforts by people in a "periphery" to resist the penetration by the "center."[1] "Penetration" here refers to the central government establishing its authority in peripheral areas and attempting to implement basic policies.

Drawing on research from a variety of sources, it is possible to develop several generalizations concerning the reasons why both elites and ordinary people in the peripheries organize politically to resist the center's penetration.[2] First, the center's instrusion may upset the balance of power between locally subordinate and superordinate groups. Especially destabilizing are actions by the center which promote a subordinate but rising group. When this occurs, members of the superordinate group will often support resistance movements.

Second, the center's intrusion often places new demands on the periphery's resources, such as military conscription, taxes, and forced production. These new burdens are especially resented when they exacerbate preexisting conflicts. Third, center penetration often imposes an alien authority structure on the local population. The new authority structure is usually less accessible to the average person than its predecessor. Under such circumstances, ordinary people in the periphery will join efforts to repel the center's intrusion. Finally, center penetration, by definition, infringes upon the authority of local elites. Their traditional prerogatives, such as the right to allocate services and patronage, are imperiled by the center's intrusion.

The empirical focus of this paper is the Boston anti-busing movement. In the following, I first describe the historical events that lead up to the emergence of the anti-busing movement. I then use the center-periphery model to explain elite and popular participation in the movement.

I.   THE BOSTON ANTI-BUSING MOVEMENT

The term "anti-busing movement" is used to refer to the collective and widespread effort that had the stated goal of preventing busing for the purpose of school desegregation in Boston and which used non-institutionalized means to achieve its goal. The anti-busing movement emerged in the fall of 1974, and over the next four years it mobilized people to join school boycotts; to support neighborhood "information centers;" to form a city-wide organization, Restore Our Alienated Rights (ROAR); and to participate in dozens of mass demonstrations, some of them violent.

A.   Historical Background to the Emergence of the Anti-Busing Movement

The Boston school busing controversy can be traced back to a 1963 confrontation between black civil rights activists and the Boston School Committee

(BSC), the biennially elected group which governs Boston's public schools.[3] At a BSC hearing in the summer of 1963, black leaders demanded that the School Committee publicly acknowledge the existence of *de facto* segregation in the schools. The BSC's refusal to do so led to a black boycott of the schools which, in turn, was met by strong white support for backlash candidates at the polls. In the fall, 1963 BSC election, Louise Day Hicks, who two years earlier projected a moderate image, ran as a "hardline" anti-integrationist. She received over two-thirds of the vote and finished a strong first.

The posture assumed by Boston's white politicians persuaded black leaders that they would have to seek support from other sources. The civil rights leaders asked the state, and later, the federal government to support their efforts to desegregate the schools. This new approach began to pay off in 1964 when Governor Peabody established the Kiernan Commission, a blue-ribbon committee charged with investigating racial discrimination in Massachusetts. The Kiernan Commission found that Massachusetts maintained 55 racially imbalanced schools, of which 45 were in Boston. Because most state legislators, other than those in the Boston delegation, supported the recommendation of the Kiernan Commission, the Racial Imbalance Act was passed. The Act required the desegregation of any school in which more than fifty percent of the student body was not white, even if this required the busing of both black and white students.

The BSC strongly opposed the Racial Imbalance Act claiming that it: (1) entailed excessive state involvement in local politics; (2) was a punitive measure directed against Boston; (3) attacked Boston's system of neighborhood schools. For the next six years the BSC avoided compliance with the Imbalance law with impunity. By 1971, however, the State Board of Education had lost its patience. Because the BSC refused to submit even a limited racial balance plan, the Board withheld $21 million in state education funds. Following this, the Board ordered the BSC to submit a plan that would end all racial imbalance in the public schools by the fall of 1973. The BSC told the Board of Education that they would comply with their demands but, in fact, continued their course of evasion. The Board responded by withholding even more state aid, the total amounting to over $50 million.

In the same period, two other government agencies began applying pressure on the BSC to desegregate the schools. First, in the fall of 1973, the Federal Department of Health, Education, and Welfare (HEW) held hearings on whether Boston operated a racially segregated school system. The Federal Administrative Judge found that a dual school system did, in fact, exist. According to federal law, this finding required HEW to cut off the $10 million in school aid annually given to Boston.

Second, in February, 1972, the NAACP filed a suit in Federal District Court alleging violation of blacks' fourteenth amendment rights. Ironically, the BSC's nine-year history of dogged resistance to the Racial Imbalance Act provided Federal Judge, W. Arthur Garrity the clearest evidence that the BSC had intentionally segregated the schools. In June, 1974, Judge Garrity ordered the desegregation of the schools using a plan devised by the State Board of Education. The state's plan required the busing of substantial numbers of both black and white students. Anti-busing activists organized a popular movement several weeks after Garrity's decision.

B.   Boston Anti-Busing Movement and the Vendée

The relevance of the center-periphery framework to the anti-busing movement can be demonstrated by considering the similarity between the anti-busing movement and the Vendée, the 1793 French counterrevolution named after the rural area in which it originated. Many of the processes underlying the two movements appear similar to each other and to those identified by the center-periphery researchers. We outline these similarities below, then more rigorously test the usefulness of the center-periphery model for understanding the anti-busing movement. Our arguments as to the Vendée are based on the careful historical and sociological research by Tilly (1964) and Moore (1966).

Tilly and Moore have identified a number of reasons why local elites in the Vendée region became involved in the counterrevolution. Similar reasons also explain local elites' participation in the Boston anti-busing movement. These reasons are consistent with the center-periphery theory proposed above.

Following the 1789 French revolution, the central government launched a three-pronged attack on the Vendée's traditionally dominant authority figure, the curé. The new government forced a reorganization of the local government; seized and sold the church's holdings; and, the pivotal measure, required all curés to swear allegiance to the revolutionary government. Whenever a curé refused to make this pledge, as almost all those in the Vendée did, the central government replaced him with one from outside the area (Moore, 1966:98–99). Because of these assaults on their position, the curés provided the counterrevolution with its leadership.

A similar process appears to have occurred in Boston. We hypothesize that an intrusion by the "center," here the federal government, imposed sharp restrictions on Boston elected officials. Such restrictions, we suggest, motivated elected officials to become involved in the anti-busing movement. Evidence supporting these claims is presented below.

Ordinary people participated in the Vendée for at least some of the reasons that would be predicted by center-periphery theory. One reason was that the center's intrusion favored an upstart group. The chief beneficiary of the 1789 revolution in the Vendée was an ascending group, the small town bourgeoisie. The benefits of the revolution devolved on the bourgeoisie as a result of the sale of the church's property. The bourgeoisie quickly bought all the land, leaving none for the peasants (Moore, 1966).

In accord with the center-periphery model, we hypothesize that the Boston anti-busing activists viewed the federal court's decision as an unjust intervention on the side of the blacks. The court's finding that a dual school system existed and its busing remedy may have looked like federal support for one side in a highly charged and long standing political controversy. The extent to which Boston residents in fact held this view will be examined empirically.

The second reason for popular participation in the French counterrevolution and possibly the Boston anti-busing movement was that the center's penetration resulted in the imposition of an "alien" authority structure. Traditionally, the curé was an extremely important authority figure to the peasants. The curé assumed great importance because "he stood at the center of the relatively few networks of cooperation that existed in this society of isolated farmhouses and scattered hamlets" (Moore, 1966:98; See also, Tilly, 1964:101–110). As noted above, the revolutionary government deliberately undercut the authority of the curés. Peasants, therefore, feared that the center's intrusion would replace the curés with authorities who would not assume their traditional role (Moore, 1966:98–99).

In Boston, we hypothesize, federal intervention imposed an alien authority structure on white residents. The federal court became involved in the routine administration of the schools. Boston residents may have felt that the court's administration was insensitive to their needs. We will assess this argument below.

Third, the center placed new demands on the periphery's resources following the 1789 French revolution and, we hypothesize, the center placed new demands on the periphery's resources following the 1974 Boston desegregation decision. In addition, in France and possibly Boston, the new demands exacerbated preexisting conflicts. The revolutionary government in France demanded higher taxes than had the old regime and instituted military conscription (Tilly, 1964: 180–181, 308–314). The latter policy was especially resented because the conscription law discriminated against those opposed to the revolution. The law exempted public officials and National Guardsmen, who were population groups most loyal to the revolution. According to Tilly (1964:309), "nothing could have been more of a goad to the rest of the people."

In Boston, residents may have felt that the federal government's busing policy placed new burdens on them. Public officials consistently asserted that busing was largely responsible for a fiscal crisis and series of tax increases that occurred in 1974. Also, public officials tended to define the acts mandated by the desegregation decree, such as riding on school buses or attending integrated classes, as disproportionately and unfairly burdensome on white students. Whether white residents also held this point of view will be examined empirically.

Finally, contributing to the uprising in the Vendée and possibly the anti-busing movement was economic strain in the periphery. The producers of grain, and to a lesser extent those of wine, did not suffer following the revolution (Tilly, 1964:212–215). There was, however, a depression in textiles, which hurt the many weavers in the region. Tilly concludes (1964:223) that "the textile crisis helped raise the level of conflict and agitation."[4] In Boston, a decline of the economic strength of the city may have made the conflict over desegregation more actue.

Having shown the relevance of the center-periphery model to the Vendée and the Boston anti-busing movement, the next step in the analysis is to examine more closely the usefulness of the center-periphery model for understanding the anti-busing movement. Before doing so, however, I briefly describe the data.

II.   DATA AND DEPENDENT VARIABLES

Data for the analysis are drawn primarily from a survey of 468 white Boston residents between 25 and 53 years old who were U.S. citizens (the "Area Survey"). To simplify the analysis and to insure than an adequate number of anti-busing activists were in the sample, the "Area Survey" was restricted to sections of the city that were predominantly white, heavily affected by the federal court's busing order, and were locations of anti-busing activities.[5] The sample was drawn from the 1977 City of Boston "Annual Listing of Residents," which provides names, addresses, birthdates, and citizenship. Respondents were selected in "clusters" of three.

We use three dependent variables. "Attitudinal support for the anti-busing movement" ("support") measures the extent to which respondents identified with the anti-busing movement and endorsed its goals and tactics. The scale was derived from two questions. First, respondents were asked how strongly they supported or opposed the following items: school boycotts to protest forced busing; the establishment of private academies for students who refused to be bused; attending anti-busing protest marches; and participating in anti-busing groups. Second, respondents were asked how much "in common" they felt with anti-busing demonstrators and the anti-busing group ROAR.

"Participation in the anti-busing movement" ("participation") measures membership in the movement and participation in its activities, based on two sets of questions. First, respondents were asked if they participated in school boycotts, the establishment of private academies, protest marches, or organized anti-busing groups. Second, respondents were asked separately if they had been active in any of nine specific anti-busing organizations. Respondents were scored a point each time they mentioned having participated in an anti-busing activity or organization.

The third dependent variable, "opposition to government actions directed against the anti-busing movement" ("oppose government control"), measures support for government constraints on the activities of the anti-busing movement. This scale is based on the assumption that if people agree with goals and tactics of a movement, they will not approve its suppression. Respondents were asked if the State Board of Education should have strictly enforced the truancy laws against boycotting students; if anti-busing demonstrators who broke the law by interfering with the busing order should have received stiff fines or worse; and whether Boston Mayor White should have refused to issue permits to anti-busing groups that wanted to demonstrate right outside the schools. Cronbach's alpha for each of the three scales is above .80, which suggests the scales are reliable.[6]

III. CENTER PENETRATION AND LOCAL ELITES' PARTICIPATION IN THE ANTI-BUSING MOVEMENT

We first examine the involvement of local elites in the anti-busing movement, using the center-periphery framework. More specifically, we assess the center-periphery hypothesis that the center's restrictions on local elites motivate their participation in anti-center movements.

In desegregating the schools, the federal court restricted city officials in a number of ways. First, Garrity's 1974 decision undercut the ability of local politicians to provide their most highly touted "service," racial segregation in the schools. Since 1965, most Boston politicians had pledged to their white constitutents that desegregation would "never" come to Boston. For nearly a decade, they were able to carry out this promise. School Committee Chairman John McDonough put it this way in 1975:

> since the Racial Imbalance Law went into effect in 1965, . . . the School Committee told the people of the city that their position was opposed to busing. When it got down to the crunch, the majority of the School Committee lived up to their promise to the people. . . . And I think this is probably the finest thing that we have done (Testimony before the U.S. Commission on Civil Rights, 1975a:466).

Thus, the 1974 desegregation order undercut the local politicians' ability to fulfill their "promises to the people."

Second, court intervention substantially reduced the patronage resources available to School Committee members. Traditionally, school employees who demonstrated their "loyalty" to the School Committee members could expect the transfers they desired and promotions. A major element of the patronage system was fund-raising "testimonial-dinners" for School Committee members. Employees who failed to succumb to the heavy pressure to buy tickets were denied advancement. Patronage especially dominated promotion in the upper echelon of the school bureaucracy. Appointment to a post in the central administration required a candidate to have a personal advocate on the Committee. Committee members supported only those individuals who had contributed to their testimonial dinners or otherwise had showed their loyalty (Edmonds, 1978:902).[7]

Moreover, a Boston Finance Commission[8] investigation into School Committee corruption revealed that in one year, 1972, 74 percent of all votes taken in School Committee meetings concerned personnel matters. According to the Commission, the School Committee's preoccupation with individual personnel decisions, rather than educational issues, is a "mark of patronage" (Boston Finance Commission, 1975:20).

The practice of promoting individuals on the basis of their loyalty to Committee members ceased with court-ordered desegregation. In order to end discriminatory hiring and assignment practices, the federal court required the School Committee to adhere to a set of formal criteria for promoting personnel and to hire certain percentages of black teachers and administrators (Edmonds, 1977:901; *Phase II Reporter*, 1975a). Employees hired in this fashion would have no reason to demonstrate their loyalty to Committee members. Thus, court intervention undercut the ability of School Committee members to use their positions for personal advantage.

Third, the court restricted local officials by directly intervening in school affairs. To insure the success of the desegregation order, Judge Garrity became deeply involved in many of the schools system's administrative affairs. Issues brought before the court during the first two weeks of October, 1975, for example, included the following: whether the School Committee should be required to appoint an associate superintendent to oversee the vocational education program; how to reduce racial tension in South Boston High School; the use of "late buses" for students staying after school; and the location of a community superintendent's office (*Phase II Reporter*, 1975b). These issues are typical of the myriad of administrative issues debated and decided in federal court. In effect, Judge Garrity assumed the role of a school administrator.

Advocates of busing have tended to minimize the importance of federal intervention in the operations of the schools. According to this line of reasoning, local officials' persistent refusal to fulfill their responsibilities forced the federal court to intervene in the daily operations of the schools. Thus local officials had only themselves to blame for the court's inordinate involvement in day-to-day affairs (See, for example, U.S. Commission on Civil Rights, 1975b; Sorgi and Smith, 1977). From the point of view of Boston politicians, however, such an argument ignores the constraints under which the city's white leadership operated. For most Boston politicians, the alternative of active compliance with the court's orders was simply not politically or personally viable.

Center-periphery theory maintains that when local leaders freedom of action and power to dispense patronage and services are restricted by the center, these leaders are likely to participate in an opposition movement. A substantial proportion of the Boston political establishment did become involved in the anti-busing movement. Several elected officials, John Kerrigan, Albert "Dapper" O'Neill, Louise Day Hicks, and Elvira "Pixie" Palladino, assumed highly visible leadership roles. Other Boston politicians regularly spoke at anti-busing functions. They included City Councilors James Michael Connelly, Gerald O'Leary, Christopher Iannella, and Frederick Langone; State Representatives William Bulger, Michael Flahrety, and Raymond Flynn; and School Committee members Paul Tierney, Patrick McDonough, and Paul Ellison. In addition, non-elected city officials participated in the movement. For example, Hick's administrative assistant on the City Council, Rita Graul, chaired ROAR during its first two years. Virginia Sheehy, employed in the School Department's central administration, held posts on the executive boards of both ROAR and the South Boston Information Center.

City officials openly displayed their involvement in the anti-busing movement. During the first year of desegregation, ROAR held its weekly meetings in the City Council's main chamber, with the press and non-members of ROAR excluded from the sessions (Bullard, Grant, and Stoia, 1981:42). For over a year, a huge sign with the letters "R-O-A-R" hung in the City Councilors' windows at City Hall.

In sum, according to the center-periphery model, center intrusion into the periphery may impinge upon the autonomy of local elites. When this occurs, local elites are likely to participate in an opposition movement. These processes appear to have occurred in Boston.

IV. CENTER INTRUSION AND THE LOCAL BALANCE OF POWER

According to the model formulated above, ordinary men and women as well as leaders resent the center's intrusion into the periphery. A person belonging to a locally superordinated group will be especially opposed to the center's intrusion if it promotes the interests of a subordinate but rising group. Most white residents of Boston felt that the federal court had unfairly sided with an upstart group, blacks.

As noted above, the 1974 desegregation ruling followed a prolonged and emotional struggle between blacks and whites. A central issue in the controversy was the existence of racial segregation in the schools. Judge Garrity ruled that a dual system did exist. Thus, Judge Garrity appeared to white residents to be siding with blacks in a long standing conflict.

To assess the extent to which white residents felt that Judge Garrity had unfairly sided with blacks, I included two questions in the Area Survey. We asked each respondent if he or she agreed with Judge Garrity's ruling that over the years, the School Committee had kept white and black children segregated. Less than one-third of the sample (31 percent) said that the Committee had segregated the schools. We then asked the sub-sample of respondents who believed that the schools had been segregated if they agreed with Judge Garrity's findings that the School Committee had deliberately segregated black and white students. Only 79 respondents, 54 percent of the sub-sample and 17 percent of the total sample, said that the School Committee deliberately segregated the schools. Thus, the vast majority of residents sampled disagreed with Judge Garrity's finding that the School Committee had willfully run a dual school system.

Furthermore, most residents also felt that Judge Garrity not only sided with blacks, but also discriminated specifically against whites by ordering busing. The extent to which white residents felt that Judge Garrity violated their rights is demonstrated by the Area Survey data. We asked each respondent, "Do you believe that court-ordered busing in Boston has or has not violated the constitutional rights of Boston citizens?" Eighty-seven percent of the sample said that busing had violated Boston residents' constitutional rights.[9]

In addition, we asked the sub-sample of respondents who said that busing had violated their rights, what those rights were. The rights that busing allegedly violated included the "right" to choose one's children's schools; the "right" not to be assigned to schools on the basis of race; and the "right" to entrust social policy decisions exclusively to locally-elected officials. Thus, most residents felt that Judge Garrity had not only sided unfairly with blacks, he had also abused whites in the process.

V.   BURDENS IMPOSED ON THE PERIPHERY

According the the center-periphery model, the center often places new burdens on the population of the periphery. These burdens are especially resented when they coincide with long-standing economic problems and are distributed inequitably.

Like many other U.S. cities, Boston faced a fiscal crisis during the 1960s and 1970s (Mollenkopf, 1975). The city's tax base had reached a peak about 1930, declined sharply over the next two decades, and had not fully recovered by 1974. The assessed value of all real property in Boston was eighty-five percent of its assessed value in 1930. While the tax base was stagnant in this period, both the costs of and demands for services and capital investment rose sharply (Mollenkopf, 1975:259). Thus, Boston residents are likely to have been especially resentful toward policies they believed imposed financial burdens on them. We examine this resentment below.

In addition, between 1950 and 1970 more than 110,000 relatively affluent whites left the city for the suburbs outside of Boston and elsewhere (Dentler and Scott, 1981:16), so that by the early 1970s Boston's "civic elite was almost completely suburbanized" (Rossell, 1977:249). Two consquences may have followed. First, business leaders and other "civic" leaders did not play the moderating role that they have elsewhere (Kirby et al., 1973). Apparently, suburban elites feared that their location in the white suburbs undercut their credibility and that only those affected by the court order were entitled to assert their stand (Leubsdorf, 1981). William Couinard, Executive Vice President of the Greater Boston Chamber of Commerce, told the U.S. Civil Rights Commission:

> it's very, very difficult for members of the business community to argue effectively with the people who live in the city that their kids should be brought from one end of town to the other, when in fact most of them live in suburbia, and for whom this problem is something which they just simply read about (Testimony before theU.S. Commission on Civil Rights, 1975b:15).

Second, because of the pattern of migration, the metropolitan area's privileged groups tended to live in the suburbs that surround Boston (Tilly, 1965:6). Judge Garrity's desegregation order did not extend beyond the city limits. Thus Boston residents may have felt that they had to assume an unfair share of the burden of desegregation.

We hypothesize that Boston residents felt that federally mandated busing was costly to them in three ways.

A. Financial Burdens

White Boston residents may have felt that busing burdened them financially. Writing several years before court-ordered busing in Boston, Pettigrew (1971) argued that the "Achilles' heel" of opposition to school desegregation is money. His survey of Boston residents revealed that citizens would accept school desegregation if failing to do so would increase their taxes.[10] "Finance," Pettigrew concluded, "offers an effective lever for social change" (1971:228). What Pettigrew did not add, however, is that the reverse may be equally true. Where social change is perceived as financially burdensome, residents will be especially resistent to change. This perception, and the association of that perception with resistance to change, occurred during the desegregation controversy.

City officials maintained that busing was extremely costly to the city. In the Spring of 1974, for example, Mayor White publicly blamed the city's deficit and a proposed tax hike on the supposed costs of desegregation.[11] Most Boston residents as well believed the politicians' argument that busing placed a heavy financial burden on the city, as can be demonstrated using the Area Survey data. We asked each respondent whether he or she thought busing resulted in Boston's property taxes going up. Respondents answering affirmatively were then asked how they felt about the causal relationship. Table 1 displays the distributions of the response to the two questions. Four-fifths of the respondents felt that busing increased their taxes. Of this group, four-fifths of them reported that they were either "very dissatisfied" or "outraged" that taxes went up because of busing.

Table 1.   Percent Expressing View that Busing Increased Taxes; Percent
Angry Because of Tax Increase

"Do you think that court ordered busing did or did not result in Boston's property taxes
going up?"

Did result in property taxes going up	81.4%
	(381)
Did not result in property taxes going up	10.5%
	(49)
Don't know	8.2%
	(38)
Total	(468)

"When you think of the tax rate going up because of busing, do you feel not especially
dissatisfied, mildly dissatisfied, very dissatisfied, or outraged?"

Not especially dissatisfied	4.2%
	(16)
Mildly dissatisfied	14.4%
	(55)
Very dissatisfied	34.1%
	(130)
Outraged	46.7%
	(178)
Don't know	0.5%
	(2)
Total	(385)

We next combine the responses to the above questions to form a scale labelled
"Taxes Up." We then correlate the Taxes Up scale with support for and participation in the anti-busing movement. The correlations between Taxes Up and
support, participation and oppose governmental control are .412, .271 and 335,
respectively.[12] The positive sign associated with each coefficient indicates that
respondents who perceived and felt angry about a rise in taxes because of busing
were especially likely to support and participate in the anti-busing movement.
Thus, the data support the center-periphery hypothesis that residents in the periphery resent burdens placed on them by the center, and this resentment will
help motivate protest participation.

B.   Threat of Violence

Another burden allegedly placed on whites because of busing was the threat of
black violence. White fear of black violence, and its connection with busing, is
graphically displayed in a "Declaration of Clarification" written by Louise Day
Hicks and two other anti-busing leaders in 1974. The widely publicized state-

ment, issued after the first week of busing, purported to explain white's resistance to busing:

[I]t is against our childrens' interest to send them to school in crime-infested Roxbury. There are at least 100 black people walking around the black community who have killed white people during the past two years. They have gone unapprehended (*Boston Globe*, 9/16/74).

The Boston firemens' union issued a similar statement reading, in part, "the good people of South Boston or any other part of Boston are justifiably worried about sending their children into these crime ridden garbage pits" (Quoted in *Boston Globe*, 10/4/74).

In addition, the fear that school integration endangers white children appears to have been an important political force, even prior to federally mandated busing. For example, in 1971 several hundred white parents protested assignment of their children to the Lee school, a newly opened elementary school in a predominantly black neighborhood. White parents argued that the neighborhood was "unsafe." Responding to the protest pressure, the School Committee voted to allow parents to transfer their children to schools in white neighborhoods (*Boston Globe* 5/25/75; Bullard, Grant, and Stoia, 1981:35).

To assess the prevalence of whites' fear of black violence, we rely on a 1975 survey commissioned by the *Boston Herald American* (8/14/75). The *Herald American* survey consisted of telephone interviews of 1,000 Boston adult residents. The interview schedule included the question, "During the [court ordered] [forced busing] last year, how many of Boston's school children were in real physical danger as a result of busing? Would you say it was a large majority, a small majority, a large minority, or a small minority?" Half of those questioned felt that a majority of students were endangered by busing.

We cannot, however, use the *Herald American* data to examine why respondents felt busing put students in danger. There may have been reasons other than the alleged lawlessness of blacks. For example, some respondents may have felt busing endangered students because desegregation gave rise to a violent anti-busing movement. Thus, the hypothesis that white residents felt that busing exposed their children to black violence cannot be tested without more direct evidence.

C. Adverse Effect on Education

Anti-busing activists claimed that desegregation adversely affected white children's education. Louise Day Hicks, for example, tirelessly argued that blacks are "culturally deprived" and thus undisciplined and less intelligent than their white classmates. Because of these traits, according to Hicks and other busing opponents, the presence of black students necessarily lowers schools' academic standards. Similarly, a School Committee member stated the belief this way:

"White children do not want to be transported into schools with a large portion of backward pupils from unprospering Negro families who will slow down their education . . ." (Quoted in Bullard, Grant, and Stoia, 1981:34).

The Area Survey did not include a question on the educational effects of busing. Two other surveys, however, did include such questions. The *Boston Herald American* survey included the question, "During the past year, would you say the quality of education in Boston Public Schools you know about was better, about the same, or worse than in previous years?" The majority of white respondents (52 percent) believed that education had worsened since the time when, one year earlier, busing had begun. Only a tiny fraction of whites interviewed (6 percent) believed that education had improved.

The distribution of responses tends to support the hypothesis that Boston residents felt that busing hurt their childrens' education. This inference, however, should be viewed with particular caution, for two reasons. First, respondents may have felt that busing itself did not cause this deterioration. They may have blamed instead, for example, the nationwide decline in the educational quality of big-city school systems in the 1970s, or the extended white student boycott. Second, even if the respondents felt that busing per se was the cause of the educational decline, the *Herald* data do not allow us to explore what aspects of busing were thought to hurt education.

Stinchcombe and Taylor's (1980) analysis of another survey of white Boston residents bears more directly on our argument. Stinchcombe and Taylor examined the relationship between the belief that students' test scores decline when they attend desegregated schools and three measures of support for anti-busing protest. The three measures are approval of a white student boycott of the schools; support for the Boston School Committee's defiance of Judge Garrity's court order; and opposition to busing for desegregation. Stinchcombe and Taylor found that respondents who believed that test scores declined under desegregation were somewhat more likely than others not holding this view to resist the desegregation order.[13] Thus, the findings are consistent with the argument that Boston residents felt that busing hurt white childrens' education, and this perception caused support of and participation in the anti-busing movement.

D.   Inequitable Distribution of Burdens

Finally, I hypothesize that white Boston residents perceived that the costs of busing were distributed inequitably to their disadvantage. As noted above, Judge Garrity's desegregation order excluded suburban areas around Boston, where privileged groups tend to live. In addition, wealthy individuals could avoid some of the costs of busing by placement of their children in private schools. Thus, Boston residents may have felt that they were forced to assume a disproportionate share of the costs of busing.

While survey data is not available to test this argument, interviews of Boston residents conducted by psychologist Thomas Cottle and psychiatrist Robert Robert Coles supports the contention. A white working class mother of several children, for example, told Cottle,

> A person says, my principle is that busing is good for all the kids involved. So you ask him, what about your kid? Will you voluntarily bus *your* kid a long way from your home just to desegregate some school somewhere? Of course the families in the suburbs are for busing, some of them. Why shouldn't they be? Their kids aren't involved and never are going to be involved (emphasis in orig., 1976:54).

Similarly, a working class father of five explained to Coles,

> My brother says that people near Harvard, the professors and doctors and lawyers and fat-cat businessmen, their kids, a lot of them,, . . . go to fancy private schools and they have nice summer homes and all the rest. Well, who has the money to afford those private schools? Not us (Quoted in Ford, 1975:459).

In sum, one factor that helped motivate popular participation in the Boston anti-busing movement was the belief that the court's desegregation order placed new and unfair burdens on the city's white residents. These burdens included increased taxes, a threat of violence against children, and worsening education.

E.   Imposition of Alien Authority

Center-periphery theory postulates that center penetration often imposes an alien, inaccessible, and deeply resented authority on the local population. Boston residents may have felt that the federal court's busing policy imposed such an alien authority structure in Boston. As we noted above, Judge Garrity became deeply involved in the routine management of the school system. Anti-busing activists frequently charged that Judge Garrity did not care about or understand the concerns of white, central city residents. In addition, under desegregation, personnel from outside the system assumed important administrative posts. Traditionally, administrative positions were filled exclusively by promotions within the system (Schrag, 1967:54–56). For example, Judge Garrity ordered control over South Boston High School placed in the hands of a court appointed receiver, and the replacement of the school's headmaster, football coach, and all full-time, non-academic administrators (*Phase II Reporter,* 1976). South Boston residents especially resented the dismissal of the headmaster, William Reid. Reid had worked in South Boston High School for over three decades, had lived in the neighborhood, and had been very popular among white students. The night Judge Garrity issued his decision the headquarters of the local NAACP was firebombed, and the day became widely known in South Boston as Black Friday (Bullard, Grant, and Stoia, 1981:52–55). The new headmaster, Jerome Winegar, was chosen by Judge Garrity and the receiver. When Winegar arrived in

Table 2.   Percent Expressing View that Busing Imposed an Alien
Authority Structure

"Because of Busing, the schools are controlled by a social and economic elite unsympathetic
to the majority of Boston residents."

	Strongly Agree	57.1%
		(254)
	Mildly Agree	21.8%
		(97)
	Mildly Disagree	12.7%
		(56)
	Strongly Disagree	8.4%
		(37)
	Don't know; Refused	—
		(22)

South Boston, he was greeted with jeers and carefully painted signs on the street
in front of the school, "Go Home Jerome" and "Winegar, We Don't Want
You" (Bullard, Grant and Stoia, 1981:54).

The Area Survey included a question tapping residents' attitudes toward the
authority system imposed by the courts. The question asked respondents if they
agreed with the statement, "Because of busing, the schools are controlled by a
social and economic elite which is unsympathetic to the majority of Boston's
residents." Table 2 shows the distribution of response to this question. Over
three-quarters of those responding expressed agreement with the statement. We
then correlated the responses to the statement with the three dependent variables.
The correlations between the item and support, participation, oppose governmental control were .424, .297, and .320 respectively.[14] The positive sign associated with the coefficients indicate that individuals who perceived that the courts
imposed an alien authority were more likely than others to support and participate in the anti-busing movement.

VI.   CONCLUSION

The center-periphery model postulates that the relationship between the center
and the periphery is of fundamental importance for an understanding of certain
protest movements. Protest occurs, according to this model, when residents in a
periphery feel the center's authority is intrusive, unresponsive, and governed by
interests opposed to those of the local group. Social movements emerge as
instruments to repel the center's intrusion and to obtain justice.

Using the center-periphery framework, we have found that the anti-busing
activists appear to have protested, in part, for the same reasons that the French

peasants protested 180 years earlier. Both movements were reacting to the center's intrusion into the community. More specifically, residents in both Boston and the Vendée resisted the center's intrusion since they felt that the center imposed new burdens and an alien authority on the local population, and promoted an upstart group. In both Boston and the Vendée, local elites were additionally motivated to protest by the center's constraints on their freedom of action.

Finally, this paper has not discussed the circumstances that lead to center penetration. I hypothesize that center penetrations occur when the actors in a center perceive a system-wide strain or crisis. The center attempts to extend its authority to or impose its standards on a peripheral area as a means of managing a crisis. Outside of a crisis situation, the center will avoid the risk of generating an opposition movement either by not infringing on the periphery or withdrawing upon initial resistance.

It could be argued, for example, that the center intervened in the operation of Boston's schools in response to the racial conflicts that erupted in most U.S. urban areas in the 1960s and early 1970s. It will be recalled that the 1974 federal court decision was the last of several attempts by state and federal agencies to desegregate the Boston schools. The various center elites may have believed that one solution to the racial crisis was to provide youth with an opportunity for interracial contact. We have seen that many white residents of Boston disagreed strongly with that solution.

ACKNOWLEDGMENTS

I thank Peter Kimball, Charles Tilly, and Mayer Zald for their helpful comments on this paper. This research was supported by grants from the National Science Foundation (No. Soc-6800621) and the Society for the Psychological Study of Social Issues.

NOTES

1. The concepts of "center" and "periphery" have been used by Shils (1975), Eisenstadt (1966), Kothari (1971), Rokkan (1970), Esman (1975), and Wallerstein (1974). Unfortunately the concepts are used quite differently. For example, Moore's (1966) analysis of the transformation of agrarian societies to industrial ones can be usefully considered as part of the center-periphery tradition. Moore defines a society's center in terms of the alliances that are necessary for the establishment of a central regime. The periphery, according to Moore's scheme, consists of those actors left out of the "nation-building alliance."

In contrast, Shils (1975) defines the center of a society as its "ultimate" or "sacred" symbols, values, and beliefs and the institutions in which they are embodied. The periphery is normally composed of recipients of the symbols and commands emitted from the center. Finally, Geertz's (1975:151) definition emphasizes that a society may have more than one center: "centers . . . are essentially concentrated loci of serious acts; they consist in the point or points in society where its leading ideas come together with its leading institutions to create an arena in which the events that most vitally affect its members take place.'' Of the available definitions of center and periphery, Geetz's is the most useful for our purposes. There are problems, however, with his definition. For example, Geertz does not provide a basis for distinguishing "serious acts" from less serious acts, or "leading ideas" from other ideas. We will not, however, attempt to resolve these conceptual problems here.

2. The analysis explicated in the next four paragraphs draws heavily on Oberschall (1973:44–45) and to a lesser extend on Eisenstadt (1966), Kornhauser (1966), and Rokkan (1970).

3. This section is based on the accounts of this period by Levy (1973), Bolner and Shanley (1974), Pettigrew (1971), Mottl (1976), Green and Hunter (1974), Ross, (1973), Rossell (1977), and Crain (1969).

4. The overall importance of the depression in textiles is difficult to assess. Tilly (1964:223) cautions that one should not reason " 'The weavers were hungry, *ergo* the Vendée revolted,' " because the formula does not "tell us how vague and various discontents were focused into extraordinarily drastic political acts." Moore (1966:95) goes further, arguing that the economic crisis in textiles explains little of the counterrevolutionary activity. He contends that the lack of contact between peasants and weavers, and the small number of weavers compared to peasants, minimized the importance of the crisis in textiles.

5. The three neighborhoods meeting these criteria are South Boston, Hyde Park and West Roxbury.

Eleven trained professional interviewers and the author conducted the interviews between December, 1977 and April, 1978. Although the interviewing period extended over several months, no important events relating to the busing controversy occurred during this period. Thus, it is unlikely that the delay between the first and last interviews introduced bias into the data. Interviewers were instructed to interview only those respondents who were selected in the sample and to make at least three attempts to interview each potential respondent. Sixty-five percent of the people selected were interviewed.

6. See Useem (1979:ch2) for a full discussion of the reliability and validity of the dependent variables.

7. The patronage system resulted in a top-heavy bureaucracy. One administrator was employed for each 3 or 4 teachers. Compared to other cities with the same number of students (e.g., Denver), Boston had four times the number of administrators (*Phase II Reporter*, 1977).

8. The Boston Finance Commission is a public agency created to oversee expenditures by the city of Boston.

9. The position that busing violates the constitutional rights of Boston citizens was taken by many public figures, including Senator Samuel Ervin. Referring specifically to the Boston desegregation decision, Ervin stated that "[t]he right of students to go to their neighborhood schools has been denied. In South Boston they are busing members of the white race into Roxbury and are busing members of the black race into South Boston. . . The equal protection clause is as clear as the noonday sun, but the judges don't seem to realize this" (*South Boston Tribune*, 12/5/74). Although the well-known legal scholar, Ronald Dworkin (1977:267), has persuasively argued that these constitutional "rights" do not exist, our concern is limited to Boston residents' beliefs about their rights.

10. At the time of Pettigrew's survey, both the federal and state governments were threatening to withhold school aid because of the city's failure to desegregate the schools.

11. Although the validity of the competing claims concerning the cost of busing is not at issue here, it is worth noting that a Boston University Law School analysis demonstrates that busing did not, in fact, place a substantial burden on the city's resources. A massive influx of federal and state aid paid for most of the cost of both busing itself and other desegregation costs (*Phase II Reporter*, 1977).

12. The association between the Taxes Up variable and the three dependent variables remained significant after controlling for five "structural" variables. When education, age, experience of

unemployment, homeownership, and having one or more child between the ages of 4 and 20 are used as control variables, the partial correlations between Taxes Up and support, participation, and oppose governmental control are .320, .176, and .317, respectively.

13. Consistent with the argument presented here, Stinchcombe and Taylor concluded that "peoples' attitudes about what will happen to test scores predict very strongly how much opposition they will show to the court order" (1980:177). The three regression coefficients, however, are only between .09 and .11.

14. These coefficients remained significant after controlling for education, age, experience of unemployment, homeownership, and having one or more child between the ages of 4 and 20. The three partial correlation coefficients are .198, .236, and .183.

REFERENCES

Bolner, James and Robert Shanley
  1974 Busing: The Political and Judicial Process. New York: Praeger.
Boston Finance Commission
  1975 Final report of an investigation into the administration, operations, and finances of the school committee of the City of Boston. Boston: Boston Finance Commission.
Boston Globe
  1974 "Statement by Mrs. Hicks, Bulger and Flaherty." September 16:4.
  1974 "Antibusing parents march in South Boston as students boycott." October 4:2.
  1975 "The first year." May 25:Section A.
Boston Herald American
  1975 "Boston's Anti-Busing Attitudes Hardened; Emotions Aroused." August 14:1.
Bullard, Pamela, Joyce Grant, and Judith Stoia
  1981 "The Northeast: Boston, Massachusetts: ethnic resistance of a comprehensive plan." Pp. 31–63 in Charles V. Willie and Susan L. Greenblatt (eds.), Community Politics and Educational Change. New York: Longman.
Cottle, Thomas J.
  1976 Busing. Boston: Beacon.
Crain, Robert L.
  1969 The Politics of School Desegregation: Comparative Case Studies of Community Structure and Policy-Making. Garden City: Aldine.
Dentler, Robert A. and Marvin B. Scott
  1981 Schools on Trial: An Inside Account of the Boston Desegregation Case. Cambridge, MA: Abt.
Dworkin, Ronald
  1977 Taking Rights Seriously. Cambridge: Harvard University Press.
Edmonds, Ronald R
  1977 "Simple justice in the cradle of liberty: desegregating the Boston Public Schools." Vanderbilt Law Review 31:887–904.
Eisenstadt, Samuel Noah
  1966 Modernization: Protest and Change. Englewood Cliffs: Prentice Hall.
Esman, Milton J.
  1975 "Communal conflict in Southeast Asia." Pp. 391–419 in Nathan Glazer and Daniel P. Moynihan (eds.), Ethnicity: Theory and Experience. Cambridge: Harvard University Press.
Ford, Maurice Deg
  1975 "Busing in Boston." Commonweal 10:456–460.

Friedman, Daniel J.
    1973   White Militancy in Boston: A Reconsideration of Marx and Weber. Lexington: D. C.
            Heath.
Glazer, Nathan
    1975   Affirmative Discrimination: Ethnic Inequality and Public Policy. New York: Basic Books.
Geertz, Clifford
    1975   "Centers, kings, and charisma: reflections on the symbolics of power." Pp. 150–171 in
            Joseph Ben-David and Terry N. Clark (eds.), Culture and Its Creators: Essays in Honor of
            Edward Shils. Chicago: University of Chicago Press.
Gottman, Jean
    1980   "Confronting centre and periphery." Pp. 11–26 in Jean Gottman (ed.), Centre and Periph-
            ery: Spatial Variations in Politics. Beverly Hills, CA: Sage.
Green, Jim and Allen Hunter
    1974   "Racism and busing in Boston." Radical America 9:1–23.
Hillson, Jon
    1977   The Battle of Boston: Busing and the Struggle for School Desegregation. New York:
            Pathfinder Press.
Jackman, Mary R.
    1977   "Prejudice, tolerance, and attitudes toward ethnic groups." Social Science Research
            6:145–169.
Kirby, David J., T. Robert Harris, Robert L. Crain, and Christine Rossell
    1973   Political Strategies in Northern School Desegregation. Lexington, MA: Lexington Books.
Kornhauser, William
    1964   "Rebellion and political development." Pp. 142–156 in Harry Eckstein (ed.), Internal
            War. New York: Free Press.
Kothari, Rajni
    1971   "Introduction: variations and uniformities in nation building." International Social Sci-
            ence Journal 23:339–354.
Leubsdorf, John
    1981   "Preface." Pp. XVII–XXXV in J. Michael Ross and William M. Berg, "I Respectively
            Disagree with the Judge's Order": The Boston School Desegregation Controversy. Wash-
            ington, D.C.: University Press of America.
Levy, Frank
    1973   Northern Schools and Civil Rights: The Racial Imbalance Act of Massachusetts. Chicago:
            Markham.
Marx, Gary T. and James L. Wood
    1975   "Strands of theory and research in collective behavior." Pp. 363–428 in Alex Inkeles
            (ed.), Annual Review of Sociology. Palo Alto: Annual Reviews.
Mollenkopf, John H.
    1975   "The post-war politics of urban development." Politics and Society 5:247–295.
Moore, Barrington, Jr.
    1966   Social Origins of Dictatorship and Democracy: Lord and Peasant in the Making of the
            Modern World. Boston: Beacon.
Morgan v. Hennigan
    1974   379 F. Supp. 410 (D. Mass.) aff'd sub nom. Morgan v. Kerrigan, 509 F.2d 580 (1st Cir.
            1974), cert. denied, 421 U.S. 963 (1975).
Mottl, Tahi
    1976   Social conflict and social movements: an exploratory study of the black community of
            Boston attempting to change the Boston Public Schools. Ph.D. dissertation, Department of
            Sociology, Brandeis University.
Oberschall, Anthony
    1973   Social Conflict and Social Movements. Englewood Cliffs: Prentice-Hall.

Pettigrew, Thomas F.
  1971   Racially Separate or Together: New York: McGraw-Hill.
Phase II Reporter
  1975a "History of Boston desegregation." Boston University School of Law, Boston, MA.
          1,1:2–5.
  1975b "Court Notes." Boston University School of Law, Boston MA 1,1:10–15.
  1976   "South Boston High Receivership: An analysis." Boston University School of Law,
          Boston, MA 1,3:2–13.
Rokkan, Stein
  1970   Citizens, Elections, Parties. New York: McKay.
  1980   "Territories, centres, and peripheries: toward a geoethnic-geoeconomic model of differ-
          entiation within Western Europe." Pp. 163–204 in Jean Gottman (ed.), Centre and Periph-
          ery: Spatial Variation in Politics. Beverly Hills, CA: Sage.
Rose, Richard
  1971   Governing Without Consensus: An Irish Perspective. Boston: Beacon.
Ross, John Michael
  1973   Resistance to racial change in the Urban North, 1962–1968. Ph.D. dissertation, Depart-
          ment of Sociology, Harvard University.
Rossell, Christine
  1977   "The mayor's role in school desegregation implementation." Urban Education 12:274–
          270.
Schrag, Peter
  1967   Village School Downtown: Politics and Education; a Boston Report. Boston: Beacon.
Shils, Edward A.
  1975   Center and Periphery: Essays in Macro-Sociology. Chicago: University of Chicago Press.
Sorgi, Donna and MaryEllen Smith
  1977   "Desegregation in Boston: the role of Boston's political leaders." University of Detroit
          Journal of Urban Law 54:465–472.
South Boston Tribune
  1974   "Editorial." March 28:2.
  1974   "Editorial" December 5:3.
Stinchcombe, Arthur L. and D. Garth Taylor
  1980   "On democracy and school integration." Pp. 157–186 in Walter G. Stephan and Joe R.
          Feagin (eds.), School Desegregation. New York: Plenum.
Tilly, Charles
  1964   The Vendée. Cambridge: Harvard University Press.
  1965   "Metropolitan Boston's social structure." Pp. 1–31 in Richard S. Bolan (ed.), Social
          Structure and Human Problems in the Boston Metropolitan Area. Cambridge, MA: Joint
          Center for Urban Studies of MIT and Harvard University.
Useem, Bert
  1979   The Boston anti-busing movement and social movement theory. PhD dissertation, Wal-
          tham, MA: Brandeis University.
U.S. Commission on Civil Rights
  1975a Hearings before the United States Commission on Civil Rights. Hearings Held in Boston,
          Massachusetts, June 16–20, 1975, Washington, D.C.: U.S. Government Printing Office.
  1975b Desegregating the Boston Public Schools: A Crisis in Civic Responsibility. Washington,
          D.C. U.S. Government Printing Office.
Vanneman, Reeve D. and Thomas F. Pettigrew
  1972   "Race and relative deprivation in the United States." Race 13:461–486.
Wallerstein, Immanuel
  1974   The Modern World System: Capitalist Agriculture and the Origins of the European World
          Economy in the Sixteenth Century. New York: Academic Press.

MOBILIZING THE TAX REVOLT:

THE EMERGENT ALLIANCE BETWEEN HOMEOWNERS AND LOCAL ELITES

Clarence Y. H. Lo

"We don't consider ourselves of the rich class. We don't consider ourselves of the lower class. . . We're middle class, but poor."

(Rutenberg and Rutenberg, 1982)

"The social work I was doing then and what I'm doing now politically all boils down to the same thing. It's all for the people. I feel I owe a debt to society. I have never worked or earned a living or anything of the sort. Life has been very good to me."

(McTyre, 1982)

". . . . [D]on't take a mink coat away from a woman. Don't give it to her if you're going to take it away, because she'll never be the same again and she might kill you in the process."

(Mason, 1982)

"The hat pin went through their wallet and into their behind, and I hope it stays sore."

(Paul Gann, *Los Angeles Times,* Oct. 25, 1976: II, 1)

"These things ought not need to be done outside the Chamber [of Commerce] . . . ."

(The *News,* Nov. 10, 1966:1)

"Of course business is politically stupid. I think they have two great inventories in business. One is political stupidity and the other is abject cowardness. I told that to the Fortune 500 . . . . I did!"

(Howard Jarvis, 1981)

Research in Social Movements, Conflict and Change, Vol. 6, pages 293–328.
Copyright © 1984 by JAI Press Inc.
All rights of reproduction in any form reserved.
ISBN: 0-89232-311-6

"[H]omeowners wanted it to be a bedroom community and the Chamber wanted it to be a business community. They aren't necessarily compatible."

(Bronston, 1982)

I. THE RISE OF A RIGHT WING TAX REVOLT

In June 1978, almost two-thirds of California voters approved Proposition 13, which drastically reduced property taxes. A number of movements arose throughout the United States to lower taxes and limit government spending (Kuttner, 1980; Rabushka, 1980). As policy makers grappled with the problems of administering health programs and financing schools, social scientists examined how limits on taxes and spending affected social policy and government decision-making.

By focusing on the consequences of tax reduction, researchers have tended to ignore the causes of tax protests. By voting for Proposition 13, the people had spoken. But who were the people and what had they really said? A few social scientists have gathered valuable information from analyzing public opinion polls and voting returns (Courant, et al., 1980; Ladd, et al., 1979; Sears and Citrin, 1982). Besides these sources of information, the history of political organizations can illuminate the origins of the tax revolt (Lo, 1982b). In California, hundreds of homeowners', taxpayers', and neighborhood associations held mass protest meetings about taxes, threatened to recall local officials, and burned their tax bills. Obtaining no relief from state or local governments, angry citizens gathered signatures to place tax reduction measures on the state ballot. In 1976, one thousand people in a school auditorium in California shouted "Strike!" But they were not militant teachers. Nor were they student protestors, but rather their parents and other taxpayers who refused to pay high property taxes (*Valley News,* July 30, 1976). As one leader put it, "I've never seen so many nice, decent people so bitter" (*Los Angeles Times,* October 25, 1976).

In this analysis, I focus on those activities to reduce taxes which can be characterized as a social movement. I study how California citizens became discontented with their institutionalized representatives (elected officials) and formed social movement associations to mobilize support to achieve change in society. (For definitions of social movements, see Smelser, 1963:1–22; Tilly, 1978:9; Turner and Killian, 1972:246). This chapter seeks to explain two important questions about the tax revolt. First, why did the tax protest movement in California take a right wing rather than a left wing course? Second, how did tax protests gain in strength and develop into the movement which succeeded in placing Proposition 13 on the ballot in California?

The first question is why the tax protest movement in California became a right wing movement, i.e., a social movement whose stated goals are to maintain order, property, status, traditional social differences, and/or economic inequality. Right wing movements may be contrasted with left wing ones, which seek to promote equality (Lo, 1982a:108). Significant left wing tax protest movements have arisen in some areas of the United States. For example, Massachusetts Fair Share, an organization based in blue collar neighborhoods, campaigned against high utility and auto insurance rates, and against tax concessions granted to businesses. Massachusetts Fair Share succeeded in obtaining voter approval for Question 1 during the November 1978 election. This measure levied a higher tax rate on business and commercial property, compared to residential property. The Ohio Public Interest Campaign proposed reductions in homeowners' property taxes, with revenues replaced by progressive taxes and the ending of exemptions for business (Kuttner, 1980:307–24). In California, a few groups such as the Citizens' Action League attempted to work for tax reforms which would benefit both homeowners and renters. Others, such as Richard Carmen, favored excluding businesses from tax reduction measures (*Alhambra Post-Advocate,* June 17, 1972, p. 1).

However, the tax revolt in California eventually produced Proposition 13, which reduced taxes for both homeowners and business. In fact, Proposition 13 left homeowners more vulnerable to rising property values. Under Proposition 13, property is assessed at full market value whenever it is sold. Residential property is sold more often than business property. In addition, landlords were not required to pass their property tax savings to their tenants through lower rents. The campaign for Proposition 13 raised many right wing themes, defended home and property, and attacked the welfare state.

A.   Constituencies of Right Wing Social Movements

What was the base of support for this right wing tax protest movement in California? During the campaign for Proposition 13, partisans advanced two opposing images of the movement. Movement leader Howard Jarvis claimed the support of hundreds of thousands of homeowners, who were fighting to save their property from government confiscation. However, one of Jarvis' critics acidly remarked, ''All you really need to know about the property tax initiative on the June ballot is that Howard Jarvis . . . is also the paid director of an association of apartment house owners in Los Angeles'' (Salzman, 1978:68).

Thus, contemporary partisans view the tax revolt either as a mass based revolt against political elites or as the machinations of local business interests. These two images correspond to the debates about other right wing movements in the U.S. (Lo, 1982a). One longstanding interpretation is that conservative movements in the U.S. are populist revolts against national elites. For example, Bell (1964) and others portrayed McCarthyism as an expression of mass status insecurity, directed against State Department elites. Senator Joseph McCarthy called those elites pampered aristocrats who sold out their country. Crawford's (1980) analysis of the new right of the 1980s continues the argument that the right is revolting against big business and the governmental establishment. Kevin Phillips (1982) argues that a populistic, conservative Republican majority feels betrayed by Ronald Reagan and will become a significant political force. Writing about local conflicts, Crain (1969) argued that the anti-fluoridation movements of the 1950s were community-wide mobilizations against city officials and the medical establishment. Similarly, Lowery and Siegelman (1981:972) suggest that the tax revolt is a mass mobilization, concerned with broad issues of lifestyle, morality, and projective self-expression.

In contrast to the notion that the populistic masses fuel the right, others have argued that right wing movements frequently have ties to elites, established institutions, or organized interests (Turner and Killian, 1972:317). Rogin (1967) argues that McCarthyism in the Midwest stemmed from local elites—prosperous farmers and business interests in the towns. Heading the protests against school busing were local politicians and the existing leaders of Home and School Associations, Parent Teachers Associations, civic groups, local newspapers, and businesses (Mottl, 1980).

Some literature has portrayed conservative social movements as uneasy combinations of both movement mobilization and local elite support. According to Lipset and Raab (1978), the Ku Klux Klan in the 1920s consisted of lower status activists (whose small town values were threatened by immigrants), combined with upper status supporters (who were concerned about the political left). In the campaigns of radio priest Charles Coughlin and Governor George C. Wallace, the intolerant allied with upper status critics of government intervention.

Sears and Citrin's (1982) careful analysis of public opinion polls also reveals a mixture of elite support and popular protest. Supporters of tax reduction initiatives in California tended to be upper income earners who owned homes. Activists who contributed money or signed petitions were likely to have high incomes. But even when demographics are controlled for, Sears and Citrin (1982:15–16, 188–206) demonstrate that support for tax protest is also correlated with symbolic hostility against blacks and the government. Symbolic predispositions quickly became mobilized when politicians clumsily reacted to higher tax assessments before the June 1978 election. The resulting mass outcry against remote, established institutions and alien values led to the two-to-one vote in favor of Proposition 13. Sears and Citrin conclude that the tax protest is both a revolt of the haves and a reawakening of the spirit of Prohibition and Populism.

Thus, the literature suggests that conservative social movements draw support from local elites, while at the same time targeting a popular mobilization against remote elites (Lo, 1982a). In the case of tax protests, *community elites* supported a movement which targeted *metropolitan elites*. Metropolitan elites consist of the political leaders of the City or County of Los Angeles, as well as the metropolitan economic elite, heavily composed of top executives from the large corporations ranked by *Fortune* magazine.

Community elites include community political elites, i.e., government officials of political units with a population of less than one hundred thousand. Community economic elites are the owners and managers of smaller businesses, especially those with fewer than fifty employees. Mills and Ulmer (1970) and Zeigler (1961) have noted how small and medium sized businesses have influenced local political issues. In particular, real estate interests frequently instigate conservative campaigns (Bouma, 1970; Hughes 1979). Owners of rental units have close ties to local and regional banks (Mollenkopf and Pynoos, 1973). In California, over half a million individuals are owners of apartment buildings of three units or more. Three hundred and sixty-five thousand Californians held real estate licenses around the time of Proposition 13. The California Association of Realtors has an annual budget of over four million dollars.

Beginning in 1957, protests against property taxes gradually formed an alliance between mobilized homeowners and community economic elites, who together opposed metropolitan elites. This alliance resulted in the successful campaign which gathered over one and one-half million signatures to place Proposition 13 on the ballot in California. However, the very success of Proposition 13 in reducing revenues produced strains in the alliance between homeowners and community economic elites—the very alliance that had supported Proposition 13. In some groups, the mobilization of homeowners came to be directed against both community economic elites and metropolitan elites. It is the rise and fall of multistrata alliances which is the focus of this analysis.

B. Emergent Multistrata Alliances

Emergent multistrata alliances can help to explain the rise and fall of social movements and their stands on issues of economic redistribution. First, emergent multistrata alliances can result in the commitment of resources that can sustain social movement activity. Particularly in the early stages of the tax revolt, homeowners' and tax protest groups were small, restricted to one community. The groups had no stable membership; they were dependent on volunteer help and contributions solicited at meetings. Donations quickly tapered off as residents lost patience with the complex haggling over tax issues, which usually brought no immediate benefits. An emerging alliance between homeowners and community economic elites brought much needed endorsements and donations of money, supplies, staff, and office space.

The emergence of multistrata alliances also has a powerful impact on the political orientation of social movements. Tax protest groups faced difficult issues which Lowi (1964) terms redistributive. What groups would receive the most tax relief? To whom would the tax burden be shifted? Frequently, tax protest groups lacked a clear understanding of these issues. For example, reform minded newspapers publicized how the San Francisco assessor took campaign contributions and then lowered tax assessments for business. Amid the widespread belief that business was not paying its fair share of taxes, the California legislature passed a bill which assessed both business and residential property at the same percentage of market value. However, this bill actually drastically shifted taxes from business onto homeowners, because businesses had, in fact, been assessed at a higher percentage compared to residences (Kuttner, 1980:1–68; Paul 1975:91–116).

Since tax protest groups generally lacked a clear analysis of redistributive questions, the goals of the groups were determined by the mix between community elites and homeowners. In the 1950s and 1960s, most tax protest groups were of two types. One was composed of community elites; the other consisted of homeowners, with little mixing between the two. The homeowners' groups can be termed isolated neo-populists. Although these groups could sometimes mobilize thousands of protestors, they lacked financial resources. Some isolated neo-populist groups expressed hostility against business elites and called for reducing property taxes for homeowners while increasing taxes for business.

The other groups, which may be termed business lobbying groups, were composed largely of community and metropolitan business elites. These groups did not welcome the active participation of homeowners and usually had difficulty in attracting the support of voters. Business lobbying groups generally sought to replace taxes on profits, property, and inventories with taxes on consumers.

In the 1950s and 1960s in California, neo-populist groups were isolated from elite support and hence could not succeed. Business lobbying groups were unpopular and thus also could not succeed. Alone, neither the neo-populists nor the business lobbying groups successfully challenged the power of the state to continue to tax and spend. The dilemmas of the business lobbyists and the neo-populists are similar to the dilemmas facing the pro-nuclear movement—in particular, the industry wing and the community wing studied by Useem and Zald (1982). What is needed is further analysis of the conditions and mechanisms that lead a movement to develop particular solutions to the dilemmas. In the case of the tax protest movement, the solution that emerged was the multistrata alliance between the business lobbyists and the neo-populists. However, this alliance was only a temporary and partial solution of the dilemma. Studying the instabilities in the alliance can illuminate historical changes in social movements.

C.   Forming the Alliance

How did these multistrata alliances emerge? As I will illustrate, in certain communities homeowners increased their affiliation with community business elites. Some businesses, who had extensive contact with customers, were familiar with the mores of the neighborhood and could provide communications networks and leadership to incipient movements. Homeowners began viewing economic elites as legitimate representatives of the entire community. Although the U.S. public's trust of business has declined in recent years, homeowners in some areas viewed community economic elites as fellow property owners and taxpayers. These emerging views were expressed in the initiative which unified the tax protest in California. Proposition 13 called for reductions in taxes for both business and residential property.

Nevertheless, the emerging multistrata alliances which placed Proposition 13 on the ballot were highly volatile. The most crucial periods were early in the history of the movement, especially when the public participation in the movement either increased or decreased drastically. At these critical times, what were the mechanisms which made and unmade the alliance between homeowners and business elites?

Eager to build their movement, tax weary homeowners sought help from community elites, particularly community economic elites. In some cases, these elites endorsed the tax protests and donated resources. But at other times, community elites refused to lend even minimal verbal support. The response of community political and economic elites to tax protests had important effects on the strength of the emerging movement.

Tilly's (1978:106–15) discussion of the authorities' response to social movements can be extended to analyze the community elites' response, and thus the emerging alliance between those elites and the protesting homeowners. According to Tilly, elites will tend to facilitate social movements when the protesting group itself is acceptable, and when the group uses acceptable tactics. Tilly operationalizes group acceptability as group power. However, in the case of tax protests, I will demonstrate that community elites will find a group acceptable when its members are wealthy. Furthermore, Tilly argues that authorities find small-scale actions more acceptable than large-scale actions. While a small riot may be more acceptable than a large one, a different pattern holds true for peaceful protests. Turner (1969) argues that small protests which pose little threat are likely to be ineffective and may be defined as deviance. Thus, I will argue that large scale protests in wealthy communities are more likely than other protests to gain the support of community elites. These are the protests which are likely to survive and to successfully influence policy in the metropolis.

II.   A COMPARATIVE STUDY OF PROTESTS AGAINST TAXES

As Tocqueville (1945) noted in 1835, "An American attends to his private concerns as if he were alone in the world, and the next minute he gives himself up to the common welfare as if he had forgotten them." The Lynds' study of Middletown (1937) and Gans' (1967) study of Levittown noted how apathy alternated with political passions. Tax protests in southern California have flared up quickly and have died just as quickly. The rhythm of tax protests is closely tied to the periodic reassessments of real estate. A California law passed in 1966 required that all property be assessed at one quarter of market value. This "reform" actually increased the tax burden on homeowners, who had generally been assessed at a lower percentage compared to businesses. Adding to the homeowners' tax burden was the rapid growth of property values. As a neighborhood was reassessed every few years, escalating property values produced higher tax bills (Kuttner, 1980:1–67; Levy, 1979; Paul, 1975). At times, citizens flooded city hall with thousands of telephone calls; they organized meetings, filed appeals of tax bills, and demanded the recall of city officials. Nevertheless, the protestors faced the problem of gaining support from civic and business leaders and then affecting government policy about taxes.

In order to compare the rise of tax protest movements in different communities, I gathered primary materials about tax protests in Los Angeles County since the Second World War. I selected the three years containing the most protest activity by consulting the *Los Angeles Times Index,* secondary sources, and the newspaper clipping ("morgue") files of three suburban dailies in Los Angeles County—The *Valley News* (Van Nuys), the *Daily Breeze* (Torrance), and the *San Gabriel Valley Tribune.* The latter three publications are the newspapers with the largest circulation in the San Fernando Valley, the San Gabriel Valley, and the southwest coastal area, the major suburban regions in Los Angeles. For the three peak years of protest—1957, 1964, and 1976—I selected the one month period containing the most activity and scanned every issue of the three suburban newspapers, looking for articles reporting the location and size of tax protest meetings and other actions.[1]

I then devised measures of the size of the protests, and also of the housing and income characteristics of the protesting communities. In addition, the newspapers and extended interviews with protest leaders provided information about the goals of the protests in each community. Some of the protests were hostile outbursts which assigned blame to government agents (e.g., drives to recall the tax assessor and the county Board of Supervisors). Others were norm oriented social movements (e.g., attempts to place a clause in the state constitution to limit the property tax rate. See Smelser, 1963:79–131).

Then, using the newspapers and interviews, I compiled information about how community economic elites and community political elites responded to the protests. In some communities, elites facilitated the protests, leading to the development of multistrata alliances with the protestors. Finally, I gathered information about the outcome of the protests—how the protests had different effects on the policies of metropolitan political elites. In each of the cases, metropolitan political elites suggested plans for tax reform and made general statements sympathizing with the protestors. The major difference was that metropolitan political elites sometimes responded by opposing the movement, sometimes by granting advantages (such as a lower tax rate), and sometimes by formal cooptation (e.g., establishing new organizations to consult with aggrieved taxpayers. See Gamson 1975:28–37).

A. Protests in 1964: Isolated Neo-populism

Of all of the protests studied, those in 1964 were the smallest and took place in the least affluent communities. As a result, community elites did not facilitate the protests. The protestors adopted expressive goals and shouted antielite sentiments. The lack of multistrata alliances produced an isolated, neopopulist group which had little effect on metropolitan political elites.

While the tax protest actions in 1964 were the smallest of the three considered (see Table 1), the activity in 1964 was significant enough to produce a political crisis for county officials, which was featured on the front page of the *Los Angeles Times*. Protestors gathered 168,000 signatures on a petition. On November 10, twelve hundred taxpayers held a mass meeting. On November 19, one thousand demonstrators rode in a caravan of buses and confronted the County Board of Supervisors. Mike Rubino, who had frantically worked to organize the protest, gave an angry speech and then collapsed from exhaustion. Rubino's efforts drove him deeply in debt. Ironically, the leader of a movement to save people's homes was forced to sell his house. After holding one more large protest meeting, activists formed an ongoing group, the Property and Homeowners of San Gabriel Valley. Periodically it became active in local politics. Fourteen years later, it gathered signatures and campaigned for Proposition 13. The group was based in Alhambra, where home values in 1960[2] were close to the median for Los Angeles County (see Table 2).

The major activity at the November 19 meeting, and the primary goal of the movement, was expressive—to vent anger. "Taxpayer after taxpayer insisted on voicing their personal complaints. . . . Some booed [Phillip] Watson [the County Assessor], some booed the Supervisors, and one man even booed a member of the protest committee who announced that the buses were ready to leave." A Supervisor tried to lecture, "No amount of rabble rousing is going to solve this very serious problem" *(Van Nuys Daily News,* November 20, 1964:1).

Suburban newspapers contained no evidence that community economic elites supported the 1964 protest. According to leader Rubino, "very few" businesses supported the movement. Rubino charged that after homeowners could not make their tax payments, real estate agents were "buying up homes cheap." Rubino (1982) alleged that the attitude of the agents was "Why should we help you? We stand to make more money."

Although two Alhambra City Council members expressed support for the protest, the community political elite generally opposed the protest mobilization. The mayor of Alhambra, Norma Yokum, established an office in Alhambra where taxpayers could file an individual appeal. Yokum then argued that it was not necessary to protest downtown and opposed Rubino's plans. Indeed, far fewer than expected attended the downtown protest on November 19, leaving Rubino to pay for the extra chartered buses. Furthermore, Mayor Yokum, who emphasized that Rubino was only a beer truck driver, helped to establish a rival group of taxpayers. The president of the group claimed to be more responsible and attempted to become president of Rubino's organization.

The outcome of the protests was not favorable, as evidenced by the purely symbolic response of metropolitan political elites. (See Table 3.) The county

Table 1.   Participation in Tax Protest Activities

1	2	3	4	5	6
		Number of		% Total	Median House
Year	Location	Meetings	Attendance	Attendance	Value ($ × 1000)
1957 (Nov. 6–Dec. 6)					
	San Gabriel Valley				
	Covina	3	2,250	23.5	7.98
	Glendora	1	500	5.22	8.19
	La Puente	1	50	0.52	6.82
	Pomona	1	200	2.09	9.16
	West Covina	1	5,000	52.22	10.4
	San Fernando Valley				
	Woodland Hills	1	275	2.87	11.2
	Other				
	Downey	1	900	9.40	8.87
	Hollywood	1	400	4.18	20+
	metropolitan-wide	1	6,000	—	—
	TOTAL	11	15,575	100%	
1964 (Nov. 10–Dec. 10)					
	Alhambra	2	2,200	91.7	15.8
	Lomita	2	200	8.33	15.1
	TOTAL	4	2,400	100%	
1976 (July 20–Aug. 20)					
	San Fernando Valley				
	Northridge	1	1,000	10.52	40.4
	Sherman Oaks	3	590	6.20	32.5
	Van Nuys	1	3,000	31.55	28.9
	Woodland Hills	1	3,000	31.55	38.1
	multi area coalitions in the SVF	4	2,350	—	—
	South Coast				
	Rolling Hills	1	800	8.41	50+
	San Gabriel Valley				
	Baldwin Park	1	40	0.42	17.2
	Covina	1	1,000	10.52	24.0
	Hacienda Heights	1	80	0.84	27.1
	TOTAL	14	11,860	100%	

Figures in column 6 derived from U.S. Bureau of the Census, 1952; 1962; 1972. House refers to owner occupied dwelling units.

Table 2. Community Consequences of Tax Protest Activity

1	2	3	4	5	6	7
Year	Location	Weighted Median House Value[a]	Col. 3 ÷ L.A. County Median	Area Attendance	Response Community Economic Elites	Response Community Political Elites
1957	San Gabriel Valley	$9,529	0.95	8,000	Some facilitation	One city council endorses
1964	Alhambra	$15,800	0.99	2,200	No support. Movement hostility to community economic elites	Hindering of mobilization by forming alternate movement
1976	San Fernando Valley Rolling Hills	$34,586 $50,000+	1.42 2.06+	9,940 800	Systematic facilitation	Few politicians endorse Facilitation: Political elites lead protest
	Covina	$24,000	0.99	1,000	No evidence of support	Few politicians endorse

303

Table 3.   Metropolitan Consequences of Tax Protest Activity

1	2	3	4	5
		Col. 2 ÷ L.A.		
Year	Weighted Median House Value[4]	County Median	Attendance (thousands)	Response of Metropolitan Political Elites
1957	$9,951	1.00	15.6	Initial offer of formal cooptation (participation in budgetary decisions)
1964	$15,750	0.99	2.4	Symbolic
1976	$34,433	1.42	11.9	Advantages granted (lower tax rate)

Board of Supervisors expressed sympathy, convened a special meeting, and proposed to limit property tax rates and provide a small exemption for senior citizens. However, no reforms were actually enacted.

A search of the documentary evidence reveals two other major periods of protest. I compared the cases, noting how protest activity had different antecedents and outcomes (Skocpol, 1979:33–40). For the other two cases, the same variables and data gathering procedures were utilized, allowing directly comparable results.

B.   Protests in 1957: The Effects of Size, the Limits of Wealth

Compared to the 1964 protests, the 1957 activity took place in neighborhoods with similar home values. Although this discouraged community elites from facilitating the movement, the 1957 actions were much larger. Consequently, some community economic elites supported the protest. However, a multistrata alliance did not emerge. Metropolitan political elites made a more favorable response in 1957 compared to 1964; they took steps to formally coopt the protestors.

In 1957, angry taxpayers gathered at protest meetings in four different areas of the county. Total attendance during the peak month of activity was over 15,500, the highest figure for the three years considered. Enthusiastic about their successes, leaders formed a county-wide coalition and urged all taxpayers to attend a central protest meeting. Six thousand heeded the call, producing the largest tax protest gathering in the history of the county. Unfortunately, the leaders held the assembly in the Los Angeles Coliseum, which seats 100,000; thus, the gathering appeared to be sparsely attended and was widely interpreted as a failure. Afterwards, the tax protests quickly tapered off (Jackson, et al., 1960).

As in 1964, taxpayers in 1957 expressed their hostility in many colorful ways. Some sent tea bags to the County Board of Supervisors reminding them that another Boston Tea Party was brewing. One thousand residents of Hollywood pledged to refuse to pay their property tax bills. As in 1964, a major strategy in 1957 was gathering signatures on petitions, but unlike 1964, the petitions were not merely expressions of protest. One petition would have recalled the County Assessor; another would have reduced a school district's tax rate back to the previous year's level.

The home values in the protesting areas (weighted by the attendance shown for each community in Table 1) were close to the median for Los Angeles County. Thus, in 1957 and in 1964, the protesting areas were of similar affluence (Table 2). However, the protests in 1957 were about six and one half times larger than those of 1964. Consequently, community political elites and community economic elites had a more favorable response to the movement.

One community city council endorsed the tax protests in 1957; another established a citizens' study commission. This contrasts to the community political elite's opposition to the mobilization in 1964. Furthermore, in 1957 there was no significant hostility between community economic elites and the movement, as there was in 1964. Some of the protest leaders in the San Gabriel Valley were small business owners. Newspaper accounts revealed the occupations of five protest leaders—two partners in a print shop, a gasoline station operator, an accountant, and a theater owner. Community economic elites sympathized with the goals of the protest, consulted with the protestors, but stopped short of actively facilitating the movement. Local Chambers of Commerce and the Covina Valley Board of Realtors urged an investigation of assessment practices and planned to study tax reform measures. The public relations committee of the Covina Realtors formed a property owners division, which homeowners could join. In 1957, there was scattered evidence of community economic elites directly facilitating movement activity. For example, the Baldwin Park Chamber of Commerce distributed protest petitions. Although the president and past president of the Covina Realtors attended an organizational meeting of the movement, the Board announced a week and a half later that it was postponing action. Community economic elites did not systematically assist the protests or even generally endorse them verbally (Jackson, et al., 1960).

County officials, at first stung by the sharpness of the protests, agreed to form "citizens" committees to cut the budget and lower taxes. But eventually, no one associated with the protests was appointed to the committees. Instead, the County Board of Supervisors appointed William Pixley and Bradford Trehnam to head two study committees. Both individuals had led taxpayer groups which criticized the protestors and defended the assessor. Trehnam was former head of the California Taxpayers' Association, whose board of directors is mainly composed of executives from large corporations ranked by *Fortune* magazine. In short, county officials offered citizens participation in budget deliberations, but never actually lowered taxes or offered any other tangible advantages. This pattern of response can be termed formal cooptation.

C.   The Protests of 1976: The Emerging Alliance

In 1976, a multistrata alliance emerged to fight for lower property taxes. Although the protests were somewhat smaller than those of 1957, the 1976 activity took place in neighborhoods of higher home values. The protestors did not simply seek to express their anger; they attempted to change the tax laws through a variety of pressures. The resulting response was more favorable— widespread facilitation from community economic elites, and tangible advantages from metropolitan political elites.

The 1976 protests flared up in three areas of Los Angeles County (compared to four in 1957). The total attendance during the peak month of protest was 11,860, somewhat less than in 1957 (see Table 1). The aim of the 1976 protests included both the expression of discontents and reforming laws. In 1976, several thousand taxpayers packed meetings that boisterously endorsed a tax strike. Several protest leaders publically burned their tax bills. Nine hundred protestors also expressed their discontent by demonstrating at a Board of Supervisors meeting. In addition, leaders collected 200,000 signatures on a petition urging governor Jerry Brown to call a special session of the State Legislature to implement property tax relief. Both Howard Jarvis and Paul Gann collected signatures for their initiatives to limit the property tax.

Community political elites sometimes aided the mobilization of protest activity. The mayors of two communities (that had the highest house values of any area studied) formed a protest group, Citizens for Property Tax Relief (CPTR). The CPTR organized numerous meetings and coordinated protest activities for the entire south bay area of Los Angeles County.

Local economic elites did much to facilitate the protests. At the first signs of discontent, the San Fernando Valley Board of Realtors placed newspaper advertisements which contained a letter protesting property taxes that could be cut out and sent to government officials. A vice-president of a local Chamber of Commerce served as the master of ceremonies for the first large protest meeting in the San Fernando Valley. Interviews with fifteen leaders of Valley homeowners' associations and groups reveals that community economic elites did much to directly facilitate the movement.

During the signature gathering campaigns in 1976 and 1977 that eventually placed Proposition 13 on the ballot, homeowners and neighborhood groups worked closely with small businesses, particularly real estate firms. A community which took the lead in organizing the entire San Fernando Valley and the west side of Los Angeles was Sherman Oaks, where the median 1970 home value in the median census tract was $32,500, above the median of $24,300 for Los

Angeles. The San Fernando Valley Coordinator for the United Organizations of Taxpayers described how advertisements and radio talk show presentations announced that petitions were available at a chain of real estate offices. Real estate boards in the San Fernando Valley gave petitions to agents, who gathered signatures from their clients. Agents telephoned homeowners about the issue of taxes, and then inquired if the person was interested in buying, selling, or trading a home. In addition, a former member of the board of directors of the United Organizations of Taxpayers related how apartment owners provided funds and a base of operations for the property tax reduction movement. While local chambers of commerce varied in their support of the movement, the Sherman Oaks Chamber of Commerce assisted the signature gathering effort. A chain of supermarkets and muffler shops served as distribution points for petitions. Several automobile dealers and retail businesses made contributions and provided office space and publicity.[3]

Compared to the protests in other years, the 1976 activities evoked the most favorable response from metropolitan political elites. The Board of Supervisors started an investigation of the Assessor and took steps to reduce the county payroll. Although the budget for the year had already been adopted, the Supervisors in an extraordinary move obtained permission from the State to re-open deliberations, resulting in a property tax reduction of about $70 for the average homeowner. Major Tom Bradley of Los Angeles led efforts to cut the city's property tax rate by about 10 percent and appeared at a protest rally "to a mixture of cheers and boos" (*Valley News*, August 15, 1976:1).

D. Elite Facilitation and Hindering of Homeowners' Protests: Theoretical Implications

The results of the comparative analysis in this section are shown in Figure 1, which builds on previous graphic models of social movements (Oberschall, 1980; Tilly, 1978:113). The horizontal axis measures the acceptability of the protesting group, operationalized as the weighted median house value for the protesting neighborhoods, divided by the median for Los Angeles County. The vertical axis measures the size of the protests, operationalized as the total attendance at meetings during peak month of activity. In 1964, the relatively small numbers and medium house values of the protestors yielded repression from community political elites and no facilitation from community economic elites. In 1957, although protests also took place in areas of medium house value, the attendance was much higher, compared to 1964. Thus, the 1957 activities produced scattered but not systematic facilitation from community economic elites and community political elites. (This is shown in Figure 1 by having the lines for facilitation come close to the point for 1957). Finally, the 1976 protests were smaller than those of 1957, but took place in neighborhoods where 1970 house values were over $34,433, or 1.42 times the median for Los Angeles County.

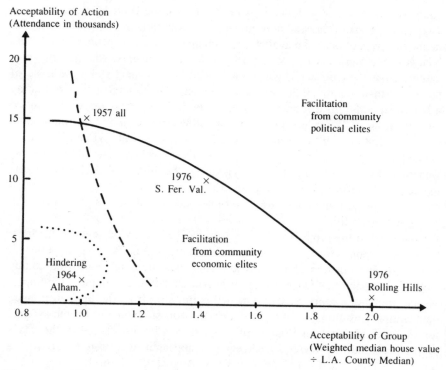

Figure 1.   Hindering and Facilitation of Tax Protests

(The owner of a $35,000 single family house would rank in the upper 21 percent of homeowners in the county, and would rank above most of the renters, who compose half the county population.) Community economic elites in 1976 strongly facilitated the protests, as did a few community political elites. For example, political elite facilitation took place in Rolling Hills, where relatively small scale actions took place in neighborhoods where house values were more than double the county average, or in the upper nine percent.

Despite the small number of cases examined here, their strategic location on Figure 1 helps to predict the types of protests which will be repressed by political elites (those encircled by the dotted line in Figure 1), facilitated by community economic elites (those to the right and above the dashed line), and facilitated by political elites (those to the right and above the solid line). One would expect that the slope of the dashed line for community economic elite facilitation would have a high negative value, indicating that economic elites respond more to the affluence of the protestors rather than their numbers. Community economic elites will join with protestors in upper middle class areas, thus forming a multistrata alliance. The slope of the solid line for community political elite facilitation would have a lower negative value, indicating that political elites respond more to the size of protests, which after all, represent the number of concerned voters. The large gap between the lines for political repression and facilitation would indicate high political tolerance (Tilly, 1978:111). For a wide range of actions in local politics, government officials neither hinder the right to organize nor assist the mobilization.

This pattern of facilitation and repression has consequences for the internal life of social movements. Community economic elites respond to the affluence of movement adherents and may provide an important source of support. Thus, leaders of tax protest movements were anxious to project an image of respectability and high status. For example, the head of the Citizens for Property Tax Relief (CPTR) constantly stressed that his association was composed of "professionals." The CPTR formed task forces to gather and disseminate statistics and other reliable information about budgets and politics (Lee, 1982). Another informant stressed that in Sherman Oaks, one's "standing in the neighborhood" was an important prerequisite for leadership (Blaine, 1982).

Furthermore, the findings of this analysis suggest that there are important differences in the political cultures of the upper middle and lower middle classes. Protests in upper middle class neighborhoods tend to be facilitated, while protests in lower middle class areas are hindered. In a lower middle class neighborhood, one would expect the residents to feel ineffective and to distrust elites. Accordingly, Wright (1976:135–43) finds that the level of political alienation among the lower middle class (i.e., self employed, clerical, and sales workers making less than $10,000 a year) is similar to the levels among manual workers. Political alienation decreases for those earning more than $10,000 a year. Similarly, Hamilton (1972) argues that the political attitudes of the working and lower middle classes are significantly different from the attitudes of the Protestant upper middle class (families whose income was above $10,000 in 1964, or in the top one fifth). The Protestant upper middle class is more likely to be conservative and Republican. Hence, one would expect them to favor an alliance with local elites.

I studied the census tracts where protest activity took place, using the decennial census immediately prior to the actions. For the tracts, I calculated the percentage of upper middle income families, i.e., those who ranked in the top one fifth of the nationwide income distribution that year. In Sherman Oaks, where local elites facilitated the protests, the percentage of upper middle income families ranged from 34 percent to 73 percent in the most affluent census tract. However in West Covina, where local elites did not facilitate, only 16 percent of the families earned upper middle incomes. In Alhambra, where local elites discouraged the protests, the percentage of upper middle income families was 25 percent. Here, as I have argued, the political alienation and the anti-business attitudes of the residents prevented the emergence of an alliance with community elites.

Finally, community elite repression and facilitation also has important consequences for more general theories about the state. Shattschneider (1960) and Offe (1972) have emphasized how elites and structures place limitations on democracy. They have described the "selective mechanisms" (such as laws, ideologies, and political procedures), which filter out expressions of the popular will and prevent many from influencing state policy. Most studies of elites have focused on the international (Useem, 1978, 1980), national, or metropolitan level (Ratcliff, 1980; Ratcliff, et al., 1979). Less familiar to academics are the realtors and small businesses which have had an important impact on defining the politics of the right.

III. HISTORICAL ANALYSIS OF BALLOT INITIATIVES TO REDUCE TAXES

Thus far, this chapter has focused on protest actions against taxes. I have utilized a comparative method, focusing on the conditions which led community elites in some areas to facilitate the protests. I will now illustrate a historical method which analyzes changes over time in one specific location. The previous section suggested that by 1976, tax protest movements had grown stronger because they began to take place in upper middle class communities. This is in accord with research which indicates that by the mid 1970s, a rapid inflation in house prices was taking place in the desirable suburbs of Los Angeles (Grebler and Mittlebach, 1979). This produced large increases in assessments and tax bills, which led to the angry protests of 1976.

Rather than focusing on protest actions, this section explains how the tax protest movement succeeded in gathering signatures which placed initiatives on the state ballot to change the tax laws. In the late 1960s and early 1970s, many tax reduction initiatives failed to get enough signatures to qualify for the ballot. Furthermore, several initiatives which were placed on the ballot then were rejected by the voters. But in 1978, Proposition 13 succeeded because a multistrata alliance had emerged between homeowners and local landed elites.

The earlier, unsuccessful initiatives were sponsored by either business lobbying groups which could not win popular support, or isolated neopopulist homeowners who could not obtain resources. Financial contributions from economic elites affected the rivalries between competing tax protest groups and leaders, as recent literature has emphasized (McCarthy and Zald, 1977; Zald and McCarthy, 1980). Howard Jarvis' major competitor was the Assessor of Los Angeles County, Phillip Watson, who also promoted state-wide tax reduction initiatives in 1968, 1972, and 1976.

A.   Watson: The Limits of Middle Level Landed Elites

Until the mid 1970s, the most prominent crusader for property tax reduction was Philip Watson, the Los Angeles County Assessor. Watson managed to win the support of local landed elites. But Watson's initiatives lost at the polls because other sections of the business community opposed him. Furthermore, he failed to win the support of homeowners.

As County Assessor, Watson had the unpleasant duty of mailing notices of increased assessments and tax bills, which sometimes provoked taxpayers to threaten him with obscenities. But in addition to being part of the problem, Watson tried to be part of the solution. Promoting plans to limit property tax rates, Watson sought support from homeowners' groups. He even courageously appeared at meetings of irate taxpayers, asking them to channel their anger into gathering signatures for his initiatives. However, Watson obtained most of his signatures from paid collectors, who were then charging about forty cents for each of the approximately half million valid signatures needed to qualify a petition.

In order to pay his signature collectors, Watson turned to large contributors. The names of these contributors and the amounts donated are listed in the archives of the California Secretary of State. As indicated in Table 4, during the campaign for the 1968 Watson initiative, 80 percent ($161,000) of the receipts were from contributions of $1,000 or more in size. Most of these large contributions came from real estate agents and boards, apartment owners, builders, developers, and farmers. However, the 1968 initiative was defeated. The opponents successfully tagged the initiative as the "landlord's tax trap," and "a big deal for the fat cats." Also opposing the initiative were major business groups, including the California Chamber of Commerce, the California Investment Bankers Association, and the powerful California Taxpayer's Association, whose board of directors mainly consists of executives from the large corporations listed in the *Fortune* 500 directory (Whitaker and Baxter, 1968).

The pattern of business support was similar during Watson's second attempt to pass a property tax reduction initiative in 1972. Land related businesses supported him, while other businesses opposed him. Real estate boards donated $260,000 and provided speakers, ads, and telephone banks for the campaign (Gillies, 1970; *California Real Estate Magazine*, 1972). The California Farm Bureau Federation contributed $200,000, another sizeable portion of the $1.04 million total funds raised. The campaign director for the 1972 Watson initiative had served as the president of the National Association of Real Estate Boards and head of the Apartment Association of Los Angeles County. Unfortunately for Watson, his 1972 initiative specified that the revenue lost from lower property taxes would be made up by increased taxes on insurance companies and liquor.

Table 4. Campaign Contributions for Tax Limitation Initiatives

Receipts of the principal campaign committees:
(in thousands of dollars)

	1 In Support Prop 9 Nov. 1968 (Watson)	2 In Support Prop 13 June 1978 (Jarvis-Gann)	3 In Opposition Prop 13 June 1978	4 For all Campaign Committees for Candidates and Ballot Propositions June 1978 Election
	Contributions of $1,000 or More by Type			*Contributions of $500 or More by Type*
Business				
Real estate: incl. boards, brokers; apartment owners, construction (U.S. private sector), developers, hotels, industrial parks, parking lots, shopping centers	76. (47%)	71. (38%)	39. (3%)	480. (4%)
Agriculture and ranches	0 (0%)	9. (5%)	0 (0%)	513. (4%)
Other corporations, incl. financial, utilities, legal	48. (30%)	44. (24%)	613. (40%)	6,354. (48%)
Labor and public employee organizations, incl. professionals, educators	0	0	820. (54%)	1,845. (14%)
Political organizations	0	22. (12%)	7. (0%)	776. (6%)
Individuals	37. (23%)	40. (21%)	35. (2%)	1,700. (13%)
Health	0	0	0	580. (4%)
Miscellaneous	0	0	0	987. (7%)
CONTRIBUTIONS SUBTOTAL	161. (100%)	186. (100%)	1,514. (99%)	13,235. (100%)
SIZE OF CONTRIBUTIONS	(thousands of dollars)			
$1,000 or more	161. (80%)	186. (8%)	1,513. (71%)	
999 or less	41. (20%)	2,093. (92%)	607. (29%)	
TOTAL CONTRIBUTIONS	202. (100%)	2,279. (100%)	2,120. (100%)	

All figures include loans and independent direct expenditures (California, Secretary of State, 1968; California, Fair Political Practices Commission, 1978). Businesses were classified by consulting the *Southern California Business Directory and Buyers' Guide, Security Dealers of North America, Directory of California Manufacturers* and Dun and Bradstreet's *Million Dollar Directory* and *Middle Market Directory*.

These two industries contributed funds to defeat the proposition (*Los Angeles Times,* September 17, 1972:1; November 1, 1972:3).

After 1972, Watson never succeeded in gathering enough signatures to place a tax reduction measure on the ballot. Beginning in June 1974, state law strictly limited the money that could be spent to gather signatures for petitions, undermining Watson's strategy of using paid rather than volunteer signature collectors. At the end of 1976, Watson was facing a city council investigation of corruption in his office, which led to his resignation a year later.

In short, Watson began with the support of established real estate interests. This provided sufficient resources to place several tax cutting initiatives on the state ballot. However, the support of local landed elites produced opposition from other sections of the business community and tarnished his appeal among the voters. Watson's initiatives lost at the polls by wide margins.

B. Jarvis and the Emerging Alliance between Homeowners and Local Landed Elites

Howard Jarvis began as a radical, anti-establishment champion of small property owners. He kept this image throughout his career. He managed to maintain his popularity among homeowners even when he obtained support from real estate businesses. This alliance between homeowners and local elites led Proposition 13 to succeed, despite the opposition from most large businesses.

Jarvis started his political career as an isolated neopopulist. Jarvis' first petition in 1968 took an even more drastic position than Proposition 13. It called for abolishing the property tax altogether. In his next attempt in 1971–72, Jarvis circulated a petition providing for a property tax levy against all previously exempt property. Any exemptions would need approval by a two-thirds vote of each house of the State Legislature. Expressing anti-establishment themes, Jarvis and other proponents attacked tax exempt foundations and trusts, proposed taxes on oil companies and insurance headquarters, and championed the small property owner unable to take advantage of tax loopholes (The *Register,* July 8, 1971; July 14, 1971; October 28, 1971; Jarvis, 1979:29).

While Jarvis was condemning the privileges of big business, apartment owners were aiding Jarvis' efforts. Charles Reynolds, president of the Orange County Apartment House Association, was at the same time the first vice president of Taxpayers Incorporated, which gathered signatures for Jarvis' tax reduction initiatives (The *Register,* March 20, 1972). In 1973, Jarvis became the Executive Director of the Apartment House Association of Los Angeles County, which donated money to the Proposition 13 campaign (Jarvis, 1979:53, 85, 89).

Campaign contribution records for Proposition 13 in 1978 reveal that Jarvis had maintained the same pattern of business support. Property related businesses gave Jarvis money; larger businesses condemned him. The campaign for Proposition 13 obtained $80,300 in contributions over $1,000 from real estate and agriculture (about the same that Watson received in 1968 from similar sources. See Table 4). Although the campaign for Proposition 13 raised $44,100 from businesses other than real estate and agriculture, the opposing No on 13 campaign raised about fourteen times this amount from businesses. Large industrial, financial, utility, and commercial corporations such as the Bank of America, ARCO, and Southern California Edison generally opposed Proposition 13.

Jarvis and the campaign for Proposition 13 succeeded in gaining contributions from thousands of homeowners. For Yes on 13, contributions under $1,000 accounted for 92 percent of the funds (compared to only 20 percent for Watson). The contrast between the Yes on 13 and the No on 13 campaigns is particularly striking. Both sides raised over two million dollars. Jarvis tapped relatively small donors; his opponents relied on business and labor organizations, contributing $1,000 or more.

Homeowners were irked at big business' opposition to Proposition 13. The California Taxpayers' Association, which is closely tied to large business, provided speakers who debated the proponents of Proposition 13. Commenting on big business groups, Virgil Elkins (1982), the Orange County Coordinator for the United Organizations of Taxpayers, remarked that, "They oppose everything that is for the people." Supporters of Proposition 13 picketed the downtown offices of the Bank of America because of its stand against Proposition 13 (Mason, 1982).

The data on campaign contributions, which demonstrate that small contributors and land based businesses backed Jarvis, is consistent with the findings of the previous section. In Los Angeles County during the 1976 protests, homeowners and community economic elites were brought together. They then gathered signatures for tax reduction measures. In other areas of California as well, local economic elites and homeowners cooperated to collect signatures in 1977 for the Jarvis-Gann initiative. In Orange County, the Coordinator for the United Organizations of Taxpayers (Elkins, 1982) told how petitions were circulated by banks, local Chambers of Commerce, Red Carpet Realtors, Century 21 Realtors, and individual real estate agents. Paul Gann's Coordinator for Southern California (New, 1982) reported that store owners and members of the Culver City Board of Realtors assisted in his signature gathering efforts. Even in neighborhoods where home values were below the county median, and where real estate agents had been reluctant to ally with tax protest movements, real estate offices helped gather signatures in 1977 (Rutenberg and Rutenberg, 1982).

However, the alliance between homeowners and small business soon developed problems. Many homeowners and voters would turn against the tax reduction movement if they thought the movement represented business. A major argument used against both Watson and Jarvis was that their reforms would produce a windfall for business. Jarvis (1979:74–75) specifically asked the California Real Estate Association not to publically endorse Proposition 13 (cf.

Useem and Zald, 1982:150). On issues other than Proposition 13 as well, the tensions between homeowners and business would surface. The democratic sentiments of homeowners would challenge landed elites as well as the government. The goals of homeowners' movements would prove to be highly volatile.

IV. THE IMPACT OF PROPOSITION 13 ON HOMEOWNERS GROUPS AND NEIGHBORHOOD DEMOCRACY

The desire for neighborhood democracy has been a fundamental impulse throughout American history (Bender, 1978; Kotler, 1969). According to Gans (1967), although residents of Levittown were cynical about the backroom deals made by powerful interests, residents expressed an abiding faith in democratic values.

As I have demonstrated, hundreds of neighborhood associations mobilized California homeowners in support of property tax limitation. These associations formed several statewide federations—Jarvis' United Organizations of Taxpayers, Gann's The People's Advocate, and the Taxpayers' Congress. Tens of thousands of volunteers, including many who had not been previously involved in politics, gathered signatures for initiatives, producing the one and one-half million signatures which placed Proposition 13 on the ballot.

Although the neighborhood associations sometimes had oligarchic leadership structures, the associations were democratic in the sense that they sought to increase citizen participation in government. Sometimes, the groups protested that government officials did not respond to their views. During a rally against taxes in 1976, protesters placed a row of empty chairs on the stage, reserved for local politicians who had been invited to the rally but who did not appear (Nerpel, 1982). But the tax reduction movement not only protested the lack of citizen participation in government; the movement took positive actions to increase participation. The Sherman Oaks Homeowners Association and the Citizens for Property Tax Relief both organized citizens' committees to examine government budgets and publicize their findings. The League of California Citizens and the Taxpayers' Congress both announced that one of their major goals was to prod local government into releasing information to the citizens.

In short, Proposition 13 was created by an alliance between homeowners, guided by democratic ideals, and local business interests. But ironically, the passage of Proposition 13 weakened this alliance on other issues such as development. At times, the invigorated democratic impulse could no longer be contained within an alliance with local elites. The history of the Monterey Park Taxpayers Association (MPTA) shows such an emerging split.

The MPTA was formed, in the words of its first president, by "the old establishment.'' These were "old time leaders who had been in power for God knows how many years.'' The original planning group was composed of about a dozen people "in city government and behind the scenes . . . businessmen and local leaders. . . . Since one of the old timers was the editor of the paper there was plenty of coverage. . . . Other members were primarily members of the local Lions Club which . . . was very powerful. If you weren't backed by the Lions Club you never got on the city council'' (Gilman, 1982). However, the first meeting was held shortly after increased property tax bills were mailed out in the fall of 1976. "It was like a lynch mob. They were out to kill anybody and everybody in government.'' On the issue of property tax reduction, homeowners worked with local business interests, who were, however, suspicious of the angry crowds. These suspicions were fully justified. Activated over the tax issue, homeowners soon began to oppose local businesses who wanted to develop Monterey Park by building a new city hall and a downtown shopping area. After the passage of Proposition 13 in 1978, revenues became scarce. Redoubling their opposition against using tax money for redevelopment, homeowners formed two new associations—the Sequoia Park Homeowners and the Residents Association of Monterey Park. These associations also opposed new condominiums, which would require increased government spending for infrastructure and services. As the president of the MPTA remarked, "Our local chamber of commerce is our enemy. . . . They promote business and . . . [that] requires customers. . . . The more the merrier. . . . They wanted developing; we wanted control.'' The board of realtors was "just murder'' (Gilman, 1982).

The issue of development split homeowners from local business interests in many communities (California. Office of Planning and Research, 1980). In Alhambra, where home values were below the county median, residents forcefully opposed redevelopment plans (Rutenberg and Rutenberg, 1982). Even in wealthier communities, where residents worked closely with local businesses on taxes and other issues, controversies over development split homeowners and business. The Beverly Glen Residents Association successfully fought the construction of new housing in the Santa Monica mountains (McQueen, 1979). The Brentwood Homeowners' Association spearheaded a coalition of several neighborhood groups, which opposed the construction of a new freeway in the westside of Los Angeles. Some homeowners' groups in affluent communities have veto power over development plans.

These findings are in accord with recent research on urban growth. Logan (1976, 1978) argues that real estate developers and business seek to attract more businesses to locate in the suburbs. However, residents in the suburbs may object to changing the character of their neighborhoods. Lower income residents are particularly harmed. However, only upper income suburbs have the political resources to successfully challenge developers. Only wealthier suburbs can restrict the number of residents and still have a sufficient tax base to finance necessary government services (cf. Molotch, 1976).

V.   CONCLUSION

The research in this chapter follows the tradition of other scholars who have used historical and comparative methods to illuminate social movements, social class, and social change. Much of this research deals with revolutions and left wing movements of the remote past in nations outside the United States (Skocpol, 1979; Tilly, 1978). The comparative study of historical cases can also illuminate conservative, contemporary, and local social movements.

Studying the protest movement against property taxes in California, I have traced the development of the alliance between homeowners and local business. This alliance succeeded in placing Proposition 13 on the ballot and passing it. Emerging multistrata alliances greatly affected the development of social movements, particularly in the suburban communities which were studied. I identified the mechanisms that lead to the formation and dissolution of multistrata alliances, and demonstrated the effects of the alliances. These findings have important theoretical implications for political sociology and social movements theory.

A.   The Formation, Consequences, and Dissolution of Multistrata Alliances

The key to understanding tax protest movements is to study the emerging alliance between the businesses and the homeowners who pay property taxes. The lack of such an alliance in the early years of the tax protest movement produced two types of tax protest groups. One type consisted of business lobbying groups and campaigns for initiatives which could utilize the mass media but which could not generate popular support. The other type was composed of homeowners' groups which protested tax increases but which lacked sufficient resources to affect policy or even survive as an organization. An alliance between local elites and homeowners formed in some areas and not in others because community elites responded differently to the protests in their areas. Thus, the mechanism for forming multistrata alliances was elite facilitation and repression of social movements. I have argued that local elites tended to respond more favorably to large protests in wealthy communities, forming emergent alliances in those areas.

Emerging multistrata alliances had a strong impact on the evolution of social movements. In some areas, the emerging alliances between homeowners and community elites led tax protest groups to combine resources (money, facilities, and technical expertise) with appeals to large numbers of voters and volunteers. These groups grew rapidly when homeowners received their tax bills each year. The groups managed to survive during the long months between the tax bills, when homeowner concern waned. These surviving tax protest groups, generally based in wealthier communities, provided leadership to other nearby groups which sprang up with the next yearly round of tax increases.

Emerging multistrata alliances affected not only the persistence of social movement organizations, but also their goals and their influence. The increasing community elite support for the protests inhibited the demands to tax corporations. Eventually, the tax protest movement in California became a right wing movement. Besides affecting the movement's stand on issues of redistribution, the emerging alliance also led the movement to successfully extract concessions from metropolitan political leaders.

Finally, I have considered two mechanisms which tended to produce the dissolution of multistrata alliances—changes in popular participation and the processes of metropolitan growth. The goals of a social movement are frequently a tenuous compromise between alliance partners; this was particularly the case for the tax protest groups. Programs for tax reduction matched the relative weight of the support from homeowners, compared to the support from community elites. Significant increases or decreases in the homeowners' participation meant that the program was no longer relevant. Then, the alliance partners would battle over a new program. The partner that lost would sometimes withdraw from the movement.

Metropolitan growth was another issue which produced tensions in multistrata alliances between homeowners and community elites. Homeowners frequently fought developers and other real estate interests that wanted to build apartment buildings, high density housing, or redevelopment projects. Homeowners in wealthy communities were particularly likely to oppose growth and hence, the landed elites who proposed it. Even though the wealthy neighborhoods produced the alliances which sustained the tax revolt, the issue of growth still made the alliances highly volatile in those areas. In general, the alliance between homeowners and community business elites holds together on issues such as reducing government spending, increasing government efficiency, excluding minorities from neighborhoods, and opposing strict rent control. The alliance between homeowners and community business elites, however, tends to fall apart on issues such as development, growth, coastal preservation, and environmental protection.

B.   Theoretical Implications for Political Sociology: Conservative Protest, Elites, and the Social System

Emerging alliances between homeowners and community economic elites led to the rise of a right wing movement to protest property taxes in California. Studying emerging alliances promises to resolve some heated debates about whether conservative movements in the United States (such as the Ku Klux Klan or the support for Father Couglin, Joseph McCarthy, or George Wallace) stem from mobilized, antielite masses or from local elites. This issue is more than an empirical one. Debates in the 1950s about the nature of right wing social movements helped to establish the theory of pluralism—tha major paradigm of political sociology for the twentieth century United States.

Pluralist social scientists generally emphasized that the right wing was a mobilized movement that challenged elites. Pluralists feared that extremist mass movements might overturn the basic consensus that underlay the institutions of the United States. Social movements might be infected with authoritarianism and intolerance, that allegedly were epidemic among the working class. The pluralists criticized social movements of both the extreme right and the extreme left. Pluralists sought to defend a moderate, liberal consensus on political principles, which would allow reasoned bargaining over a limited range of interests.

The leftist critics of the pluralists (Rogin, 1967) were much more sympathetic to social movements in the United States. Gamson (1975:130–43) argues that social movements need to be combat ready in order to be effective. They may need to resort to violence to overcome the barriers to participation in the political arena. According to the leftist critics, democracy in the United States was not a fragile experiment. Rather it was a fortress that the disenfranchised needed to storm.

The findings of this chapter have a number of implications for the debates over pluralist political theory. Some tax protest movements have tended to undermine the pluralist consensus. Some movements have displayed hostile intentions, disrupted political processes, and have caused drastic effects. Many tax protest activists had the attitude, "I'm all for Jarvis and I don't give a damn what happens to the system" (*Glendale News Press,* June 6, 1978). The California state legislature became bogged down in haggling over tax relief for homeowners, stimulating the direct citizen action of Proposition 13. California voters in 1978 could choose between Proposition 13 and a more moderate proposition drafted by the state legislature. Voters chose the more drastic solution. And finally, the success of tax reduction measures produced fiscal crises, which sometimes required emergency measures which short circuited established patterns of bargaining.

My forthcoming book, *Small Property and Big Government: Homeowners' Protests against Property Taxes and Toxic Dumps,* examines the extent to which tax protests in other states were mobilized movements which challenged pluralist institutions. A tax protest group in Florida gathered signatures on a petition which due to a mistake in drafting, would have reduced the property taxes on a $50,000 home to twenty cents. Even after this error was discovered and publicized, enough disgruntled homeowners signed anyway and the initiative qualified for the ballot (Kuttner, 1980:299). In Massachusetts, a drastic tax cutting measure, Proposition 2½, passed, while in Michigan, a more moderate initiative was adopted.

Thus, the rise of the tax protest movement indicates that the pluralists have correctly pointed to a problem of enduring significance. At times, social movements can be expressive, rather than rational, and can sometimes directly challenge the political order. The pluralists emphasized that this challenge stemmed from the mobilized populace. However, this chapter has pointed to the limits of the power of mass mobilization. Without assistance, irate citizens in California could only produce short lived protests with little impact on government policy.

Radical critics emphasize the power of elites to create change. However, this chapter has also pointed to the limits of elite power. Without popular support, business elites in California failed to significantly reduce the tax burden. Only through popular mobilization could business elites gain sufficient power to defeat the state by drastically reducing state revenues and halting the growth of spending. Thus, this analysis suggests that it is important to study the process whereby mutually suspicious groups can form an alliance to create major insitutional change.

C.   Emergent Alliances: The Implications for Theories of Social Movements

Through studying tax protest movements, I have developed an approach to analyzing social movements which can be elaborated and contrasted to other contemporary theories. My approach differs from the prevailing paradigm of social movements, resource mobilization theory. Resource mobilization theory could benefit from increased attention to the diversity of resources in different historical situations, the structural mediation of grievances, and the emergence of goals in social movements.

1.   A Historicist View of Resource Mobilization Theory

Resource mobilization theory emphasizes that the success of a social movement depends upon professional leaders who gather resources from groups other than the beneficiaries of a movement. Resource mobilization theorists have studied how movement beneficiaries relate to sympathizers and resource donors. Jenkins and Perrow (1977) for example, argue that the farmworkers' movement depended on resources from liberal, labor, and church groups. But as Perrow (1979) points out, certain formulations of resource mobilization theory may only be valid for a limited historical period—the years between 1965 and 1970.

Certain versions of resource mobilization theory, which are grounded in studies of left wing movements of the 1960s in the United States, need modification in order to explain right wing movements or movements during different periods of time. Professionalism may not lead to success of a movement; professionalism may even be absent during crucial stages of a movement. For example, the tax protests in California grew rapidly and developed a right wing orientation without such professionals. Only after the passage of Proposition 13 in 1978 was the tax protest movement dominated by paid political consultants and advertising agencies. Although the professionals led another campaign (dubbed "Jaws II") to cut the California income tax, they were soundly defeated.

Conscience constituencies (such as fundamentalist churches) which support right wing movements may differ significantly from the liberal denominations which support the left wing movements studied by resource mobilization theorists. As I have argued elsewhere (Lo, 1982a) there is no simple correlation between the growth of the resources of the fundamentalist churches and their support for conservative political movements. What is required is not only an analysis of resources, but also an understanding of belief systems about the millennium and about the preparations the faithful must make.

As this chapter demonstrates, important resources for tax protest movements flowed from particular sectors of small business. The flow of resources to other right-wing movements may depend upon conflicts within the business community, and the willingness of some business groups to mobilize popular support. Elsewhere, I have investigated divisions in the business community about military spending, and more generally, about the state and political processes (Lo, 1982c). The perceptions of businesses about their own interests affect their support of right wing movements.

2. The Importance of Mediated Grievances and Popular Support

Resource mobilization theory has argued that grievances are only a secondary factor in explaining the rise of social movements. Social movement activity may not be preceded by increases in grievances. According to resource mobilization theory, a sufficient level of grievances usually exists for extended times so that the rise of a movement is caused by changes in leadership or outside support (Jenkins and Perrow, 1977; McCarthy and Zald, 1977). But as I have argued, tax protest movements were the product of the interaction between community leaders and aggrieved citizens who provided popular support. A strong popular base is particularly important for social movements which attempt the difficult task of diminishing the steady increase in government spending. Popular grievance connot be treated as a constant or as a background factor.

However, it is widely recognized that increased grievances do not necessarily produce the mobilization of a social movement. What is needed is a theory of the mediations between grievances and mobilization—that is, a theory that explains why grievances produce mobilization in some cases but not in others. Collective behavior theory stresses the individual, social psychological mechanisms that mediate between hardship and movement mobilization. For example, Turner and Killian (1972:251) emphasize that for a social movement to arise, individuals must perceive hardships as injustices. Individuals must sense worsening conditions for themselves, compared to other significant groups (cf. McCarthy and Zald, 1977; Marx and Wood, 1975:380).

The research in this chapter suggests a different approach to specifying the conditions that must be met for grievance to produce mobilization. Researchers may discover important mediating mechanisms by focusing on communities and their structure rather than on individuals and their psychology. As I have demonstrated, an increase in taxes for a working class suburb has different political consequences than the same reassessment in a wealthy neighborhood. The lack of a simple connection between grievances and mobilization should not lead researchers to conclude that grievances are unimportant. Rather, researchers should examine the pattern of deprivations closely, studying where in the social structure the hardship occurs and what spatial locations and historical periods are particularly affected (Schwartz, 1976:164; Walsh, 1981).

3. Emergent Alliances Produce Emergent Goals

Resource mobilization theory emphasizes that beneficiaries of a social movement must make alliances with other groups and elites which provide resources. McCarthy and Zald (1977:1216, 1232) do point out that these outside groups may have values which differ from the beneficiaries, may have a fluctuating commitment to the movement, and may have loyalties to other groups. But on the whole, resource mobilization theory emphasizes the effects of alliances on the strategy of social movements (Useem and Zald, 1982).

My research has emphasized that alliances effect not only the means of achieving goals, but also how the goals themselves evolve. Future research can approach other social movements in a similar way, studying the basic goals that a movement pursues—whether it seeks to gain power, to embody new values, to express frustration, or to offer channels of participation (Turner and Killian, 1972:269–307; Turner, 1981).

Schwartz (1976), for example, argues that large farmers and political elites caused the Southern Farmers Alliance to drastically change its goals. E. P. Thompson (1966) describes how the shifting alliances between English factory workers, displaced artisans, middle class reformers, and publicists eventually produced a movement that fought for democratic goals. The alliances created and broken in social movements will also shape the emerging consciousness of the middle classes in the United States. C. Wright Mills, pondering the political direction of the middle classes in 1951, could see only their political apathy (324–51). The social movements of the 1970s and 1980s will be the making of the American middle class.

ACKNOWLEDGMENTS

The author wishes to thank Marianna King, Janice Schuler, and Lynn Spigel for their research assistance, the U.C.L.A. Academic Senate for funding, and Joseph Gusfield, Ivan Light, Seymour Martin Lipset, Laurie Castro Lo, Gary T. Marx, Neil J. Smelser, Sam Surace, and Maurice Zeitlin for their advice and encouragement.

NOTES

1. Newspaper articles containing only announcements of future meetings were not tallied. Attendance figures are the average of the numbers recorded in press accounts. In three instances when no figures were given, the attendance was estimated from the capacity of the meeting place and the description of the audience (such as "packed" or "overflow").

2. For each neighborhood where no aggregate census statistics were available, the census tracts were listed which fell entirely within the neighborhood. Using the U.S. Bureau of the Census (1952; 1962; 1972) report immediately prior to the activity, I listed the median house value (owner-occupied dwelling units) for each tract. The house value shown in Table 1 is the median for the census tracts composing the neighborhood.

3. The information was gathered from in-depth interviews with leaders including the founder of a citizens group, two current presidents of homeowners' associations, the public affairs director of a medium sized corporation, the founding co-editor of a tax protest newspaper, and two leaders of the signature gathering and campaign efforts in behalf of Proposition 13.

4. The figure for each year in column 3, Table 2 represents the weighted average:

$$\sum_{j=1}^{n} \frac{A_j}{A_t} M_j$$

For each neighborhood j, A_j is the attendance for all events in the neighborhood (shown in column 4, Table 1). A_t is the total L. A. County attendance that year (less events not attributable to a specific neighborhood). M_j is the median house value for the neighborhood (shown in column 6, Table 1 as described in footnote 2 above).

REFERENCES

Alhambra Post Advocate (CA.)
    1972 "Carman has a better mousetrap." June 17:1.
Bell, Daniel (ed.)
    1964 The Radical Right. New York: Doubleday.
Bender, Thomas
    1978 Community and Social Change in America. New Brunswick, N.J.: Rutgers University
          Press.
Blaine, Joyce
    1982 Interview, August 6, with Community Research Project, Los Angeles, CA: Sociology
          Department, University of California Los Angeles.
Bouma, Donald H.
    1970 "Analysis of the social power position of a real estate board." Pp. 367–377 in M. Aiken
          and P. E. Mott (eds.), The Structure of Community Power. New York: Random House.
Bronston, Jim
    1982 Interview, September 9, with Community Research Project, Los Angeles, CA: Sociology
          Department, University of California Los Angeles.
California. Office of Planning and Research
    1980 The Growth Revolt: Aftershock of Proposition 13? Sacramento, CA.
California Real Estate Magazine
    1972 "Action plan formed for 'yes' vote on proposition 14." Sept.:8.
Courant, Paul N., Edward M. Gramlich, and Daniel L. Rubinfeld
    1980 "Why voters support tax limitation amendments: the Michigan case." National Tax Jour-
          nal 33 (March):1–20.

Crain, Robert L., Elihu Katz, and Donald B. Rosenfeld.
  1969   The Politics of Community Conflict. Indianapolis, IN: Bobbs-Merrill.
Crawford, Alan
  1980   Thunder on the Right: The New Right and the Politics of Resentment. New York:
          Pantheon.
Elkins, Virgil
  1982   Interview, March 18, with Community Research Project, Los Angeles, CA: Sociology
          Department, University of California Los Angeles.
Gamson, William A.
  1975   The Strategy of Social Protest. Homewood, IL: Dorsey.
Gans, Herbert J.
  1967   The Levittowners: Ways of Life and Politics in a New Suburban Community. New York:
          Pantheon.
Gillies, Dugald
  1970   "Major tax reform proposals expected for 1970." California Real Estate Magazine,
          January:5.
Gilman, Irving
  1982   Interview, August 2, with Community Research Project, Los Angeles, CA: Sociology
          Department, University of California Los Angeles.
Glendale News Press
  1978   "Tax protestors dump tea and see." June 6:1.
Grebler, Leo and Frank G. Mittlebach
  1979   The Inflation of House Prices: Its Extent, Causes, and Consequences. Lexington, MA: D.
          C. Heath.
Hamilton, Richard F.
  1972   Class and Politics in the United States. New York: Wiley.
Hughes, Everett Cherrington
  1979   The Growth of an Institution: The Chicago Real Estate Board. New York: Arno Press.
  [1931]
Jackson, Maurice and Eleanora Peterson, James Bull, Sverre Monsen, and Patricia Richmond.
  1960   "The failure of an incipient social movement." Pacific Sociological Review 3
          (Spring):35–40.
Jarvis, Howard
  1981   Interview, August 14, with Community Research Project, Los Angeles, CA: Sociology
          Department, University of California Los Angeles.
Jarvis, Howard with Robert Pack
  1979   I'm Mad as Hell. New York: Berkley Publishing.
Jenkins, J. Craig and Charles Perrow
  1977   "Insurgency of the powerless: farm worker movements (1946–1972)," American So-
          ciological Review 42:249–68.
Kotler, Milton
  1969   Neighborhood Government. Indianapolis, IN.: Bobbs-Merrill.
Kuttner, Robert
  1980   The Revolt of the Haves: Tax Rebellions and Hard Times. New York: Simon & Schuster.
Ladd, Everett Carll, Jr. with Marilyn Potter, Linda Basilick, Sally Daniels, and Dana Suszkiw
  1979   "The polls: taxing and spending." Public Opinion Quarterly 43 (Winter):126–35.
Lee, James K.
  1982   Interview, July 30, with Community Research Project, Los Angeles, CA: Sociology De-
          partment, University of California Los Angeles.
Levy, F.
  1979   "On understanding Proposition 13." The Public Interest, 56 (Summer):66–89.

Lipset, Seymour M. and Earl Raab
  1978   "The message of Proposition 13." Commentary 66 (Sept.):42–46.
Lo, Clarence Y. H.
  1982a "Countermovements and conservative movements in the contemporary U.S." Annual
          Review of Sociology 8:107–34.
  1982b "The appeal of tax protest organizations in the United States, 1945–1978." Paper present-
          ed to the World Congress of the International Sociological Association, August, 1982,
          Mexico City.
  1982c "Theories of the state and business opposition to increased military spending." Social
          Problems 29 (April):424–438.
Logan, John R.
  1976   "Industrialization and the stratification of cities in suburban regions." American Journal of
          Sociology 82(2):333–352.
  1978   "Growth, politics, and the stratification of places." American Journal of Sociology
          84(2):404–16.
Los Angeles Times
  1972   "Voters facing dilemma over property tax limit proposal." September 17:I, 1.
  1972   "State employes assn. spends $1.6 million backing prop. 15." November 1:I, 3.
  1976   "Revolt of taxpayers looms as county prepares to mail bills" October 25:II, 1.
Lowery, David and Lee Sigelman
  1981   "Understanding the tax revolt: eight explanations." American Political Science Review 75
          (December):963–74.
Lynd, Robert S. and Helen Merrell Lynd
  1937   Middletown in Transition: A Study in Cultural Conflicts. New York: Harcourt, Brace and
          World.
McCarthy, John D. and Mayer N. Zald
  1977   "Resource mobilization and social movements: a partial theory." American Journal of
          Sociology 82:1112–1141.
McQueen, William Robert James
  1979   Community Groups in the Eastern Santa Monica Mountains: With Special Reference to the
          Beverly Glen Residents Association. M.A. Thesis, University of California Los Angeles,
          Department of Geography.
McTyre, Eunice
  1982   Interview, July 15, with Community Research Project, Los Angeles, CA: Sociology De-
          partment, University of California Los Angeles.
Marx, Gary T. and James L. Wood.
  1975   "Strands of theory and research in collective behavior." Annual Review of Sociology
          1:363–428.
Mason, Dorothy
  1982   Interview, July 22, with Community Research Project, Los Angeles, CA: Sociology De-
          partment, University of California Los Angeles.
Mills, C. Wright
  1951   White Collar: The American Middle Classes. New York: Oxford.
Mills, C. Wright and Melville J. Ulmer
  1970   "Small business and civic welfare". Pp. 124–154 in M. Aiken and P. E. Mott (eds.), The
          Structure of Community Power. New York: Random House.
Mollenkopf, John and Jon Pynoos
  1973   "Boardwalk and Park Place: property, ownership, political structure, and housing policy at
          the local level." Pp. 57–76 in J. Pynoos, R. Schafer, and C. Hartman (eds.), Housing in
          Urban America. Chicago: Aldine.

Molotch, Harvey
  1976   "The city as a growth machine: toward a political economy of place." American Journal of
         Sociology 82 (2):309–332.
Mottl, Tahi L.
  1980   The analysis of counter movements. Social Problems 27 (June):620–35.
Nerpel, Jane
  1982   Interview, March 4, with Community Research Project, Los Angeles, CA: Sociology
         Department, University of California Los Angeles.
New, Bill
  1982   Interview, June 18, with Community Research Project, Los Angeles, CA: Sociology
         Department, University of California Los Angeles.
News, The (Van Nuys, CA.)
  1966   "New buildings will raise skyline for Sherman Oaks." November 10:1.
Oberschall, Anthony
  1980   "Loosely structured conflict: a theory and an application." Pp. 45–68 in L. Kriesberg
         (ed.), Research in Social Movements, Conflicts and Change, Vol. 3. Greenwich, CT: JAI
         Press.
Offe, Claus
  1972   "Political authority and class structures: an anaylsis of late capitalist societies." Interna-
         tional Journal of Sociology 2:73–108.
Paul, Diane B.
  1975   The Politics of the Property Tax. Lexington, MA: D. C. Heath.
Perrow, Charles
  1979   "The sixties observed." Pp. 192–211 in Mayer N. Zald and John D. McCarthy (eds.), The
         Dynamics of Social Movements: Resource Mobilization, Social Control, and Tactics.
         Cambridge, MA: Winthrop.
Phillips, Kevin
  1982   Post Conservative America. New York: Random House.
Rabushka, Alvin
  1980   The Tax Revolt. Stanford, CA.: Hoover Institution Press.
Ratcliff, Richard E.
  1980   "Capitalist class impact on lending behavior of banks." American Sociological Review
         45:553–570.
Ratcliff, Richard E., Mary Elizabeth Gallagher, and Kathryn Strother Ratcliff
  1979   "The civic involvement of bankers: an analysis of the influence of economic power and
         social prominence in the command of civic policy positions." Social Problems 26:298–313.
Register, The (Santa Ana, CA.)
  1971   " 'Forces' blocking public vote on property tax amendment." July 8:A, 1.
  1971   "Jarvis amendment may win key point." July 14:D, 4.
  1971   "Jarvis petition." October 28:B, 6.
  1972   "Jarvis amendment triumph predicted." March 20:A, 1.
Rogin, Michael
  1967   The Intellectuals and McCarthy: The Radical Specter. Cambridge, MA: MIT Press.
Rubino, Mike
  1982   Interview, January 21, with Community Research Project, Los Angeles, CA: Sociology
         Department, University of California Los Angeles.
Rutenberg, Marie and John Rutenberg
  1982   Interview, July 14, with Community Research Project, Los Angeles, CA: Sociology De-
         partment, University of California Los Angeles.
Salzman, Ed
  1978   "Dear landlord: you have a friend in Howard Jarvis." New West. February 27:68.

Schwartz, Michael
  1976   Radical Protest and Social Structure: The Southern Farmers Alliance and Cotton Tenancy, 1880–1890. New York: Academic Press.
Sears, David O. and Jack Citrin
  1982   Tax Revolt! Something for Nothing in California. Cambridge, MA: Harvard University Press.
Shattschneider, Elmer E.
  1960   The Semisoverign People: A Realist's View of Democracy in America. New York: Holt, Reinhart, and Winston.
Skocpol, Theda
  1979   States and Social Revolutions: A Comparative Analysis of France, Russia, and China. Cambridge, England: Cambridge University Press.
Smelser, Neil J.
  1963   Theory of Collective Behavior. New York: Free Press.
Thompson, E. P.
  1966   The Making of the English Working Class. New York: Vintage Books.
Tilly, Charles
  1978   From Mobilization to Revolution. Reading, MA: Addison-Wesley.
Tocqueville, Alexis de.
  1945   Democracy in America. New York: Vintage.
  [1835]
Turner, Ralph H.
  1969   "The public perception of protest." American Sociological Review 34 (December):815–31.
  1981   "Collective behavior and resource mobilization as approaches to social movements: issues and continuities." Pp. 1–24 in Louis Kriesberg (ed.), Research in Social Movements, Conflict, and Change, Vol. 4. Greenwich, CT: JAI Press.
Turner, Ralph H. and Lewis M. Killian
  1972   Collective Behavior. Second Edition. Englewood Cliffs, N.J.: Prentice-Hall.
U.S. Bureau of the Census
  1952   U.S. Census of the Population, 1950. Vol. 3. Census Tract Statistics. Chapter 28. Los Angeles, California and Adjacent Area. Selected Population and Housing Characteristics. Washington, D.C.: Government Printing Office.
  1962   U.S. Census of Population and Housing, 1960. Census Tracts. Final Report PHC (1)-82. Los Angeles-Long Beach, California Standard Metropolitan Statistical Area. Washington, D.C.: Government Printing Office.
  1972   Census of Population and Housing. Census Tracts. Los Angeles-Long Beach, California Standard Metropolitan Statistical Area. Washington, D.C.: Government Printing Office.
Useem, Michael
  1978   "The inner group of the American capitalist class." Social Problems 25:225–40.
  1980   "Which business leaders help govern?" Pp. 199–225 in G. William Domhoff (ed.), Power Structure Research. Beverly Hills, CA: Sage Publications.
Useem, Bert and Mayer N. Zald
  1982   "From pressure group to social movement: organizational dilemmas of the effort to promote nuclear power." Social Problems 30 (Dec.):144–156.
Van Nuys Daily News (CA.)
  1964   "Aroused Alhambrans lambaste supervisors over jump in taxes." November 20:1.
Valley News (Van Nuys, CA.)
  1976   "Angry area taxpayers shout 'strike!' at mass meeting on assessment hikes." July 30:1.
  1976   "3,000 at rally cheer call for tax strike in December." August 15:1.

Walsh, Edward J.
  1981   "Resource mobilization and citizen protest in communities around Three Mile Island."
         Social Problems 29 (Oct.):1–21.
Whitaker and Baxter, Public Relations and Campaign Management.
  1968   "Vote no on prop 9." San Francisco, November 5.
Wright, James D.
  1976   The Dissent of the Governed: Alienation and Democracy in America. New York: Academic Press.
Zald, Mayer N., and John D. McCarthy
  1980   "Social movement industries: competition and cooperation among movement organizations." Pp. 1–20 in L. Kriesberg (ed.), Research in Social Movements, Conflicts and Change, Vol. 3. Greenwich, CT.: JAI Press.
Zeigler, Luther Harmon.
  1961   The Politics of Small Business. Washington D.C.: Public Affairs Press.

AUTHOR INDEX

SUBJECT INDEX